# Object Orientation and Prototyping in Software Engineering

# THE OBJECT-ORIENTED SERIES

D. Coleman, P. Arnold, S. Bodoff, C. Dollin, H. Gilchrist, F. Hayes and P. Jeremaes
*Object-Oriented Development: The Fusion Method*

S. Cook and J. Daniels
*Designing Object Systems*

B. Henderson-Sellers
*A Book of Object-Oriented Knowledge*

B. Henderson-Sellers and J. Edwards
*Book Two Object-Oriented Knowledge: The Working Object*

H. Kilov and J. Ross
*Information Modelling: An Object-Oriented Approach*

P. Krief
*Prototyping with Objects*

K. Lano and H. Haughton
*Object-Oriented Specification Case Studies*

J. Lindskov Knudsen, M. Löfgren, O. Lehrmann Madsen and B. Magnusson
*Object-Oriented Environments: The Mjølner Approach*

M. Lorenz
*Object-Oriented Software Development: A Practical Guide*

M. Lorenz and J. Kidd
*Object-Oriented Software Metrics*

B. Meyer
*An Object-Oriented Environment: Principles and Applications*

B. Meyer
*Eiffel: The Language*

B. Meyer
*Reusable Software: The Base Object-Oriented Component Libraries*

B. Meyer
*Object Success: A Manager's Guide to Object Orientation, its Impact on the Corporation, and its Use for Reengineering the Software Process*

B. Meyer and J.-M. Nerson (eds)
*Object-Oriented Applications*

D. Mandrioli and B. Meyer (eds)
*Advances in Object-Oriented Software Engineering*

O. Nierstrasz and D. Tsichritzis
*Object-Oriented Software Composition*

G. Pomberger and P. Blaschek
*An Object-Oriented Approach to Software Engineering*

R. Rist and R. Terwilliger
*Object-Oriented Programming in Eiffel*

P. J. Robinson
*Hierarchical Object-Oriented Design*

R. Switzer
*Eiffel: An Introduction*

K. Waldén and J.-M. Nerson
*Seamless Object-Oriented Software Architecture: Analysis and Design of Reliable Systems*

R. Wiener
*Software Development Using Eiffel: There Can Be Life Other Than C++*

(Various editors)
*Proceedings of TOOLS Conferences, 4 to 16: Technology of Object-Oriented Languages and Systems*

# Object Orientation and Prototyping in Software Engineering

**Gustav Pomberger and Günther Blaschek**
Johannes Kepler University, Linz, Austria

Translation by Robert Bach

PRENTICE HALL
London New York Toronto Sydney Tokyo Singapore
Madrid Mexico City Munich

First published 1996 by
Prentice Hall Europe
Campus 400, Maylands Avenue
Hemel Hempstead
Hertfordshire, HP2 7EZ
A division of
Simon & Schuster International Group

Printed and bound in Great Britain by TJ Press (Padstow) Ltd,
Padstow, Cornwall

Library of Congress Cataloging-in-Publication Data

Pomberger, Gustav, 1949-
[Grundlagen des Software Engineering. German]
Object Orientation and prototyping in software engineering/
Gustav Pomberger and Günther Blaschek : translated by Robert Bach.
p. cm. -- (Prentice-Hall object-oriented series)
Translation of: Grundlagen des Software engineering.
Includes bibliographical references and index.
ISBN 0-13-192626-8 (pbk.)
1. Software engineering. 2. Object-oriented programming (Computer science) I. Blaschek, Günther, 1957- . II. Title. III. Series.
QA76.758.P6515 1996
005.1--dc20 96-17527
CIP

British Library Cataloguing-in-Publication Data

A catalogue record for this book is available from the British Library

ISBN 0-13-192626-8

1 2 3 4 5 00 99 98 97 96

# Table of Contents

# Foreword

This book addresses anyone who plans, develops and implements software, anyone who wants to or needs to come to terms with fundamental questions regarding the design of larger software system. This includes primarily professional software developers, university educators, and students of computer science and related fields.

The authors have accumulated many years of experience in the application and development of methods and tools for rationalizing the production of software and for improving its quality. The experience of numerous research projects, practical project work under commercial conditions, and frequent discussions with colleagues and clients collectively provided fertile soil for the genesis of this book.

Software engineering is the area of computer science that deals with the production of large software systems, researches the necessary scientific methods, and develops tools that support or even enable the production, documentation and maintenance of large software systems. Software development is a demanding activity whose problems cannot be solved by common sense alone. In addition to the mastery of technical skills, a methodical approach proves especially necessary. This book strives to provide the reader with the basic knowledge required for carrying out software projects and shows how the development process can be systematized and rationalized and how the quality of software products can be improved.

Although the authors have strived to handle the entire software development process and all associated aspects, we are aware that each component area cannot be treated with equal attention and in the same depth. Thus this book contains core and peripheral aspects. Prototyping, object-oriented software construction, modularization techniques, and phase models are presented in great detail; only an overview is provided for aspects related to project management, cost projection, and tools.

We have incorporated *prototyping and object-oriented software development* into the title of our book because we assess these techniques as particularly important. At the appropriate locations in the book we discuss how these techniques affect the software development process; hence their treatment extends throughout the book. Since the application of object-oriented programming demands extensive detailed knowledge, we present the fundamentals of this technique in depth in a dedicated chapter.

We illustrate important methods and principles using simple examples. Furthermore, an extensive practice-oriented example shows how to employ both tried and novel design and implementation techniques in a software project. For the large example we selected the simulation of a portal robot, an extensive and challenging task that justifies the isolation of various subtasks in order to show how to tackle them with adequate solution strategies.

The book is structured in two short chapters, followed by two long and detailed chapters, and finally two brief closing chapters. For our examples, we have chosen a notation that proves self-explanatory and simple; therefore we spare the reader an explicit explanation to its syntactic and semantic aspects.

The first of six chapters of the book circumscribes its scope and defines the terms software engineering, prototyping and object-oriented programming.

Chapter 2 identifies the attributes that characterize the quality of software products and the measures necessary for quality assurance. The remainder of the book then treats concrete aspects of such measures toward quality assurance. We do not handle metrics or methods for the measurement of software quality because we are convinced of the lack of practical applicability of proposals in this direction to date.

In Chapter 3, the most extensive part of the book, we present the phases of a software project in their respectively due detail. The chapter begins by describing the most important phase models and discussing their advantages and drawbacks, their differences and commonalities. Then we dedicate one section each to the phases problem analysis, system specification, design, implementation, testing, documentation, and maintenance. Here we introduce the most important methods and techniques and use examples to illustrate their application.

Chapter 4 is dedicated to object-oriented programming. With the help of object-oriented techniques, programs can frequently be developed in a fraction of the time that would be needed with a conventional approach, and the resulting software systems are significantly more maintainable. The authors therefore put priority on presenting the theoretical, technical and organizational fundamentals of object-oriented programming so completely that after careful perusal the reader can begin to apply these concepts practically.

Chapter 5 addresses the management of software projects and serves to round out the overview. It outlines the goals and tasks of project management and aspects of cost estimation.

If software engineering is to meet the demands of an engineering discipline, it must provide tools that simplify or accelerate the development, testing, maintenance and documentation of programs or improve their quality. Chapter 6 summarizes the tools provided by modern software development environments and how they support the activities of the software development process.

Gustav Pomberger
Günther Blaschek

# Acknowledgments

It is our honor and pleasure to express our gratitude for the plentiful help, many suggestions and much advice that we received.

We are particularly indebted to Prof. Dr. Peter Rechenberg, to whom we are bound by many years of good cooperation and who very exactingly and critically perused the manuscript. We are grateful to him for numerous suggested improvements and ideas. Without his contribution this book would have suffered in quality.

We also owe gratitude to Prof. Dr. Hanspeter Mössenböck and Dr. Alois Stritzinger for their conscientious review of the manuscript and the resulting suggestions for improvements; to Prof. Dr. Niklaus Wirth for our ongoing exchange of ideas, which repeatedly offered a rich source of inspiration; to our colleagues whose research results influenced the content of this book; and Ms. Brigitte Taurer, Mrs. Gabriele Thürriedl and Ms. Ulli Knoll for their support in the production of the manuscript.

We also thank the C. Doppler Association as well as Siemens AG in Munich, Germany, for their generous support of our research projects, which represent a significant basis for this book, and to Prentice Hall for their good cooperative spirit, for their patience, and for the freedom that they allowed us in preparing this book.

Chapter 1

# Scope

## 1.1 The development of software engineering

The first computers were used in the application domains of science and technology. Rather than devising complex new algorithms, a programmer's job originally consisted of formulating already known algorithms in a specific programming language to allow them to execute on a given machine. Aside from the mastery of a programming language, the programmer required no particular knowledge for this task. The program author was usually the user. Programs were used only occasionally, and their requirements seldom changed afterwards. The only problem was guaranteeing correctness and efficiency. The tasks to be solved were relatively simple compared to today's, and there were few coding errors. Programming errors only became a real problem when efforts turned to devising software systems to solve complex scientific, technical and commercial tasks.

Nowadays multiple persons work on producing software systems for many users. The task description and the requirements frequently change even during the program design phase, and they continue to change even after the software system has long since been in use. In addition to correctness and efficiency, the major problems encountered in the development of large software systems came to include the mastery of complexity, interface specification, reliability, flexibility, documentation, maintainability and project organization. Too little theoretical foundation and too few methodological aids were known in both the technical and the organizational realm. Programmers' qualifications did not suffice to adequately solve the problems. Collectively this created such difficulties in the production of software that in 1965 the *software crisis* became a buzzword.

Hardware development never experienced a corresponding crisis. Although this does not imply that hardware never has errors, practice has shown that problems arising in the use of computer systems usually emanate from faulty software. Dijkstra describes this situation as follows:

> To put it quite bluntly: as long as there were no machines, programming was no problem at all; when we had a few weak computers, programming became a mild problem, and now that we have gigantic computers, programming has become an equally gigantic problem. In this sense the electronics industry has not solved a single problem; it has only created them—it has created the problem of using its products [Dijkstra 1972a].

Previously developed programming methodologies could not keep pace with the features of new computer generations. The growing economic importance of software production and the enormous expansion of the data processing branch have pressed the demand for improved *programming techniques* ever more into the focus of research interests in the field of computer science.

The striving to develop an improved programming technique encountered its first setback in research at the two software engineering conferences sponsored by NATO in Garmisch, Germany, in 1968 [Naur 1969] and in Rome in 1969 [Buxton 1969]. At these conferences programs were defined as industrial products, and the challenge was issued to move away from the *art* of programming and toward an *engineering* approach to software development.

Since these conferences there have been efforts to apply scientific approaches throughout software production as an integrated process. The research limelight has fallen on questions of specification, methodical program development, structuring of software systems, reusability of software components, project organization, quality assurance, documentation, requirements for software development tools, and automatic generation of software.

## 1.2 The term software engineering

What is behind the term *software engineering*? Is this just a new name for programming or a new methodology? When it was coined, the term software engineering was meant to be provocative and was intended to show that software production needed to assume the nature of an engineering discipline. Nevertheless, we still lack a generally recognized, stable definition of the term.

Boehm defines software engineering as follows:

> Software Engineering: The practical application of scientific knowledge in the design and construction of computer programs and the associated documentation required to develop, operate, and maintain them [Boehm 1979].

Dennis offers this definition:

> Software engineering is the application of principles, skills and art to the design and construction of programs and systems of programs [Dennis 1975].

Parnas writes:

> Software engineering is programming under at least one of the following two conditions:
> (1) More than one person is involved in the construction and/or use of the programs and
> (2) more than one version of the program will be produced [Parnas 1974].

Fairley provides the following definition:

> Software Engineering is the technological and managerial discipline concerned with the systematic production and maintenance of software products that are developed and modified on time and within cost estimates [Fairley 1985].

Sommerville tells us:

> Software engineering is concerned with building software systems which are larger than would normally be tackled by a single individual, uses engineering principles in the development of these systems and is made up of both technical and non-technical aspects [Sommerville 1985].

Bauer defines:

> [The aim of software engineering is] to obtain economically software that is reliable and works efficiently on real machines [Bauer 1975].

New and different problems accompany the production of *larger software systems* as compared with the production of *smaller programs.* Producing larger systems bears similarities to the production of other technical products. The major problems are:

- Definition of requirements
- Mastering complexity
- Decomposition of a system into subsystems
- Specification of interfaces between subsystems
- Reusability of components; development of semi-finished products
- Project organization, especially for divided-labor system development
- Efficiency
- Documentation and maintainability of the overall solution
- Modifiability and extensibility
- Portability and adaptability to other hardware platforms

Common sense alone cannot solve all these problems. Instead, it is necessary to scientifically study the whole complex in order to determine the prerequisites for methods and tools to support software production. The field of *software engineering* thus needs to provide methods, tools, standards and aids that enable us to manage the technical and organizational problems that arise in the production of software. The goal is to produce and use qualitatively acceptable software with economically feasible effort.

On this basis we define the term *software engineering* as follows:

> Software engineering is the practical application of scientific knowledge for the economical production and use of high-quality software.

## 1.3 The term prototyping

For more than a decade the literature has been reporting on software projects that used prototypes to clarify user requirements and development problems. Yet an analysis of the publications demonstrates that we have reached no consensus on the meanings of prototype and prototyping in software engineering.

Agreement prevails that software prototypes must be *executable*. The controversy begins with the question of whether a prototype must be directly executable or whether it can be simulated instead. Near agreement also prevails that software prototypes, in contrast to other prototypes, e.g., in the machine industry, must be realized *fast* and *cheap*. Some propose developing *real* prototypes in the sense of patterns that have all the important features of the planned product, and then using this as the specification for the actual product development process; this amounts to conventional prototyping as in other technical disciplines. Others believe that software prototyping should be an *incremental development process*: we quickly implement several basic functions that are clear from the start, we let the user test and evaluate these, then we improve them and implement additional user requirements until the product is complete, yielding an *evolutionary software development* process.

Many emphasize that prototypes are important components of software development with respect to quality assurance and risk reduction, and that economical prototyping proves impossible without appropriate tools.

Due to the lack of a generally recognized definition of the term, we need to establish what we mean by *prototype* and *prototyping* in this book. Based on Boar [Boar 1984] and Connell and Shafer [Connell 1989], we define the terms as follows:

> A *software prototype* is an executable model of the proposed software system. It must be producible with significantly less effort than the planned product. It must be readily modifiable and extensible. The prototype need not have all the features of the target system, yet it must enable the user to test all important system features before the actual implementation. *Prototyping* encompasses all activities necessary for the production of such prototypes.

Prototyping has several goals. This leads us to distinguish among *different types of prototyping* as well as *different types of prototypes* (see [Bischofberger 1992]). The literature often presents the following classification for prototyping (compare [Floyd 1984]):

- Exploratory prototyping
- Experimental prototyping
- Evolutionary prototyping

**Exploratory prototyping**. The *goal* of exploratory prototyping is a system specification that is as complete as possible. Its *purpose* is to introduce developers to the application domain, to discuss various possible solutions with the users, and to clarify the feasibility of the proposed system in the given organizational environment. Its *approach* begins with initial ideas about the proposed system and develops a prototype that makes it possible to test these ideas on the basis of real application examples to determine the required functionality. The determinants are not the quality of the prototype but its functionality, its easy modifiability, and its rapid development. The prototype is realized jointly by the users and the developers. Exploratory prototyping is a method for supporting problem analysis and system specification.

**Experimental prototyping**. The *goal* of experimental prototyping is a complete specification of subsystems as a foundation for the implementation. Its *purpose* is to prove experimentally the suitability of subsystem specifications, of architecture models, and of solution ideas for various system components. Its *approach* works from initial ideas about the decomposition of the system to develop a prototype for simulating the mutual effects among system components; application examples help to test the interfaces of individual system components and the flexibility of the system decomposition with respect to extensibility. The same quality requirements apply as with exploratory prototyping. The prototypes for carrying out the experiments with architecture models are realized primarily by the developers. Experimental prototyping supports system and component design. (Experimentation also plays a central role in exploratory prototyping.)

**Evolutionary prototyping**. The *goal* is incremental software development, which means a stepwise constructive development according to the following *approach*: First, develop a prototype for the user requirements that are clear from the start. The result serves as the base system for the user and for the next step, in which new user requirements are integrated and the process begins anew. Thus system development loses the nature of a completed task and becomes a process that accompanies the application throughout its development. This is easier said than done. Here the specification problem is somewhat ameliorated, but the problem of system design is by no means solved, for an incomplete specification can be the very reason that the usefulness of a decomposition cannot be evaluated. This approach does not distinguish between a prototype and the product, yet the designation prototyping applies because the initial versions can hardly be considered a practically usable product. In evolutionary prototyping the prototypes are not simulated and generally not thrown away, but they evolve stepwise to the final product.

We distinguish the *types of prototypes* as:

- Complete and incomplete prototypes
- Disposable and reusable prototypes

A *complete prototype* is a prototype in the conventional sense in which all important functions of the proposed system are complete and available. The experience gained in the production and application of the prototype and the prototype itself form the basis for final system specification. Complete prototypes are seldom produced for software systems. An *incomplete prototype* permits the examination of the usefulness and feasibility of *individual* aspects (e.g., user interface, system architecture, system components) of the proposed system.

We speak of a *disposable prototype* if the prototype implementation is not reused in the production of the target system, but instead serves "only" as an executable model. With a *reusable prototype*, significant parts of the prototype can be employed in the implementation of the target system.

## 1.4 The term object-oriented programming

In retrospect we can view the 1970s as the age of *structured programming*. This was the time of the Goto controversy, which began with the article "Goto Statements Considered Harmful" [Dijkstra 1968]. Structured programming owes its assimilation into practice to programming languages like Algol and Pascal, which encouraged the writing of programs with comprehensible control structures. But structured programming amounts to more than the avoidance of Goto statements; it also encompasses decomposing the problem at hand into subproblems, for example, by using the method of stepwise refinement [Wirth 1971], and the resultant structuring of the program in procedures.

In the 1980s interest focused on *module-oriented programming*. Large software systems could no longer be written in one piece by a single programmer, but had to be developed and implemented in teams. The module supplanted the procedure as the central structural element. The decomposition of the problem into largely independent components became the focus of the design phase; the delimitation of the individual subtasks and the specification of their interfaces gained particular importance. Thanks to languages like Modula-2 and Ada, the resulting decomposition was also reflected in the implementation.

It has become clear that the 1990s will be the decade of *object-oriented programming*. An interesting aspect of this development is that the concept of object-oriented programming is no new invention; in fact, it was introduced in the early 1970s with the languages Simula and Smalltalk. Nevertheless, fifteen years elapsed before this concept attracted interest outside academic circles. Object-oriented extensions of existing programming languages, such as C++ and Object Pascal, contributed significantly to this development.

While structured and module-oriented programming afford means for qualitative improvement of programs, object-oriented programming serves primarily as a vehicle for boosting productivity. This becomes possible due to the extensibility and reusability of object-oriented software systems. Object-oriented techniques make it possible to develop many programs in a fraction of the time required for conventional programming, and the resulting products prove more maintainable. As we will show later, some programs that would have been unthinkable with conventional means due to high costs can be developed with minimal effort using an object-oriented approach.

Taken strictly, the term object-oriented *programming* is inadequate since it encompasses more than a programming method. Since this approach also encompasses the design phase, a more appropriate descriptor would be object-oriented *software development*. This term never gained broad acceptance, however, so that in this book we also refer to object-oriented programming and employ the popular acronym OOP.

Object-oriented programming builds on the idea of putting data at the focus of a program. In conventional program development we design the algorithms first and then give consideration to which data we need to process. By contrast, in object-oriented development we invert this sequence: we begin with the data and then consider which operations on them are necessary and useful. The resulting program amounts to a network of data – the objects – that communicate with one another. Rather than remaining passive data on which actions are carried out as in the conventional view, objects take on an *active* role by carrying out actions themselves and inducing actions in other objects.

As with data types, objects of the same kind are combined in object *classes*. Every object belongs to a class; a class determines the structure and behavior of its objects. Classes can be ordered hierarchically. For example, the class of rectangles forms a subset of the class of polygons, which is a subset of the class of graphical elements, which also includes lines and circles. These relationships between classes reflect more than a thought model. Based on an existing class, we can create a new class by simply describing how the new class will differ from the existing one. The new class will inherit all other properties from the existing class. This *inheritance* provides the key to boosting productivity. Features that are needed repeatedly only need to be implemented once and then apply to an entire subtree of classes.

Other fundamental concepts of object-oriented programming include polymorphism and dynamic binding. *Polymorphism* allows, for example, that a variable need no longer be limited (as in Pascal, for example) to the data of *one* specific type, but can stand for objects of *various* classes that can differ in structure and behavior. Such flexibility is made possible by *dynamic binding*, which guarantees that an operation on the variable at run time will invoke those actions that are defined in the class of the current object.

The use of OOP becomes especially efficient with the availability of a supply of frequently needed classes (a *class library*). Program development then begins to resemble the design of an electronic device. No one today would consider soldering together a computer from individual transistors, resistors and capacitors, yet frequently software continues to be designed according to this principle, where almost all components are reinvented over and over again. Object-oriented programming enables us to design software by easily combining available components to increasingly large units and adapting them to changing requirements. Beyond this, *application frameworks* make it possible to adapt software systems with a prefabricated standard behavior to the specific requirements at hand, a method that provides many advantages, especially in the development of interactive programs.

Object-oriented programming has become a focus of research in computer science worldwide. Nevertheless (or perhaps precisely for that reason), no consensus has been reached on the prerequisites for a programming language to be labeled object-oriented. The fact that it has become fashionable to write about object-oriented programming contributes nothing in the way of clarity. Some authors speak of object orientation with as little as a data capsule, while others use the language Smalltalk as a measure and make the presence of metaclasses a precondition. We take the point of view that the truth lies somewhere between these extremes. In agreement with many experts in the field of OOP, we see object orientation as present if the following features are included:

- Data abstraction
- Object identity
- Inheritance
- Polymorphism
- Dynamic binding

The consequences of these preconditions for labeling a language object-oriented are treated in detail in Chapter 4.

Chapter 2

# Quality attributes of software products

In the previous chapter we noted that software production has the nature of an engineering discipline and bears many similarities to the manufacture of other technical products. Software products are produced by multiple persons for multiple users and increasingly serve as components of complex technical and business systems. This means that the functionality and reliability of the software product serve as prerequisites for the functionality of the overall system of which the software is a part. This makes it quite natural that we ask how the kinds of quality requirements that are widespread in industry today can be applied to software products, and how this quality can then be assured.

Software quality is by no means a precisely defined term. However, experts do agree that the quality of a software product extends far beyond merely its correctness. What quality attributes arise from the quality requirements and determine the quality of a software system? How can we measure these attributes? What consequences result for software engineering from quality requirements?

The computer science community largely agrees on quality attributes. The above questions have been discussed for a long time (compare [McCabe 1976], [Boehm 1976], [McCall 1977], [Boehm 1978], [Ramamoorthy 1982], [Arthur 1985], [Dobbins 1987], and [Wallmüller 1990]). To date we can scarcely measure software quality attributes as we would measure the quality of machines because we lack appropriate methods and metrics.

This chapter identifies which attributes characterize the quality of software products and which measures need to be undertaken to assure quality. The remainder of the book then treats concrete aspects of such measures toward quality assurance. In the authors' view, the research results in the development of metrics for measuring the fulfillment of quality criteria remain too immature; hence this book does not treat the area of software metrics.

## 2.1 Software quality attributes

The quality requirements on software products have been embodied in the definition of quality attributes. But in practice we often encounter unsolved problems that emanate primarily from two areas: we lack a generally recognized definition of the terms *quality* and *quality attributes*, and an unambiguous, objective evaluation of the quality of a software product proves impossible. Yet quality must be a goal of software development and affects not only the *planning* but also the *execution* and the *testing* of software production. Figure 2.1 shows the most important quality attributes for software products. This taxonomy and the succinct descriptions of the terms give the reader an overview.

Software quality aspects have been discussed for many years. Some of the following software quality aspects date back to Kopetz [Kopetz 1976]. Note that software quality is a broad and important field that has been addressed by standardization bodies such as ISO (especially in ISO 9000), ANSI and IEEE and by authors such as Wallmüller [Wallmüller 1995] and Schmauch [Schmauch 1994].

**Correctness**. By the *correctness* of a software system, we mean the software system's fulfillment of the specifications underlying its development. Hence the correctness of a

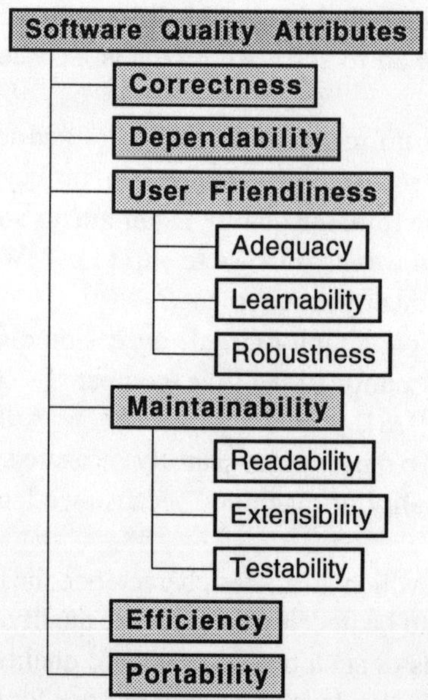


Figure 2.1: Software quality attributes

| n \ P | p 0.99 | 0.95 | 0.90 |
|---|---|---|---|
| 1 | 0.99 | 0.95 | 0.90 |
| 10 | 0.90 | 0.60 | 0.35 |
| 50 | 0.61 | 0.08 | 0.01 |
| 100 | 0.37 | 0.01 | 0.00 |

Figure 2.2: Resultant probability of correctness

software system refers to the agreement of *program code* with *specifications* and is thus independent of the actual application of the software system.

The correctness of a program becomes especially critical when it is embedded in a complex software system. Let *p* be the probability that an individual program is correct; then the probability *P* of correctness of the software system consisting of n programs is computed as $P=p^n$. If *n* is very large, then *p* must be nearly 1 in order to allow *P* to deviate significantly from 0 (see Figure 2.2; compare [Dijkstra 1972b]).

**Reliability**. A program's *reliability* derives from its correctness and its availability. We defined the correctness of a software system above without making any statement about the time interval in which the system must fulfill its specifications. The behavior over time for the fulfillment of a given specification depends on the reliability of the software system.

Reliability of a software system is defined as the probability that this system fulfills a function (determined by the specifications) for a specified number of input trials under specified input conditions in a specified time interval (assuming that hardware and input are free of errors). A software system can be seen as reliable if this test produces a low *error rate*. The error rate (i.e., the probability that an error will occur in a specified time interval) depends on the frequency of inputs and on the probability that an individual input will lead to an error.

**User friendliness**. We see user friendliness as a superordinate term for adequacy, learnability and robustness of a software system.

The requirement of *adequacy* encompasses the following three factors.

(1) The *input* required of the user should be limited to only what is necessary. The software system should expect information only if it is necessary for the functions that the user wishes to carry out. The software system should enable flexible data input on the part of the user and should carry out plausibility checks on the input. In dialog-driven software systems, we vest particular importance in the uniformity, clarity and simplicity of the dialogs.

(2) The *performance* offered by the software system should be adapted to the wishes of the user with consideration given to extensibility; i.e., the functions should be limited to those in the specification.

(3) The *results* produced by the software system:
The results that a software system delivers should be output in a clear and well-structured form and be easy to interpret. The software system should afford the user flexibility with respect to the scope, the degree of detail, and the form of presentation of the results. Error messages must be provided in a form that is comprehensible for the user.

The *learnability* of a software system depends directly on the design of user interfaces and on the clarity and simplicity of the user instructions (tutorials or user manual). The user interface should present information as close to reality as possible and permit efficient utilization of the software's features. The user manual (see Section 3.7.1.1) should be structured clearly and simply and be free of all dead weight. It should explain to the user what the software system can do, how the individual functions are activated, what relationships exist between functions, and which exceptions might arise and how they can be corrected. In addition, the user manual should serve as a reference that supports the user in quickly and comfortably finding the correct answers to questions.

The *robustness* of a software system is the characteristic that reduces the impact of operational mistakes, erroneous input data, and hardware errors.

A software system is robust if the consequences of an error in its operation, in the input, or in the hardware, in relation to a given application, are inversely proportional to the probability of the occurrence of this error in the given application.

This means that errors that we expect to occur frequently (e.g., erroneous commands, typing errors) must be handled with particular care, while less frequent errors (e.g., power failure) can be handled more laxly, but still must not lead to irreversible consequences.

**Maintainability**. The *maintainability* of a software systems refers to its suitability for debugging (localization and correction of errors) and for modification and extension of its functionality. This definition indicates that maintainability depends on the readability, the extensibility and the testability of a software system.

The *readability* of a software system depends on its form of representation, on programming style and consistency, on the readability of the implementation language, on the structuredness of the system, and on the quality of the documentation, but also on the tools available for inspection of the software system.

By *extensibility* we mean the attribute of a software system that allows us to make required modifications at the appropriate locations without undesirable side effects. This quality depends particularly on the structuredness (modularity) of the software systems and on the possibilities that the implementation language provides for this purpose, as well as on the readability (to find the appropriate location) of the code, the availability of comprehensible program documentation, and the available tools.

The *testability* of a software system is its suitability for allowing the programmer to follow program execution (run-time behavior under given conditions) and for debugging.

The testability depends primarily on the modularity and the structuredness of the software system. Modular, well-structured programs prove more suitable for systematic, stepwise testing than monolithic, unstructured programs. Testing tools and the possibility of formulating consistency conditions (assertions) in the source code reduce the testing effort and provide important prerequisites for the extensive, systematic testing of all system components.

**Efficiency**. The *efficiency* of a software system refers to the ability of a software system to fulfill its purpose with the best possible utilization of all necessary resources. The term *resources* is taken very broadly and encompasses time, storage, transmission channels, and peripherals.

**Portability**. By the *portability* of a software system we mean the ease with which it can be adapted to run on computers other than the one for which it was designed. Thus the portability of a software system depends on its degree of hardware independence. Such factors as the choice of the implementation language and the extent of exploitation of specialized system functions and hardware properties determine the degree of machine independence. Thus the portability largely depends on whether the software system is organized such that its system-dependent elements are collected in easily interchangeable program components. We consider a software system to be portable if the effort required for porting it proves significantly less than the effort necessary for a new implementation.

## 2.2 The importance of quality criteria for software production

The quality requirements on a software product refer not only to the finished (ready-to-use) product. In fact, the quality of the finished product depends on the quality of the intermediate products; i.e., the quality requirements encompass all levels of software production. Poor quality in intermediate products (e.g., architecture design) always proves detrimental to the quality of the final product.

We distinguish quality attributes and their importance for the software production process according to:

- Quality attributes that affect the end product
- Quality attributes that affect intermediate products

We distinguish the quality attributes of *end products* according to Bons and van Megen [Bons 1982] as follows:

- Quality attributes that affect their *application*: These influence the suitability of the product for its intended application (correctness, reliability and user friendliness).

- Quality attributes related to their *maintenance*: These affect the suitability of the product for functional modification and extensibility (readability, extensibility and testability).
- Quality attributes that influence their *portability*: These affect the suitability of the product for porting to another environment (portability and testability).

We distinguish the quality attributes of *intermediate products* (compare [Bons 1982]) as follows:

- Quality attributes that affect the transformation: These affect the suitability of an intermediate product for immediate transformation to a subsequent (high-quality) product (correctness, readability and testability).
- Quality attributes that affect the quality of the end product: These directly influence the quality of the end product (correctness, reliability, adequacy, readability, extensibility, testability, efficiency and portability).

## 2.3 The effects of quality criteria on each other and on time and costs

Figure 2.3 shows the mutual effects of quality criteria and their effects on costs and time (compare [Bons 1982]). Figure 2.2 shows that the demand to fulfill a certain quality

| Attribute \ Effect on | Correctness | Dependability | Adequacy | Learnability | Robustness | Readability | Modifiability/extensibility | Testability | Efficiency | Portability | Development time | Service life | Development costs | Operating costs | Maintenance costs | Porting costs |
|---|---|---|---|---|---|---|---|---|---|---|---|---|---|---|---|---|
| Correctness | | + | 0 | 0 | + | 0 | 0 | 0 | 0 | 0 | – | + | – | + | + | 0 |
| Dependability | 0 | | 0 | 0 | + | 0 | 0 | 0 | – | 0 | – | + | – | + | + | 0 |
| Adequacy | 0 | 0 | | + | 0 | 0 | 0 | 0 | + | – | – | 0 | – | + | + | – |
| Learnability | 0 | 0 | 0 | | 0 | 0 | 0 | 0 | – | 0 | – | 0 | – | + | 0 | 0 |
| Robustness | 0 | + | + | 0 | | 0 | 0 | + | – | 0 | – | + | – | + | + | 0 |
| Readability | + | + | 0 | 0 | + | | + | + | – | + | + | + | + | 0 | + | + |
| Modifiability/extensibility | + | + | 0 | 0 | + | 0 | | + | – | + | – | + | + | 0 | + | + |
| Testability | + | + | 0 | 0 | + | 0 | + | | – | + | + | + | + | 0 | + | + |
| Efficiency | – | – | + | – | – | – | – | – | | – | – | + | – | + | – | – |
| Portability | 0 | 0 | – | 0 | 0 | 0 | + | 0 | – | | – | + | – | – | + | + |

Figure 2.3: Mutual effects between quality criteria and their effects on time and costs ("+": positive effect, "–": negative effect, "0": no effect)

requirement triggers measures in the software development process that could be bound to costs and time (e.g., improving the correctness, reliability, and user friendliness), but normally these save money and time during the maintenance and operation of the software product (e.g., due to better readability and testability). However, such a requirement could also contradict other quality criteria (e.g., because increased reliability normally has a negative effect on the efficiency of a system).

## 2.4 Quality assurance measures

Software quality does not evolve on its own. It requires a number of measures to guarantee that the final product has acceptable quality. The most important measures are:

(1) Constructive measures:
- Consistent application of methods in all phases of the development process
- Use of adequate development tools
- Software development on the basis of high-quality semifinished products
- Consistent maintenance of development documentation

(2) Analytical measures:
- Static program analysis
- Dynamic program analysis
- Systematic choice of adequate test cases
- Consistent logging of analysis results

(3) Organizational measures:
- Use of approach models
- Continuous education of product developers
- Institutionalization of quality assurance

The following chapters present methods, techniques, principles and tools for translating the above measures into quality assurance and for rationalization of the software development process.

Chapter 3

# The phases of a software project

When confronted with a complex task, we try to systematically order our approach to solving it, i.e., to define an approach model. Such an approach model then regulates our solution process, dividing it into comprehensible subtasks and thus enabling stepwise planning, execution, decisions and control.

We naturally apply this basic idea of systems engineering to our approach to the development of software. As with other projects, we divide software projects into individual phases. These phases collectively and their chronological sequence are termed the *software life cycle*.

## 3.1 Phase models

Phase models have been described in numerous variants (see [Fairley 1985], [Sommerville 1985], [Pomberger 1986], [Pressman 1987]). In essence they postulate the following phases of the software development process:

- Requirements analysis and planning
- System specification
- System and component design
- Implementation and component test
- System test
- Operation and maintenance

The approach model underlying the phase model of software development is based on the principle that for each phase we can clearly define which results must be achieved and that a given phase can only begin on completion of its predecessor. Using this strictly sequential approach is intended to make software projects more planable, organizable and controllable. However, reality shows that such a purely sequential approach can hardly ever be carried out. This realization led to the development of model variants that relaxed this strictly sequential approach. In addition, new methods and techniques arose to ameliorate the software development process (e.g., prototyping to improve the specification process, object-oriented programming to improve the design and implementation process); these had their effects on our approach to the software development process and required deviations from the classical phase model. Although in practice it will scarcely be possible to apply a phase model consistently in its pure form, a systematic approach certainly improves a software project's chances of success. This section describes today's most important phase models.

### 3.1.1 The classical sequential software life-cycle model

The term *software life cycle* suggests a time span in which a software product is developed and used, extending to its retirement. It also suggests the structuring of this time span into phases and their associated activities and results, and the establishment of the sequence of and the relationships between these phases. The cyclical nature of the model expresses that the phases can be carried out repeatedly in the development of a software product. Figure 3.1 shows the *classical* (and accordingly idealized) *sequential phase model* of the software life cycle.

The remainder of this subsection describes the goals, the most important activities, and the products of the phases of the software life cycle without detailed treatment of the methods and techniques that need to be employed to achieve these goals. For more detail, we refer the reader to the subsequent chapters of this book.

**Requirements analysis and planning**. For a domain targeted for a software solution, the *goal* of the analysis and planning phase consists of determining and documenting which steps (activities) need to be carried out, the nature of their mutual effects, which parts are to be automated, and which resources (technical, personnel, financial and temporal) are available for the realization of the project.

The most important *activities* are completing the requirements analysis, delimitating the problem domain, roughly sketching the components of the target system, making an initial estimate of the scope and the economic feasibility of the planned project, and creating a rough project schedule.

The *products* of the analysis and planning phase are the user requirements, the project contract, and a rough project schedule.

**System specification**. The *goal* of the specification phase is a contract (the requirements definition) between the client and the software producer that precisely specifies what the target software system must do and the premises for its realization.

The most important *activities* are specifying the system and compiling the requirements definition, establishing an exact project schedule, validating the system

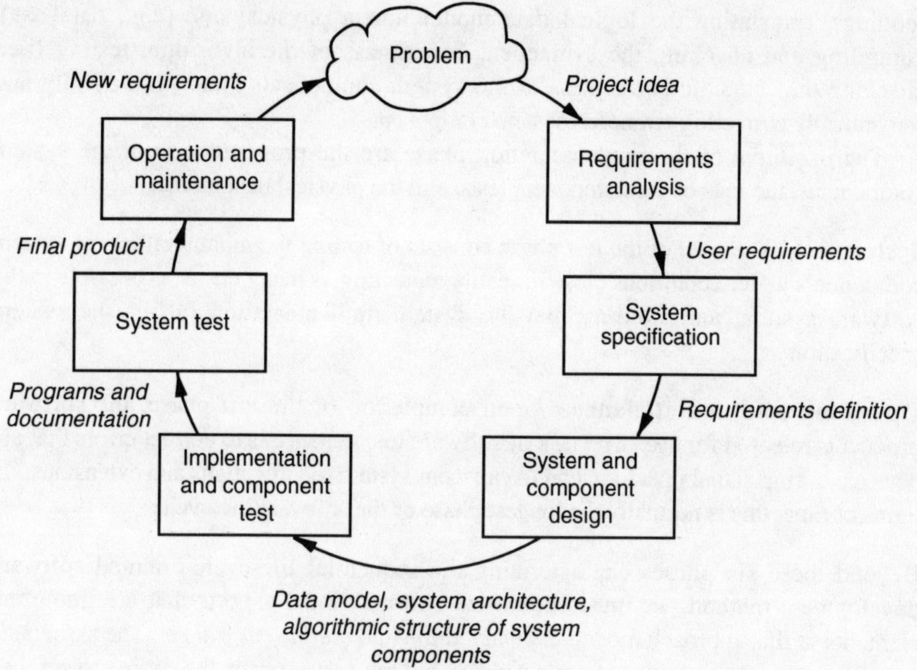


Figure 3.1: The classical sequential software life-cycle model

specification, (i.e., inspecting the completeness and consistency of the requirements and examining the technical feasibility), and justifying the economic feasibility of the project.

The *products* of the specification phase are the requirements definition and the exact project schedule.

**System and components design**. The *goal* of the design phase consists of determining which system components will cover which requirements in the system specification and how these system components will work together.

The most important *activities* are designing the system architecture (i.e., defining the system components by designing their interfaces and specifying their mutual effects) and, if needed, designing the underlying logical data model; designing the algorithmic structure of the system components; and validating the system architecture and the algorithms to realize the individual system components.

The *products* of the design phase are the descriptions of the logical data model, the system architecture and the algorithmic structure of the system components, as well as the documentation of the design decisions.

**Implementation and component test**. The *goal* of the implementation phase is to transform the products of the design phase into a form that is executable on a computer.

The most important *activities* encompass completely refining the algorithms for the individual components, transferring the algorithms into a programming language (coding), translating the logical data model into a physical one (e.g., database), compiling and checking the syntactical correctness of the algorithm, testing (i.e., checking the semantic correctness of the system components), and syntactically and semantically correcting erroneous system components.

The *products* of the implementation phase are the program code of the system components, the logs of the component tests, and the physical data model.

**System test**. The *goal* of the test phase consists of testing the mutual effects of system components under conditions close to reality, detecting as many errors as possible in the software system, and assuring that the system implementation fulfills the system specification.

**Operation and maintenance**. Upon completion of the test phase, the software product is released for use. The task of software maintenance is to correct errors that are detected during actual operation and to carry out system modifications and extensions. In terms of time, this is normally the longest phase of the software life cycle.

Beyond these six phases characterizing the sequential life-cycle-oriented software development method, we must emphasize two additional aspects that are important elements of this approach model: *documentation* and *quality assurance*. The associated activities do not form an actual project phase, but must accompany the entire project, i.e., must be carried out in all phases.

During the development phases the *documentation* should enable communication among the persons involved in the development; upon completion of the development phases it supports the utilization and maintenance of the software product. Furthermore, documentation reflects the course of the project for the purpose of calculating production costs and for improved planning of future projects.

*Quality assurance* encompasses analytical, design and organizational measures for quality planning and for fulfilling quality criteria such as correctness, reliability, user friendliness, maintainability, efficiency and portability.

### The life-cycle-oriented software development approach

The procedure in software development according to the life-cycle model is based on the principle of top-down decomposition of black boxes, i.e., on stepwise refinement (see Figure 3.2).

Each phase requires well-defined products (usually in the form of documents) as input. These products are processed in phase-related processes – for which certain methods and tools are employed – and the products are output to the next phase.

The phases are clearly delimited, and we only leave a given phase after its products have been accepted in verification and validation steps. Verification and validation are separate processes: the verification step tests whether a phase product (e.g., the system architecture) fulfills the system specifications, while the validation step tests whether the

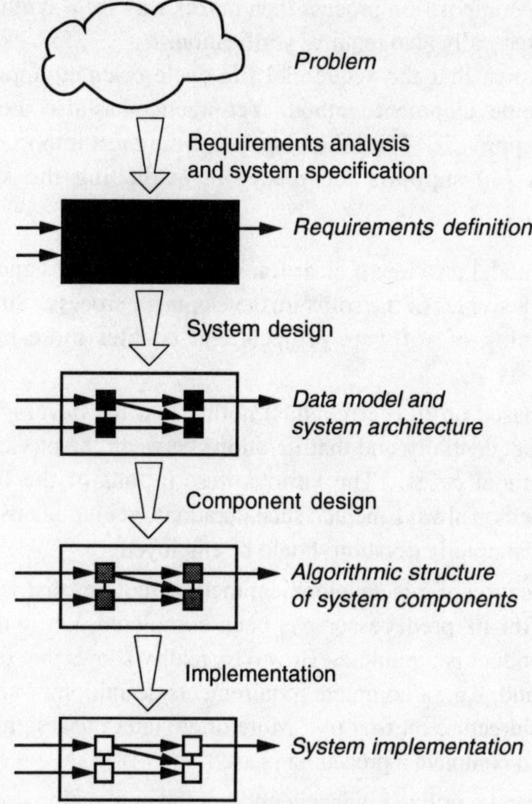


Figure 3.2: Stepwise refinement in the life-cycle model
(compare [Zave 1984])

product in its current form actually meets the client's wishes (since the specifications could be incorrect).

The approach according to the software life-cycle model characteristically describes the system from the outside first (during the analysis and specifications phase). We first ask *what* the system must do; *how* this is to be achieved is initially of no importance. The system itself is seen as a black box whose behavior is defined exactly from the outside and whose inner structure is not specified further.

Next, in the design phase, we continue in the same way by specifying the decomposition of the system into its components, describing *what* these components must do, and defining their necessary cooperation, but we do not state *how* they will actually be realized. Once this process is complete, i.e., the interfaces of all system components are defined, the developers need only consider the component specifications to design the algorithmic structure of the system components. This approach supports the successive reduction of complexity of both the development process and the product itself. Next the algorithms must be coded in a programming language and tested individually. The decomposition process then makes way for a synthesis of the system components, which naturally also requires verification.

Studies have shown that the sequential life-cycle-oriented approach is the most widespread software development method. Yet practice has also shown the limits and weaknesses of this approach. The following list of the most important advantages (+) and disadvantages (−) supports the reader in evaluating the suitability of this development method.

+ The life-cycle model provides a clear framework that defines and distinguishes the most important activities of the software development process. Such an organization eases the planning of software projects and enables more exact estimates of development costs.

− The model is based on the (erroneous) notion that the development process can usually elapse sequentially and that iterations between the phases prove necessary only in exceptional cases. The various descriptions of the life-cycle-oriented development method always include such iterations, yet it remains unclear when and according to what criteria iteration should be employed.

− The strict application of this development method requires that we can only begin a given phase after its predecessor has been completed, i.e., when the respective intermediate product is complete. However, reality shows that only in exceptional cases can we land, e.g., a complete requirements definition or an error-free design of a system architecture on first try. More often, later phases provide the information necessary to complete a preceding phase.

+ The approach can be utilized independently of the application domain, project size, and complexity of the target product.

+ The structuring of the development process provided by the model encourages a structuring of the product that largely adheres to today's recognized software engineering principles.

− The strict separation of the individual phases is an inadmissible idealization. In reality the encompassed activities overlap, and the mutual effects between the phases prove much more complex than the sequential model can express.

In summary, we see that the life-cycle-oriented software development method certainly provides an important foundation for an engineering-based approach, but with certain serious drawbacks. The software life-cycle model describes activities, their sequence, and the nature of the intermediate products (phase results). The model's defined activities are certainly necessary, but perhaps not adequate, and they cannot be circumvented even by an ingenious method. Using this approach model in practice shows that we sometimes need to diverge from this idealized, purely sequential approach, and that we cannot define the goal of a system development fully independently of the subsequent solution.

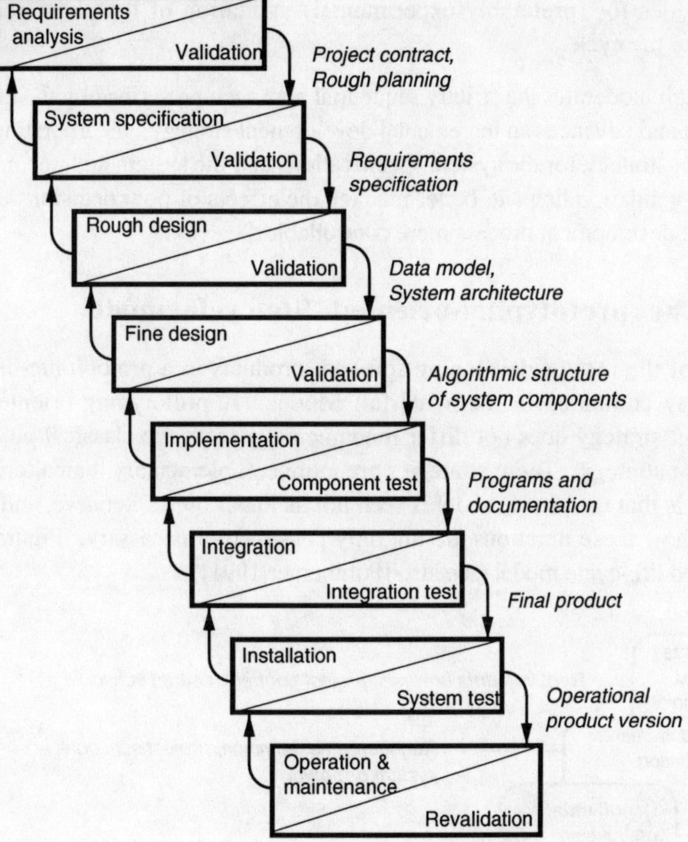


Figure 3.3: The Waterfall Model

## 3.1.2 The Waterfall Model

Experience with the application of the classical sequential software life-cycle model has led to the development of variants that primarily concern the subdivision of the phases and statements about the mutual effects between the phases. One of the best-known variants is the Waterfall Model represented in Figure 3.3 (see [Royce 1970]).

Developed in the 1970s, the Waterfall Model represents an experience-based refinement of the classical sequential software life-cycle model. Essentially it incorporates two extensions:

(1) It introduces iteration between the phases along with the restriction of providing iterations, if possible, only between successive phases in order to reduce the expense of revision that results from iterations over multiple phases.

(2) It provides for (preferably experimental) validation of the phase results in the software life cycle.

This approach moderates the strictly sequential approach prescribed by the classical life-cycle model and advances an incremental development strategy. Incorporating a stepwise development strategy for the system specifications and the system architecture as well as phase-wise validation helps to better manage the effects of poor decisions and to make the software development process more controllable.

### 3.1.3 The prototyping-oriented life-cycle model

The seeds of the idea of developing software products in a prototyping-oriented way were already contained in the Waterfall Model. A prototyping-oriented software development strategy does not differ fundamentally from the classical phase-oriented development strategy. These strategies are more complementary than alternative. The new aspect is that the phase model is seen not as linear but as iterative, and it specifies where and how these iterations are not only possible but necessary. Figure 3.4 shows this modified life-cycle model (see also [Pomberger 1991]).

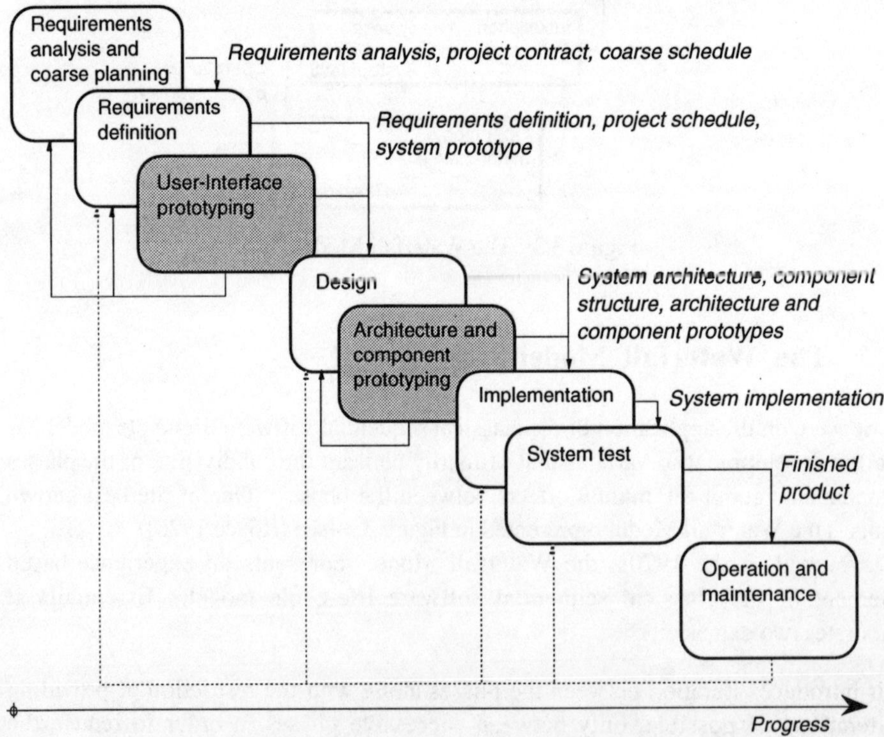


Figure 3.4: Prototyping-oriented software life cycle

The prototyping-oriented development method (as the authors see it) deviates from the conventional development method according to the sequential life-cycle model primarily in its approach and the products of the individual phases of the life cycle. The phase distinction is maintained, but with the difference that requirements analysis and system specification overlap significantly in time, and design, implementation and testing tend to merge. The phases are thus no longer distinct parts of a continuous development process. Hence we speak of activities rather than phases because we no longer have the complete separation of subtasks, as the classical software life cycle requires.

Prototype construction is an iterative process (see Figure 3.5). First a prototype is produced (preferably with tool support) on the basis of the results of preceding activities. During the specification phase a prototype of the user interface is developed that encompasses significant parts of the functional requirements on the target software system. Experiments are conducted on this prototype that reflect real conditions of actual use in order to determine whether the client's requirements are fulfilled. Under conditions close to reality, software developers and users can test whether the system model contains errors, whether it meets the client's preconceptions, and whether modifications are necessary. This reduces the risk of erroneous or incomplete system specifications and creates a significantly better starting point for subsequent activities. We essentially introduce a life cycle within the life cycle in order to achieve better system specifications.

The same applies to subsequent activities: After the design of the system architecture has attained a certain level of complexity, an architecture prototype is used (before the start of the implementation phase) to test whether the design decisions are on target. Here again, we introduce a subcycle into the overall life-cycle model. This allows experimental testing of the quality of the chosen system decomposition, the completeness and correctness of the component interfaces, and the extensibility of the system

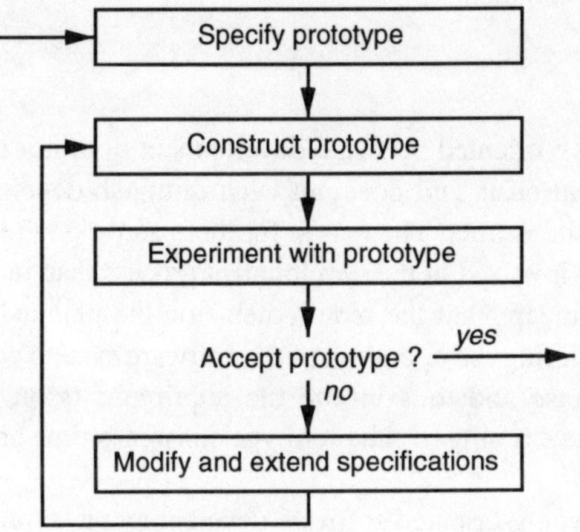


Figure 3.5: Prototyping activities

architecture, under conditions close to reality. This significantly reduces the risk of having to make extensive and expensive modifications during implementation.

This leads us to another significant difference between the two approaches. According to the classical life-cycle-oriented development method, implementation occurs *as late as possible*, only after all details of the specification and design process have been clarified. In the prototyping-oriented development method, by contrast, implementation (of a prototype) takes place *as early as possible*. This is because practice has shown that we are more likely to achieve our goal if the system specifications and the system architecture are developed stepwise on the basis of a model that permits representation of the dynamic behavior of the system, in other words, with executable prototypes rather than mere written descriptions.

The overlapping of the individual activities (see Figure 3.4) and the nature of the products (which are no longer mere descriptions but executable prototypes) significantly reduce the risk of wrong decisions, and the effects achieved with intermediate results through experiments make quality assurance easier.

For the general approach in prototyping-oriented software development, it does not matter whether the prototypes (for the user interface, the system architecture or individual components) are throw-away or reusable; the goals are risk reduction, successful quality assurance, and benefiting from the learning effect of experimentation under real conditions. With respect to the rationalization of the expensive production process, reusable prototypes are desirable, leading to an evolutionary development strategy. The extent to which this goal can be achieved depends primarily on the quality of the employed prototyping tools (see Chapter 6).

In the following we summarize quantitative and qualitative aspects of prototyping-oriented software development (compare [Bischofberger 1992]). In addition, we provide answers to a number of questions that keep recurring in connection with prototyping-oriented software development.

### Costs

As a rule, prototyping-oriented software development does not achieve a reduction in software development costs and does not even diminish development time. In fact, sometimes the opposite is true. The reason for these surprising results is that the user is much more intensely involved in the development process than in conventional software development. This means that the requirements on the planned software system that normally arise only during the operation of the software system come to light already in the specification phase and thus inflate the requirements on the planned product. Furthermore, the user's testing of the prototype consumes time and demands additional resources.

However, prototyping-oriented software development generally leads to a reduction in the overall costs of the software life cycle primarily because the high costs of maintenance, and usually the operating expenses as well, can be reduced because of an improvement in quality. The system specifications reflected in a prototype prove more adequate than a written requirements definition and provide a better basis for design and implementation. The proportion of perfective and adaptive maintenance, which Lientz and Swanson [Lientz 1980] calculate at approximately 80% of maintenance costs (see Section 3.7.2) can be pronouncedly reduced. Early experiments with the user interface lead to an ergonomically improved product, which has a positive effect on operating costs.

**Quality**

Prototyping-oriented software development, when carried out by experts, reaps a significant improvement in the quality attributes *user friendliness*, *functional adequacy*, *modifiability and extensibility*, *correctness* and *reliability* and is thus an extremely efficient quality assurance measure.

Prototyping proves especially well suited for experimentally testing various aspects of ergonomic design of user interfaces and for obtaining early indications of the actual user requirements. The user friendliness can already be determined before the design and implementation and can be increased more cost-effectively than on the finished product. This produces a cost-effective improvement in the quality attribute user friendliness.

User interface prototypes permit experiments close to reality and thus support functional exploration. Many requirements only become clear with the application to a concrete case; prototyping in the specification process supports the definition of functional requirements especially well.

The more precise and complete a system specification is, the more secure is the basis for the design and implementation. This makes it easier to achieve the goals of correctness, reliability, modifiability and extensibility of a software product (assuming, naturally, that software engineering principles are upheld during design and implementation).

A prototyping-oriented design validation permits evaluation of the adequacy of a decomposition before its implementation and encourages a willingness to redesign to achieve architectural improvements.

The prototyping-oriented approach improves not only the quality of the product, but also the quality of the development process. A precise system specification enables precise estimation of the required design, implementation and testing effort and thus significantly improves *planability* of software projects and helps keep them *on schedule*. Furthermore, prototyping supports the division of labor in software development especially well because it reduces communication difficulties between future users and software engineers and among the software engineers themselves. An experimentally tested model validation, as the prototyping-oriented approach provides, reduces the number of uncertain assumptions in a software project and thus reduces the risk of a flop.

**Risks**

However, although prototyping significantly reduces risk factors in the software development process, it also introduces new risk factors.

Experience has shown that prototyping can unnecessarily *inflate the specification process* and sometimes threatens never to let it end – the more the users have, the more they want.

There is a real danger of *delivering a system prototype* rather than a final product. Observations have shown that when users are confronted during the specification process with prototypes that already exhibit a large part of the required functionality, then users prefer to use this diminished and still immature functionality immediately rather than to wait for the clean and efficient implementation, for which the prototype only serves as a model. This leads to negligence of software engineering principles during system implementation and thus to the danger of deterioration in the quality attributes, especially structure, extensibility and efficiency.

Another risk factor is *price justification*. Conventional software development takes a long time before presenting the user with an executable program. Prototyping-oriented software development inverts this relationship: the user can experiment with prototypes very early and in them already finds part of the functionality in satisfactory form. This creates the false impression that the production of a software product has become much simpler and requires less effort than previously. Hence the client cannot understand the actual effort required to complete the final product from a working prototype.

### 3.1.4 The Spiral Model

In the Spiral Model, Boehm [Boehm 1988] defined a software development model that combines the above models or includes them as special cases. Boehm's model makes it possible to choose the most suitable approach for a given project. Figure 3.6 shows this variant of the software life-cycle model.

The radial expansion in Figure 3.6 represents the cumulative costs to a certain point in time, and the angular dimension refers to progress on the project in the respective spiral cycles. Each cycle encompasses the same sequence of steps for each part of the target product and for each stage of completion.

A spiral cycle begins with the establishment of the following points:

- Goals for and requirements on the (sub)product (application domain, functionality, modifiability, etc.)
- Alternatives to realization of the (sub)product (alternative solution A, alternative solution B, reuse, purchase, etc.)
- Constraints and restrictions (costs, deadlines, interfaces, etc.)

The next step evaluates the proposed solution variant with respect to the project goals and applicable constraints, emphasizing the detection of risks and uncertainties. If such are

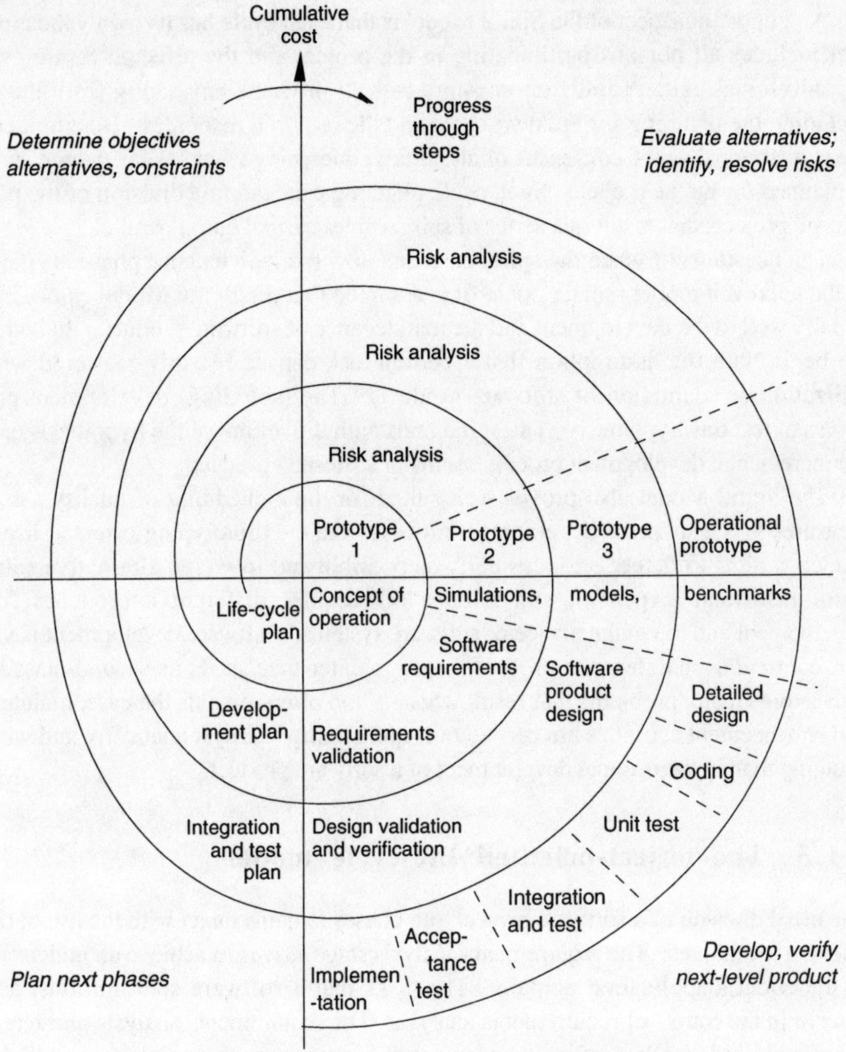


Figure 3.6: Boehm's Spiral Model [Boehm 1988]

found, measures and strategies are considered to reduce these risks and their effects. Here prototyping provides the primary remedy; for example, given uncertainty about the scope, the design of the user interface, or the data model for a database, prototypes help to clarify these aspects.

This approach continues in a clockwise direction; i.e., the next step follows according to the classical phase model, with each step again preceded by a risk analysis and complemented by prototyping-oriented validation accompanied by the maintenance or creation of a project schedule (costs, time, required resources) for the next cycle.

An important aspect of the Spiral Model is that each cycle has its own validation step that includes all persons participating in the project and the affected future users or organizational unit. Validation encompasses all products emanating from the cycle, including the planning for the next cycle and the required resources. Boehm identifies the primary goal as the consensus of all parties concerning what has been done and what is planned for the next cycle. Such cycle planning can lead to a division of the projects into subprojects that result in a series of spiral cycles carried out in parallel.

The questions of when the spiral ends and how the maintenance phase is embedded in the approach model remain open. It is assumed that the Spiral Model can be applied equally well to the development and the maintenance of software products. In both cases we begin with the assumption that a certain task can be feasibly mastered with the utilization or adaptation of software products. The (spiraling) development process serves to test this hypothesis. The spiral ends with the refutal of the hypothesis or when the incremental development process results in a finished product.

The Spiral Model also proves well suited for the embedding of quality assurance measures in the software development process; like the prototyping-oriented life-cycle model, it aims to detect errors as early as possible and to weigh alternative solutions (with justifiable expense); and it does not require different approaches for the development and the maintenance of software systems. Software development is viewed as a continuous maintenance process; hence maintenance sheds its second-class status. This avoids many problems that result when, as too often remains the case, maintenance and enhancement activities are carried out significantly less systematically and with less planning than in the original development of a software product.

### 3.1.5 The object-oriented life-cycle model

The usual division of a software project into phases remains intact with the use of object-oriented techniques. The requirements analysis stage strives to achieve an understanding of the client's application domain. The tasks that a software solution must address emerge in the course of requirements analysis. The requirements analysis phase remains completely independent of any implementation technique that might be applied later. Similarly, in the system specification phase the requirements definition describes *what* the software product must do, but not *how* this goal is to be achieved.

One point of divergence from conventional phase models arises because implementation with object-oriented programming is marked by the assembly of already existing components. This has the following consequences:

- Design can no longer be carried out independently of the later implementation because during the design phase we must consider which components are available for the solution of the problem. Design and implementation become more closely associated, and even the choice of a different programming language can lead to completely different program structures.

- The duration of the implementation phase is reduced. In particular, (sub)products become available much earlier to allow testing of the correctness of the design. Incorrect decisions can be recognized and corrected earlier. This makes for closer feedback coupling of the design and implementation phases.
- The class library containing the reusable components must be continuously maintained. Savings at the implementation end are partially lost as they are reinvested in this maintenance. A new job title emerges, the class librarian, who is responsible for ensuring the efficient usability of the class library.
- During the test phase, the function of not only the new product but also of the reused components is tested. Any deficiencies in the latter must be documented exactly. The resulting modifications must be handled centrally in the class library to ensure that they impact on other projects, both current and future.
- Newly created classes must be tested for their general usability. If there is a chance that a component could be used in other projects as well, it must be included in the class library and documented accordingly. This also means that the new class must be announced and made accessible to other programmers who might profit from it. This places new requirements on the in-house communication structures.

Figure 3.7 shows the object-oriented life-cycle model. Do not misinterpret the diagram: the release of new components after their testing does not create a cycle within the particular project. The class library serves as a tool that extends beyond the scope of an individual project because classes provided by one project can increase productivity in subsequent projects. The actual software life cycle recurs when new requirements arise in the company that initiate a new requirements analysis stage.

In the object-oriented approach model, the class library plays such a central role that we want to visualize its management in Figure 3.8.

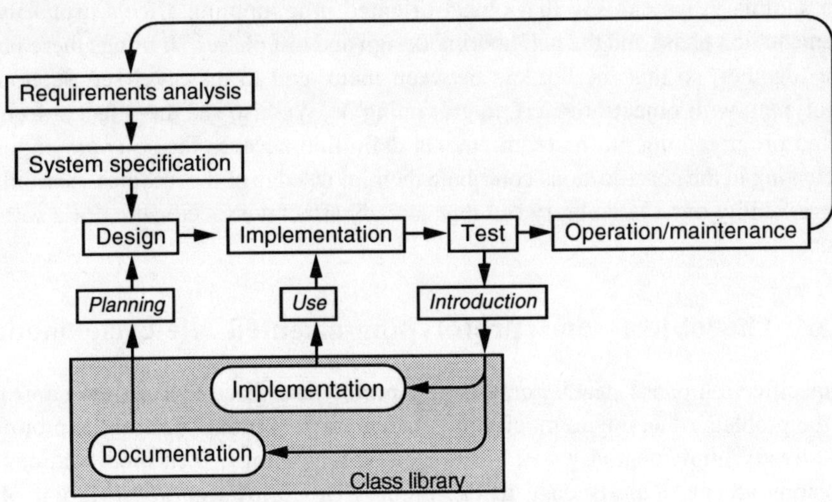


Figure 3.7: Object-oriented life-cycle model

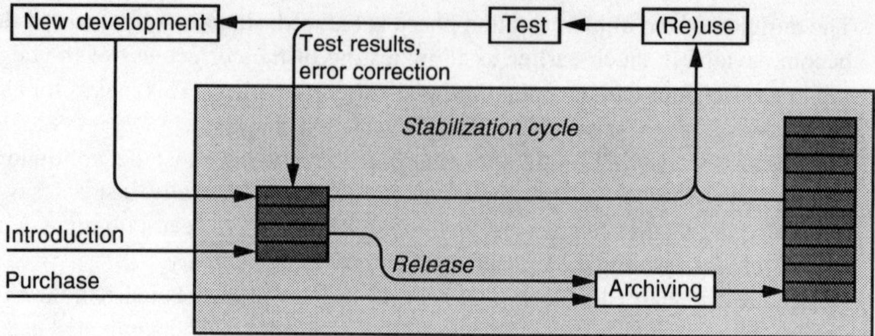


Figure 3.8: Stabilization of classes

A class that has been declared reusable enters the class library for the first time upon its release after testing. However, it is not immediately archived, but is placed in interim storage as an immature class. Before the class is declared as mature, it must pass a trial by fire by being reused a certain number of times. Thus a class repeatedly goes through a *stabilization cycle*. With each reuse, test documentation records how well the class has proven its suitability. Errors are corrected immediately in cooperation with the class librarian, who also collects feedback. The class librarian is responsible for declaring a class as mature and officially archiving it.

Mature classes no longer need to be monitored so strictly. Nevertheless, they can become obsolete or be replaced in part or as a whole by newer classes. The introduction of a new class can trigger the restructuring of the class library. If interface changes result, it might become necessary to rethink already archived classes. In this case a specialist or a design team (independent of all other projects) undertakes such redesign.

In summary, we can say that object-oriented programming affects primarily the implementation phase and the neighboring design and test phases. It brings these phases closer together, so that the borders between them tend to dissolve (see Section 4.8 "Prototyping with object-oriented programming"). We also see the effects of object-oriented programming on the requirements definition because the software engineers participating in the specifications contribute their knowledge of the technical possibilities. The availability of a class library can thus already affect the specification of a software product.

### 3.1.6 The object- and prototyping-oriented life-cycle model

The specification phase steadily creates new prototypes. Each time we are confronted with the problem of having to modify or enhance existing prototypes. If the prototypes were already implemented with object-oriented technology, then modifications and extensions are particularly easy to carry out. This allows an abbreviation of the specification phase, which is particularly important when proposed solutions are repeatedly discussed with the client. With such an approach it is not important whether the prototype serves solely specification purposes or whether it is to be incrementally developed to the final product. If no prototyping tools are available, object-oriented programming can serve as a substitute tool for modeling user interfaces. This particularly applies if an extensive class library is available for user interface elements.

For incremental prototyping (i.e., if the produced prototype is to be used as the basis for the implementation of the product), object-oriented programming also proves to be a suitable medium. Desired functionality can be added stepwise to the prototypes without having to change the prototype itself. This results in a clear distinction between the user interface modeled in the specification phase and the actual functionality of the program. This is particularly important for the following reasons:

- This assures that the user interface is not changed during the implementation of the program functionality. The user interface developed in collaboration with the client remains as it was defined in the specification phase.
- In the implementation of the functionality, each time a subtask is completed, a more functional prototype results, which can be tested (preferably together with the client) and compared with the specifications. During test runs situations sometimes arise that require rethinking the user interface. In such cases the software life cycle retreats one step and a new user interface prototype is constructed. Experience has shown that this new prototype can usually be extended by the already implemented functionality, without significant modifications.

With the use of a prototyping tool, how the tool works proves decisive with regard to whether object-oriented programming brings rewards. Most prototyping tools generate code from a user interface description (which was input as text or interactively developed) that realizes the specified user interface. The quality of a prototyping tool can be measured in terms of its possibilities for specification of dialog behavior and the structuredness of the generated program code. Newer tools already employ the features of object-oriented programming; they generate object classes for the various user interface elements and usually build on an existing class library. Such tools provide a seamless transition to an object-oriented development style. They employ the extensibility of the class library to generate user interface prototypes; the extensibility of the prototype provides the means for constructing the final product.

Figure 3.9 depicts the software life cycle with a combination of prototyping and object-oriented software development. For the sake of simplicity, we have omitted the stabilization cycle described in Section 3.1.5.

Since the user interface and the functional parts of the program are largely decoupled, two cycles result that share a common core. The integration of the functional classes and the user interface classes creates a prototype that can be tested and validated. This places new requirements on the user interface and/or the functionality, so that the cycle begins again.

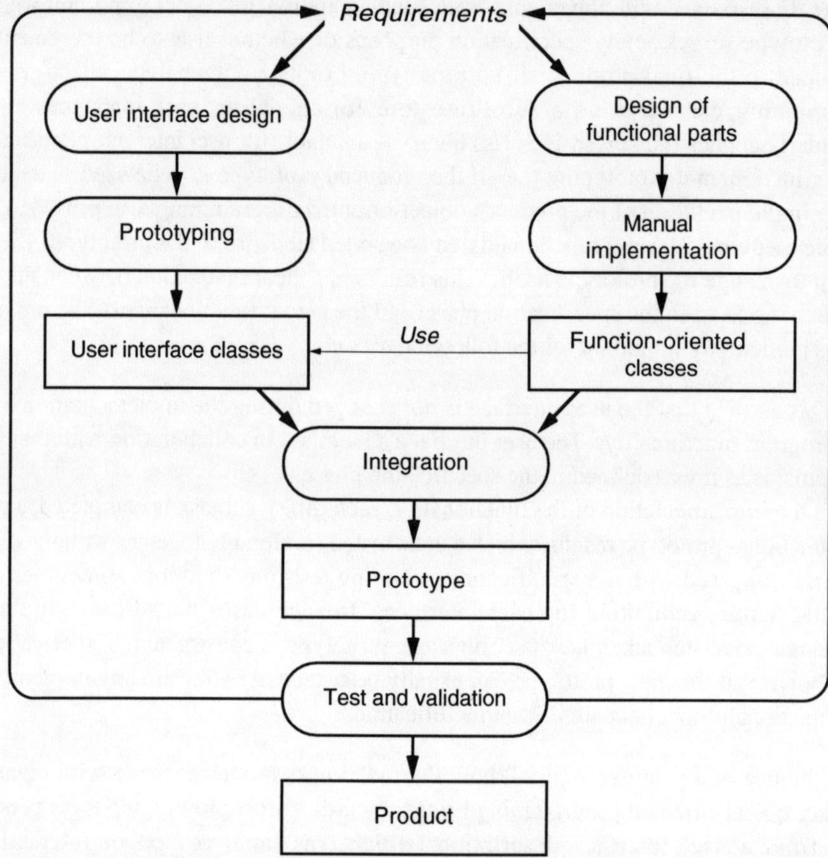


Figure 3.9: Software development with prototyping and object-orientation

## 3.2 Requirements analysis

A widespread misconception holds that the client can explain the requirements to the developer in such a way that the latter understands them without difficulty. The first goal of a software project is to have the client and software developer agree on what actually is to be done. The scope of the problem must be identified and delimited, and the requirements and the scope of provided goods and services must be defined. The goal of *requirements analysis* is to determine which tasks are to be handled with computer support and under what environmental conditions.

Usually clients and software engineers have little knowledge of the other's field and first need to bridge their communication gap. Here it pays to discuss the problem to be solved with as many persons as possible: the later users of the planned product, the project leader, and any other project participants. This is the surest approach to establishing which features the software product must have; sometimes it proves valuable to determine what is *not covered.*

Which activities are necessary in the analysis phase depends to a large extent on the specific case. Nevertheless, several generally applicable guidelines help in systematizing the process. We restrict our discussion to a concise description of the most important of these activities.

When some area of a company seeks a software solution, but lacks a clear task description, a *requirements analysis* is necessary in order to determine what is to be automated. The requirements analysis phase encompasses activities to analyze the current (organizational) system and the affected company operations, and to collect the user's wishes. The analyst needs to determine who is the actual client; in some cases the client's requirements diverge significantly from those of the future users. Only knowledge of both (possibly different) sets of requirements can guarantee a satisfactory overall solution.

We recommend a stepwise approach to requirements analysis. First comes the *system delimitation*, then the *system investigation*, and finally the *system description.* The term *system* means a structured interconnection of mutually influencing processes that obey certain rules.

Not every software project begins with a requirements analysis. In many cases we do not have an existing system that is to be automated, hence there is no existing system to be investigated; or the client is capable of compiling a requirements definition (see Section 3.3) without the preceding requirements analysis phase. In such a case we omit the requirements analysis phase of the software life cycle.

### 3.2.1 System delimitation

The purpose of *system delimitation* is to achieve clarity about which components to include in the analysis and which to consciously exclude. Note that this is often not clear from the start. The first task description for a software project is usually kept very general, such as the following: "A cost accounting system is to be implemented to monitor the cost developments." System delimitation needs to define the scope of services contained in such a vague description. For instance, system delimitation requires defining the scope of the project as a simple line-oriented accounting system or a cost accounting system encompassing periodical achievement computations.

Another goal of system delimitation is to determine the environmental conditions that are relevant for the product. Many projects make the mistake of paying too little attention to the system delimitation and the definition of environmental conditions; on introduction of the software product, this results in extensive modifications and adaptations in many parts of the environment. Only after it is clear what is to be automated and which functions are to be excluded can the actual requirements analysis begin.

### 3.2.2 System analysis

*System analysis* is the actual core of *requirements analysis*. On the one hand, requirements analysis should handle only parts of the system that already exist. On the other hand, note that the following often occurs in practice: A department of a company is seeking a software solution for a certain range of tasks. For personal reasons or because they are not convinced of the feasibility, the employees keep their wishes to a minimum. When the finished software product is introduced and the users have achieved a certain level of confidence in using it, they soon begin to place new demands on the software product. This finally results in a software system in which the magnitude of add-on components by far exceeds that of the original version. The quality of the software product suffers, especially if the original version was poorly structured and not modular enough. This requires the analyst to always keep more problems in mind than the user raises independently. If future extensions can be foreseen in the requirements analysis stage, this affects the design of a software product regarding its easy extensibility. During system analysis the analyst must examine the *application domain*, the *information flow*, as well as all *weaknesses* of the existing system. We introduce a rough systematization for this analysis and classify the analysis activities as follows:

- Structural analysis
- Operational analysis
- Communications analysis
- Document analysis
- Data analysis
- Flow analysis
- Weakness analysis

**Structural analysis**. The purpose of *structural analysis* is to clearly understand the organizational structure of a system or company department that is seeking a software solution. This is important in order to be able to present the software concept later to all involved. Structural analysis needs to provide insight into:

- The organizational structure of the system or department being analyzed
- The system hierarchy
- The type and extent of connections to other system components or departments
- The number and qualifications of system users

Tools for representing the structural analysis include organizational diagrams, process flow diagrams, and hierarchy diagrams.

**Operational analysis**. The purpose of *operational analysis* is to analyze the nature and scope of the tasks (operations) that occur in the system or department being analyzed and special aspects of the internal flow of these operations. Hence we must determine the following:

- What is done? (Which operations occur in the domain being analyzed?)
- Who or what carries out these operations?
- When and how often are these operations carried out?
- What is the purpose of each operation?

For each operation we compile a description with the following contents:

- Data and information used (signals, card files, records, forms, instructions, etc.)
- Data and information produced
- Flow of operations (processing algorithm)

Here it is important to learn all (decision making) rules that regulate the cooperation of the various processes or that guide managers and personnel in deciding whether automation is feasible and for which operations. Flow diagrams provide a tool for representing functional flow, with everything else described in prose.

**Communications analysis**. *Communications analysis*, in contrast to operational analysis, handles the informal relationships between individual operations. Interesting aspects include the form (e.g., communications logs in technical application domains or per telephone, in writing, and orally in commercial application domains), the type (e.g., synchronous or asynchronous communication in technical domains, meetings, conferences, and reference to files or archives in commercial domains), and the frequency of communication between operational units. For each operation a communications matrix represents the form, the type and the frequency of its application.

**Document analysis**. The purpose of *document analysis* is to analyze all documents and protocols that are used and produced in the analyzed domain. The results of this analysis form the basis for the subsequent specification of the form of input and output for the individual operations. For each document we create a description with the following contents:

- Designation
- Contents
- Purpose (control form, job sheet, production instructions, ...)
- Degree of formalization, structuredness
- Distribution
- Archiving

In addition, we create a utilization matrix (depicting which operations employ and produce which documents).

**Data analysis**. The purpose of *data analysis* is to achieve clarity about the range and types of data to be processed. The following analyses need to be carried out:

- Data volumes, grouped according to files and individual data
- Ranges of the data

- Data storage media to be used
- Ordering structures, numbering systems, sorting criteria
- Frequency of processing
- Frequency of modification
- Type and requirements of data storage
- Growth of data volumes
- Data interdependencies (relations, consistency constraints, sequence of creation, etc.)

**Flow analysis**. *Flow analysis* provides information about the sequence in which the operations need to be carried out and about data flow between the operations. Suitable means of representation for the results of this analysis include hierarchy diagrams, flow diagrams and data flow diagrams.

**Weakness analysis**. From the results of the preceding analysis steps, we can now determine shortcomings, omissions and redundancies of the system. *Weakness analysis* tries to search the individual operations as well as the overall system in order to establish the weaknesses of the existing system.

### 3.2.3 System description

The goal of *system description* is to order the results obtained from system delimitation and system analysis (i.e., matrices, flow diagrams, process diagrams, hierarchy diagrams, and verbal descriptions) and to structure them and add explanatory notes so that they represent a *self-contained* and *complete* system description. We have no generally applicable answers for the scope and the structuring of a system description because this depends on the complexity and the nature of the analyzed system. It is important that the system be described from outside inward, i.e., first the system delimitation and the functionality of the system as seen from the outside, then the individual functions and their interplay.

### 3.2.4 Analysis techniques and tools

No one has yet succeeded in developing techniques for the problem analysis phase that are methodical in nature and generally applicable. The most likely reason is the broad range of application domains that software products cover.

The choice of a useful approach and of tools for requirements analysis depends on the type, the size and the goals of a particular project. In one frequently used approach, analysts address detailed questions in *survey forms* to all affected employees of the company or department. This requires that the analysts have exact preliminary knowledge of the application domain in order to be able to generate useful and complete survey forms.

Individual and group *interviews* prove to be simpler and more flexible, but more difficult to process and document.

One recommended approach is the *report method*. The client's personnel prepare written reports about the application domain and provide all relevant facts for the analyst. The advantage is that the personnel deliver greater precision and consistent cooperation in the analysis phase. However, writing usable (i.e., well-structured, clear and precisely formulated) reports requires much experience that the personnel lack; furthermore, personnel often present their own area as much too important and complicated, resulting in a distorted picture.

Certainly the most enlightening (and also most expensive) approach to requirements analysis places the analyst to *work directly* in the respective application domain over an adequate period of time.

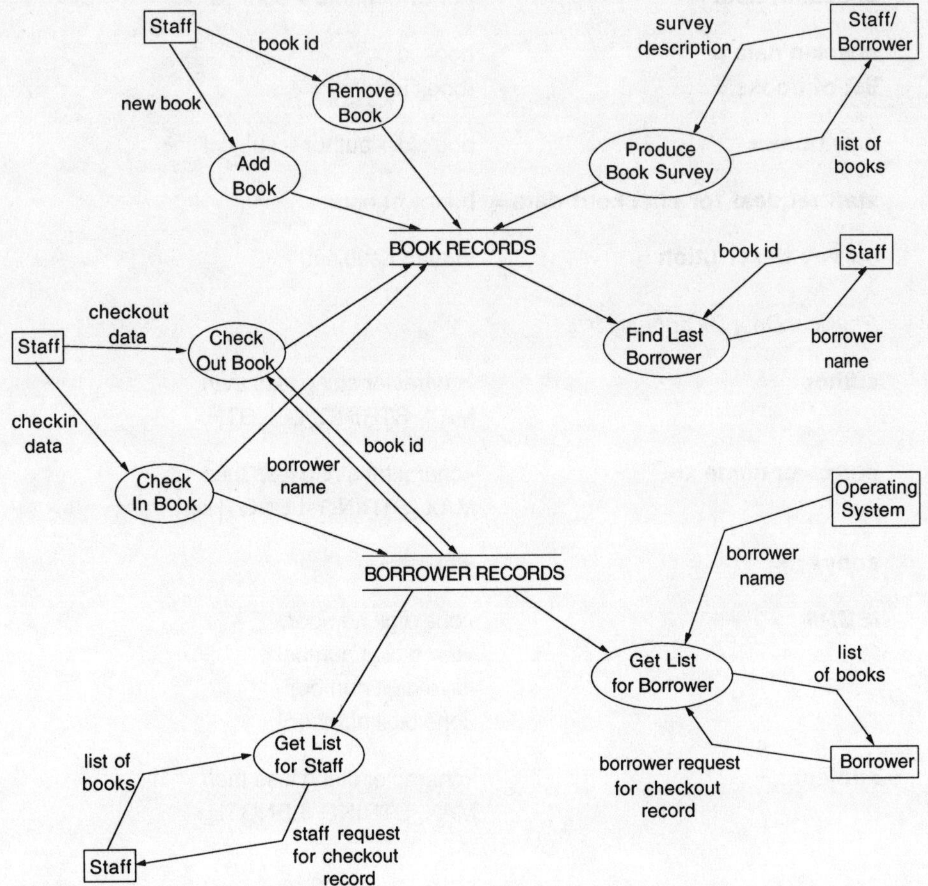


Figure 3.10: A data flow diagram for a library information system (from [Kerth 1987])

*Logical Data Dictionary – Files*

| | |
|---|---|
| **BOOK RECORDS** = | {book id + author + subject + status flag + borrower name} |
| **status flag** = | ["checked out" I "available"] |
| **BORROWER RECORDS** = | {borrower name + 0 {book id} MAX NR} |

*Logical Data Dictionary – Data Flow*

| | |
|---|---|
| **book id** = | ISBN# + copy# |
| **borrower request for checkout record** = | <TRIGGER – no data required> |
| **checkout data** = | borrower name + book id |
| **checkin data** = | book id |
| **list of books** = | {book id} |
| **new book** = | book id + author + subject |
| **staff request for checkout data** = | borrower name |
| **survey description** = | [author I subject] |

*Physical Data Dictionary*

| | |
|---|---|
| **author** ::= | <character string less than MAX_STRING_LENGTH> |
| **borrower name** ::= | <character string less than MAX_STRING_LENGTH> |
| **copy#** ::= | <Integer> |
| **ISBN#** ::= | <one digit number> "_" <three digit number> "_" <five digit number> "_" <one digit number> |
| **subject** ::= | <character string less than MAX_STRING_LENGTH> |

Figure 3.11: Data dictionary for a library information system (from [Kerth 1987])

**Add Book**
Get *book id*, *author* and *subject* from staff member;
Create a new entry in BOOK RECORD using *book id*, *author* and *subject*;
In this new entry, set status flag to "available" and set *borrower name* to "NONE".

**Remove Book**
Get *book id* from staff member;
Remove this entry from BOOK RECORD.

**Checkout Book**
Get *borrower name* from staff member;
Using the *borrower name*, determine from BORROWER RECORD the number
    of books currently checked out to this borrower;
If the number < MAX NR THEN
    Get *book id* from staff member;
    Using *book id*, in BOOK RECORD change the *status* flag to "checked out" and
    Set the borrower name to the *borrower name* entered by the staff member;
    Using *borrower name*, in BOOK RECORD, append the *book id*;
ELSE
    The borrower has reached his/her limit of books that can be checked out;
    Inform the staff member that the limit has been reached.

Figure 3.12: Specifications for a library information system (excerpt) in stylized prose ([Kerth 1987])

A number of specialized tools have been developed to support the analysis phase, the best-known being the SA (structured analysis) method. The two variants of the SA method were described by Gane and Sarson [Gane 1979] and by DeMarco [DeMarco 1978]. The scope of this book does not permit detailed treatment of the application of these tools, which are limited in their applicability anyway. The following example to represent the analysis results for a library information system will give the reader an impression of the formalisms employed in SA:

First the system to be analyzed is described with data flow diagrams using the following four symbols:

- *Arrows* to represent data flow
- *Circles* to represent processes that transform the data
- *Rectangles* to represent external entities (sources or targets for data)
- *Double bars* to represent data storage (files, databases).

The symbols are labeled according to simple rules. The restriction to these four symbols and the lack of a representation of mechanisms to describe processes result in simple, easy-to-read diagrams (see Figure 3.10). The diagrams are developed *top down*. After refinement, a data lexicon is compiled describing the files logically and physically and reflecting the data flows (see Figure 3.11). Decision tables, decision trees and stylized prose (or pseudocode) help to specify the processes more exactly (see Figure 3.12).

While SA is suited primarily for commercial applications, *SADT (Structured Analysis and Design Technique)* proves more generally applicable. This technique (see [Schoman 1977], [SoftTech 1976]) encompasses a graphical description language along with a method for employing it. Top-down and function-oriented, SADT supports the creation of both activity models and data models. SADT extensions also permit the description of control flows ([Ross 1985]).

## 3.3 System specification

The computer science world lacks consensus on the meaning of the term *system specification (or requirements definition)* and on the distinction of the specification phase from its neighboring phases, requirements analysis and design. Fairley [Fairley 1985] and Pressman [Pressman 1987] consider requirements definition to be a component of requirements analysis, while Sommerville [Sommerville 1985] views *software specification* as a subphase of the design process.

Various more or less synonymous terms find usage in identifying the system specification phase. For example, the literature employs *requirements definition*, *requirements specification*, *concepts definition* and *functional specification*. The term requirements definition also designates the result of this phase.

We employ the term *system specification* to mean the activities involved in the preparation of a contract between the client and the software developer that exactly specifies what the planned software system must do and which premises apply to the realization. We use *requirements definition* to mean the document which results from this specification process.

### 3.3.1 Structure and contents of the requirements definition

Based on the ANSI/IEEE guide to *Software Requirements Specification* [ANSI 1984], we recommend the following sectional organization of the requirements definition:

(1) Initial situation and goals
(2) System application and system environment
(3) User interfaces
(4) Functional requirements
(5) Nonfunctional requirements
(6) Exception handling
(7) Documentation requirements
(8) Acceptance criteria
(9) Glossary and index

The section *initial situation and goals* contains a general description of the initial situation with references to the requirements analysis (if it was carried out), the project goals, and a delimitation of these goals with respect to the system environment.

The section *system application and system environment* describes the prerequisites that must apply for the system to be used. Here we mean the description of all information (data, forms, etc.) that are necessary for the employment of the system, but are not part of the implementation (i.e., information provided from the outside). Furthermore, this section also contains specifications of the number of users, the frequency of use, and the jobs of the users.

The section *user interfaces*, one of the most important parts of the requirements definition, documents how the user communicates with the system. The human/machine interface (screen structures, dialog windows, interaction mechanism) needs to be presented here as the user will later use them. The quality of this section largely determines the acceptance of the software product.

The *functional requirements* define the system functionality expected by the user. Good specifications of system functionality contain only the necessary information about these functions. Any additional specifications, such as about the solution algorithm for a function, distracts from the actual specification task and restricts the flexibility of the subsequent system design. The definition of the functional requirements also contains all necessary specifications about the type, amount and expected precision of the data associated with each system function. Only exact determination of value ranges for data permits a plausibility check to detect input errors.

The *nonfunctional requirements* enumerate all requirements of nonfunctional nature, such as reliability, portability, and response and processing times. For the purpose of the feasibility study (see Section 3.3.5), it is necessary to weight these requirements and to provide detailed justification.

The section *exception handling* discusses the effects of various kinds of errors and the required system behavior upon occurrence of an error. Developing a reliable system means considering possible errors in each phase of development and providing appropriate measures to prevent or diminish the effects of errors. Thus measures for exception handling must already be described (as far as possible) in the specification phase.

The *documentation requirements* establish the scope and nature of the documentation. The documentation of a system provides the basis for both the correct utilization of the software product (user manual) and for system maintenance.

The *acceptance criteria* establish the conditions for inspection of the system by the client (acceptance test). The criteria refer to both functional and nonfunctional requirements. We recommend establishing acceptance criteria for each individual system requirement. If no respective acceptance criteria can be found for a given requirement, then we can assume that the client is unclear about the purpose and value of the requirement.

The requirements definition constitutes a document that provides the basis for all phases of a software project and contains preliminary considerations about the entire software life cycle. The specifications are normally not read sequentially, but serve as a reference for lookup purposes. Hence, a glossary of terms used and an extensive index prove practical.

### 3.3.2 Quality criteria for requirements definition

As a contract between client and software developer, the requirements definition must be precise and formulated understandably for all its target readership. For the client the specifications must describe the target system as it is to appear for the users. From the viewpoint of the software developers the specifications must provide all information necessary for the design and implementation of the system. The requirements definition also provides the basis for project management, for setting development schedules, for resource allocation, for establishing project standards, and for estimating development costs.

We therefore identify the following quality criteria for the requirements definition:

- It must be *concrete* and *complete.*
- It must be *consistent* and *unambiguous.* (That is, it cannot contain contradictory requirements and must be unambiguous for everyone involved in the development process.)
- It should be *minimal.* (That is, it should be free of redundancy and contain only information that is absolutely necessary for the implementation of the system.)
- It should be *readable* and *comprehensible.*
- It must be readily *modifiable.* (In the course of system development, it must be possible to handle new requirements and to modify already defined functions, without threatening the consistency of the requirements definition.)

### 3.3.3 Fundamental problems in defining requirements

The fundamental problems that arise during system specification are (see also [Keller 1989]):

- The goal/means conflict
- The determination and description of functional requirements
- The representation of the user interfaces

**The goal/means conflict in system specification**. The primary task of the specification process is to establish the *goal* of system development rather than to describe the means for achieving the goal. The requirements definition describes what a system must do, i.e., which functions the planned system should provide, but not how the individual functions are to be realized.

The most important reasons for separating *what* from *how* are:

- Specifications that concentrate on the goal of development remain short and comprehensible.
- Concentration on realization details distracts from the actual task of specification (defining the functional scope).
- Handling questions related to implementation at the time of specification camouflages the danger of realization-specific restrictions of system requirements and limits the freedom of the system developer.

Unfortunately this separation of *what* from *how* also has a number of drawbacks, the most important being:

- The quality of the requirements definition suffers. The completeness and unambiguity of the requirements definition can normally be achieved only with the knowledge of whether and how individual system functions can be realized.
- The form of representation of the requirements definition remains inadequate. What/how separation restricts the description of the most important aspect of a software system, its dynamic behavior, to static (i.e., verbal) forms. This inflates the size of the requirements definition and leads to communication problems between users and developers.

*Prototyping-oriented system specification* retains the advantages of the what/how separation while eliminating its drawbacks. If we describe the most important aspects of the dynamic behavior of a software system not in words but in the form of a prototype (as described in Section 3.1.3, "The prototyping-oriented life-cycle model"), the size of the requirements definition can be reduced, the completeness and unambiguity of the requirements definition can be improved, and the communication problems between users and developers can be ameliorated without constraining the freedom of the developer and without needing to concentrate overly on the implementation details.

**Determining and describing the functional requirements**. Practice shows that we are seldom able to determine all the functional requirements of a software system without experimenting. Describing functional requirements in the form of text is extremely difficult and leads to very lengthy specifications. Here, too, prototyping-oriented system specification proves helpful. A system model on the user interface level serving as an executable prototype supports the exploration of functional, nonfunctional and interaction-related requirements. It simplifies the determination of dependencies between system functions and abbreviates the requirements definition. A prototype that represents the most important functional aspects of a software system represents this system significantly better than a verbal description could do.

**Designing the user interfaces**. User interfaces represent a user-oriented abstraction of the functionality of a system. Their design measurably influences the acceptance of a software product.

The graphical design of screen layouts requires particular effort and only affects one aspect of the user interface, its appearance. The much more important aspect, the dynamics behind a user interface, can hardly be depicted in purely verbal specifications. Therefore the user interface components of the requirements definition should always be realized as an executable prototype.

We have shown that it makes sense to use prototypes for system specification. The goal is to depict the user interfaces, the functional requirements, and exception handling in the form of prototypes. It usually suffices to implement a user interface prototype that simulates the most important functional aspects and exception handling. For software system specification where data management plays an important role, the underlying data model should also be specified in the form of a prototype.

### 3.3.4 A model for prototyping-oriented system specification

Figure 3.13 shows the general approach for prototyping-oriented system specification. The analysis, description and evaluation of the requirements forms the backbone of the specification process. Employing a prototype to model the target software system can ease all three tasks.

**General approach**: The circled numbers in the following description refer to Figure 3.13.

① *Determining the basic requirements* (*rough specifications*). Users and system developers discuss the initial situation and the goals; they roughly sketch the task description.

② *Production and evaluation of a base prototype*. Based on the rough specifications, the system developers construct the initial prototype, which models the most important functional and data-related properties of the target system. The system developers present the (base) prototype to the users. Their presentation emphasizes explaining the concepts for modeling the user interface, assumptions about the basic functions, and a discussion of the permissible simplification for the modeling. The base prototype primarily serves the purpose of clarifying whether the system developers fundamentally understand the users' rough specifications. This base prototype might be thrown away repeatedly and reconstructed.

③ *Evaluation/adaptation cycle* Once the base prototype has been accepted by everyone engaged in the system specification process, this prototype is extended and employed for functional exploration. All requirements that emerge from this process but cannot be realized in prototypes are documented in writing. Parallel to the

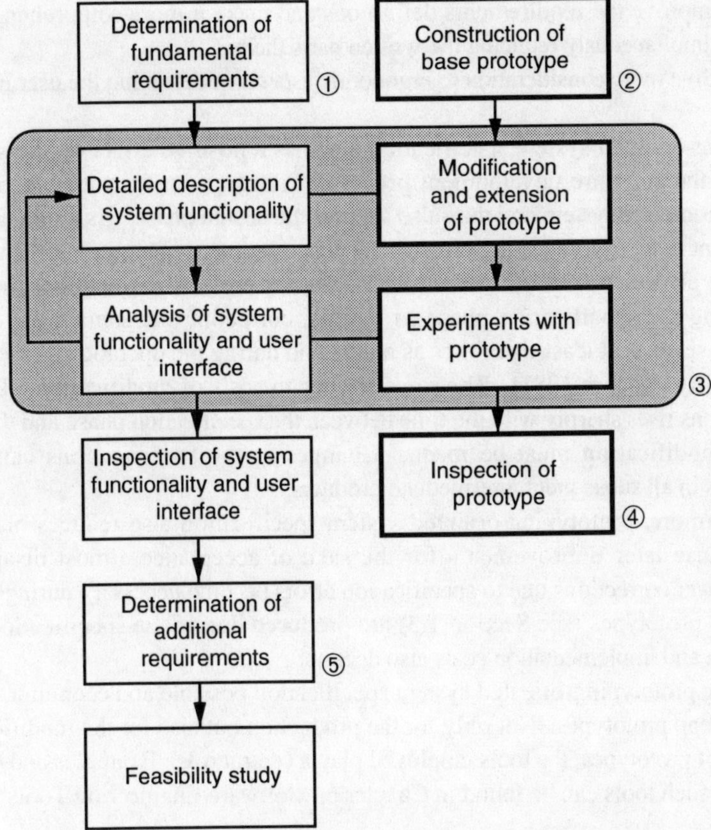


Figure 3.13: The prototyping-oriented system specification process

extension and analysis of the prototype, all specification-relevant knowledge gained from the experiments with the prototype is documented; i.e., the written part of the requirements definition is complemented.

④ *Acceptance of the prototype.* Once the user and system developer agree on the scope of the functionality, the nonfunctional requirements and the user interface, the prototype is frozen. This prototype version then provides the basis for the design, implementation and acceptance of the system under development.

⑤ *Completion of the requirements definition.* After the acceptance of the prototype the requirements definition is completed, i.e., all parts that do not involve prototyping are completed (e.g., description of conditions affecting utilization and environment, documentation requirements and acceptance criteria, as well as glossary and index).

This approach enables us to:

- Avoid problems in the specification process

- Improve the requirements definitions and make it more comprehensible while simultaneously reducing the written parts thereof
- Give more consideration to ergonomic aspects in designing the user interface

Prototyping-oriented system specification also has a positive effect on the subsequent phases of the software development process. Prototypes offer valuable tips for the decomposition of a system and thus also support the design phase. As a rule they deliver a significant reduction in testing effort. The cost of correcting an error depends on how much time elapses before it is detected. Taking the costs of correcting a specification error during the specification phase as a basis, correcting the same error during the testing phase costs at least five times as much, and during the operation phase the factor becomes fifty [Boehm 1981]. The same applies to costs of modification. The cost of modifications rises sharply with the time between the specification phase and the phase in which a modification must be made. Changes in the specifications can result in adaptations in all subsequent intermediate products.

Furthermore, prototyping-oriented system specification also reduces maintenance costs because later improvements for the sake of acceptance almost disappear and because fewer corrections due to specification errors become necessary during operation. If reusable prototypes (see Section 1.3) are produced during the specification process, then design and implementation costs also decline.

Making prototyping-oriented system specification possible and economical requires fast and cheap prototypes. Not only for the production but also for the modification and extension of prototypes, the tools employed play a central role. Examples and evaluation criteria for such tools can be found in Chapter 6, "Software Engineering Tools".

### 3.3.5 Feasibility study

Before the requirements definition becomes a contract between the client and the software developer, there must be assurance that the requirements definition is complete and correct and that fulfilling the requirements is technically and economically feasible. (This might have already taken place during the production of the prototype.)

The concluding feasibility study thus encompasses the following:

- *Checking the completeness of the requirements*. The client must confirm that all functional and nonfunctional requirements and all constraints are covered.
- *Examination of consistency of requirements*. The requirements must not contradict one another.
- *Evaluation of technical feasibility*. The technical feasibility depends on the availability of appropriate hardware and software technology that can deliver the required services. Furthermore, the feasibility also depends on whether the system environment can provide the expected information in the required quantity and precision.

- *Examination of personnel requirements.* Suitably qualified personnel must be available for both the production and the operation of the system.
- *The economic feasibility.* Naturally a cost/benefit analysis must determine whether the project can be realized with economically justifiable costs.

## 3.4 Design

The quality of a software product derives from the quality of its design. This bestows particular importance on the design phase in the software life cycle. The *purpose of the design* is to establish the *architecture of a software system*, with the goal of fulfilling the quality requirements with a cost-effective implementation.

Difficulties begin because the concept of good design is not readily definable. Depending on the application domain and the specific project situation, a design might be considered good if it results in an inexpensive implementation; in another case the criterion might be an extremely compact system architecture that operates with minimal resources; or the quality criteria might be the comprehensibility, maintainability and extensibility of the resulting architecture. In the following we consider maintainability and extensibility to be the most important criteria for the evaluation of the quality of a design. The management of resources and the efficiency of the implementation provide additional quality attributes to which designer must always attend. An efficient system architecture implies keeping the costs of required resources and the operating costs as low as possible.

The design of a software systems is a creative process. To master design, the designer must possess a comprehensive understanding of the problem as well as the ability to apply software engineering methods and principles, as well as imagination and creativity. The architecture of a software system normally evolves iteratively: in a series of design steps based on an initial rough design, an overall system structure emerges that is adequate to solve the problem.

In the design phase the system architecture is designed with the goal of availing the functionality set down in the requirements definition and of guaranteeing that the architecture can be adapted easily to changing requirements. In a rough overview, the designs process encompasses the following activities (compare [Sommerville 1985]):

- Adequate decomposition of the overall system into subsystems and specification of the mutual effects between the subsystems
- Decomposition of the subsystems into components (modules) and specification of the requirements on these components, i.e., specification of component interfaces
- Design of the algorithms to provide the functionality defined in the component interfaces

This section presents methods and techniques for mastering design problems, that is, for decomposing systems into subsystems and subsystems into components, and handles questions regarding the internal structure of system components. First we give an overview of various design techniques; then we explore some of these design techniques and their methodical foundation in detail and demonstrate their application with an example. In addition, we discuss certain design aspects such as the design of user interfaces and modularization criteria with their due attention.

### 3.4.1 Design techniques

The expert design of a software system requires a systematic approach. One of the most important principles for mastering the complexity of software systems is the *principle of abstraction.* With respect to approach we distinguish top-down and bottom-up design.

The fundamental idea of *top-down design*, which goes back to Dijkstra [Dijkstra 1969] and Wirth [Wirth 1971], postulates that the design activity must begin with the analysis of the requirements definition and should not consider implementation details at first. On the basis of knowledge gained from the analysis of the requirements definition, a project is decomposed into subprojects, and this procedure is repeated until the subtasks have become so simple that an algorithm can be formulated as a solution. Top-down design thus becomes a successive concretization of abstractly described ideas for a solution. Abstraction proves to be the best medium to render complex systems comprehensible; the designer is involved only with those aspects of the system that are necessary for understanding before the next step or during the search for a solution.

*Bottom-up design* proceeds in the reverse direction. The fundamental idea is to perceive the hardware and layer above it (from the operating system to the complete application) as an abstract machine. An abstract machine is a set of basic operations that permits the modeling of a system or subsystem. Bottom-up design begins with the givens of a concrete machine and successively develops one abstract machine after the other by adding needed attributes, until a machine has been achieved that provides the functionality that the user requires.

The design process is influenced not only by the design approach but also by the criteria used to decompose a system. Numerous decomposition principles have been proposed. Essentially, these decomposition principles can be classified into the following three groups.

(1) *Function-oriented decomposition.* A function-oriented system perspective forms the core of the design. Based on the functional requirements contained in the requirements definition, a task-oriented decomposition of the overall system takes place. The most important methods and principles proposed for this approach are credited to Wirth (stepwise refinement [Wirth 1971]) and Yourdon and Constantine (structured design [Yourdon 1979]).

(2) *Data-oriented decomposition.* The design process focuses on a data-oriented system perspective. The design strategy orients itself to the data to be processed. The underlying idea is that the structure of a software system should reflect the structure of the data to be processed. The decomposition of the system thus stems from the analysis of the data. The most important methods and principles were proposed by Jackson [Jackson 1975], Warnier [Warnier 1974] and Rechenberg [Rechenberg 1984a].

(3) *Object-oriented decomposition.* An object-oriented system perspective provides the focus of the design. A software system is viewed as a collection of objects that communicate with one another. Each object has data structures that are invisible from outside and operations that can be executed on these data structures. The decomposition principle orients itself to the unity of data and operations and is based on Parnas' principle of information hiding [Parnas 1972] and the principle of inheritance derived from Dahl and Nygaard [Dahl 1966]. The methodological foundation of the design approach has not yet been researched adequately; the interested reader will find work in this direction in Abbott [Abbott 1983], Meyer [Meyer 1988], Wirfs-Brock [Wirfs-Brock 1989], Coad and Yourdon [Coad 1990], Booch [Booch 1991] and Rumbaugh et al. [Rumbaugh 1991].

This section has roughly sketched the approaches and decomposition principles that are important for systematic design of the architecture of a software system. More detail on each design approach and how to apply its underlying thought model in concrete cases is described in Sections 3.4.5 to 3.4.7 on the basis of the task description in Section 3.4.2. In the design of the user interface of a software system, other aspects apply than in the design of the functional components. In Section 3.4.4 the reader will find general guidelines for the design of user interfaces and their application to the task described in Section 3.4.2.

Choosing an appropriate design approach can be a difficult job that demands at least as much instinctive feel as the design process itself. In the past there have been repeated efforts to develop generally applicable design principles that are equally suitable for all kinds of tasks. However, experience has shown that some design approaches prove more adequate for certain application domains, while they fail in others. We are convinced that the most suitable design method should be applied for each project on an individual basis. In the following sections we will show that this applies not only to a project as a whole, but also to subprojects.

## 3.4.2 Task description for a design example

This section gives the rough specifications for a software product whose components will be developed in the following sections using various techniques. Our example task will simulate the motion of a portal robot (e.g., an industrial robot for spot welding). Figure 3.14 shows such a portal robot.

A portal robot consists of a portal that moves longitudinally along a pair of tracks. The crossbeam of the portal supports a carriage that moves at a right angle across the path of the portal. The carriage supports a gripper that moves up and down. The actual tool rests at the bottom of the gripper (e.g., a spot-welding pistol).

**Simulation of a portal robot**

The motion of a portal robot is to be simulated on a computer screen. The robot is to be represented schematically on the screen: orthographically in front, top and side views as well as isometrically. Figure 3.15 shows the required forms of display.

The trajectory is to be described in a simple language that permits the formulation of its linear and circular components. During the simulation each motion component will be decomposed into linear steps of equal length.

- Linear motion to point (*x, y, z*) in *n* steps: n L (x, y, z)
- Circular motion to point (*x, y, z*) via point (*x1, y1, z1*) in n steps:
  n C (x1, y1, z1) (x, y, z)

The purpose of the steps is twofold: First, for the sake of simplicity, we reduce a circle to a polygon. Second, as in the example of a welding robot, we can describe a trajectory with equidistant stops (e.g., welding points) in one line of descriptive code rather than having to write each subtrajectory separately.

The description of the trajectory begins with a starting point (*x0, y0, z0*). The end point of a motion component simultaneously serves as the starting point of the next motion component. The trajectory description is terminated with the letter E.

Each coordinate can be specified in absolute or relative terms. The number 10 indicates an absolute position (10 mm from the origin of the coordinate system). A

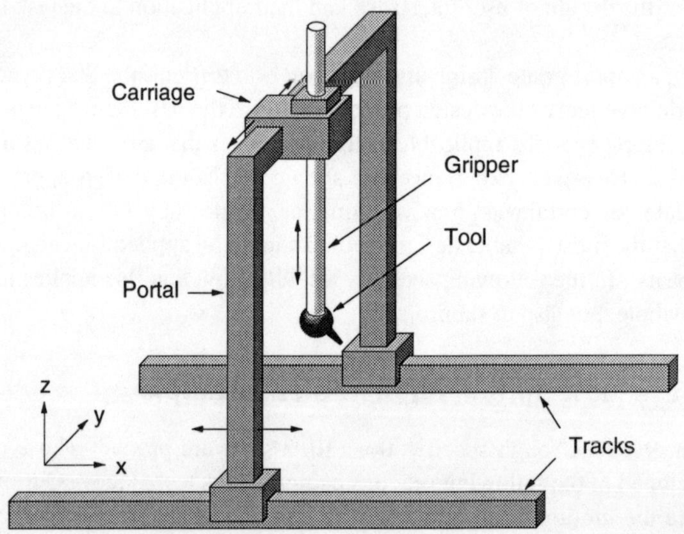


Figure 3.14: Structure of a portal robot

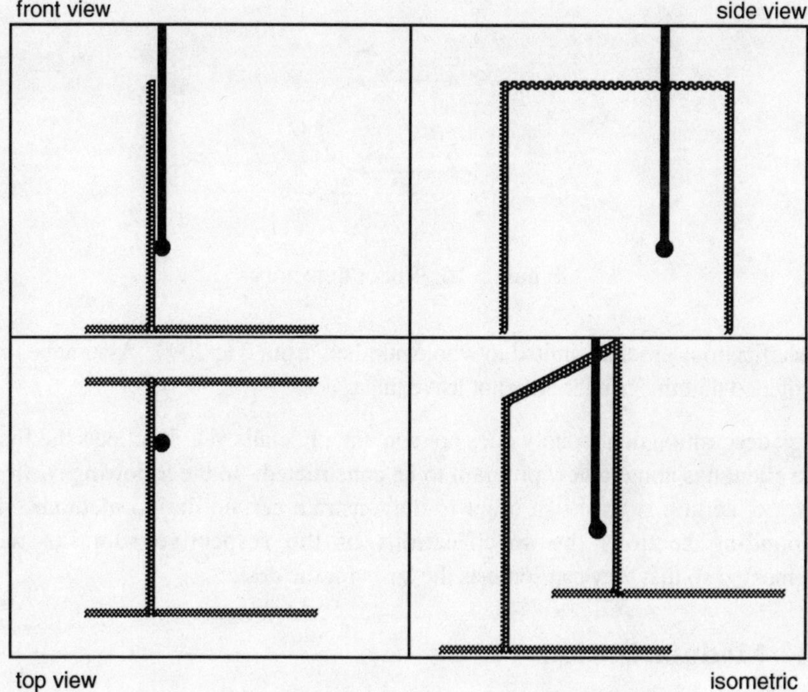


Figure 3.15: Orthographic sketch of a portal robot

relative coordinate is represented by a number with a preceding sign. +10 indicates a movement of 10 mm from the starting point of the motion component. For both linear and circular motions, all relative specifications refer to the starting point of the respective step.

*Example of trajectory description:*

| | |
|---|---|
| (100,100,100) | *starting position (A)* |
| 10 L (+400,0,0) | *linear motion to point B* |
| 20 C (700,300,100) (500,500,100) | *circular motion to point D via point C* |
| 10 L (–400,0,0) | *linear motion to point E* |
| E | *end of trajectory* |

Figure 3.16 shows the robot trajectory as defined by this description (top view).

The software product developed for this purpose must enable the input of a complete trajectory description and display the motion on the screen. It should be possible to stop the process from the dialog and/or to follow the sequence stepwise.

*Constraints*

The motion of the robot's gripper is to be limited to a cube with an edge length of 2 meters. The positioning precision is assumed to be 1 millimeter. All coordinate

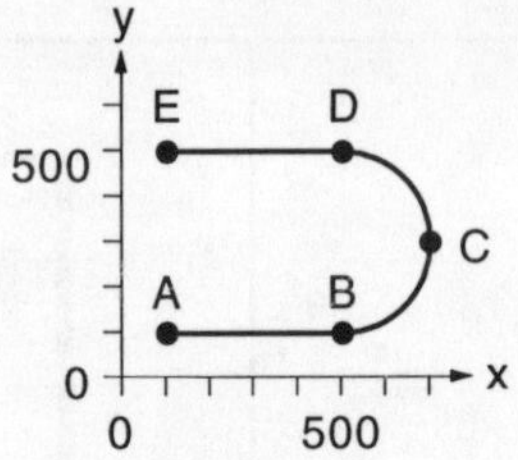


Figure 3.16: Robot trajectory

specifications are thus limited to whole numbers from 0 to 2000. Assurance must be provided that the gripper does not leave this space.

This task description deliberately does not contain all details yet. It reflects the first idea that the client has about a new program to be constructed. In the following sections we will extract certain subtasks in order to demonstrate certain design methods. In the corresponding sections thc specifications of the respective subtasks will be complemented so that they can serve as the basis for the design.

### 3.4.3 Modularization

The first design step in the realization of a larger software project consists of decomposing the task into separate subtasks in such a way that they can be solved as independently of one another as possible. Such a decomposition is a prerequisite for teamwork, allowing various team members to tackle the individual subtasks simultaneously. This requires defining the interfaces between the subprojects at the start of the design phase. After completion of the solutions to the subtasks, they combine to yield the overall solution as long as each implementation adheres to the initially defined interfaces.

Interface definition is a difficult job that requires much experience. Every interface between a pair of subtasks implies a potential problem in the integration of the partial solutions into the overall solution. Thus the interfaces must be specified so precisely that misunderstandings are precluded as far as possible. If the interfaces are incomplete (i.e., if they do not suffice to solve the problem), this requires revision in the course of the project. This can cause modifications in the design of subprojects that are already underway. Experience has shown that interface modifications in larger projects can hardly be avoided because the designers cannot know all the details and special cases at the start of the project. This is unpleasant for all project participants, but need not be a catastrophe as long as the necessity for an interface modification is recognized in time. Interface specifications that permit different interpretations present a greater danger. This can result in incompatibilities between subprojects that are only recognized when they are integrated into the overall solution. Such incompatibilities can cause erroneous program behavior that might only be detected through extensive testing, and even then the cause of the error can be difficult to pinpoint.

#### 3.4.3.1 Guidelines for modularization

Many modularization errors can be avoided from the start by following a few rules. Thus this section presents a definition of the term *module* and some guidelines for modularization. Then several examples will show the content and structure that interface specifications should have.

Goos [Goos 1973] and Dennis [Dennis 1973] offer a definition of the term module that encompasses the following four points:

- A module is a collection of operations and data for the realization of a distinct task.
- A module's communication with its environment must take place only via a precisely defined interface.
- The integration of a module into a software system must not require any knowledge of the inner workings of the module.
- The correctness of a module must be testable without any knowledge of its embedding in a software system.

The first point states that a module contains not only operations to realize subtasks, but also the data necessary to do so. In this context, equate operations to procedures and data to variables. A module combines procedures and the variables that they collectively use to a larger abstract unit. The second point states that the interplay of multiple modules is defined by a clearly specified interface. More precisely, there are two interfaces: the *export interface* specifies what a module makes available to other modules; the *import interface* specifies what the module uses from other modules. In the design phase only the export interface is of interest; it contains all specifications about how a module can be used. The import interface becomes important only during testing and documentation because the union of all import interfaces reveals where a given module is used. When we speak of an interface in the present section on design, we always mean the export interface. Figure 3.17 shows the contents and the interfaces of a module.

Every module makes some of its operations available to other modules. Other operations are used only internally by the module. The same applies to the module's data, some of which are available to the outside while others are hidden in the module and thus protected from outside access. Software engineering generally views exported variables as a safety risk that should be avoided whenever possible. We will handle this aspect in more detail in the discussion of abstract data structures (data capsules).

One of the most difficult problems in modularization is the question of which operations should be combined with which data to form a module. The following aspects should be considered to attain good modularization:

- Module closure and module binding

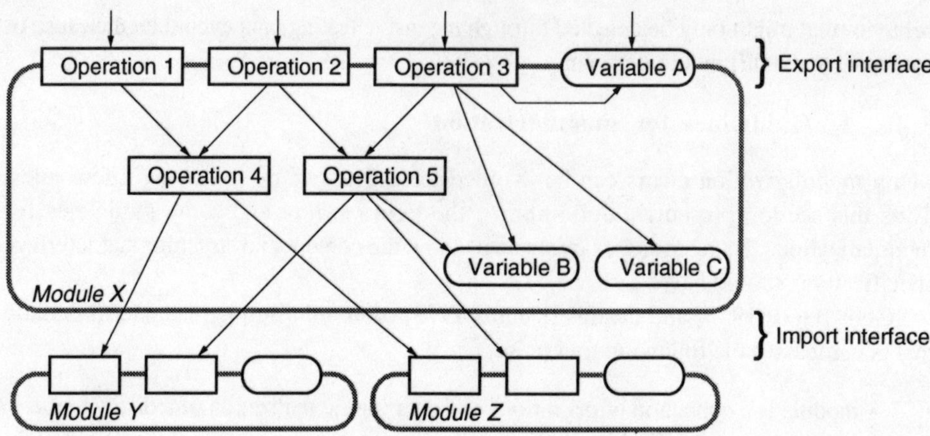


Figure 3.17: A module's interfaces

- Module coupling
- Minimality of the module interface
- Module size
- Testability
- Freedom from interference
- Import frequency
- Frequency of use
- Module hierarchy

By *module closure* we mean that a module is responsible for a restricted task. The term *module binding (cohesion)* is closely related and means the sum of the relationships between operations of a module. Depending on the kind of module, modularization can put either the operations or the data in the foreground.

- A *functionally oriented module* collects the operations required for the solution of a subtask into one unit.
- A *data-oriented module* is packaged around the data. The module's interface results from contemplating which operations should be provided on these data.

In both a function- and a data-oriented module, the binding between the operations and the data should be as strong as possible. This means that there should be no operations or data without a relation to one another.

*Module coupling* expresses how strongly different modules are interconnected. Stronger module coupling requires more interfaces that have to be watched. This increases the danger of misunderstandings and errors. Furthermore, changes in the requirements definition usually have ramifications for many modules. Weak module coupling can therefore be seen as a measure of module independence. Strong module coupling often indicates that logically related operations have been spread over multiple modules. This also indicates weak module binding. A primary cause of strong module coupling is global (exported) data. The presence of global data alone leads to the undisciplined use of module interfaces. In particular, uncontrolled modification of such data can result in errors that are impossible to find. Figure 3.18 shows how module coupling and module binding depend on the number of modules in a software system.

The less modules a software system contains, the weaker the module coupling tends to be. In the extreme case (when there is but a single module that contains all operations) module coupling is zero and module binding is maximal. On the other hand, if each operation were packaged in its own module, there would be no module binding (no relation within a module), but module coupling would be maximal. If we add the complexities that ensue from module coupling and module binding, the resulting curve of the sum reaches its minimum with an average number of modules. The exact location of this minimum depends on the kind of software system.

The *minimality of the interface* is closely related to module coupling. Smaller module interfaces reduce the danger of strong module coupling. A minimum interface is characterized by all of the following:

- As little as possible global data (preferably none)
- As little as possible exported procedures
- As few as possible parameters

With strong module binding, all procedures in a module are related to one another. The larger the number of exported procedures, the greater is the danger of misuse of the module (e.g., by incorrect invocation sequence or erroneous interpretation of mutual effects). The more parameters a procedure has, the more difficult it becomes to use them. In such a case a decomposition into multiple procedures can provide a solution.

*Module size* is often seen as a simple criterion for modularization. Usually a maximum size in lines or pages is specified. While it is true that a small module is easier to comprehend and thus easier to use and to test, the complexity of a module depends on

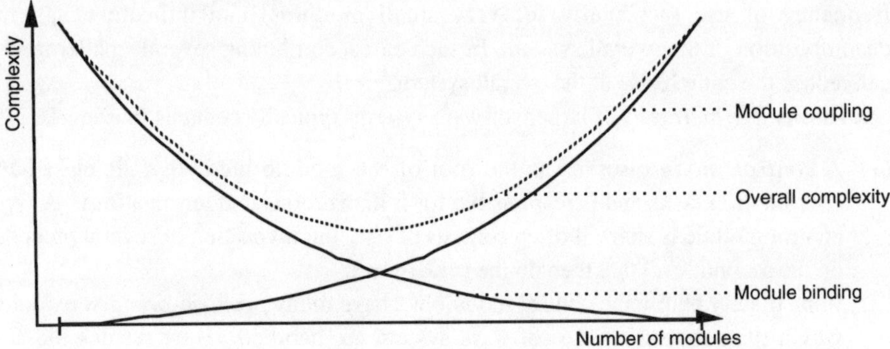


Figure 3.18: The relationship between module coupling and module binding

more than its raw size. In particular, data-oriented modules can be many pages long, yet they are generally easy to understand because the operations working with the data are usually short. Thus it would be an error to begin decomposing into multiple modules once a certain number of pages has been attained and thereby sacrifice the strong module binding which results from the data orientation. Hence we cannot make generally applicable statements about the size of modules; its importance in modularization is often overrated.

Good *testability* of a module requires that its correctness can be tested without any knowledge of its embedding in the overall system. This means that strong module coupling (when a module is related to many other modules) negatively affects its testability. A narrow module interface also enhances the testability of the module.

*Freedom from interference* indicates that a module must have no undesired side effects on other modules. Only by avoiding such side effects can we guarantee that a module can be replaced with another module with the same interface definition without changing anything in the overall system. Thus freedom from interference is an important criterion for the modifiability and extensibility of a software system. If one module handles multiple tasks or one task is distributed across multiple modules, freedom from interference has not been attained.

A module's *import frequency* reflects how many other modules are used in its implementation. A high import frequency can indicate strong module coupling and thus possible interference. On the other hand, a low import frequency often occurs with extremely large modules that combine all operations required for the solution of a subtask. This frequently occurs when a module is repeatedly extended in the course of a project. In such cases the designer should find strongly related operations within the module and combine them to a new module.

The *frequency of use* of a module indicates how many other modules use it. A high frequency of use of the modules of a software system indicates generality and high reusability. On the other hand, a high frequency of use for an individual module can occur even if this module is a mere collection of unrelated operations. If the frequency of use is particularly high, the module's binding strength should be tested. A low frequency of use (especially for very small modules) can indicate exaggerated decomposition of the overall system. In such cases, combining several smaller modules can reduce the complexity of the overall system.

The *module hierarchy* of larger software systems typically contains four levels:

(1) A *control module* serves as the root of the module hierarchy. It must handle coordination tasks and is responsible for initializations and terminations. A typical control module is short; it often consists of only the invocation of several procedures on the second level that then do the actual work.

(2) Immediately below the control module we have many *problem-oriented modules* in which the subtasks of the software system are handled. Here resides the actual algorithm for solving the problem.

(3) The third level contains mostly *auxiliary modules* with frequently used operations. This level also contains modules for the implementation of data structures. Examples include the management of lists and tables.
(4) The bottommost layer encompasses modules for *communication with the hardware and the operating system.* Here we find, e.g., modules for input/output as well as for mathematical functions and string operations. These modules are generally not problem-specific, but are used in many software systems. They are usually not written by the application programmer, but are available in a library.

Good modularization should make this distinction of levels clearly recognizable. In a top-down design such a hierarchy develops almost automatically. However, there can be deviations that depend on the nature and scope of the task. For example, for extremely algorithm-oriented tasks the second layer plays an important role. Above all in small software systems, the second and third levels can merge. Hence strict guidelines are difficult to formulate: good modularization largely depends on the skill and experience of the designer.

From the very start the attributes of the programming language to be used, of the operating system, or even of the underlying hardware can encroach on the modularization. This is one of the most frequent errors in program design. As a result, unnecessarily many details are incorporated in the rough design, and they also filter down to the module interfaces. This produces strong module coupling, which has a negative impact on debugging and maintenance. Furthermore, machine-specific details are so strongly rooted in the design that porting it to another target machine produces immense difficulties. For the purpose of high reliability and maintainability, it pays to observe the above criteria during modularization.

In object-oriented design, the difficulty is finding the right classes to solve the task at hand. If this succeeds, modularization hardly presents a problem. If a separate module is provided for an object class, data-oriented modularization ensues automatically. The resulting modules are usually very small and display strong module binding and weak module coupling. For object-oriented design, different rules apply regarding the minimality of interfaces. The more extensive a module interface is, the more operations are possible with objects of the respective class and the better are the chances of attaining reusability.

Little changes in the module hierarchy for object-oriented design. We still have a control module handling the coordination of the overall system, and there are still base modules (base classes) for communication with the operating system and the hardware. The most striking difference with respect to conventional design is that the second layer is much reduced or even lacking. The object classes (which represent data structures) constitute the largest portion of the third layer; this is also where most of the algorithmic work is done.

### 3.4.3.2 Abstract data structures and abstract data types

Modules find one of their most important applications in the formation of data capsules. Recall that unrestricted access to common data presents a prime source of errors. Figure 3.19 shows how complex the relationships can become when only three operations access three common sets of data.

Such a situation occurs in almost every larger software system. Its error-proneness is relatively low if the operations share only simple data (e.g., numbers). The matter becomes critical if the data also have a complex structure, i.e., if data are structured in a superordinate abstract unit. Complex relationships can already exist between the component data of such a structure. This means that an unintentional change in one of the variables can destroy the consistency of the entire data structure. In the situation depicted in Figure 3.19, these consistency conditions must be observed in every individual operation. If for whatever reason the data structure must be modified, this change must also be reflected in each operation. If even a single operation is overlooked, this can result in incorrect behavior of the entire software system.

To prevent such errors from the start, more complex data are best designed as *abstract data structures*. This means that the whole of the data is specified during design only by its interface (based on the operations that should be possible on this data structure). The result of the design is a collection of operations that access shared data (whose specific structure is unknown). The operations are packaged in a module together with the data (see Figure 3.20).

Access to the data is possible only with the help of dedicated operations. We call these *access operations* or *access routines*. Indirect access has its price in terms of efficiency, but this seldom impacts negatively on the speed of the overall system. However, such software organization has a very positive effect on maintainability. Since the specific structure of the data is known only in the access routines, they alone are affected by any modification in the data structure. All responsibility for the consistency of the data structure is concentrated at one location. Section 3.4.3.3 gives two examples of abstract data structures.

An abstract data structure can only be used to implement *one* set of data. It is not possible to work with multiple copies of such a data structure simultaneously. An *abstract data type*, on the other hand, makes it possible to work with multiple sets of data of the same kind while still enjoying the advantages of data encapsulation. As with abstract data structures, access routines are used, whereby the data are no longer encapsulated in the module, but each operation is passed as a parameter. The following

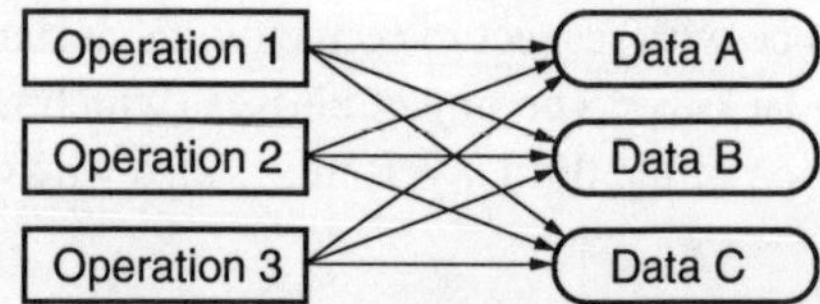


Figure 3.19: Multiple operations accessing common data

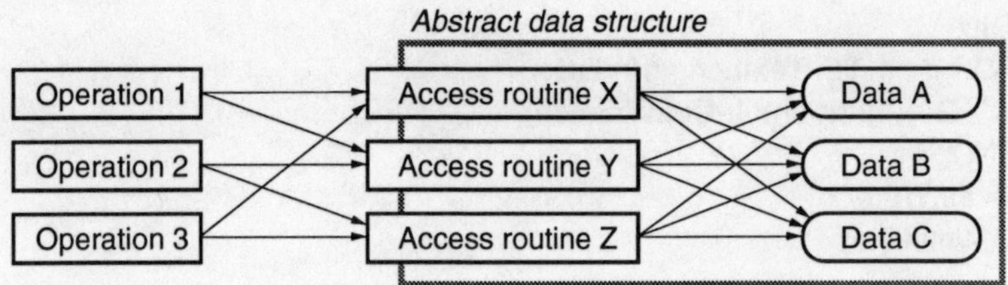


Figure 3.20: Multiple operations accessing an abstract data structure

example shows how the interface of an abstract data type Text can be specified. We employ the concept of opaque types (as used in the programming language Modula-2).

```
DEFINITION MODULE TextMod;

  TYPE Text;

  PROCEDURE NewText (VAR t:Text);
  PROCEDURE DisposeText (VAR t:Text);
  PROCEDURE AppendChar (VAR t:Text; ch:CHAR);
  PROCEDURE GetChar (t:Text; index:CARDINAL; VAR ch:CHAR);
  PROCEDURE TextLength (t:Text): CARDINAL;
  PROCEDURE InsertChar (VAR t:Text; before:CARDINAL; ch:CHAR);
  PROCEDURE DeleteChar (VAR t:Text; index:CARDINAL);

END TextMod.
```

In the following definition module the name Text is defined only as a data type. The specific structure of variables of this type remains hidden from the user. The following program fragment shows how the module TextMod can be used in order to read a text and output the text lines in reverse order.

```
PROCEDURE ReadLine(VAR t:Text; VAR ok:BOOLEAN);
VAR ch:CHAR;
BEGIN
  InOut.Read(ch);
  ok := InOut.Done;
  IF ok THEN
     NewText(t);
     WHILE InOut.Done & (ch # InOut.EOL) DO
        AppendChar(t,ch); InOut.Read(ch)
     END
  END
END ReadLine;

PROCEDURE WriteLine(t:Text);
VAR i:CARDINAL; ch:CHAR;
```

```
BEGIN
   FOR i:= 1 TO TextLength(t) DO
      GetChar(t,ch); InOut.Write(ch)
   END;
   InOut.WriteLn
END WriteLine;

VAR
   line: ARRAY [1..1000] OF Text;
   n: CARDINAL;
   ok: BOOLEAN;

BEGIN
   n := 0;
   REPEAT
      INC(n);
      ReadLine(line[n],ok)
   UNTIL NOT ok;
   WHILE n>1 DO
      DEC(n);
      WriteLine(line[n]);
      DisposeText(line[n])
   END;
   ...
```

Note that for each line a new element of the abstract data type Text is created using the procedure NewText; at the end DisposeText disposes of them. This approach is typical for working with abstract data types because they are usually realized using dynamic data structures. This examples also shows that the concrete realization of the data type Text need not be known in order to use it. The concrete data structure (which is hidden in the module TextMod) could be an array, a linked list, or even a file.

Unfortunately, abstract data types cannot be formulated in all programming languages as elegantly as in Modula-2. In Ada, e.g., the concrete data structure must be declared in the interface specification, as the following example shows.

```
package TEXT_PACKAGE is

   type TEXT is private;

   procedure NEW_TEXT (t: out TEXT);
   procedure DISPOSE_TEXT (t: in out TEXT);
   procedure APPEND_CHAR (t: in out TEXT; ch: in CHARACTER);
   ...
```

```
private
    type TEXT_CHUNK;
    type TEXT is access TEXT_CHUNK;
    type TEXT_CHUNK is record
                len: INTEGER;
                txt: array (1..1024) of CHARACTER;
                next: TEXT_CHUNK;
    end record;

end TEXT_PACKAGE;
```

Ada guarantees security because, when variables of type TEXT are used, the compiler forbids access to components of these variables (declared as private).

Other programming languages (e.g., C) provide no possibility for declaring abstract data types. Here the programmer must rely on using a concrete data type. One standard solution consists of assigning a unique number for each example of the abstract data type. The user of the abstract data type then works with whole numbers; the implementation might use a table to map the external onto the internal representation.

### 3.4.3.3 Application to the design example

The beginning of modularization should be to achieve an overview of the required functionality in the form of a block diagram or – even better – of a state transition diagram. Our task description indicates that the software system will contain two components that will communicate with the user: a text editor (for creating trajectory descriptions) and the actual simulator (to display the robot and its motions on the screen). The editor should be available immediately upon launching the program, and the simulation can be started from there. From the user's viewpoint it would be desirable to return to the editor after a simulation in order to make modifications in the trajectory and try a new simulation. Figure 3.21 shows a possible example of program flow.

The task description refers to decomposing each trajectory component into steps and meeting certain constraints. This means that we also need an analysis component that reads the trajectory description that the user inputs and checks it for errors; from a correct trajectory description, this component generates a list of single steps. In case of an error, a message is displayed and the user is prompted to correct the error. Figure 3.22 shows the program flow with this extension.

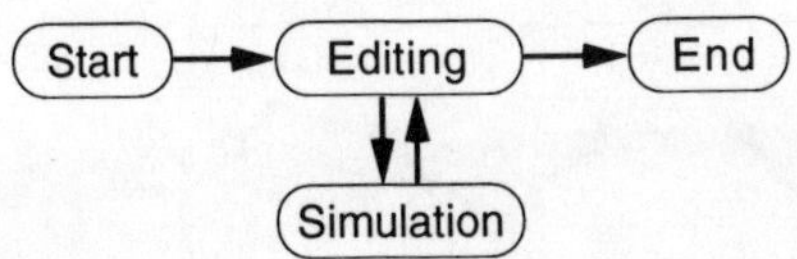


Figure 3.21: State transition diagram of the robot simulation (initial version)

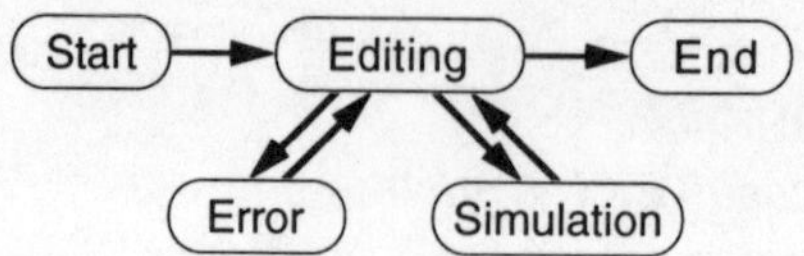


Figure 3.22: State transition diagram of the robot simulation with error handling

Hence we have established that the software system will contain a main module, an editor, an analyzer and a simulator. Figure 3.23 shows the control flow and the data flow among these four components.

If we provide a separate (data-oriented) module for the text entered by the user and for the list of single steps, we can derive our first design of the module hierarchy from the block diagram almost without modifications. The only components that need to be added are modules for the output of error messages, for the graphic display of the robot, and for communication with the user. In order to stay as independent of the target machine as possible, we provide only one input/output block. We will postpone the structuring of this block until we know exactly which operations we need. The module hierarchy now takes the form depicted in Figure 3.24. The modules are represented as rectangles; the arrows express import relationships.

This rough design already clearly reflects the hierarchy in the four levels identified above. The sole task of the main program is to invoke its directly subordinate operations in the correct sequence. The algorithmic work is vested in level 2, and the modules for managing data are located in level 3. The input/output block (which will likely decompose into several modules later) forms the base of the hierarchy. Because read/write operations almost always depend on the target machine and its operating system, it makes sense to implement the necessary input/output operations ourselves and to package them in appropriate modules. The respective procedures will then be quite short and only invoke the appropriate operating system routines. Such an approach has the advantage that the superordinate levels are completely independent of the target machine and its operating system. Porting to another computer requires reimplementation of level 4 only.

Our rough design does not reflect the final module structure yet. In particular, we have to assume that the three main components – editor, analyzer and simulator – will

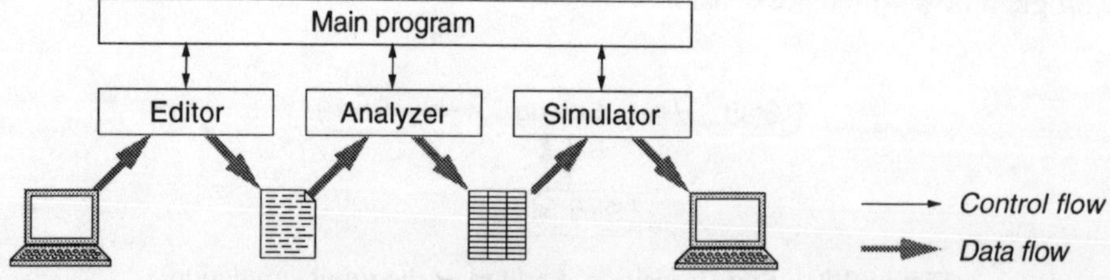


Figure 3.23: Block diagram of the robot simulation

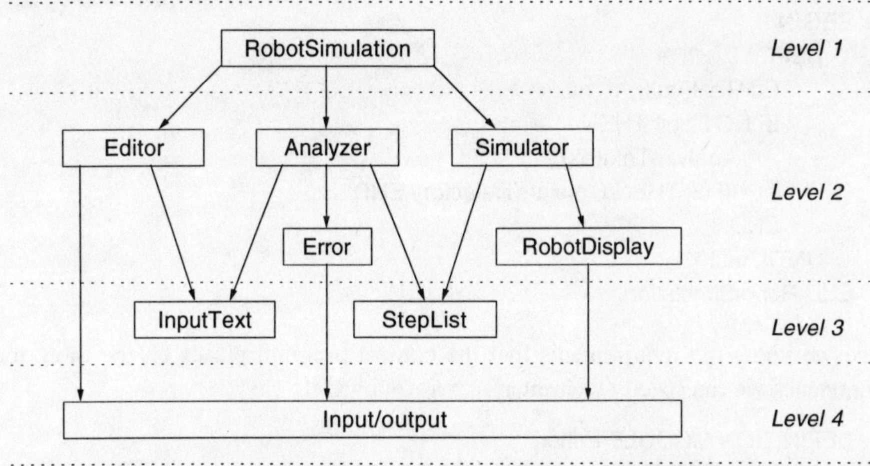


Figure 3.24: Module hierarchy of the robot simulation

prove so complex that each cannot be realized in a single module. However, we can postpone the decomposition of these modules until we handle each respective component. We can later approach the solution of these subproblems as we did the structuring of the overall problem solution. Each component then decomposes into a main program and a number of additional modules.

To complete our rough design, we need to specify the module interfaces. Before we begin this task, we should consider which information we will need in the main program to fulfill the required control tasks. We assume that the user will execute control from the editor. There are two ways to terminate editing: the user can request an analysis of the trajectory description followed by a simulation, or quit the program. In order to distinguish these two cases, a boolean variable parameter *quit* suffices. In the module hierarchy specified above, we already determined that the analyzer would directly invoke the error module if the input text is incorrect. The only information that the analyzer needs from the main program is whether the analysis was successful. We also introduce this in a boolean variable parameter *ok*. The simulator, on the other hand, requires no variable parameter. It retains control until the user explicitly terminates the simulation. The main program must then invoke the editor again. Given these considerations, our initial design of the main program takes the following form:

```
MODULE RobotSimulation;

FROM Editor         IMPORT EditText;
FROM Analyzer       IMPORT AnalyzeText;
FROM Simulator      IMPORT SimulateTrajectory;

VAR quit,ok:BOOLEAN;
```

```
BEGIN
  REPEAT
    EditText(quit);
    IF NOT quit THEN
      AnalyzeText(ok);
      IF ok THEN SimulateTrajectory END
    END
  UNTIL quit
END RobotSimulation.
```

Since we know the requirements that the control program places on the three main components, we can specify their interfaces as follows:

```
DEFINITION MODULE Editor;
  PROCEDURE EditText (VAR quit:BOOLEAN);
END Editor.

DEFINITION MODULE Analyzer;
  PROCEDURE AnalyzeText (VAR ok:BOOLEAN);
END Analyzer.

DEFINITION MODULE Simulator;
  PROCEDURE SimulateTrajectory;
END Simulator.
```

We have undertaken a function-oriented modularization; each module is responsible for a self-contained task.

The specification of the interface of the error module proves more challenging since we need to make assumptions about which error types might arise. A simple solution consists of coding the type of error as a text and the error position as the indices of the first (first) and of the last (last) characters of the erroneous text segment in the trajectory description. The interface of the error module thus takes the following form:

```
DEFINITION MODULE Error;
  PROCEDURE ReportError (message:ARRAY OF CHAR; first,last:CARDINAL);
END Error.
```

The interface definitions become increasingly more difficult to design as we delve deeper into the program hierarchy. The specification of the interface of the error module already required making assumptions that might not be adequate to the problem. This can result in unnecessarily restricting the implementer of the analysis components, which would mandate a revision of the error interface. The display component (module RobotDisplay) is used exclusively by the module Simulator. The required display operations emanate from the requirements that evolve during the development of the module Simulator: Only then does it become possible to specify the interface of the module RobotDisplay.

The interface definitions for the modules of level 3 prove just as difficult. For example, in order to completely establish the interface of the text module, we first need information about which text operations the editor and the analyzer need to handle their tasks. At this design stage, however, this is not yet possible. The best solution is to set up an abstract model for the trajectory description and to leave the details to the designers of the editor and the analysis component. Hence we introduce an abstract data structure InputText. The same applies for the interface of the step list. The following example shows what the interfaces of the modules InputText and StepList could look like:

```
DEFINITION MODULE InputText;

(* Text manipulation *)
  PROCEDURE GetLength(): CARDINAL;
     (* Returns the number of characters in the input text *)
  PROCEDURE GetCharacter (i:CARDINAL): CHAR;
     (* Returns the character at position i *)
  PROCEDURE ReplaceChar (i:CARDINAL; ch:CHAR);
     (* Replaces the character at position i with character ch *)
  PROCEDURE InsertChar (i:CARDINAL; ch:CHAR);
     (* Inserts character ch before the character at position i *)
  PROCEDURE DeleteChar (i:CARDINAL);
     (* Removes the character at position i, shifts all subsequent characters left *)

(*Text display*)
  PROCEDURE OpenTextWindow;
     (* Opens a window to display and input text on the screen *)
  PROCEDURE CloseTextWindow;
     (* Closes a window that was opened with OpenTextWindow *)
  PROCEDURE GetCursorPosition(): CARDINAL;
     (* Returns the index of the character at the current cursor position *)
  PROCEDURE SetCursorPosition (i:CARDINAL);
     (* Locates the cursor at the character at index position i *)

END InputText.

DEFINITION MODULE StepList;

TYPE
  Coordinate = [0..2000];
  Position = RECORD x,y,z:Coordinate END;
```

```
    PROCEDURE DeleteList;
        (* Initializes the step list to empty *)
    PROCEDURE ListLength(): CARDINAL;
        (* Returns the number of steps in the step list *)
    PROCEDURE AppendStep (pos:Position);
        (* Appends to the step list the step to position pos *)
    PROCEDURE GetStepTarget (i:CARDINAL; VAR pos:Position);
        (* Returns the target position pos of the step at index i *)
  END StepList.
```

For both modules we have followed the data capsule principle; since we only need *one* input text and *one* step list, we opted against abstract data types for the sake of simplicity.

## 3.4.4 User interface design

The design of the user interfaces is a subtask of the design phase. Strictly speaking, this design task should largely be part of the specification phase, because program operation must be anchored in the requirements definition. Nevertheless, we handle the design of user interfaces in the section on design.

In this section we introduce the most important principles for designing user interfaces and then show how they can be applied to the task presented in Section 3.4.2. We assume that the target computer on which the software system is to be implemented meets several fundamental requirements for the design of a modern graphical user interface (GUI), in particular:

- Graphical monitor
- Mouse
- Window technology
- Menus

In the 1970s Xerox's Palo Alto Research Center (PARC) developed the first software systems employing these graphical user interface elements. Since then this technology has proven itself in many application domains, and today it can be found on most computers. The Apple Macintosh operating system and Microsoft Windows serve as examples of GUIs. In the following sections we mention several determinants of the comfort of such a graphical user interface. Space limitations do not allow detailed treatment of the associated concepts. We refer interested readers to [Apple 1987], [Betts 1987] and [Laurel 1990].

### 3.4.4.1 Modes

Interactive programs of the past almost always employed modes. A program mode in this sense is a situation in which the user can only execute a limited number of operations. Note that programs also always have internal states during their execution, but these normally do not affect the operation.

The motto "avoid modes" had a deciding influence on the design of user interfaces. It was recognized that modes restrict the user and force the user to deviate from a normal way of working. Consider the following simple program for the division of two numbers.

```
MODULE Division;

FROM RealInOut IMPORT ReadReal, WriteReal;
FROM InOut IMPORT Done, WriteString, WriteLn;
VAR
   numerator,denominator: REAL;

BEGIN
   WriteString("numerator="); ReadReal(numerator); WriteLn;
   IF NOT Done THEN RETURN END;
   WriteString("denominator="); ReadReal(denominator); WriteLn;
   IF NOT Done THEN RETURN END;
   WriteString("quotient="); WriteReal(numerator/denominator); WriteLn;
END Division.
```

When the program runs, the following dialog ensues (user input being indicated with underlining):

```
numerator = 25
denominator = 3.1415926
quotient = 7.957747
```

The program passes through two subsequent modes. In the first mode only the numerator can be input; in the second mode, only the denominator. The input of each number can be confirmed with the return key or interrupted with the escape key. Program execution resembles a question-and-answer game in which the computer takes the leading role. The user can only answer the computer's questions or terminate program execution. On inputting the denominator, if the user observes that the value of the numerator is incorrect, the only possible corrective action is to terminate the program and then restart it. For such a simple program this might not be serious; imagine, however, that the user had input numerous data into the program (e.g., personnel data). In such situations (which unfortunately can still be found all too frequently today) the human feels like a servant of the computer; the user rejects the program because it fails to make work easier. Figure 3.25 shows how the division example could be designed with improved user friendliness.

Now the user can enter the numerator and denominator in any order and correct an entry as well. The user can repeatedly request computation of a quotient and finally end the program.

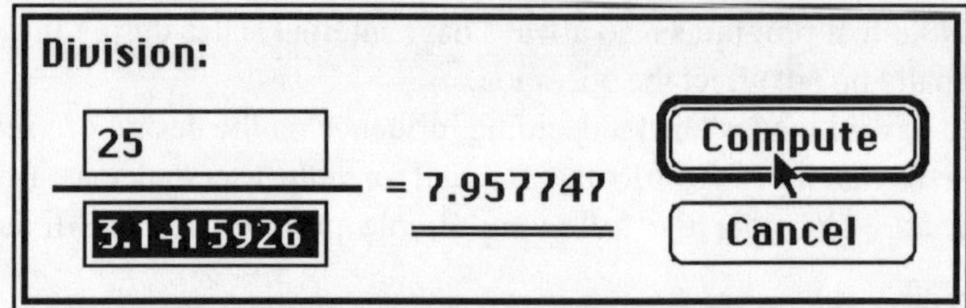


Figure 3.25: Dialog window for division

For the implementer, this type of user dialog demands more programming effort unless a suitable tool (interface builder) or specialized language features are available. There is but a single program mode, in which the user can decide what will happen next. The task of the program consists of reading and correctly interpreting user input (both keyboard input and pointing operations with the mouse). For the program, user input is an event to which it must react in an appropriate way. This leads to the concept of *event-driven programming*.

Unfortunately, it is not possible to avoid all types of modes. One goal of user interface design should be to eliminate all modes that the user perceives as particularly irritating. Window technology can provide valuable services here. With the help of windows, the user can process various subtasks simultaneously in different windows. Figure 3.26 shows a text editor, a calculator and a drawing program in three windows.

It is clear that this represents three different modes: The user can either input text or work on a drawing or make computations, depending on which window is active (in the foreground). These modes do not represent significant restrictions for the user for two

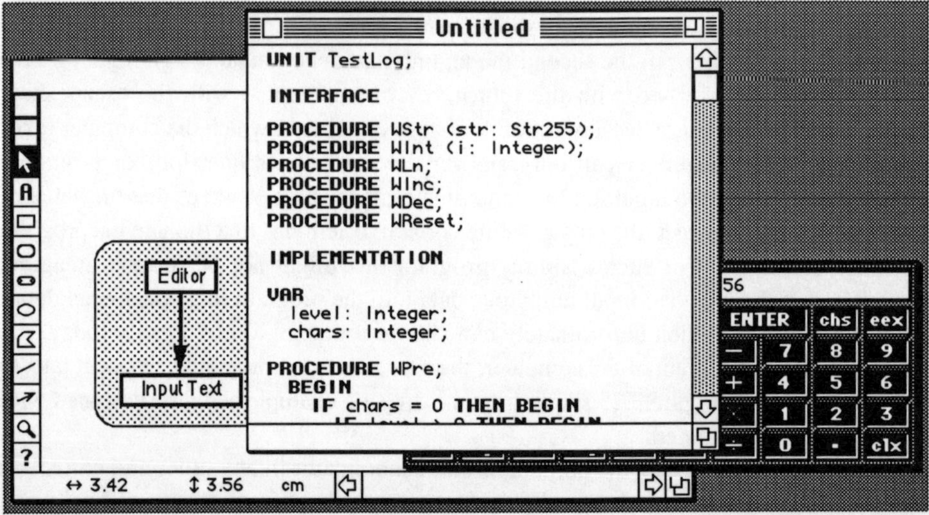


Figure 3.26: Screen snapshot with multiple windows

reasons: First, they reflect the way people work; as a rule, a person working at a desk likewise cannot simultaneously write, draw and compute. Second, the user can easily and deliberately change modes; for example, to switch from writing mode to computation mode, it suffices to click on the calculator in the background and thereby activate it.

### 3.4.4.2 Elementary operations

The key to avoiding modes is the decomposition of the overall user dialog into elementary operations. What this means can best be explained using the example of text editors. The first interactive text editors were command line-oriented and were controlled with a command language. For example, moving the first three lines of a text to a position before the tenth line requires a command similar to "move 1-3,10". This operation only appears to be simple, which we can recognize by its three parameters (start and end of the text area to be moved, target position). In modern text editors the same operation is decomposed into four elementary operations:

- Selection of the first three lines
- Menu command "cut"
- Move the cursor to the start of (former) line 10
- Menu command "paste"

This *cut-copy-paste principle* permits the user a change of mind or corrections after each elementary operation. One characteristic of this principle is that the user first determines what is to be manipulated and only then what is to occur, while inversely in command languages the user first established the operation and then specified the parameters.

However, there are situations where we cannot avoid additionally specifying parameters for a command. Searching for and replacing character strings in texts serves as an example that can best be solved with a dialog window, as shown in Figure 3.27.

Since such dialog windows for inputting additional parameters represent modes, they should be avoided in user interface design whenever possible.

### 3.4.4.3 Menus

The requirement to decompose the user dialog into elementary operations also means that the input of commands should take place via a minimum of individual actions. Menu

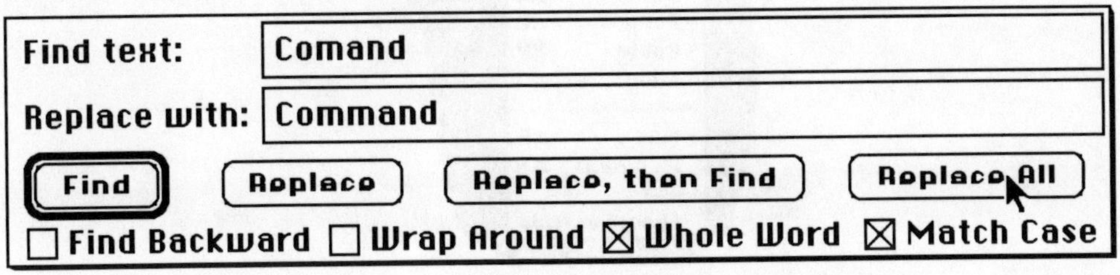

Find text: Comand
Replace with: Command
Find | Replace | Replace, then Find | Replace All
☐ Find Backward ☐ Wrap Around ☒ Whole Word ☒ Match Case

Figure 3.27: A dialog for global replacement in texts

commands provide a means to achieve this goal. While the first modern user interfaces worked with pop-up menus (pressing a certain mouse key activated a menu with commands at any screen position), pulldown menus have come to dominate because of their ease of use. They characteristically have a constantly displayed menu bar (normally a single line at the top) with the names of all available menus. The user can click on the menu bar with the mouse to display all the commands belonging to a menu and can select a command, likewise with the mouse (see Figure 3.28). Pop-up menus prove more efficient because they can appear at any position and thus require less mouse movement. Pulldown menus permit better structuring (including hierarchically) of an extensive set of commands and are easier to use with a single-button mouse.

In contrast to former systems where commands had to be input in text form, menus make it significantly easier for the user to work with a system. Learning to use a program no longer requires mastering a command language; instead, the user can view the available commands at any time. Especially for lay persons and occasional users, this means relief in terms of what must be remembered. The operation of the program no longer demands the user's attention, so that the user can concentrate more fully on the actual task at hand.

We divide menu commands into three classes according to their functionality:

- Immediately executable commands
- Commands with parameters
- Commands for switching modes

We use the example in Figure 3.28 to explain these classes of commands.

Directly executable commands include all menu commands that require no parameters or that operate on the current selection. Examples include *Cut* and *Paste*. Such commands are examples of elementary operations: With a simple mouse click the user causes the program to carry out an action that normally involves processing data.

Commands with parameters are similar in effect to those in the first class. They differ primarily in the user actions that are required to execute them. An example is the command *Find* to locate certain characters, such as in a text editor. This command has an

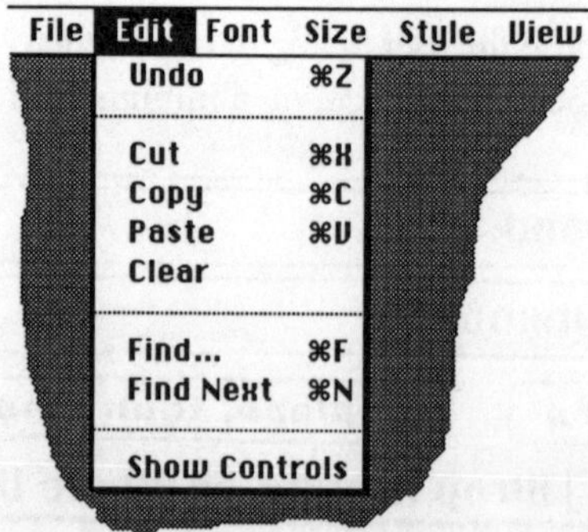


Figure 3.28: Pulldown menu

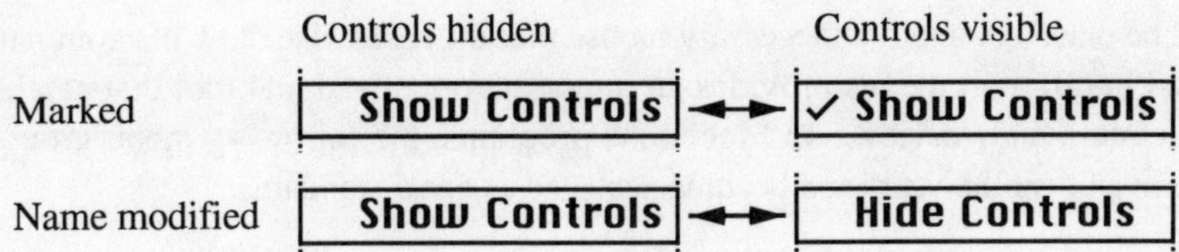


Figure 3.29: Modes of a menu command

implicit parameter, the position where searching is to begin (normally the current cursor position). The execution of the command prompts the user to input additional parameters (the characters to be found, search direction, etc.). Input prompting is normally handled via a dialog window (see Section 3.4.4.4). The execution of such a command thus requires several sequential inputs from the user. To simplify the repeated execution of a command with the same parameters, it can be useful to use a dedicated, immediately executable menu command. Such an example is *Find Next*.

Instead of manipulating data, the menu commands of the third class cause a change in mode that affects subsequent commands or the way in which data are displayed. Examples include switching between insert and overwrite mode and the command *Show Controls* in a text editor to display normally invisible control characters. Such menu commands characteristically toggle a certain mode on repeated executions. Because of this dual function, the user needs a means of knowing what effect the next execution of the command will have. Two approaches address this type of feedback: either the menu command has some kind of mark that shows whether the associated mode is currently on or off, or the wording of the command is adapted to the current mode, so that its name indicates the effect of executing the command again. Figure 3.29 shows how this could be realized with the *Show Controls* example.

A frequent argument against menu commands is that they are primarily intended for lay persons, and that menus hinder the practiced user's work. This argument is partially true; it is true that the flow of work is interrupted when a hand leaves the keyboard and moves to the mouse for the execution of a menu command. Most menu systems provide shortcuts for executing menu commands with special key combination. Nevertheless, this option should be used sparingly. We recommend introducing keyboard shortcuts only after extensive testing with typical users.

A frequently neglected task in the design of a menu system is the choice of appropriate wording for the menu commands. Apply the rule that the commands should be as short as possible, yet still pregnant. Developers in German or French are confronted with a more difficult problem with respect to brevity than colleagues developing in English. Independent of the language used, pregnant menu commands result from using verbs to describe the action to be carried out. The command "Show Controls" is clearer than simply "Controls".

In the design of a menu system, similar commands should be grouped together and under the same menu. The more frequently a command is used, the higher in the menu it should be placed to avoid unnecessary mouse motion. Likewise, how the commands are grouped in different menus provides an important organizational tool that can help the user maintain an overview. In Macintosh programs, the following menu groups have been proven over the years and become accepted as quasi-standards:

| | |
|---|---|
| *File* | File operations, e.g., Open, Close, Print and Save documents |
| *Edit* | Editing operations, e.g., Cut, Copy, Paste and Clear |
| *View* | Selection of display form, e.g., Show Controls |
| *Format* | General formatting aids, e.g., justification and line spacing |
| *Font* | Choice of available fonts |
| *Style* | Font styles, e.g., Bold, Italic, Underline |
| *Size* | Size of font |
| *Pen* | Line attributes |
| *Windows* | Display and reorganization of windows |

Many menu commands can only be executed in certain modes. For example, the command *Copy* only makes sense if something is selected in the active window. There are three basic possibilities for handling the situation where such a command is invoked in a mode where it cannot be executed.

- *The command has no effect.* This variant is easiest to implement, but can cause confusion and frustration for the user when the command fails to function in certain situations.
- *An error message is displayed.* This possibility is preferred over the first because the user can be advised why the execution of the command is impossible. If the same situation arises repeatedly, however, the recurring error message tends to irritate the user.
- *The command is disabled.* The best choice is to prevent the selection of a senseless command from the start. To achieve this goal, the command should not be removed from the menu, which would confuse an occasional user and cause a search in vain for the command. It is better to mark nonexecutable commands as disabled in some suitable form (e.g., struck through or in another color).

#### 3.4.4.4 Dialog windows

The term *screen mask* emanates from a time when strongly mode-oriented dialog programs were the rule. In every state the user could enter the requested information in respective fields. The purpose of such dialog windows in today's dialog programs remains the same, although their appearance has changed through the use of window technology. As a result, on-screen forms are no longer viewed as elementary means for managing user dialog, but are primarily used to provide additional parameters for commands. The dialog window for global search-and-replace in Figure 3.27 shows such an example.

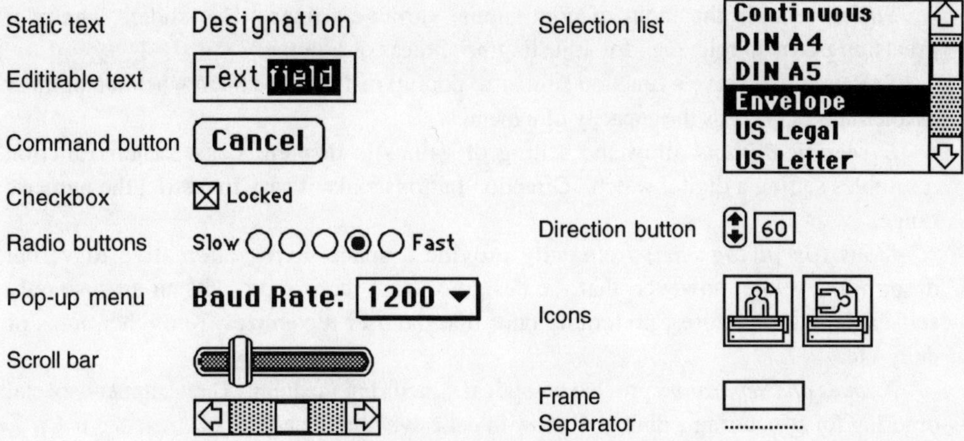


Figure 3.30: User interface elements

In contrast to former screen masks, the forms used today contain not just fields for text input, but also new elements such as buttons and checkboxes. The user interface thus tends to resemble the switching panel of a technical device more than a form. Figure 3.30 shows which user interface elements have become the primary accepted standards (inspired by the user interface of the Apple Macintosh).

*Static text* is used for titles, labels and explanations. Dialog windows should be structured to minimize static text. In particular, avoid long explanations by means of adequate labeling of the elements available to the user.

As far as possible, use *editable text* only for inputting character strings (e.g., names). For the input of numbers, other user interface elements (e.g., direction keys and slide switches) do a better job of eliminating errors.

*Command buttons* trigger immediate action. Typically an input dialog window contains an OK button to confirm an input and a Cancel button to abort an action.

*Checkboxes* permit the selection of boolean values. Examples include Find Backward and Match Case in the search dialog window in Figure 3.27.

*Radio buttons* allow the selection of one alternative from a set of mutually exclusive possibilities. Use this design element when the user is to select from a range of more than two elements as well as to replace the checkbox in cases where the meaning cannot be described by the boolean values true and false, e.g., "Baud Rate: ○ 1200 ◉ 2400". By contrast, in "Grid Display: ○ Off ◉ On" this interface design element is not applied properly.

*Pop-up menus* provide an alternative to radio buttons. A mouse click on a framed area presents a list of available possibilities from which the user can select. Compared to radio buttons, pop-up menus require less space and can be arbitrarily (even dynamically) extended. That they normally do not display all available options proves to be a disadvantage.

*Sliders* enable the input of continuous, variable values. Use sliders wherever precision plays no role, e.g., for adjusting brightness or volume.

*Selection lists* serve a function similar to pop-up menus. Use them when the number of alternatives exceeds the capacity of a menu.

*Direction buttons* allow the setting of values in discrete steps. Their function resembles setting a digital watch. Direction buttons make it easy to restrict the numeric range.

*Icons (or pictograms)* frequently provide a space-saving alternative to verbal description. Note, however, that the design of such icons represents an art; use only self-explanatory pictures, preferably ones that the user recognizes from other areas of daily life.

*Frames and separators* provide an optical structuring medium. They augment spacial ordering for structuring a dialog window in cohesive functional blocks.

Whenever possible, avoid extensive dialog windows with numerous individual elements. They become time-consuming to use because the user must control every adjustment, even to set only a single field. To assure a good overview, limit input dialog windows to not more than ten individual elements. If more settings are required, divide these among several dialog windows (invoked from the main dialog window with respective commands).

In most cases it makes sense to save settings that were made (possibly even across session boundaries) and to treat them as defaults on the next invocation of the same command. The reason is that various invocations of the same command usually occur with similar parameters. This enables the user to ignore most of the settings on repetition of a command.

Modern graphical user interfaces with windows and menus have come to dominate not only because of their user friendliness, but also for aesthetic reasons. No one disputes that working with an attractive screen is more fun and so is perceived as less of a burden than character-oriented communication with the computer. Designers of newer systems thus pay particular attention to achieving an appropriate look. The graphical capabilities of monitors are exploited, e.g., to give windows and buttons a plasticity like three-dimensional objects (see Figure 3.31). Use such design possibilities only if they are standard in the target environment. It would be wrong to sacrifice the uniformity of a user interface for purely aesthetic reasons.

#### 3.4.4.5 Color and sound

Today's computer monitors can simultaneously display millions of colors. This possibility has lured many programmers into making the user interfaces of their programs as colorful as possible. However, studies have shown that the excessive use of color distracts the user from what is relevant. Hence we provide the following guidelines for the design of color user interfaces [Apple 1987].

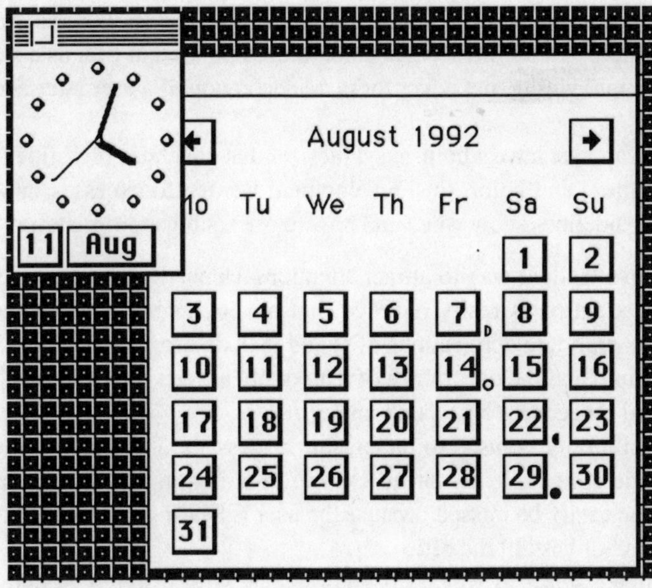


Figure. 3.31: Plasticity of a user interface

- About one person in twenty is colorblind in some way. To avoid excluding such persons from using a program, color must not serve as the sole source of information. For example, highlighting an error in a text with red effectively flags it for most people, but is scarcely recognizable, if at all, to a red-green colorblind user. Another form of highlighting (e.g., inversion of the text) should be preferred over color.
- Longitudinal studies have shown that black writing on a white background proves most readable for daily work. For a black background, amber proves the most amicable to the eyes. Writing in red and blue proves least readable because these colors are at opposite ends of the visible spectrum for humans. Because of the extreme wave length of these colors, their focal point is not exactly on the retina of the eye, but in front of or behind it. Although the eye automatically adapts to reading red or blue text, the resulting strain causes early fatigue. Experts recommend avoiding red and blue to display text.
- Red serves as a danger signal. However, because the user's eye is drawn to red, it would be wrong to employ red to mark dangerous actions. Color "support" in such a case would have the reverse effect.
- Light blue on a white background is hard to read, especially for small objects or thin lines. Thus important things should never be displayed in light blue. Still, this effect can be exploited, for example, to set grid lines in the background as unimportant.

- In general, color should only be used where the task expressly requires it, such as in graphic editors. In all other cases color should be used at best as a supplementary means for highlighting, but never for mere decoration of a user interface.

Many newer computers have a built-in synthesizer that generates high-fidelity sound. As with color monitors and color, this development has led to excesses in sound output. The following guidelines show when and how to use sound appropriately.

- Sound is an excellent way to attract attention. Hence it should only be used when the user's attention is really required, but never as simple background for other actions. Appropriate applications of sound include error situations (e.g., paper out while printing) and the occurrence of temporally uncertain events such as the end of an extended procedure (e.g., data transfer).
- Sound should only be used to underscore a message displayed on the screen, but never as the sole indicator of an exception situation. Otherwise an important message can easily be missed because the user is hearing-impaired, works in a loud environment, or has left the office.
- It might make sense to signal different events with different sounds. However, observe that only a user with musical training or talent can discern signals with similar pitch.
- Avoid loud and shrill sounds. Imagine a large office where every few minutes another computer trumpets an alarm. For the same reason, avoid sounds with more than three sequential tones; such signals become irritating when heard too often.
- Even in particularly pressing emergencies, never, under any circumstances, employ a long, continuous sound or, even worse, an enduring staccato. Such sounds can create panic and evoke erroneous action from the user. It is better to use a short, unintruding sound and to repeat it at intervals of one minute until the user reacts.

#### 3.4.4.6 Consistency

When planning which user interface elements to use in a software system, give particular attention to consistency. Frequently new user interface elements are introduced or the function of existing ones is changed to enable the user to work more efficiently with the program. Such ideas often do contribute to simplification of work procedures. However, it is more important to have the user encounter a known environment free from surprises. This means that similar things should have a similar look and that different things should differ in appearance. In particular, this implies the following:

- Menu commands with similar functions should have the same nomenclature and the same location even in different programs.
- Shortcut keys for menu commands should always be consistent. Rather than introduce a nonstandard key combination, leave the menu command without a shortcut.

- Buttons with similar functions should have similar labels and the same relative position in different dialog windows.
- Dialog windows for the input of similar functions should have a consistent look.

A typical user works with various programs on the same computer. The acceptance of a new program significantly depends on whether the user encounters similar interface functionality as in other familiar programs. Every deviation as well as every omission can mean an irritation factor. For example, if the user is accustomed to interrupting any action by pressing a given key combination, then irritation results when this key has no function or a different function in a new program.

The greater the internal consistency of a user interface and its consistency with the user interfaces of other programs, the less effort is required for learning to use the new program. In many cases this can replace extensive user's manuals. On the other hand, the obligation to maintain consistency, like any form of standardization, can also restrict possibilities for user interfaces. Thus revolutionary ideas would never be implemented for the sake of uniformity. Whether a new idea justifies deviation from consistency can best be determined by means of experiments with typical users working on prototypes.

#### 3.4.4.7 Prototyping

Paper and pencil provide an inadequate medium for designing a user interface for a new program. They permit noting the planned structure of dialog windows and the description of anticipated commands and their functionality. However, this exhausts the possibilities of such a static description.

The dynamics of a program cannot be described statically. To avoid unpleasant surprises in the implementation phase, it is important to also define the behavior of the program as early as possible. A prototype serves as the best medium for specifying a user interface because it allows playing through the typical steps in working with the planned program. In such an experimentation phase, most questions regarding operation can be discussed and solved together with the client.

It is clear that the implementation of a prototype means additional effort. Frequently weeks pass before the implementation of the first prototype for the most important user interface elements, and this prototype might prove useless within the first hours of experimentation. Still, the time invested in the production of the prototype is not lost; even a negative experience is valuable because it helps to avoid later (more expensive) errors in the implementation phase.

The use of appropriate tools can reduce the effort for implementing prototypes. Many software products are available today that support the interactive description (usually in graphical form) of the user interface. Most of these tools generate the source code of a program that implements the user interface from a user interface definition. The time required to implement a prototype thus shrinks from weeks to hours. (Chapter 6 handles prototyping tools and their features in more detail.)

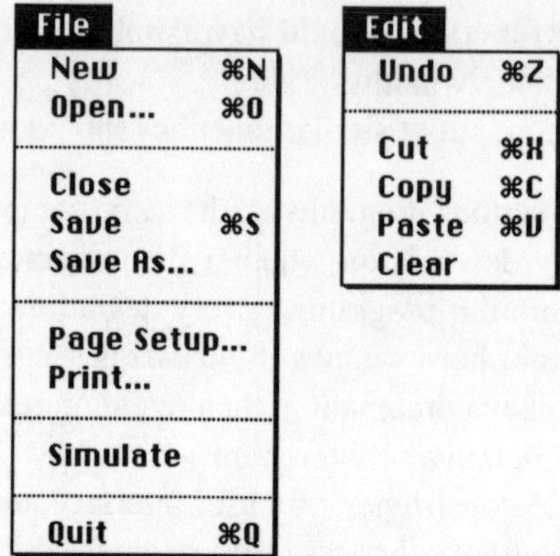


Figure 3.32: Robot simulator menus

#### 3.4.4.8 Application to the design example

This section describes the user interface for our robot exercise in enough detail to serve later as the design basis for the implementation. We assume that the implementation will be on a Macintosh computer and that we will employ a prototyping tool to model the user interface. The early selection of a target machine is important to us because we want to adhere to the rules for designing user interfaces that apply for this computer.

The following illustrations are excerpts of screens that are displayed during the execution of our prototype of the robot program. As explained above regarding static representation, this does not reveal all details because the dynamic aspect is lacking. However, we will strive to compensate for this shortcoming with extensive specifications based on the Figures.

We will use two windows for our exercise: a text window for inputting the trajectory description and a simulation window for monitoring the trajectory. In order to make the robot control (run, stop, step) as realistic as possible, we will provide the respective buttons in the simulation window. We will tackle the design of this window last, but we can already assume that we will not need menu commands for robot control. Thus the standard menus File and Edit suffice, as shown in Figure 3.32.

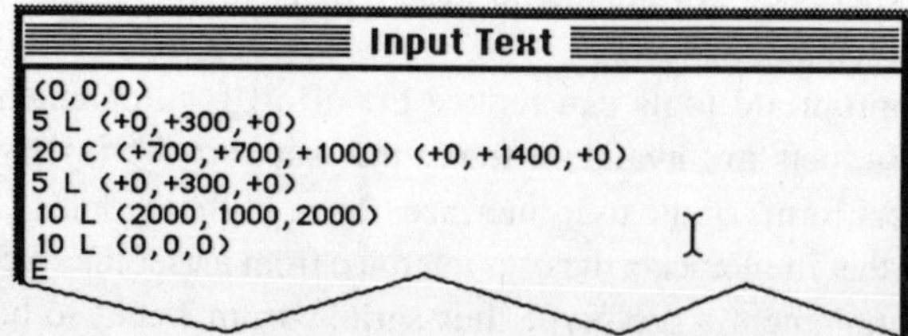


Figure 3.33: Text window for inputting trajectory descriptions

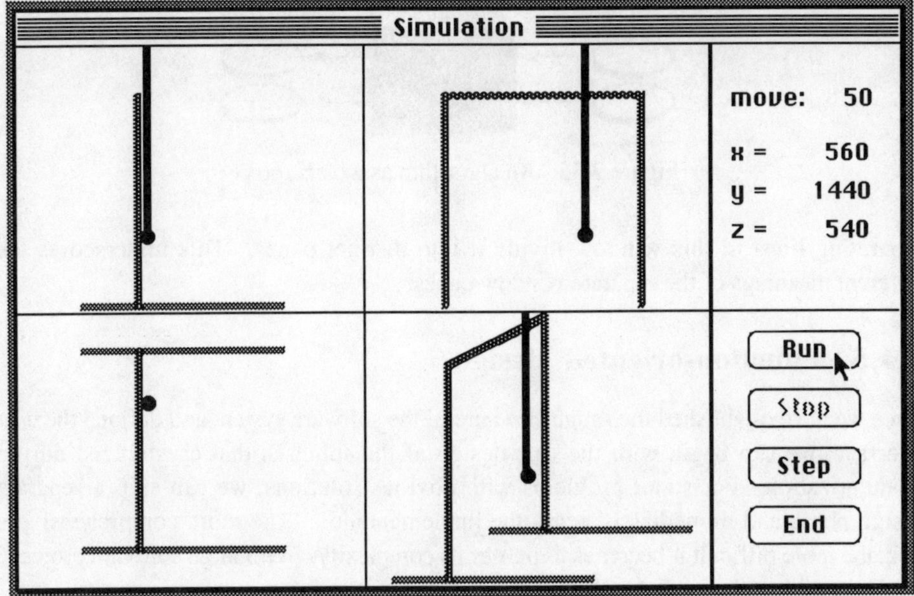


Figure 3.34: User interface of the robot simulation

Both menus adopt the usual Macintosh organization of commands. Most of their commands are for opening, saving, printing and processing a trajectory description. The only application-specific command is *Simulate* in the File menu.

A trajectory description is edited in a simple text window. We will not describe the editing features at this point, but simply show how this window is presented to the user and the font in which the text is displayed (Figure 3.33).

The major part of our design work will be on the simulation window for observing and controlling the trajectory of the robot. According to the task description, the trajectory is to be monitored in front, top and side views and isometrically. Thus it makes sense to reserve most of the space within this window for the simulation display. Additionally, we would like to follow the trajectory numerically as well as graphically. Thus, although it is not required in the task description, we will also display the x, y and z coordinates and the current step number. We need three buttons to control the trajectory simulation: one for starting and one for stopping the robot, and one for single-stepping. We will also provide a button to end the simulation and return to the editor. We also want the buttons to mutually (de)activate one another as needed . For example, the Stop button should be deactivated if the robot is not currently moving. On the other hand, while a trajectory is being carried out, the buttons Run and Step should be deactivated. This mutual effect on the part of commands is a dynamic aspect of the program. It can best be specified and controlled during a test run of the prototype. Figure 3.34 shows the finished user interface for the robot simulation. Note that

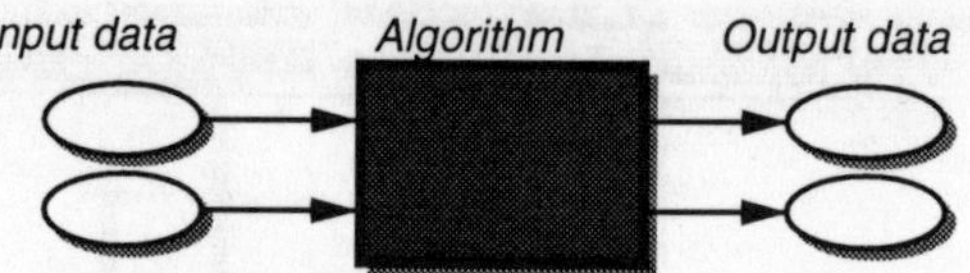


Figure 3.35: An algorithm as a black box

separating lines in this window divide it into distinct panes. This underscores the different meanings of the separate window panes.

## 3.4.5 Function-oriented design

Once we have established the rough structure of the software system and defined the user interface, we can begin with the fine design of the subtasks that crystallized during modularization. For small problems with obvious solutions, we can skip a separate design phase and immediately begin the implementation. The more comprehensive a task, the more difficult it becomes to master its complexity. With large software projects, it is impossible to keep all details in mind simultaneously.

The core question in the design of larger software systems is how to begin with the solution of the task. A novice to software engineering will immediately tackle subtasks that appear interesting, depending on personal tastes and capabilities. Usually these are core problems for which the designer already has a vague solution idea. This can even go so far that refined algorithms and concrete data structures are already set down to the last detail at the very beginning of the design stage. However, because the exact interrelationships within the overall problem are not yet known at this stage, such an approach can lead to errors that have to be corrected later.

### 3.4.5.1 Stepwise refinement

Most known design methods are function oriented, which means that they focus on the algorithm to solve the problem. The underlying thought model is illustrated in the sketch in Figure 3.35.

Imagine the algorithm as a mathematical function that computes results on the basis of given parameters. At the start of the design stage the algorithm is still a *black box* whose contents are unknown. The more difficult the task to be solved, the more extensive, generally, is its solution algorithm. Thus it makes sense to proceed as with the modularization, i.e., to decompose the task into mutually independent subtasks, whereby the algorithms for the solution of subtasks again should be viewed as black boxes. The resulting overall solution thus becomes a network of cooperating subalgorithms, as Figure 3.36 shows.

Wirth [Wirth 1971] termed this principle of problem solving *stepwise refinement*. The idea behind stepwise refinement encompasses two simple rules:

- Decompose the task into subtasks.
- Consider each subtask independently and decompose it again into subtasks.

Continue the ongoing decomposition of large tasks into smaller subtasks until the subtasks become so simple that they can readily be expressed with statements in the selected programming language. Solving a task using this approach is characterized as follows:

- For each (sub)task, begin with the identification of its significant components. However, merely specifying the subtasks will not suffice; it must be clear whether and how the solutions to these subtasks can assimilate into an overall solution. This means that the initial design of an algorithm certainly can contain control structures. The interconnection of the (yet unknown) subsolutions can and should already be specified at this stage by means of sequential, conditional and repeated execution.
- Treat details as late as possible. This means, after the decomposition of a task into appropriate subtasks, waste no thoughts yet on what the solutions of these subtasks could look like. First clarify the interrelationship of the subtasks; only then tackle the solution of each subtask independently (i.e., by neglecting to a large degree its embedding in the overall system). This ensures that critical decisions are made only after much information is available about the interrelationship of the subtasks. This makes it easier to avoid errors with grave consequences.
- A continuous reduction of complexity accompanies the design process when using the principle of stepwise refinement. For example, if a task A is solved by the sequential solution of three subtasks B, C and D, there is a temptation to assess this decomposition as trivial and of little use. In actuality, however, the solution to each respective subtask is demonstrably simpler than the solution to the overall task. In some cases an apparently insolvable problem seems to solve itself when we apply repeated decomposition into subproblems.
- The subtasks become increasingly concrete and their solution requires increasingly detailed information. This means stepwise refinement not only of the algorithms but also the data with which they work (represented as small circles in Figure 3.36). The concretization of the data should also be reflected in the interfaces of the subsolutions. In the initial design steps, we recommend working with abstract data structures or abstract data types whose concrete structure is defined only when the last subtasks can no longer be solved without knowledge thereof.

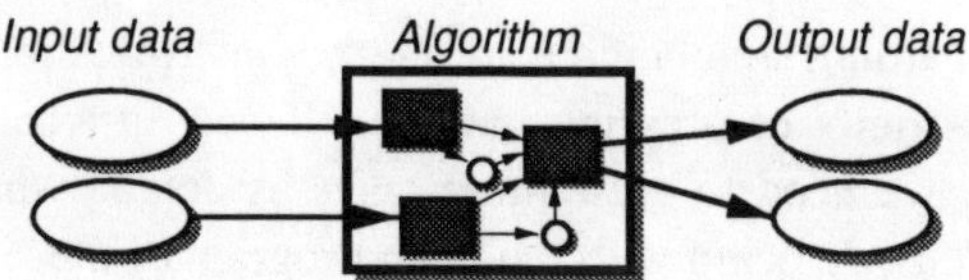


Figure 3.36: Result of the first refinement step

- During stepwise refinement the designer must constantly check whether the current decomposition can be continued in the light of further refinement or whether it must be scrapped.

As simple as this procedure seems at first glance, we must warn against rash optimism. The most important decomposition decisions are made at the very start, when the designer knows the least. Hence the designer is hardly able to apply stepwise refinement consistently. If the design falters, the designer is tempted to save the situation by incorporating special cases into already developed subalgorithms. However, this leads to a patchwork whose inadequacies can prove to be catastrophic when modifications in the task description require rethinking the design. Here it is better to backtrack several steps in the design to find the incorrect design decision. Although this requires resolving some subproblems, it probably leads to better structuring of the overall solution. The additional effort required to correct the error should not be construed as lost time; indeed, it enables the collection of valuable information that can be of use in later design decisions.

### 3.4.5.2 Application to the design example

As an example of the use of stepwise refinement, in this section we show how to realize parts of the simulator (see Section 3.4.3.3). We will not solve the entire simulation task; in order to demonstrate the principle of stepwise refinement, we limit ourselves to solving part of the simulation task to such an extent that procedures emerge that could easily be implemented in a concrete programming language.

In Section 3.4.3.3 we specified the following interface definition for the simulator:

```
DEFINITION MODULE Simulator;
   PROCEDURE SimulateTrajectory;
END Simulator.
```

The task description suggests that the procedure SimulateTrajectory has the following subtasks:

- Initialization: open the window.
- Reading user input: here we are interested only in mouse clicks.
- Interpretation of user input: execute desired actions.
- Termination: close the window.

The main problem regarding simulation is the correct interpretation of user input, which in our case consists strictly of pressing buttons. Based on what we have said about stepwise refinement, we need to view these tasks as details whose solution we will postpone for now. Thus we begin with the main program of the simulator and consider its constituent subtasks. The first design step will be to specify a provisional algorithm for running a simulation. This algorithm need not be complete and correct; we simply want to have a basis for planning the further approach. We assume that the simulation will be decomposed into continuously running single steps, between which user input will be accepted. Our initial algorithm design could look like this:

```
Initialize;
ReadInput(↑input);
while input ≠ endButton do
   InterpretInput(↓input);
   ReadInput(↑input);
end;
Terminate
```

This initial design already shows that we will not likely get far with the solution of the task without thinking about the representation of user input. In Section 3.4.4.8 we stated that the control of the simulation would occur via the buttons Run, Stop, Step and End. Furthermore, note that pressing the Run button causes the simulation to run independently until the Stop or End button is clicked. This means that the action InterpretInput not only needs to know which button was clicked, but also whether any user input took place. This information permits the following declaration of the data type UserInput:

```
TYPE
   UserInput = (runButton, stopButton, stepButton, endButton, noButton);
```

For running the simulation, this means that the action ReadInput will not wait until the user has clicked a button, but immediately returns with the code noButton if there has been no user input since the last time input was polled. This information suffices to completely formulate the procedure SimulateTrajectory:

```
PROCEDURE SimulateTrajectory;
VAR
   input: UserInput;
BEGIN
   Initialize;
   ReadInput(input);
   WHILE input # endButton DO
      InterpretInput(input);
      ReadInput(input)
   END;
   Terminate
END SimulateTrajectory;
```

This completes the first design step. The action SimulateTrajectory has been refined; new actions (Initialize, ReadInput, InterpretInput and Terminate) resulted that have yet to be refined.

This poses the question of which subtask of the design process we should tackle next. There are four approaches:

- Refinement of subtasks in *sequential order*: This approach is particularly appropriate when an algorithm decomposes into sequentially executable subtasks and the products of one subtask simultaneously provide the input data for the next. In our case this is appropriate because the first action of our algorithm is responsible for establishing a useful initialized state for the subsequent actions. However, we do not yet know which conditions need to be met for these actions to function. In particular, there are no clues about what states variables need to be set during initialization alongside the opening of the window.
- Refinement in the order of the *data flow*: For many tasks the structure of the input data determines the sequence of the algorithm. This is particularly the case when determining which subsequent actions are possible depends on the analysis of the input data. Particularly with dialog programs, in which a broad range of user input determines program flow, this approach best leads to the goal.
- Conclusions drawn from desired *output data*: Especially in business applications, we often know only which results are needed. Which input data we need might emerge only after we know the algorithm for the computation of the results. In such cases it makes sense to begin the process of stepwise refinement with the last algorithms (those that provide the final results).
- Refinement according to the *Hardest-First* method: Stepwise refinement can often lead to wrong decisions based on inadequate information. In order to acquire as much detailed information as early as possible, especially for complex interrelationships, it pays to begin with the most difficult subtask. This at least prevents erroneous assumptions stemming from the refinement of other subtasks from complicating the solution of the most complex subtask. Unfortunately, we cannot always assess which subtask will be the most difficult.

Based on these criteria, the next step is to refine the action ReadInput. Since the solution of this task requires knowledge of window management and handling buttons, we will omit this solution for didactic reasons. Instead we will tackle the operation InterpretInput. Its task is to decide, based on user input, which action is to be executed next. We use a case statement for our algorithm, which invokes further actions that have yet to be refined. The operation InterpretInput simply decides *which* operation needs to be executed for a given user input, and it delegates the solution of these subtasks to subsequent procedures. Thus the algorithm has the following structure:

```
PROCEDURE InterpretInput(input:UserInput);
BEGIN
```

```
  CASE input OF
      runButton:      StartTrajectory
    | stopButton:     StopTrajectory
    | stepButton:     TakeSingleStep
    | endButton:      (*no action*)
    | noButton:       RunAutomaticMode
  END
END InterpretInput;
```

Reacting to user input depends on the possibilities that the user has (see Figure 3.34). If the user clicks the *Run*, *Stop* or *Step* button, a trajectory must be started or stopped, or a single step must be executed. Pressing the *End* button requires no further action. Actually, we need not treat this case here since the procedure InterpretInput is not invoked after the *End* button is pressed. As long as the user does not press a button, any trajectory that has been started continues. The procedure RunAutomaticMode handles this. This procedure is invoked over and over again during lulls in input and executes a single step each time.

Please note that we are exaggerating the principle of stepwise refinement here for didactic reasons. In practice we probably would have already incorporated the case distinction in this step in the algorithm SimulateTrajectory. The algorithm would only have grown slightly in length and would not have sacrificed clarity. Nevertheless, our consistent adherence to the method of stepwise refinement has its advantages. In this way we produce simple algorithms that are usually immediately comprehensible. Furthermore, many design decisions remain recognizable in the final program, which eases familiarization with the program, particularly during maintenance.

The algorithmic formulation of the procedure InterpretInput concludes another design step. This completes the distinguishing and handling of user input; we have provisionally delayed specifying what should happen for specific user input and have defined four new subtasks (StartTrajectory, StopTrajectory, TakeSingleStep, RunAutomaticMode) for this purpose.

To be able to solve the current subtasks, we need to think about how communication should take place between the individual algorithms. For the execution of a single step, we need to know how many steps have already been carried out. Furthermore, the procedure to solve the subtask RunAutomaticMode must know whether a trajectory has been started or stopped (through invocation of one of the procedures StartTrajectory or StopTrajectory). Hence in the simulation module we introduce two local variables, which all procedures of the module can access:

step
: Number of the last executed subtrajectory (single step). For each single step, this variable is incremented by 1.

running
: This boolean variable indicates whether a simulation is running without the user's assistance. Its value is set to true when the Run button is pressed and false when the Stop button is pressed.

The variable running is a state variable. It is set by the actions StartTrajectory and StopTrajectory as follows:

```
PROCEDURE StartTrajectory;
BEGIN
   running := TRUE
END StartTrajectory;

PROCEDURE StopTrajectory;
BEGIN
   running := FALSE
END StopTrajectory;
```

As long as the user does not press a button, we need to check whether the variable running has the value true. If so, the robot must make a single step. The action RunAutomaticMode thus takes the following form:

```
PROCEDURE RunAutomaticMode;
BEGIN
   IF running THEN
      TakeSingleStep
   END
END RunAutomaticMode;
```

This completes refinement of the user dialog to the extent that only the action TakeSingleStep remains. The task of this action is to move the robot to the next position stored in the step list. Thus we use the data capsule StepList specified in Section 3.4.3.3 with the following interface:.

```
DEFINITION MODULE StepList;
TYPE
   Coordinate = [0..2000];
   Position = RECORD x,y,z:Coordinate END;

   PROCEDURE DeleteList;
      (*  initialize step list to empty  *)
   PROCEDURE ListLength(): CARDINAL;
      (*  returns number of steps  in step list  *)
   PROCEDURE AppendStep (pos:Position);
      (*  appends the step to position pos to the step list  *)
   PROCEDURE GetStepTarget (i:CARDINAL; VAR pos:Position);
      (*  returns the target position pos of the step at index i  *)
END StepList.
```

Using the procedures exported by module StepList, the algorithm TakeSingleStep takes the following form:

```
PROCEDURE TakeSingleStep;
VAR
   pos: Position;
BEGIN
   step := step + 1;
   GetStepTarget(step,pos);
   MoveRobot(pos)
END TakeSingleStep;
```

With the information acquired so far, we can finally detail the initialization action. During initialization the state variables step and running must be assigned practical values, the simulation window must be opened, and the robot must be moved to its start position. We assume that the entry 0 in the step list contains the start position. The algorithm thus takes the following form:

```
PROCEDURE Initialize;
VAR
   pos: Position;
BEGIN
   step := 0;
   running := FALSE;
   OpenSimulationWindow;
   GetStepTarget(0,pos);
   MoveRobot(pos)
END Initialize;
```

Terminating the simulation involves only closing the simulation window, so that this algorithm consists of a single procedure invocation:

```
PROCEDURE Terminate;
BEGIN
   CloseSimulationWindow
END Terminate;
```

Thus we have solved the significant problems of the simulation task. Only the three actions OpenSimulationWindow, CloseSimulationWindow and MoveRobot remain. However, we can consider these operations as independent subtasks and undertake their design when we tackle the input/output tasks.

In the design so far we have neglected two subproblems: We have not considered what should happen when the robot has made the last single step, and we have no provisions for mutual (de)activation of the control buttons. The two subproblems can be solved together by introducing a new action SetButtonActivation. We can completely derive which buttons need to be deactivated from the two state variables step and running. The following table shows which buttons may be clicked based on the values of these two state variables:

| | step<ListLength() | step=ListLength() |
|---|---|---|
| running=FALSE | run step end | end |
| running=TRUE | stop end | |

The table shows that the *End* button must always be activated. We only need to set it to this state once (during initialization) and can forget it afterwards. When the last step has been carried out (step = ListLength()) the variable running must no longer be true. This constraint can be incorporated in the action SetButtonActivation, which then takes the following form:

```
PROCEDURE SetButtonActivation;
BEGIN
  IF step = ListLength() THEN
     running := FALSE;
     DisableButton(runButton);
     DisableButton(stepButton);
     DisableButton(stopButton)
  ELSIF running THEN
     DisableButton(runButton);
     DisableButton(stepButton);
     EnableButton(stopButton)
  ELSE
     EnableButton(runButton);
     EnableButton(stepButton);
     DisableButton(stopButton)
  END
END SetButtonActivation;
```

Now we only need to assure that the procedure SetButtonActivation is invoked at the right locations. We can easily identify these locations based on our considerations so far: SetButtonActivation must be invoked wherever the value of either of the two state variables running and step is changed. The complete simulation module (with all declarations) now takes the following form:

```
MODULE Simulator;

FROM StepList IMPORT
  Position, ListLength, GetStepTarget;
FROM UIElements IMPORT
  UserInput, ReadInput, DisableButton, EnableButton;
FROM RobotDisplay IMPORT
  OpenSimulationWindow, CloseSimulationWindow, MoveRobot;
```

```
PROCEDURE SetButtonActivation;
BEGIN
   IF step = ListLength() THEN
        running := FALSE;
        DisableButton(runButton);
        DisableButton(stepButton);
        DisableButton(stopButton)
   ELSIF running THEN
        DisableButton(runButton);
        DisableButton(stepButton);
        EnableButton(stopButton)
   ELSE
        EnableButton(runButton);
        EnableButton(stepButton);
        DisableButton(stopButton)
   END
END SetButtonActivation;

PROCEDURE Initialize;
VAR
   pos: Position;
BEGIN
   step := 0;
   running := FALSE;
   OpenSimulationWindow;
   EnableButton(endButton);
   SetButtonActivation;
   GetStepTarget(0,pos);
   MoveRobot(pos)
END Initialize;

PROCEDURE StartTrajectory;
BEGIN
   running := TRUE;
   SetButtonActivation
END StartTrajectory;

PROCEDURE StopTrajectory;
BEGIN
   running := FALSE;
   SetButtonActivation
END StopTrajectory;
```

```
PROCEDURE TakeSingleStep;
VAR
   pos: Position;
BEGIN
   step := step + 1;
   SetButtonActivation;
   GetStepTarget(step,pos);
   MoveRobot(pos)
END TakeSingleStep;

PROCEDURE RunAutomaticMode;
BEGIN
   IF running THEN
       TakeSingleStep
   END
END RunAutomaticMode;

PROCEDURE InterpretInput(input:UserInput);
BEGIN
   CASE input OF
       runButton:      StartTrajectory
   |   stopButton:     StopTrajectory
   |   stepButton:     TakeSingleStep
   |   endButton:      (*no action*)
   |   noButton:       RunAutomaticMode
   END
END InterpretInput;

PROCEDURE SimulateTrajectory;
VAR
   input: UserInput;
BEGIN
   Initialize;
   ReadInput(input);
   WHILE input # endButton DO
       InterpretInput(input);
       ReadInput(input)
   END;
   Terminate
END SimulateTrajectory;
```

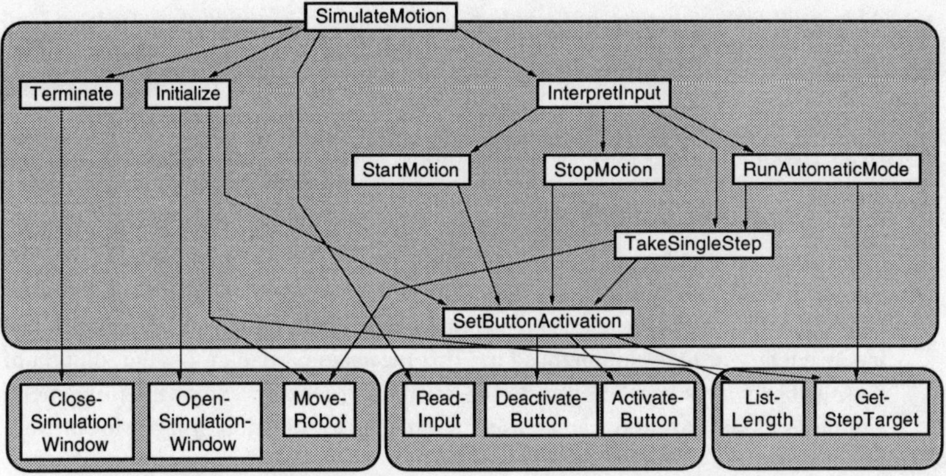


Figure 3.37: Invocation hierarchy of the simulation procedures

```
PROCEDURE Terminate;
BEGIN
   CloseSimulationWindow
END Terminate;

END Simulator.
```

In this final version of the simulation module we have introduced several other modules that we assume provide the actions that have not been refined yet. This is also typical for stepwise refinement. The more refinement progresses, the more information becomes available about unresolved subtasks. Often new subactions evolve (e.g., DisableButton and EnableButton) for which a fitting place in the module hierarchy needs to be found. Thus stepwise refinement and modularization cannot be viewed independently; above all in the design of larger software systems, these processes take place in parallel and influence each other.

The invocation hierarchy of the procedures that resulted from our stepwise refinement is depicted in the diagram in Figure 3.37, which represents module borders with rounded rectangles. Note that the combination of yet unrefined actions into modules does not simply happen as a byproduct of stepwise refinement. Achieving the modularization depicted above required additional reflections that we have not detailed here.

The stepwise refinement in our exercise produced a number of subtasks that still need to be solved. At first glance one might infer that no real work has been done. Nevertheless, we have achieved respectable partial success:

- The simulation task was decomposed into nine subproblems of relatively low complexity. Once we know the interrelationship of these subtasks, each component subalgorithm is easy to understand.

- Above all, the subtasks of opening and closing the window, activation and deactivation of buttons, and moving the robot have been postponed. In this way we were able to clearly decouple the running of the user dialog from the underlying graphical operations (especially from the graphical representation). Such decoupling is an advantage especially when the program is later ported to another target machine.
- The solution of the remaining subtasks is assuredly simpler than the overall task. Most subsolutions can be formulated with just a few lines of code. Only the subproblem MoveRobot proves more difficult. Here we can again use stepwise refinement as a means to reduce the complexity. The remainder can be developed independently of the solution thus far. This means in particular that the solution of these subproblems can be entrusted to another developer. Stepwise refinement, similar to modularization, can be used as a means for division of labor in software production.

### 3.4.6 Data-oriented design with attribute grammars

Stepwise refinement is an algorithm-oriented approach; the data take a back seat. In practice we too often forget that data also have to be concretized stepwise along with the algorithms. Several software engineers have recognized that the structure of the algorithms can be derived from the structure of the data to be processed. Examples include the Jackson and LCP methods ([Jackson 1975], [Jackson 1983], [Warnier 1974]). These techniques have been described and discussed extensively in the literature. Therefore we do not treat them in more detail here, but refer the interested reader to the cited literature. Instead, we introduce the general method of attribute grammars from the area of compiler design, which we believe receives much too little attention in practice. Knuth [Knuth 1968] introduced attribute grammars for the static description of attribute dependencies in a syntax tree. In this section we orient ourselves to the ideas of Rechenberg and employ his notation from [Rechenberg 1984a] and [Rechenberg 1985a].

In practice we often find task descriptions that require processing a stream of structured input data. Examples include unformatted input of number sequences, account data in business programs, and operational data in production systems. Such tasks can be elegantly specified, developed and documented with the help of attribute grammars. Using attribute grammars requires theoretical knowledge from the areas of formal languages and compiler design. Thus, before we show the application of attribute grammars in Section 3.4.6.4, we first need to cover the basics of compiler design.

Compiler design is one of the best theoretically founded areas of computer science. In a narrow sense, compiler design handles the translation of one programming language to another (usually a machine language). However, it has been shown that the techniques of compiler design can be applied wherever an adequately structured input data stream is to be processed. If its structure adheres to certain rules, a *grammar* can be specified to unambiguously describe these rules. Such a grammar not only serves as a static means of describing such a language, but also provides the basis for the design of an analyzer that tests whether given input data abide by the rules of the language. Furthermore, the grammar rules can be complemented with *semantic actions* that determine which operations to carry out on reading input data. In the following, we first describe the structure of context-free grammars and how to design analysis programs from them. Then we handle how to attach attributes to such grammars and show how to apply this technique in practice using the analysis component of our design task.

#### 3.4.6.1 Context-free grammars

Similarly to sentences in natural languages, structured input data consists of "words" called *symbols*. In the theory of formal languages we distinguish *terminal symbols* and *nonterminal symbols*. Terminal symbols are atomic components of the sentences of a language that cannot be decomposed further. Examples include the words and punctuation marks in natural languages. We do not consider blanks in a sentence to be symbols; they simply serve to separate neighboring symbols, but have no meaning themselves.

Terminal symbols are further separated into *simple terminal symbols* and *terminal classes*. In natural languages every punctuation mark (e.g., a comma) is a simple terminal symbol. Each such punctuation mark stands alone and does not need to be described further. By contrast, the words of a sentence form a terminal class *word*. The words "a" and "text" both belong to this terminal class. They differ in length, their constituent letters, and meaning.

Nonterminal symbols are used for organizing grammars. They combine multiple terminal symbols and possibly other nonterminal symbols into a larger abstract unit. For example, we could describe a subordinate clause in a natural language by means of a dedicated nonterminal symbol. For each nonterminal symbol there is a *derivation rule* that describes how it can be reduced to other symbols. To formulate derivation rules, we use Wirth's EBNF (*extended Backus-Naur form*), which employs the following conventions:

- A derivation rule begins with the name of the nonterminal symbol to be defined, followed by an equal sign and the actual definition. The complete rule ends with a period.
- For clearer distinction, we start nonterminal symbols with capitals and write terminal symbols with lower-case letters. *AuxClause* would thus be a nonterminal symbol and *word* a terminal symbol. If a terminal symbol is represented by a fixed character sequence, we put this sequence in quotation marks, e.g., ":=".
- Symbols that must occur in a certain order are written in sequence separated by blanks. The rule $A = xy$ means that the nonterminal symbol $A$ must always have the form $xy$ (the symbol $x$ immediately followed by $y$).

- A vertical bar separates alternatives. The rule $B = x|y$ means that the nonterminal symbol $B$ consists of either an $x$ or a $y$. The sequential order of symbols has precedence over the alternative bar. The rule $C = xy|zw$ means that the nonterminal symbol $C$ consists of either $xy$ or $zw$.
- Parentheses are used to group parts that belong together. For example, they can be used to override the above precedence rules. The rule $D = x(y|z)w$ means that the nonterminal symbol $D$ always begins with an $x$ and ends with a $w$, and in the middle it contains either a $y$ or a $z$.
- Brackets indicate possible omissions (options). The rule $E = x[y]z$ means that the non-terminal symbol $E$ consists of an $x$ and a $z$, between which there can (but need not) be a $y$.
- Braces designate repetition. The parts in braces can be repeated any number of times, or they can be omitted. The rule $F = x\{y\}z$ means that the nonterminal symbol $F$ consists of one $x$ and one $z$, between which any number of $y$s can occur, i.e., $xz$, $xyz$, $xyyz$, ...

A complete context-free grammar consists of four parts:

- List of *terminal symbols*
- List of *nonterminal symbols*
- *Derivation rules* for each nonterminal symbol
- Specification of the *start symbol*, a special nonterminal symbol that describes the complete input text

As an example to clarify context-free grammars, we will describe a subset of natural language sentences using a context-free grammar. We will limit ourselves to simple sentences with a main clause and an optional auxiliary clause, and we permit only the punctuation marks comma, period, exclamation mark and question mark.

- Terminal symbols: word, ",", ".", "!", "?"
- Nonterminal symbols: Sentence, MainClause, AuxClause
- Derivation rules:
  Sentence = MainClause [AuxClause] ("." | "!" | "?").
  MainClause = word {word}.
  AuxClause = "," word {word}.
- Start symbol: Sentence

One aspect of EBNF is that it provides no means of describing the minimum or maximum number of repetitions. The frequent case that a construct $x$ must occur at least once is thus formulated as $x\ \{x\}$. The rule for a main clause thus indicates that a main clause consists of a word that can (but need not) be followed by any number of additional words. According to these rules, the following examples are valid sentences:

Run!

Do you think it is cold?
Where there is a will, there is a way.
This sentence are correct.
wrdlbrmft Klapumpfen, ruls puff klump Wurgl.

According to our rules, the last two examples are also valid sentences, although they offend our sense of language. This is because our grammar only specifies the sequence of the individual symbols that combine to make a sentence. Additional conditions that result from the context cannot be specified. This is why such grammars are called context-free.

#### 3.4.6.2 Design of a language analyzer

In order to be able to process an input text, we need an analysis program that determines whether the input text adheres to our grammar. The design of a language analyzer for a grammar is possible only if the grammar fulfills certain requirements. For the grammar to make sense at all, we must assure that every nonterminal symbol can be reached from the start symbol and that the grammar contains no cyclical rules. The following grammar violates both these requirements:

```
A = a B.
B = b A.
C = c B.
```

If *A* is the start symbol, there is an endless loop between rules *A* and *B*. The only sentence upholding this grammar would be an endless sequence of *a*s and *b*s. The grammar contains cyclical derivation rules. Furthermore, the rule for *C* is obviously superfluous since it can never be reached from the start symbol *A*.

Aside from such senseless constructs, decidability is the most important criterion for the design of a language analyzer. This condition requires that for every alternative it must be possible with the help of the next input symbol to decide the alternative with which the analysis must continue. Note that an alternative arises not only where the context-free grammar contains a vertical bar; option brackets and repetition braces also require such a case distinction. For example, if we had written the rule for a main clause in the form

```
MainClause = {word} word.
```

then for a given word that we encounter during our analysis of a main clause, we could not decide whether this word is a repeated element or already the last word of the main clause. We do not handle this problem in detail at this point, but refer the interested reader to the literature ([Aho 1972], [Knuth 1965], [Lewis 1976]).

In the design of an analysis program (in the area of compiler design, also termed a *syntax analyzer*) an algorithm is formulated for each nonterminal symbol to recognize this nonterminal symbol on the basis of the appropriate derivation rules. Here we assume a *lexical analyzer* that reads the input text characterwise and returns a terminal symbol with each invocation. For our example of natural language sentences, we would use the following data type:

```
TYPE Symbol = (word, comma, period, exclamation, question, error, eof );
```

One of the tasks of the lexical analyzer is to filter out the meaningful characters from the input text. Blanks and possibly end-of-line character need to be skipped. When a period is read, the lexical analyzer must return the appropriate kind of symbol. When a letter is read, subsequent letters must be skipped and the symbol type *word* is returned. When the input text contains no further symbols, the lexical analyzer returns a special end symbol. When an impermissible character is found in the input text, the lexical analyzer returns a special error symbol. The following module contains a complete lexical analyzer for our example language:

```
DEFINITION MODULE LexicalAnalyzer;

TYPE Symbol = (word, comma, period, exclamation, question, error, eof );

VAR sym: Symbol;

PROCEDURE InitLex;
PROCEDURE ReadSymbol;

END LexicalAnalyzer.
```

---

```
IMPLEMENTATION MODULE LexicalAnalyzer;

FROM InOut IMPORT Read, Done;

VAR ch: CHAR;

PROCEDURE InitLex;
BEGIN
  Read(ch)
END InitLex;

PROCEDURE ReadSymbol;
BEGIN
  WHILE Done & (ch<=" ") DO Read(ch) END;
  IF NOT Done THEN sym := eof; RETURN END;
  CASE ch OF
     "A".."Z","a".."z":
        REPEAT
```

```
                Read(ch)
            UNTIL NOT Done OR (((ch<"A") OR (ch>"Z"))
                & ((ch<"a") OR (ch>"z")));
            sym := word
    |    ",":    Read(ch); sym := comma
    |    ".":    Read(ch); sym := period
    |    "!":    Read(ch); sym := exclamation
    |    "?":    Read(ch); sym := question
        ELSE Read(ch); sym := error
    END
  END ReadSymbol;

  END LexicalAnalyzer.
```

The lexical analyzer exports the variable sym, which describes the current symbol. The current symbol is needed in all procedures of the syntax analyzer; although exported variables are frowned upon in software engineering, this exported variable proves to be the most convenient and efficient medium to make the current symbol available. The value of the variable sym may only be used, but not modified, in the syntax analyzer.

The lexical analyzer employs a local character variable ch, which at any time contains the next character of the input text that has not been processed. Each time a punctuation mark is recognized, the procedure Read must be invoked in order to read the next character of the input text. The initialization procedure InitLex must assure that the variable ch contains the first character of the input text before the first invocation of ReadSymbol.

The first action of the procedure ReadSymbol is to skip meaningless characters. By testing whether ch<=" ", not only blanks but also control characters such as tabulators and carriage returns are ignored.

For every derivation rule of the grammar, we write a function procedure that returns a boolean result whose value indicates whether the nonterminal symbol was recognized. On entering the recognition procedure, the global variable sym receives the first symbol to be recognized by the procedure. On successful termination of a recognition procedure (result = true) the variable sym contains the first symbol that does not belong to the currently recognized nonterminal symbol. On nonrecognition of a terminal symbol (result = false), the variable sym contains the symbol producing the error. The transformation of an EBNF rule into a recognition procedure can occur completely systematically according to the following rules:

```
  NTS = ...     PROCEDURE NTS():BOOLEAN;
                BEGIN
                    ...
                    RETURN TRUE
                END NTS;
```

```
... a ...         IF sym # a THEN RETURN FALSE END;
                  ReadSymbol;

... A ...         IF NOT A() THEN RETURN FALSE END;

... (x | y) ...   IF sym IN L(x) THEN
                      recognize x
                  ELSIF sym IN L(y) THEN
                      recognize y
                  ELSE
                      RETURN FALSE
                  END;

... [x] ...       IF sym IN L(x) THEN
                      recognize x
                  END;

... {x} ...       WHILE sym IN L(x) DO
                      recognize x
                  END;
```

L(x) means the set of *terminal start symbols* of the construct x, which means all terminal symbols with which x can begin. The boolean expression sym IN L(x) is true if x can begin with the current symbol sym (i.e., if there is a chance to completely recognize x). A repetition without a possibility for omission can be recognized in the following way:

```
... x {x} ...     REPEAT
                      recognize x
                  UNTIL NOT (sym IN L(x));
```

With the help of these rules, we can formulate the syntax analyzer for recognizing natural-language sentences as follows:

```
DEFINITION MODULE SyntaxAnalyzer;
   PROCEDURE InitSynt;
   PROCEDURE IsSentence():BOOLEAN;
END SyntaxAnalyzer.

IMPLEMENTATION MODULE SyntaxAnalyzer;
FROM LexicalAnalyzer IMPORT Symbol, sym, InitLex, ReadSymbol;

PROCEDURE InitSynt;
BEGIN
   InitLex
   ReadSymbol
END InitSynt;

PROCEDURE IsMainClause():BOOLEAN;
BEGIN
```

```
    IF sym # word THEN RETURN FALSE END;
    ReadSymbol;
    WHILE sym = word DO
        ReadSymbol
    END;
    RETURN TRUE
  END IsMainClause;

  PROCEDURE IsAuxClause():BOOLEAN;
  BEGIN
    IF sym # comma THEN RETURN FALSE END;
    ReadSymbol;
    IF sym # word THEN RETURN FALSE END;
    ReadSymbol;
    WHILE sym = word DO
        ReadSymbol
    END;
    RETURN TRUE
  END IsAuxClause;

  PROCEDURE IsSentence():BOOLEAN;
  BEGIN
    IF NOT IsMainClause() THEN RETURN FALSE END;
    IF sym = comma THEN
        IF NOT IsAuxClause() THEN RETURN FALSE END;
    END;
    IF sym = period THEN
        ReadSymbol
    ELSIF sym = exclamation THEN
        ReadSymbol
    ELSIF sym = question THEN
        ReadSymbol
    ELSE
        RETURN FALSE
    END;
    RETURN TRUE
  END IsSentence;

  END SyntaxAnalyzer.
```

Note that when an error occurs, the procedure IsSentence only returns the result FALSE. After an unsuccessful invocation of the syntax analyzer, we cannot determine the type of error or its location. However, we need this information in order to correct the error in the input text. A simple solution consists of displaying a message in the event of an error. Normally on nonrecognition of a terminal symbol an error procedure is invoked and only then is the recognition procedure terminated with RETURN FALSE, e.g.:

```
  IF sym # word THEN Error(wordExpected); RETURN FALSE END;
```

The error procedure has an input parameter that specifies the type of error. This information can be used to output an explanatory text (e.g., "Word expected in line n at position m"). The error position can be determined with the help of additional access routines of the lexical analyzer.

Another drawback of our syntax analysis module is that it aborts execution on occurrence of the first error. In many cases this proves inadequate because the remaining text is not checked. Sometimes we want an analyzer that processes the rest of the input text after an error and detects all errors. The difficulty is locating a position in the input text where the analysis can reasonably be continued. In the area of compiler design, various methods are used for such a *recovery*. Detailed treatment of these techniques exceeds the scope of this book; hence we refer the interested reader to the literature on compiler design ([Aho 1986], [Waite 1984], [Wirth 1986]).

#### 3.4.6.3 Attribute grammars

A context-free grammar describes only the syntax of a language; thus a syntax analyzer can only check whether an input text is syntactically correct. Processing an input text (i.e., determining results from it) requires additional actions. In solving this task, we again borrow from compiler design, where attribute grammars describe translation processes. In a broader sense any program that generates an output text from an input text can be viewed as a translator, so that this method is applicable to many other tasks as well.

A context-free grammar can be extended to an attribute grammar by adding:

- Semantic actions
- Semantic routines
- Attributes
- Context conditions

*Semantic actions* describe operations to be executed during the recognition of the input text. *Attributes* describe properties of grammar symbols. *Context conditions* are rules that extend beyond the syntactic rules and that the input text must fulfill. We will describe this aspect of an attribute grammar in more detail below and show how it finds expression in the syntax analyzer.

Semantic actions are inserted directly at the appropriate locations in the context-free grammar. Borrowing from [Dobler 1990], we bracket them in « and ». A semantic action immediately after a grammar symbol means that it is to be executed upon recognition of this symbol. In our example grammar for natural-language sentences, for example, if we want to count the words of a main clause and to output this count at the end of the main clause, we can express this in the following rule:

```
MainClause =        word        « count := 1 »
                    { word      « count := count +1 »
```

```
}                    « WriteCard(count,1); WriteLn »
.
```

After the first word the variable count is initialized to 1, and it is incremented by 1 after each subsequent word; at the end of the rule (once we establish that no further word is coming) it is output. We can readily find the respective locations in the recognition procedure. The semantic actions are simply inserted into the procedure:

```
PROCEDURE IsMainClause():BOOLEAN;
VAR count:CARDINAL;
BEGIN
   IF sym # word THEN RETURN FALSE END;
   count := 1;
   ReadSymbol;
   WHILE sym = word DO
      count := count + 1;
      ReadSymbol
   END;
   WriteCard(count,1); WriteLn;
   RETURN TRUE
END IsMainClause;
```

Note that the semantic actions are executed *before* the next symbol is read. For our simple counting exercise this plays no role, but later we will encounter situations in handling attributes where the current terminal symbol is needed to carry out a semantic action.

In the notation we use here, command sequences of any length are permissible as semantic actions. If semantic actions are needed at multiple locations or if individual actions become too complex and thus inflate the attribute grammar too much, then individual subactions are implemented as procedures and invoked at the suitable locations in the attribute grammar. Such procedures are called *semantic routines*. In terms of program logic, they belong to the analyzer, but they are implemented elsewhere (usually in another module). In order to make the relationship clear, the semantic routines must be labeled as such and need to be documented together with the attribute grammar.

With semantic actions and semantic routines we can make the execution of any operations dependent on the structure of an input text. In most cases, however, this does not suffice because we cannot exchange data between semantic actions of different rules. Global variables provide one solution, but at the price of the associated problems. Furthermore, difficulties arise when the grammar contains recursive rules. A better solution is to define data exchange between rules via clear interfaces, as with procedures. Here we provide each nonterminal symbol with attributes. Attributes are similar to parameters in procedures and can be grouped as input and output attributes, with the latter occurring more frequently. Output attributes describe properties of the nonterminal symbols. In our example the length of a sentence could serve as an output attribute of the nonterminal symbol Sentence. Borrowing from Rechenberg and Mössenböck [Rechenberg 1985a], we write attributes subscripted after the symbol name and use an up or down arrow to indicate input or output attributes, respectively. A sentence with an output attribute that specifies how many words it contains would be written as $\text{Sentence}_{\uparrow\text{words}}$. We use this notation everywhere the nonterminal symbol occurs, i.e., both in its definition and with its use. The following example shows how counting the words of a sentence with attributes and semantic actions can be written.

```
Sentence↑words =        MainClause↑words
                        [ AuxClause↑w        « words := words + w »
                        ]
                        ("." | "!" | "?").
```

In this rule the word count of a sentence stems from the word count of the main clause. If an auxiliary clause follows, its word count is added to that of the main clause. To make this work, both the rules for a main clause and for an auxiliary clause must be provided with an output attribute. The rule for a main clause takes the following form:

```
MainClause↑words =      word                 « words := 1 »
                        { word               « words := words + 1 »
                        } .
```

The rule for an auxiliary clause has a similar structure. The analogy between grammar rules and procedures and between attributes and parameters makes the realization of an attribute grammar rule almost automatic. The respective procedures for recognizing a sentence and a main clause are specified here:

```
PROCEDURE IsSentence(VAR words:CARDINAL):BOOLEAN;
VAR w: CARDINAL;
BEGIN
  IF NOT IsMainClause(words) THEN RETURN FALSE END;
  IF sym = comma THEN
     IF NOT IsAuxClause(w) THEN RETURN FALSE END;
     words := words + w
  END;
  IF sym = period THEN
     ReadSymbol
  ELSIF sym = exclamation  THEN
     ReadSymbol
  ELSIF sym = question  THEN
     ReadSymbol
  ELSE
     RETURN FALSE
  END;
```

```
    RETURN TRUE
  END IsSentence;

  PROCEDURE IsMainClause(VAR words:CARDINAL):BOOLEAN;
  BEGIN
    IF sym # word THEN RETURN FALSE END;
    words := 1;
    ReadSymbol;
    WHILE sym = word DO
        words := words + 1;
        ReadSymbol
    END;
    RETURN TRUE
  END IsMainClause;
```

Now, if we approach the task of computing not the length of a sentence but the mean length of its words, then our tools thus far do not suffice because we lack the necessary information about the words. We can overcome this by providing the terminal class word with an output attribute that specifies its length. Such attributes only make sense for terminal classes, but not for the terminal symbols themselves, since they each have but a single notation anyway.

To calculate the mean length of the words of a sentence, we need the word count and the number of characters in the sentence. Thus to solve our task we have to give the rules for main and auxiliary clauses each an additional output attribute characters. The terminal class word also gains an attribute length. The rule for a main clause now takes the following form:

```
MainClause↑words ↑characters =
                          word ↑characters        « words := 1 »
                          { word ↑length          « words := words + 1;
                                                    characters := characters + length
»
                          } .
```

Terminal classes with attributes cannot be implemented in the syntax analyzer in the same way as nonterminal symbols because there are no recognition procedures for terminal classes. Thus we need to extend the interface to the lexical analyzer in such a way that the syntax analyzer can access the attributes of the last terminal symbol that was recognized. For efficiency reasons, global variables are used that are exported from the lexical analyzer. For each relevant attribute of a terminal class there is such a variable that is set by the lexical analyzer when a symbol of this class is recognized. It is clear that the attribute values are to be read but not modified by the syntax analyzer.

The following example shows how the lexical analyzer of Section 3.4.6.2 must be extended so that after recognition of a word it makes its contents and its length available. The new parts are highlighted by italic.

```
DEFINITION MODULE LexicalAnalyzer;

TYPE Symbol = (word, comma, period, exclamation, question, error, eof);

VAR
   sym: Symbol;
   contents: ARRAY [0..39] OF CHAR;
   wordLength: CARDINAL;

PROCEDURE InitLex;
PROCEDURE ReadSymbol;

END LexicalAnalyzer.
```

---

```
IMPLEMENTATION MODULE LexicalAnalyzer;

FROM InOut IMPORT Read, Done;

VAR ch: CHAR;

PROCEDURE InitLex;
BEGIN
   Read(ch)
END InitLex;

PROCEDURE ReadSymbol;
BEGIN
   WHILE Done & (ch<=" ") DO Read(ch) END;
   IF NOT Done THEN sym := eof; RETURN END;
   CASE ch OF
       "A".."Z","a".."z":
           wordLength := 0;
           REPEAT
               IF wordLength<40 THEN
                   contents[wordLength] := ch; INC(wordLength)
               END;
               Read(ch)
           UNTIL NOT Done OR (((ch<"A") OR (ch>"Z"))
               & ((ch<"a") OR (ch>"z")));
           sym := word
   |   ",":    Read(ch); sym := comma
   |   ".":    Read(ch); sym := period
   |   "!":    Read(ch); sym := exclamation
   |   "?":    Read(ch); sym := question
       ELSE Read(ch); sym := error
```

```
    END
  END ReadSymbol;
  END LexicalAnalyzer.
```

For the sake of simplicity, we have restricted word length to 40 characters; longer words are simply truncated at the 41st character.

The above rule for recognition of a main clause can now be implemented as follows:

```
FROM LexicalAnalyzer IMPORT ..., wordLength, ...;

PROCEDURE IsMainClause(VAR words,characters:CARDINAL):BOOLEAN;
BEGIN
   IF sym # word THEN RETURN FALSE END;
   words := 1;
   characters := wordLength;
   ReadSymbol;
   WHILE sym = word DO
      words := words + 1;
      characters := characters + wordLength;
      ReadSymbol
   END;
   RETURN TRUE
END IsMainClause;
```

Note that each invocation of ReadSymbol produces the possibility of a modification of the global attribute value. The attributes of the current terminal symbols are thus only available until the next invocation of ReadSymbol. If they are needed for a longer time, they must be stored in local variables.

A context-free grammar can only describe the permissible sequence of symbols. A context-free grammar for a programming language, for example, can only specify where identifiers are permitted. The additional constraints that each identifier must be declared before its first use and that it can only be utilized in accordance with its declaration, cannot be expressed in this way. However, attributes and semantic actions can be employed to check correctness constraints that go beyond pure syntax. In the theory of compiler design we use *context conditions* that are integrated at the appropriate locations in the attribute grammar. The following example shows simplistically how such context conditions could appear for an assignment operation in a programming language.

```
Assignment =        identifier↑name          CC: AlreadyDeclared(name)
                                             CC: IsVariable(name)
                                             « varType := TypeOf(name) »
                    ":="
                    Expression↑exprType      CC: exprType = varType
                    ";" .
```

The abbreviation CC stands for context condition. The first condition states that the identifier name must already be declared; the second condition assures that name designates a variable. Only if both conditions are fulfilled can the semantic action be executed. After we recognize the expression that is to be assigned to the variable, we test whether it is of the same type as the variable. This example clearly shows why we speak of *context* conditions: each individual condition tests the correctness of relationships *between* symbols that are not expressed in the context-free grammar.

Note that the context conditions simply specify where which constraints must apply, but not what is to happen if a constraint is not fulfilled. A similar situation already arose in our context-free grammar, which only specifies the structure of sentences in our language, but leaves the handling of errors open. In translating this into a program, the context conditions create great difficulties. For handling syntax errors, many methods are known that have been utilized successfully in compilers. On violation of context conditions (semantic errors), we have to decide what to do on a case-by-case basis. The simplest approach is terminating processing upon the first error and leaving the correction of the error to the user. But if the analysis is to be continued for any reason, then any attribute values must be corrected such that we can avoid indirect resultant errors during further analysis. If the first context condition is not fulfilled in the above rule, for example, then to continue we could assume that the identifier has been declared as a variable. Here we also have to assure that varType contains a sensible value, which could lead to a resultant error on checking the last context condition.

### 3.4.6.4 Application to the design example

In the preceding sections we have used small examples to show how attribute grammars can be created and then translated into programs. In this section we will round out the picture by applying the technique of attribute grammars to the analysis component of our robot task. Figure 3.38 shows this subtask as a block diagram.

What we have is a translation of a trajectory description to a step list. Note that this is merely a transformation of the representation: both forms of representation describe the same trajectory; they differ only in their outer form.

The first step is to set up the context-free grammar for the language of the input text. As a reminder we repeat the relevant parts of the task description (see Section 3.4.2):

> The trajectory is described in a simple language that permits the formulation of linear and circular subtrajectories. For the simulation, each subtrajectory is decomposed into linear steps of equal length.

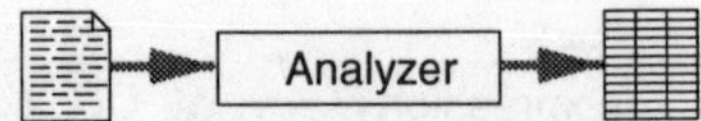


Figure 3.38: Block diagram of the analysis task

- Linear trajectory to point (*x*, *y*, *z*) in *n* steps: n L (x, y, z)
- Circular trajectory to point (*x*, *y*, *z*) via an intermediate point (*x1*, *y1*, *z1*) in *n* steps: n C (x1, y1, z1) (x, y, z)

The trajectory description begins with a start position (*x0*, *y0*, *z0*). The end point of a subtrajectory is the starting point of the next subtrajectory. The trajectory description is terminated with the letter E.

Any coordinate can be specified in absolute or relative terms. The number 10 indicates an absolute position (10 mm from the origin of the coordinate system). A relative coordinate is specified with a number with a leading sign. +10 indicates a movement of 10 mm from the relative origin of the subtrajectory. For both a linear and a circular path, all relative specifications refer to the starting point of the respective subtrajectory.

...

*Constraints*

The gripper of the robot is to be restricted to a cubic space of dimension 2 meters. Positioning precision is assumed to be 1 mm. All coordinate specifications are thus restricted to whole numbers from 0 to 2000. We must assure that the gripper does not trespass beyond this cube.

First we must clearly define the symbols that constitute a trajectory description. For reasons of efficiency, in a compiler we would leave the skipping of blanks and the recognition of numbers (including the transformation of a sequence of digits into the respective numeric value) to the lexical analyzer. Thus only commas, the signs + and –, and the letters L, C and E would be terminal symbols; numbers are a terminal class with the numeric value as the output attribute. For didactic reasons, we exaggerate some to reach the solution to our task and so decide to treat each individual character of the input text as a terminal symbol. The numbers make up a terminal class; the output attribute is the numeric value.

These initial considerations lead us to the following list of terminal symbols:

- Terminal class digit ↑value
- Letters "L", "C" and "E"
- Signs "+" and "–"
- Parentheses "(" and ")"
- Comma ","
- Blank " "

For the design of the context-free grammar itself, we recommend a top-down approach as with stepwise refinement. Thus we begin with the complete input text and decompose it to its components:

A trajectory description begins with a starting position followed by any number of trajectories and terminates with the letter E.

TrajDescription = Position { Trajectory } "E" .

A position consists of three coordinates separated by commas and enclosed in parentheses:

Position = "(" Coordinate "," Coordinate "," Coordinate ")" .

A trajectory always begins with the step number followed by "L" or "C" and one or two positions:

Trajectory = Number ( "L" Position | "C" Position Position ).

We represent a coordinate with a number, possibly with a leading sign:

Coordinate = [ "+" | "–" ] Number .

A number is a sequence of digits of any length, but with at least one digit:

Number = digit { digit } .

The grammar we have specified so far does not consider that the input text may also include blanks. We want to permit blanks everywhere except within a number and between a number and its sign. Since our simple language does not require blanks to separate symbols, blanks can be omitted. Since we also want to permit larger white spaces with multiple blanks, we introduce a new terminal symbol that describes a white space of any length (including zero):

Blank = " " { " " } .

This terminal symbol can now be inserted wherever white space is permitted. This applies to the following locations:

- Beginning of the input text
- After the terminal symbols "L", "C", "E", "(", ")" and ","
- After a number

The complete context-free grammar now takes the following form:

```
TrajDescription =  Blank Position { Trajectory } "E" Blank .
Position =         "(" Blank Coordinate
                   "," Blank Coordinate
                   "," Blank Coordinate
                   ")" Blank .
Trajectory =       Number ( "L" Blank Position | "C" Blank Position Position ) .
Coordinate =       [ "+" | "–" ] Number .
Number =           digit { digit } Blank .
Blank =            " " { " " } .
```

For adding attributes to the grammar, we recommend first considering which attributes we will need for the individual nonterminal symbols. The rule for the trajectory description requires no attributes; the result of the analysis is the step list. In our stepwise refinement in Section 3.4.3.3 we already defined the interface of the module for managing the step list. We can enter the individual steps with the help of the procedure StepList.AppendStep. The internal structure of the step list is of no importance for its use. To make the following attribute grammar more comprehensible, we repeat the interface of the module StepList here:

```
DEFINITION MODULE StepList;

TYPE
  Coordinate = [0..2000];
  Position = RECORD x,y,z:Coordinate END;

  PROCEDURE DeleteList;
     (*  initialize empty step list *)
  PROCEDURE ListLength(): CARDINAL;
     (*  returns the number of steps in the step list *)
  PROCEDURE AppendStep (pos:Position);
     (*  appends a step to position pos to the step list *)
  PROCEDURE GetStepTarget (i:CARDINAL; VAR pos:Position);
     (*  returns the target pos of the step at index i *)

END StepList.
```

A trajectory requires a starting point (which results from the end point of the preceding trajectory) and returns its end point (which is required as the starting point for the subsequent trajectory). Analogously, a position reflects a point in three-dimensional space (of data type StepList.Position). To assure that the position can be computed correctly when it contains relative coordinate specifications, we also need an input attribute that contains the starting point of the current trajectory. The approach is similar for an individual coordinate: an input attribute specifies the starting value, and an output attribute returns the computed value of the coordinate. The following alphabetical list gives the attribute symbols:

*Terminal symbols:*

digit $\uparrow$value

recognizes a digit with a value value (0 to 9)

*Nonterminal symbols:*

Trajectory $\downarrow$pos0 $\uparrow$pos

recognizes a linear or circular subtrajectory beginning at position pos0, appends the steps necessary for its execution to the step list, and returns the end point of the subtrajectory in pos; pos is simultaneously the starting point for the next subtrajectory. pos and pos0 are of data type StepList.Position.

TrajDescription

recognizes a sequence of trajectory descriptions and generates a step list from it.

Coordinate $\downarrow_{v0}$ $\uparrow_{v}$

recognizes an individual (*x*, *y* or *z*) coordinate with the value v. v0 is the value of the respective coordinate at the start of the current subtrajectory; relative coordinate specifications refer to this value. v0 and v are of data type StepList.Coordinate.

Blank

recognizes a white space consisting of any number (including 0) of blanks.

Position $\downarrow_{pos0}$ $\uparrow_{pos}$

recognizes a position and returns its coordinates in pos. pos0 is the starting point of the subtrajectory; relative coordinate specifications refer to this position. pos and pos0 are of data type StepList.Position.

Number $\uparrow_{value}$

recognizes a whole number with the value value (of data type INTEGER).

We recommend always preparing such a list of the attribute symbols. First, this forces the developer to precisely consider the purpose of the individual symbols and the actions required to process them. Second, such a list simultaneously serves as part of the documentation of a translating process; this list proves its worth, especially for long grammars with one hundred or more rules.

The sole terminal symbol that we have introduced is digit because this symbol is the only one with attributes. The meanings of the other symbols need not be explained separately because they derive directly from the grammar. By contrast, we listed all nonterminal symbols, even those without attributes, because they can describe complex rules with extensive actions.

With thc information thus far, we can insert the semantic actions in the above rules. In the following we specify each rule separately and insert comments on the design decisions necessary for understanding it.

```
TrajDescription =
        Blank                  « pos0.x := 0; pos0.y := 0; pos0.z := 0 »    ①
        Position ↓pos0 ↑pos    « DeleteList; AppendStep(pos);                ②
                                 pos0 := pos »                               ③
        { Trajectory ↓pos0 ↑pos « pos0 := pos »                              ④
        } "E" Blank .
```

① These statements serve to initialize the starting position. More precisely, this corrects an omission in the task description, which stated that a position specification always refers to the starting point of the respective step. There was no specification of whether the starting position also permits relative coordinate specifications and, if so, to what they refer. We correct this omission by permitting relative specifications and having them refer to point (0,0,0) of the coordinate system.

② After the recognition of the starting point, we initialize the step list (see Section 3.4.3.3) by first clearing it and then appending the starting position (as step number 0). For the sake of simplicity we omit the module name before a procedure name; i.e., we write AppendStep instead of StepList.AppendStep.

③ The rule for Trajectory expects the starting point of the subtrajectory in the attribute pos0. This assignment sets the value correctly.

④ The end point of a subtrajectory is simultaneously the starting point of the next subtrajectory. This statement assures that pos0 contains the correct value in the repetition of the loop. Further semantic actions are not required after the recognition of a subtrajectory because the step list has already been extended during the recognition.

```
Position ↓pos0 ↑pos =
    "(" Blank Coordinate ↓pos0.x ↑pos.x                              ①
    "," Blank Coordinate ↓pos0.y ↑pos.y
    "," Blank Coordinate ↓pos0.z ↑pos.z ")"
    Blank .
```

① No semantic actions are required here. The recognition of a position is limited to the recognition of the three coordinates. The output attribute pos is set by simply transferring the output attribute from Coordinate.

```
Trajectory ↓pos0 ↑pos =
    Number ↑n              CC: (n>=1) & (n<=1000-ListLength())       ①
    ( "L" Blank
      Position ↓pos0 ↑pos  « LinearTrajectory(n,pos0,pos) »          ②
    | "C" Blank
      Position ↓pos0 ↑posTr                                          ③
      Position ↓pos0 ↑pos  « CircularTrajectory                      ②
                               (n,pos0,posTr,pos,ok) »
                           CC:ok                                     ④
    ) .
```

① After recognizing the number of steps n, we must test whether the value of n is permissible. Hence we provide a context condition in which we prescribe that the number of steps must be at least 1 and at most 1000-ListLength(). ListLength is a function procedure of the module StepList. The second part of the condition assures that the step list does not overrun with the appending of a subtrajectory.

② We use two procedures (LinearTrajectory and CircularTrajectory) to append single steps. In particular, the algorithm for decomposition of a circular trajectory into single steps is so complex that it would unnecessarily inflate the attribute grammar. By introducing semantic routines, we keep the rules short and comprehensible. To understand the rules, the reader only needs to know what the semantic routines mean. The routines are documented separately in the next section.

③ The first position specification in a circular trajectory describes the transition point, designated as posTr. posTr is a local variable that is used only within this rule.

④ The semantic routine CircularTrajectory returns a boolean value ok, which specifies whether the end points of all single steps of the trajectory are within the robot coordinate system. This context condition tests whether the circular trajectory keeps within the robot's restricted coordinate system. A linear trajectory does not require such a test because all intermediate points automatically lie within the permissible limits if the starting and end points are valid (which is assured by the following rule for recognition of a coordinate). However, it is easy to specify three points within a cube such that the intersecting circle is partially outside the cube.

```
Coordinate ↓v0 ↑v =
                          « sign := 0 »                      ①
    [ "+"                 « sign := +1 »                     ②
    | "–"                 « sign := –1 »
    ]
    Number ↑v             « if sign # 0 then                 ③
                              v := v0 + sign*v
                            end »
                          CC:  (v >= 0) & (v <= 2000)        ④
```

① The local auxiliary variable sign enables us to know which sign preceded the number after the number has been recognized. sign is initialized to 0 to indicate that no sign has been recognized yet.

② On recognition of "+" or "–" the variable sign receives the value +1 or –1, respectively. If there is no leading sign, sign retains the value 0.

③ Upon recognition of a number with the value v, we need to test whether it has a leading sign, i.e., whether this is a relative coordinate specification. Multiplication of v by sign results in the value that must be added to v0 in order to attain an absolute coordinate specification.

④ At the end we still need to test whether a coordinate is in the permissible range between 0 and 2000. In general the rule applies that context conditions should be recognized as early as possible. This is especially important for output attributes. If possible, their correctness should already be tested in the rule that returns the attribute.

```
Number ↑value =
    digit ↑value                                              ①
    { digit ↑w                « value := value*10 + w »        ②
    }
    Blank .
```

① The value of a single-digit number results from the value of the digit. Note that no semantic action is required to express this relationship; in the case of a single-digit number the output attribute of digit is simply reused as the output attribute of number.

② A number is read from left to right. To compute the numeric value we use the Horner rule, treating each digit as a coefficient of the polynomial

$$A(x) = a_n x^n + a_{n-1} x^{n-1} + ... + a_1 x + a_0$$

where x is 10 in the base 10 system, and then calculate

$$A(x) = (...(( a_n x + a_{n-1})x + a_{n-2} )x + ... + a_1)x + a_0$$

This completes attribution. For the sake of completeness we need to specify the semantic routines LinearTrajectory and CircularTrajectory. We combine them in the new module Trajectories and provide its commented interface:

```
DEFINITION MODULE Trajectories;

FROM StepList IMPORT Position;

PROCEDURE LinearTrajectory (n:INTEGER; pos0,pos:Position);
(* Appends the steps required for the execution of the linear trajectory from pos0
   to pos to the step list.  n is the number of steps.  *)

PROCEDURE CircularTrajectory
   (n:INTEGER;
    pos0,posTr,pos:Position;
    VAR ok:BOOLEAN);
(* Appends the steps required for the execution of the circular trajectory from
   pos0 to pos to the step list.  The arc is described completely by the points
   pos0, posTr and pos.  n is the number of steps;  the output parameter ok
   specifies whether the end points of all single steps lie within the robot's
   coordinate system.  *)

END Trajectories.
```

We do not provide algorithmic solutions for the procedures LinearTrajectory and CircularTrajectory because this encompasses primarily the solution of a geometric problem, and the development of these algorithms would offer no further software engineering insights. However, the reader should note that the algorithms are far from trivial.

We translate this attribute grammar into modules according to the rules identified above. First we specify the lexical analyzer, which is quite short due to the simplicity of our symbols:

```
DEFINITION MODULE LexicalAnalyzer;

TYPE Symbol =
  (digit, lSymbol, cSymbol, eSymbol, plus, minus, leftParenthesis,
  rightParenthesis, comma, blankChar, error, eof);

VAR
  sym: Symbol;
  digitValue: INTEGER;  (*attribute of digit*)

PROCEDURE InitLex;
PROCEDURE ReadSymbol;

END LexicalAnalyzer.
```

---

```
IMPLEMENTATION MODULE LexicalAnalyzer;

FROM InputText IMPORT GetLength, GetCharacter;

VAR textPos: CARDINAL;   (*position of the last character read from input text*)

PROCEDURE InitLex;
BEGIN
  textPos := 0
END InitLex;

PROCEDURE ReadSymbol;
VAR ch:CHAR;
BEGIN
  IF textPos = GetLength() THEN sym := eof; RETURN END;
  INC(textPos);
  ch := GetCharacter(textPos);
  CASE ch OF
    "0".."9":     sym := digit; digitValue := ORD(ch) – ORD("0")
  | "L", "l":     sym := lSymbol
  | "C", "c":     sym := cSymbol
  | "E", "e":     sym := eSymbol
  | "+":          sym := plus
  | "–":          sym := minus
  | "(":          sym := leftParenthesis
```

```
    |   ")":       sym := rightParenthesis
    |   ",":       sym := comma
    |   0C.." ":   sym := blankChar (*all control characters (TAB, CR, ...)
                                      and blanks*)
        ELSE       sym := error
    END
  END ReadSymbol;

  END LexicalAnalyzer.
```

We do not specify the complete syntax analyzer, but concentrate on the rule for recognition of a coordinate in order to show how context conditions are handled:

```
  PROCEDURE CoordinateOK (v0:INTEGER; VAR v:INTEGER): BOOLEAN;
  VAR sign:INTEGER;
  BEGIN
    sign := 0;
    IF sym = plus THEN
        sign := +1; ReadSymbol
    ELSIF sym="–" THEN
        sign := –1; ReadSymbol
    END;
    IF NOT Number(v) THEN RETURN FALSE END;
    IF sign # 0 THEN v := v0 + sign*v END;
    IF (v<0) OR (v>2000) THEN
        ReportError("invalid coordinate value"); RETURN FALSE
    END;
    RETURN TRUE
  END CoordinateOK;
```

If the context condition is not fulfilled, an error is reported and processing is aborted as with a syntax error. The procedure ReportError is intended not only to tell the user which error occurred, but also to identify the error location.

Since implementing an attribute grammar as a translator is a routine activity, it can be automated, i.e., handled by a program. Such programs are called *compiler generators* or *compiler compilers*. They process an attribute grammar and generate a program from it that tests the syntactic correctness of an input text and executes the semantic actions during analysis. In recent years intense research has been done in this area, so that today multiple compiler compilers are available for various domains and target machines (e.g., YACC [Johnson 1975], GAG [Kastens 1982], HLP [Koskimies 1984] and Coco-2 [Dobler 1990]). To round out the picture, we will show how an attribute grammar must be formulated in order to be processed by the compiler compiler Coco-2. We selected Coco-2 because it is one of the newest developments.

```
  COMPILER Robot
```

```
SEM <<                                                                          ①
  FROM StepList IMPORT
      Coordinate, Position, DeleteList, AppendStep, ListLength;
  FROM Trajectories IMPORT
      LinearTrajectory, CircularTrajectory;
  FROM Error IMPORT
      ReportError;
  >>

CHARACTER SETS                                                                  ②
  decimalDigit = "0" .. "9".

TOKENS                                                                          ③
  "L". "C". "E".
  "+". "–".
  "(". ")".
  ",". " ".

TOKEN CLASSES                                                                   ④
  digit <<VAR value:INTEGER>> =
      decimalDigit              LEX   <<value := ORD(tokenStr[1]);>>            ⑤

NONTERMINALS                                                                    ⑥
  Robot.
  InputText.
  Position <<pos0:Position; VAR pos:Position>>.
  Trajectory <<pos0:Position; VAR pos:Position>>.
  Coordinate <<v0:Coordinate; VAR v:Coordinate>>.
  Number <<VAR value:INTEGER>>.
  Blank.

RULES                                                                           ⑦
  Robot =
          Input text .
  Input text =
                                LOCAL <<VAR pos0:Position;>>                    ⑥
          Blank                 SEM <<                                          ⑨
                                    pos0.x := 0; pos0.y := 0; pos0.z := 0;
                                    >>
          Position <<pos0,pos>>
                                SEM <<
                                    DeleteList; AppendStep(pos);
                                    pos0 := pos;
                                    >>
```

```
            { Trajectory <<pos0,pos>>
                                SEM <<pos0 := pos;>>
            }
            "E" Blank .

      Position <<pos0:Position; VAR pos:Position>> =
            "(" Blank Coordinate <<pos0.x,pos.x>>
            "," Blank Coordinate <<pos0.y,pos.y>>
            "," Blank Coordinate <<pos0.z,pos.z>> ")"
            Blank .
            Trajectory <<pos0:Position; VAR pos:Position>> =
                                LOCAL <<
                                      VAR
                                         n:INTEGER;
                                         posTr:Position;
                                         ok:BOOLEAN;
                                      >>
            Number <<n>>        SEM << (*CC*)                          ⑩
                                      IF (n<1)
                                      OR (n>1000 – ListLength()) THEN
                                         ReportError
                                      END;
                                      >>
            ( "L" Blank
              Position <<pos0,pos>>
                                SEM <<
                                      LinearTrajectory(n,pos0,pos);
                                      >>
            | "C" Blank
              Position <<pos0,posTr>>
              Position <<pos0,pos>>
                                SEM <<
                                      CircularTrajectory
                                         (n,pos,pos0,posTr,pos,ok);
                                      (*CC*)
                                      IF NOT ok THEN ReportError END;
                                      >>
            ) .

      Coordinate <<v0:Coordinate; VAR v:Coordinate>> =
                                LOCAL <<VAR sign:INTEGER;>>
                                SEM <<sign := 0;>>
```

```
        [ "+"                SEM <<sign := +1;>>
        | "-"                SEM <<sign := -1;>>
        ]
        Number <<v>>         SEM <<
                                IF sign<>0 THEN
                                  v := v0 + sign*v
                                END;
                                (*CC*)
                                IF (v<0) OR (v>2000) THEN
                                  ReportError
                                END;
                                >>

    Number <<VAR value:INTEGER>> =
                             LOCAL <<VAR v:INTEGER;>>
        digit <<value>>
        { digit <<v>>        SEM <<value := value*10 + v;>>
        } .
    Blank =
        " " {" "} .

END Robot.
```

① From the attribute grammar Coco-2 generates a compiler that uses other modules. At the beginning of the attribute grammar we must therefore list the source modules for imported data types and procedures.

② Character sets can be declared under CHARACTER SETS to simplify the description of the terminal symbols. In this case we only need the set of digits.

③ In the section TOKENS we list the (simple) terminal symbols. The symbols can be designated by their names or, as here, by character strings.

④ The terminal classes are declared in the section TOKEN CLASSES. In addition to their names, they have one or more attributes, which are enclosed in angular brackets in Coco-2.

⑤ A digit is defined as an element of the set decimalDigit. An alternative would be an explicit listing in the form "0" | "1" | "2" | ... | "9". Following the reserved word LEX we specify the statements for computing the output attributes. tokenStr is a variable provided by the lexical analyzer that contains the last terminal symbol read as a character string.

⑥ The section NONTERMINALS must contain declarations of all nonterminal symbols occurring in the grammar. Among other things, this list serves to check whether the grammar is complete.

⑦ The section RULES – the main part of the attribute grammar – contains all rules for nonterminal symbols.

⑧ Each rule is translated into a respective analysis procedure. After the reserved word LOCAL and enclosed in angular brackets, all declarations can be included that are visible only in the procedure. These declarations are usually employed, as here, for local variables.

⑨ Contrary to the notation introduced above, semantic actions are enclosed in angular brackets after the reserved word SEM. The compiler compiler embeds the semantic actions at the appropriate locations in the generated compiler. Thus it is important that both the declarations and the statements reflect the rules of the implementation language (here Modula-2).

⑩ Coco-2 has no language element to describe context conditions. Context conditions must be programmed out, as with a manually written syntax analyzer. In particular, we have to specify what is to happen if a context condition is violated. We have highlighted context conditions with comments in the form (*CC*).

### 3.4.7 Object-oriented design

Function-oriented design begins with the actions to be carried out. Ideally the data to be processed should be refined stepwise while the overall task is decomposed stepwise into subtasks. This proves successful as long as the quantity and the complexity of the data involved remain low. Once there is a need to process much data with complex structure, the result becomes incomprehensible because the data are usually accessed from many scattered locations. This has a negative effect on the modifiability, testability and maintainability of the product. Data encapsulation and modularization can offer only limited alleviation once the size of the task exceeds a certain dimension. For large-scale projects it pays to focus more on the data and to build the design around the data.

Concentrating on the actions finds expression in function-oriented design in that it focuses on the *verbs*. For example, the following procedure might result for a traffic light control:

```
PROCEDURE Toggle (VAR light:TrafficLight; col:Color);
```

By contrast, object-oriented design focuses on the *nouns*. In this case the object TrafficLight would play a central role.

Object-oriented design requires the designer to think differently than with function-oriented design. Since the focus is on the data, the algorithms are not considered at first; instead the objects and the relationships between them are studied. The fundamental problem in object-oriented design consists of finding suitable classes for the solution of the task. The next step is identifying the relationships of these classes and their objects to each other and defining the operations that should be possible with the individual objects.

The literature presents various approaches to object-oriented analysis and object-oriented design. Some authors recommend using the *entity/relationship model* for modeling the interaction of objects; others employ *semantic networks* for this purpose. Research in the area of object-oriented design remains far from completion; none of the recommended methods has yet been able to gain general acceptance. The interested reader will find descriptions of these methods in [Booch 1991], [Coad 1990], [Heitz 1988], [Rumbaugh 1991], [Wasserman 1990], [Wilson 1990], [Wirfs-Brock 1989] and [Wirfs-Brock 1990].

We are convinced that most of the recommended methods scarcely offer more than healthy common sense. As a rule these methods emphasize a certain notation. They give the impression that, if we just use the right notation, everything else is automatic. The design of larger software systems remains a difficult task – even with the use of object-oriented techniques. Hence we cannot offer any all-round approach; instead, we employ an elementary method for identifying the objects required for a solution, the Abbott method.

#### 3.4.7.1 The Abbott Method

In object-oriented design we try to quickly identify the objects involved in a task. These could be data (e.g., texts), forms (e.g., order forms), devices (e.g., robot) or organizational aids (e.g., archive). Abbott [Abbott 1983] showed that verbal specifications can serve as the basis of the design. He recommends an approach that looks for various kinds of words (nouns, verbs) in the specifications and derives the design from them. Abbott employs the approach to form abstract data structures and to define the operations required on them. It has been shown that this approach can also be used for object-oriented design. The approach employs the following schema:

- *Filtering out nouns*
  The relevance of a noun depends on its usage:
  - *Generic terms* (e.g., person, automobile, traffic light) play a central role. Every such term is a candidate for a class.
  - *Proper nouns* serve as identifiers for specific objects (e.g., Paris, *War and Peace*, Salvador Dali). They can indirectly contribute to forming classes since every proper noun has a corresponding generic term (e.g., city, book, painter).
  - *Quantity* and *size units* (e.g., gallon) and *material descriptors* (e.g., wood) as well as *collective terms* (e.g., government) usually prove unsuitable for forming classes.
  - *Abstract terms* (e.g., work, envy, beauty) likewise prove unsuitable.
  - *Gerunds* indicate actions. They are treated like the verbs from which they derive.
- *Seeking commonalities*
  In real tasks descriptions many related nouns usually occur, such as “department manager” and “supervisor”, “author” and “writer”, “auto” and “vehicle”, “street”

and "one-way street". In such cases the analyst first must determine whether the terms are really distinct, or whether they indicate the same class. The answer to the question "Same or different?" generally emanates from the task description. For example, for a traffic simulation it would be of no importance whether only cars or arbitrary vehicles utilize a street. For a program to manage license plates and registrations, this difference would certainly play a role. In any case, the criterion for distinguishability is the question of whether the elements of the class in question have differing attributes.

If we find that two related terms designate different things, then we need to clarify what relation they have to one another. Often we find a subset relation that finds expression in sentences like: "Every auto is a vehicle." This *is-a relation*, discussed in more detail in Section 3.4.7.2, is the most important criterion for the design of class hierarchies.

- *Finding the relevant verbs*
  Verbs denote actions with objects. In contrast to the function-oriented approach, here these actions are not viewed in isolation, but always in connection with objects of certain classes. For example, the verb "toggle" belongs to a traffic light, and "accelerate" is associated with a vehicle. Assignment to a certain class proves easy for intransitive verbs because they are bound only to the subject of the sentence (e.g., wait). Transitive verbs and sentence structures that connect multiple nouns present more problems. For example, the statement "The *auto* is to be displayed on the *screen*" does not indicate whether the action "display" should be assigned to the screen or the auto. Unfortunately, such questions arise often in object-oriented design. A usual solution to the problem is to assign the action to both classes in question, and then during implementation to base one of the two operations on the other.

Naturally, strict adherence to these rules does not provide a generally applicable recipe that guarantees a good design. Above all, the decision as to which nouns to select as the basis for classes, and the problem of assigning actions to classes often present difficulties. Likewise, the scope and the quality of the available specifications influence the resulting design. Sparse specifications that leave numerous details open often force the designer to complement the task description according to personal conceptions. The result can be a collection of classes that have little to do with the original problem domain. Overly exhaustive specifications, on the other hand, harbor the danger of too many classes and often encumber the designer with unnecessary details. Specifications formulated in the terminology of the problem domain prove to be an advantage. This forces the designer to project into the role of the client, resulting in classes whose meaning the client also understands.

If prototyping was used in the specification phase, then only part of the requirements definition is in the form of a verbal description. This means that the prototype also must be used for the identification of objects. Prototypes prove especially suitable here because they are visible models of the system to be implemented. For example, all interaction elements displayed on the screen of a user interface prototype become candidates for objects.

With a little practice and intuition, handling specifications according to the Abbott Method produces a natural object-oriented decomposition of the overall problem. The resulting classes have clear interfaces that can largely be handled independently. In analogy to stepwise refinement, detailed specifications can be made for each class and again handled according to the same scheme. The objects that are viewed at first as black boxes thereby take increasingly concrete form. The algorithmic design of the actions usually exposes additional classes that only peripherally have anything to do with the original problem. In the design of a simulation program for a traffic light control, for example, classes might evolve in the following sequence:

(1) Directly from the specifications:
TrafficLight, Auto, Street, Intersection, Time, Statistics
(2) From the design of the classes in (1):
Lane, Direction, Color, Histogram
(3) During the algorithmic design of the operations:
Event, Generator, Queue, List, Quantity, Matrix

The original classes still relate directly to the problem domain, while the last classes are meaningful only for the implementation. A top-down approach according to Abbott thus allows us to largely close the chasm in abstraction (the semantic gap) that often occurs between the client's application domain and the world of the implementor.

#### 3.4.7.2 Design of class hierarchies

A particular characteristic of object-oriented programming is that the classes (= data types) are hierarchically structured. This approach has the organizational advantage that similar things are recognized and combined under a common superordinate term. This produces a tree structure in which the general (abstract) terms are near the root and the leaves represent the specialized (concrete) terms. Figure 3.39 shows an example class hierarchy for motor vehicles.

The class MotorVehicle determines the general attributes of the classes derived from it. For example, independent of the type of vehicle, every vehicle has a brand name, a model, a series number, a power rating for the motor, and much more. Every auto (since it is also a vehicle) also has these attributes. In addition, it has further attributes such as the number of passengers, the number of doors, etc. This scheme can be continued to any extent. Each specialization stage adds further attributes to the general ones.

Another characteristic of a class hierarchy is the extension of functionality with increasing specialization. A convertible, for example, permits all actions that are possible with a car. In addition, its roof can be folded down.

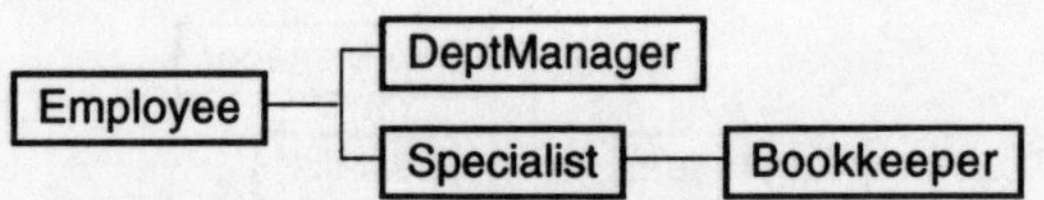


Figure 3.40: Class hierarchy of employees

The most important relation in a class library is the is-a relation. Since the class Car is a subset of the class Auto, every car (object of class Car) *is* an auto. This relation represents the first criterion for designing class hierarchies. Often, however, there are multiple possibilities for assignment. For example, the class StationWagon could also be a subset of commercial vehicles for the transport of goods as reflected in the class Truck. Such ambiguities can impede the search for an adequate common superordinate term.

Such a class hierarchy has two consequences for implementation:

- *Inheritance*: Attributes and operations defined for a general class automatically apply to the more specialized classes derived from it. For example, if Auto has a function that computes the top speed from the wind resistance value and the engine data, then this function is also valid for all objects of derived classes (e.g., Car, StationWagon).
- *Polymorphism*: A program fragment that functions for objects of a class K can also work with objects of a class derived from K even though such objects have different attributes (structure, behavior) from K objects. This is possible because derived classes only *add* attributes, but can never *remove* any. This results in a flexibility that can be achieved only with arduous effort with conventional programming.

Both these characteristics need to be considered in the design of class hierarchies. For example, if a personnel management system employs the terms employee, department manager, specialist and bookkeeper, a software designer needs to consider the context in which objects of these classes are used and which attributes and operations can be inherited between classes. If a bookkeeper is viewed as a specialist in a particular area, then the hierarchy in Figure 3.40 could result:

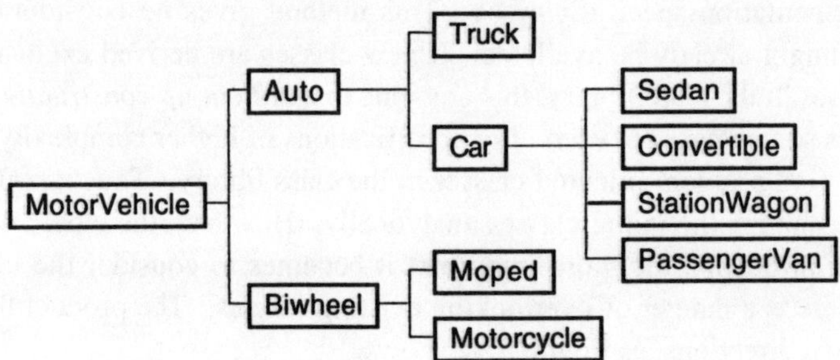


Figure 3.39: A class hierarchy for motor vehicles

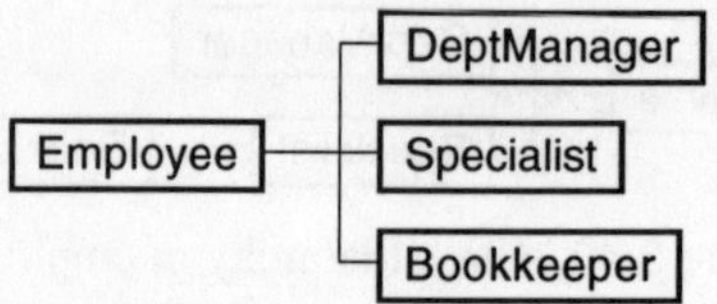


Figure 3.41: Flattened class hierarchy of employees

However, if a bookkeeper differs from other specialists (e.g., because a specialist works on a productivity basis and might be awarded a bonus which a bookkeeper does not receive), then this hierarchy proves unsuitable, suggesting a flatter structure such as that in Figure 3.41.

Yet it is just as likely that there are no differences at all that are relevant to the task at hand, so that we might be able to dispense with any differentiation of employees.

Often specifications employ terms that are similar in many ways, yet differ significantly in certain details. Such an example arises in a program to display rectangles and circles. These geometric shapes have attributes that could be handled collectively (e.g., line thickness, fill pattern, movement on the screen), yet they cannot be combined fruitfully in an is-a relation. In such cases a common superordinate class, or *superclass*, must be created, e.g., GeomFigure. The attributes common to a circle and a rectangle (e.g., line thickness, color, fill pattern) are then transferred to the common superclass, and only the specialized attributes and operations (center and radius, width and height, drawing operations) are implemented in the derived classes. The common superclass represents an abstraction of the specialized classes. In this context we speak of *abstract classes*.

The availability of a collection of prefabricated classes (a class library) can save a great deal of implementation and even design work. A little luck might even produce a fitting class, or at least a more general class from which the desired class can be derived by inheritance and specialization. In this case two activities in opposing directions characterize the design procedure: top-down analysis and bottom-up synthesis.

The Abbott Method is a *top-down analytical method* because we begin with the design of the application-oriented classes starting with the task description and progress to the implementation-specific classes. This method gives no consideration to any classes that might already be available. If new classes are derived exclusively on the basis of classes in the class library, this amounts to a *bottom-up constructive approach*. The truth lies somewhere between. For specifications of higher complexity, a designer can scarcely find problem-oriented classes in the class library. Thus it makes sense in any case to establish the initial classes analytically. However, the closer we get to the implementation details, the more important it becomes to consider the class library; otherwise there is a danger of overlooking existing classes. The product thus tends to grow from two directions, as Figure 3.42 shows.

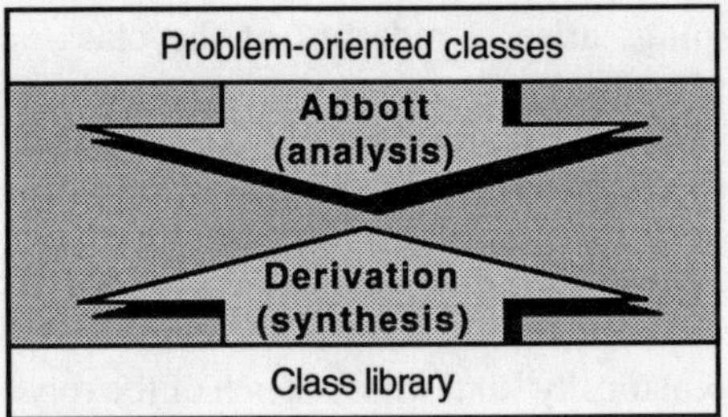


Figure 3.42: Mixed top-down and bottom-up software construction with object-oriented design

### 3.4.7.3 Generalization

Reusability plays a central role in object-oriented programming. Here we distinguish reuse within a program and between programs. Within a program reuse is realized with inheritance. High reuse results almost as a side effect of the design of the class hierarchy by the introduction of abstraction levels. A class library as the basis of implementation is the most important medium for achieving high reuse between programs. Usually such a class library is provided by the compiler manufacturer. If similar tasks are to be solved frequently, similar subtasks crystallize repeatedly that can be solved in the same way in different programs. This suggests striving for as much generality as possible in every class in order to assure high reusability in later projects. Above all the following measures prove useful toward this goal:

- *Far-sighted extensions*: In the development of a new class, more should be implemented than just the attributes absolutely necessary for the solution of the immediate task. Developers should also plan ahead and give consideration to the contexts in which the class might also be used.
- *Factoring*: When it is predictable that a class will later have alternatives with similar behavior, abstract classes should be planned from which the future classes can be derived. Especially when there is a large abstraction gap between existing (base) class and the new class (e.g., between graphic elements and editable text), intermediate classes should be introduced (e.g., non-editable text).
- *Simple functions*: Since existing functions that are not precisely suitable must be reimplemented (overwritten) in the derivation of new classes, complex operations should be avoided. It is better to decompose complex operations to smaller ones during their design; the simpler operations can then be overwritten individually as needed.

The highest possible generality can be achieved most easily if the design of reusable classes is handled by independent design teams that are not directly involved in the current project. Still, only actual reuse can determine whether this goal has been achieved. If shortcomings arise, a redesign of the class needs to be considered (stabilization cycle, see Section 3.1.5).

#### 3.4.7.4 Application to the design example

Section 3.4.2 specified the display components very briefly with the statement "The robot is to be represented schematically on the screen: orthographically in front, top and side views as well as isometrically" and with a sketch of the robot (Figure 3.43).

In this section we show how an object-oriented solution to this subtask can be designed. We assume that no class library is available, i.e., that the design will proceed purely top-down.

In the solution of this task we limit ourselves to the identification of the classes necessary for the display of the robot and their interfaces. In Chapter 4 we show how these classes can be implemented.

In order to be able to apply the Abbott Method, we first need extensive verbal specifications such as the following:

> A portal robot, consisting of a foundation and a portal with a vertical gripper arm, is to carry out linear trajectories. After every subtrajectory the robot is to be drawn schematically on the screen: orthographically in front, top and side views as well as isometrically.
>
> The foundation consists of two rails, the portal of three beams (two vertical and one horizontal). The gripper arm is to be represented by a beam and a ball (for the gripper).

The following list shows *all* nouns and verbs that occur in these specifications in alphabetical order. We have not yet filtered according to the criteria in Section 3.4.7.1.

*Nouns:*

ball, beam, front view, foundation, gripper arm, isometric, portal, portal robot, rail, side view, subtrajectory, top view, trajectory,

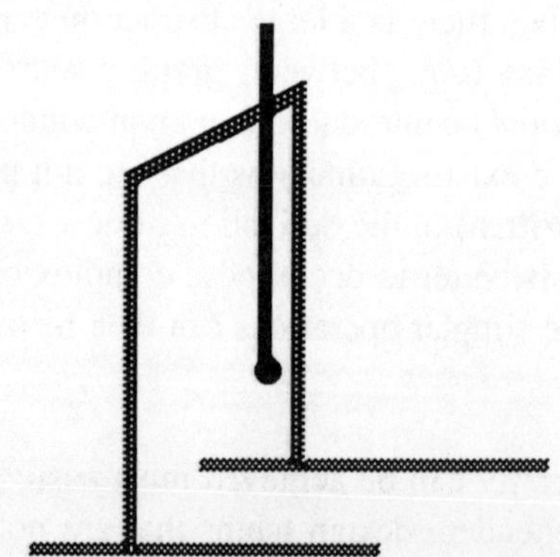

Figure 3.43: Structure of the portal robot

*Verbs:*

carry out, consist (of), draw, represent

Our first task is to distinguish the significant nouns from the unimportant ones. Here it makes sense to begin with concrete terms that play an important role in the specifications. In our case these are the robot and its components:

ball, beam, foundation, gripper arm, portal, portal robot, rail

The noun "trajectory" occurs in connection with the verb "carry out". We can derive the action "carry out trajectory", or simply:

move

The four views occur in connection with the verb "draw". We can conclude that four drawing operations will be required:

draw front view
draw isometric view
draw side view
draw top view

This leaves us with one last noun, "subtrajectory". In the specifications this word occurs in the formulation "after every subtrajectory"; this means it is used to describe the chronological progression, which is presently of lesser interest.

Hence we only have two verbs to deal with: the phrase "consists of" describes not an action, but a state (more precisely, a relation between objects). It is not yet of importance at the beginning of the design, but must be considered in the later design of the object structures. The verb "represent" is used in the specifications as a synonym for draw; it contributes nothing new to our design.

The next step is to derive the classes from the relevant nouns. In principle, we could introduce a class for each term, but the specifications contain two terms whose meaning can hardly be distinguished for our simulation: rail and beam. This can be tested by replacing the word "beam" with "rail" in the specifications. The term rail can thus be eliminated as a candidate for a class. This leaves us with six terms whose commonality consists of being concrete parts that must be drawn and most of which can be moved. Thus we introduce an abstract class Part, from which all other parts will be derived. A further abstraction results from the realization that the various parts can be divided into elementary (i.e., not further decomposable) and composite parts. This leads to the hierarchy in Figure 3.44.

Compositeness is a significant attribute that indicates additional attributes and operations. In particular, a complex part consists of a number of elements of data type Part, whereby it is possible that new parts could be added or removed at run time, so that the structure of a complex part can change dynamically. Adding such operations that at first glance seem superfluous is typical of long-range planning in object-oriented design.

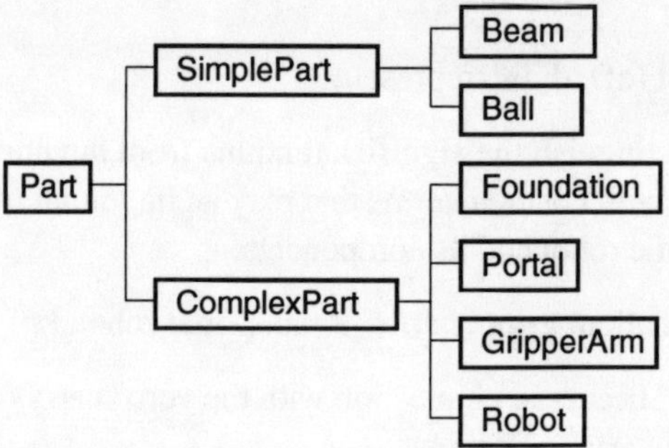


Figure 3.44: Class hierarchy of robot parts (initial design)

By contrast, the simple parts ball and beam share no commonalities that are not already defined in the class Part. Thus we can conclude that the class SimplePart is superfluous. This leads to the simplified class hierarchy in Figure 3.45.

The remaining task is to specify the interfaces of the classes. Here we will specify all operations and their parameters for each class. For derived classes we do not repeat the inherited functions and only specify the added operations.

We specify the general interface of a part as follows:

```
Part
    move (↓dx:Integer, ↓dy:Integer, ↓dz:Integer)
    drawFrontView (↓r:Rectangle)
    drawTopView (↓r:Rectangle)
    drawSideView (↓r:Rectangle)
    drawIsometric (↓r:Rectangle)
```

Note that Part is an abstract class. The form of a part remains undefined until further specialized. For this reason the operations defined in class Part cannot be implemented there, but must be delayed for more concrete classes.

The above interface specifies only the names of the operations and the number and data types of the parameters. The interface says nothing about how the operations are to be realized. The exact specification of a class in our sense must thus contain additional verbal explanations so that they facilitate the further application of the Abbott Method.

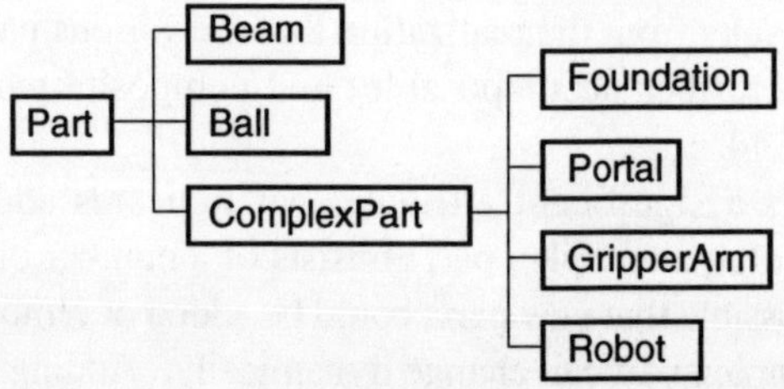


Figure 3.45: Class hierarchy of robot parts (final version)

To show what degree of detail is necessary, we provide the detailed specifications of the first two operations:

move (↓dx:Integer, ↓dy:Integer, ↓dz:Integer)

Moves the part by (dx,dy,dz) units relative to its current position. The motion is not displayed on screen, but only effects a state transition of the part.

drawFrontView (↓r:Rectangle)

Draws the part in the front view (i.e., in a projection along the *y* axis) in the current window within the rectangle defined by r. This effects a transformation of real coordinates to screen coordinates, so that point $(x,y)=(0,0)$ is displayed at the bottom left corner and point $(x,y)=(2000,2000)$ at the right top corner of rectangle r.

If we continue the Abbott Method with these specifications, we soon encounter additional nouns (e.g., position, screen, window, rectangle) that also represent potential classes. However, we will not continue the method and will concentrate instead on the further design of the parts.

Once the interface definition of a class has been established (for the time), we tackle the next class. To help retain an overview, we recommend continuing with a class derived from Part above. As there are multiple candidates, we should again begin with an abstract class, in our case ComplexPart.

A complex part inherits all operations from class Part and additionally contains the operations needed to manage its constituent parts:

```
ComplexPart
    partCount ' Integer
    simplePart (↓num:Integer) ' Part
    addPart (↓t:Part)
    removePart (↓num:Integer)
```

The operations simplePart and removePart expect as parameter the number of the part to be returned or removed. We assume that the constituent parts of a complex part are numbered. If part number $i$ is removed from a complex part with $n$ individual parts, then the parts with numbers $i+1$ to $n$ are assigned numbers $i$ to $n-1$.

To complete the specification of the class, the error behavior would have to be specified (e.g., if the parameter num of the operation simplePart is smaller than 1 or larger than the number of constituent parts).

The elementary parts beam and ball require several operations with which their extension and position in space can be requested and changed:

```
Beam
    start ' Position
    end ' Position
```

```
    thickness ‘ Integer
    setStart (↓pos:Position)
    setEnd (↓pos:Position)
    setThickness (↓d:Integer)
```

The position of a beam in space is defined by the coordinates of its starting and end points. Here the designation start and end are arbitrary since the two ends of a beam cannot be distinguished. We assume that a beam has a square cross-section whose dimension is specified by the attribute thickness. Each attribute has one operation each for querying and changing its value.

```
Ball
    center ‘ Position
    radius ‘ Integer
    setCenter (↓pos:Position)
    setRadius (↓d:Integer)
```

A ball can be described most simply by specifying its center and it radius. Here, too, we provide each attribute with one operation each for querying and changing its value.

For the complex parts foundation, portal, gripper arm and robot, we provide no operations to change all possible attributes, but only an initialization operation to bring these parts into their defined initial state. The primary task of this initialization is to assemble the complex parts from their constituent simple parts. Only for the robot do we provide an additional operation to query its current position (i.e., the position of the gripper arm in space). These considerations result in the following interfaces for these parts:

```
Foundation
    initialize (↓length:Integer, ↓width:Integer)
Portal
    initialize (↓height:Integer, ↓width:Integer, ↓x0:Integer)
GripperArm
    initialize (↓length:Integer, ↓pos:Position)
Robot
    initialize (↓length:Integer, ↓width:Integer, ↓height:Integer, ↓pos:Position)
    gripperPosition ‘ Position
```

It makes sense to assign the same name to initialization operations for all parts; however, they do require different parameters. This shows that the same operations cannot always be factored into a common abstract superclass.

For all initialization operations we assume that the left end of the front foundation rail is at position (0,0,0), the origin of the coordinate systems. To circumvent this simplifying constraint, we would have to pass the actual origin coordinates to each procedure.

Each part is initialized by the specification of its size. The foundation has only width and length. Since it is immobile, no other specifications are necessary. The portal can move longitudinally, so that we also need a specification of the initial distance from the origin. Analogously, the initialization of the gripper arm requires its position in three-dimensional space.

This terminates the object-oriented design of this subtask for the present. Compared with a conventional design with stepwise refinement, we can make the following observations:

- *Information hiding* was consistently upheld. The design only specifies the interfaces of the objects, but leaves the structure and the implementation of the operations open. This assures a high measure of security without giving particular attention to this aspect.
- The interaction of the different types of objects was considered during the design, but scarcely affects the result. This applies to both the relationships between objects (e.g., the components of a robot) and the invocation of algorithms (e.g., procedures for moving the robot). This *loose coupling* proves particularly advantageous for later modifications and extensions.
- Instead of a main program there is a multitude of operations that can be invoked as needed. This fact often creates difficulties for novices because they do not see the *embedding* in the overall system and thus believe they have lost the connection. However, it is typical of object-oriented design to specify only *what* can be done with objects, but not *when* something actually happens.
- The design is *flexible* and almost arbitrarily *extensible*. For example, additional elementary parts (e.g., surfaces and cubes) or composite parts (e.g., frames, tables and any kind of shaped bodies) can be added with little effort. The appearance of a robot can thus be changed at any time, even after completion of the implementation.
- Several classes are largely independent of the simulation task. This applies above all to the abstract classes and the elementary parts. These classes can be reused without changes in later projects with similar task descriptions (e.g., for CAD applications). It is also possible to design a new, more specialized robot that inherits the significant attributes from the class designed here, but to add new operations (e.g., automatic protocoling of all trajectories).
- The result of the design (the system architecture) differs fundamentally from the result of a functional decomposition and represents a more comprehensible abstraction of the real system (which reduces the semantic gap).

Our design effort produced a number of classes that can be viewed as modules. Object-oriented design can thus rightfully be termed a modularization technique. By concentrating on the kinds of objects, our decomposition in mutually independent components evolved almost as a side effect. Section 4.9 will show that the implementation of the classes presents no particular difficulty.

**Summary**

The goal of Section 3.4 was to acquaint the reader with various design techniques (function-oriented, data-oriented and object-oriented design). Hence we designed individual components for our example task (portal robot) with the techniques best suited to the respective components:

- The analyzer for the trajectory description was designed with attribute grammars because this technique serves well for the translation of a structured input stream (trajectory description) to an internal representation (step list).
- The control of the simulation was designed functionally using the method of stepwise refinement because the handling of user input in event-driven programming naturally leads to a multitude of small procedures. This part of the task description could also have been designed with object-oriented means, but for didactic reasons we chose a functional design approach.
- The display of the robot was designed in an object-oriented way because this technique proves best suited to modeling occurrences in the real world.

## 3.5 Implementation

By the term *implementation* of a software system we mean the transformation (coding) of the design results into programs that are executable on a certain target machine. A good implementation reflects the design decisions. In particular, the implementation should ensure the following:

- The decomposition structures, data structures and identifiers selected and established during the design procedure need to be easily recognized in the implementation.
- The abstraction levels of the design (the classes, modules, algorithms, data structures and data types) must also be feasible in the implementation.
- The interfaces between the components of a software system should be explicitly described in the implementation.
- It must be possible to check the consistency of objects and operations already with the compiler (before the actual testing phase).

The degree to which these characteristics are fulfilled depends on the choice of the implementation language and on the programming style.

### 3.5.1 Choice of implementation language

The question of which is the "right" programming language has always been a favorite topic of discussion in programming circles. Actually, the choice of a programming language for the implementation of a project frequently plays an important role. In the ideal case, the design should be carried out without any knowledge of the later implementation language so that it can be implemented in any language. Unfortunately, in practice this is seldom feasible because certain constraints (such as the client's restrictions or the availability of compilers) require a certain programming language from the start. Thus we can generally assume that the implementation language is generally known at the beginning of a project. This knowledge has an enormous influence on the design and thus on the final product because every programming language is founded on its own thought model that partially determines the solution [Rechenberg 1990]. For example, the availability or lack of certain language elements in different languages can lead to the evolution of completely different designs. A Basic programmer would never dream of using abstract data types, for example, and a Fortran programmer would avoid recursive algorithms in a design because the implementation language does not support recursion.

Time has seen the birth of thousands of programming languages triggered by advances in software engineering (and vice-versa). Thus newer programming languages are more likely to reflect the state of the art and prove more suitable for the production of high-quality software products. Nevertheless, there is no "best" programming language that is equally suited for all tasks. A developer must observe many criteria in order to choose the optimum implementation language for a particular task under given circumstances. In this section we deliberately refrain from favoring any specific programming language, but only list characteristics that could have an influence on the choice of an implementation language. We consider the following quality criteria for programming languages:

- Modularity
- Documentation value
- Data structures
- Control flow
- Efficiency
- Security
- Portability
- Dialog support
- Specialized language elements

The *modularity* of a programming language is the degree to which it supports modularization of programs. The decomposition of a large program into multiple modules is a prerequisite to carrying out large software projects. Without modularization, division of labor in the implementation becomes impossible. Furthermore, as of a certain size, monolithic programs become unmanageable: they are difficult to maintain and document and they impede implementation with long compile times. Languages such as standard Pascal (which does not support modules) prove unsuitable for large projects.

If a language supports the decomposition of a program into smaller units, there must also be assurance that the components work together. If a procedure is invoked from another module, there must be a check of whether the procedure actually exists and whether it is used correctly (i.e., whether the number of parameters and their data types are correct). We distinguish languages with *independent compilation* (e.g., C and Fortran), where this check takes place only upon invocation at run time (if at all), and languages with *separate compilation* (e.g., Ada and Modula-2), where each module has an interface description that provides the basis for checking its proper use already at compile time. The earlier an error can be detected, the less its correction costs. In the worst case the compatibility of two modules can be checked only partially or not at all, because this can lead to errors that surface only at run time, when they might cause irreparable damage. The larger a software project and the more people involved, the greater is the importance of intermodular interface checking.

The *documentation value* of a programming language affects the readability and thus the maintainability of programs. The importance of the documentation value rises for longevous programs and for software that the client continues to develop. High documentation value results, among other things, from explicit interface specifications with separate compilation (e.g., in Ada and Modula-2). Likewise the use of keywords instead of special characters (e.g., BEGIN...END in Pascal rather than {...} in C) has a positive effect on readability because the greater redundancy gives less cause for careless errors in reading. Since programs are generally written only once but read repeatedly, the minimum additional effort in writing pays off no later than in the maintenance phase. Likewise the language scope influences the readability of programs. Extensive languages with numerous specialized functions (e.g., Ada) are difficult to grasp in all their details, thus encouraging misinterpretations. Languages of medium scope (e.g., Pascal and Modula-2) harbor significantly less such danger.

Primarily when complex data must be processed, the availability of *data structures* in the programming language plays an important role. Older languages such as Basic, Fortran and Cobol offer solely the possibility to combine multiple homogeneous elements in arrays or heterogeneous elements in structures. Recursive data structures are difficult to implement in these languages. Languages like C permit the declaration of pointers to data structures. This enables data structures of any complexity, and their scope and structure can change at run time. However, the drawback of these data structures is that they are open and permit unrestricted access. Primarily in large projects with multiple project teams, abstract data structures take on particular meaning. Although abstract data structures can be emulated in any modular language, due to better readability, preference should be given to a language with its own elements supporting this concept. Beyond this, object-oriented languages offer the feature of extensible abstract data types that permit the realization of complex software systems with elegance and little effort. For a flexible and extensible solution, object-oriented languages provide a particularly good option.

Another quality attribute of programming languages is the availability of language elements for *structuring control flow*. Languages like Basic, C and Fortran include variations of a Goto statement, which programmers can employ to create unlimited and incomprehensible control flow structures. In Pascal the use of the Goto statement is encumbered because the target must be declared explicitly. In Eiffel, Modula-2 and Smalltalk there is no Goto statement at all, which forces better structuring of the control flow.

In technical applications additional possibilities for control flow can play an important role. These include the handling of exceptions and interrupts as well as parallel processes and their synchronization mechanisms. Many programming languages (e.g., Ada and Eiffel) support several of these concepts and thus permit simpler program structures in certain cases. Note, however, that every deviation from sequential flow is difficult to understand and thus has a negative effect on readability.

The *efficiency* of a programming language is often overrated as a criterion. For example, the programming language C bears the reputation that it supports the writing of very efficient programs, while object-oriented languages are accused of inefficiency. However, there are few cases where a language is in principle particularly efficient or especially inefficient. Optimizing compilers often generate excellent code that an experienced Assembler programmer could hardly write better. For time-critical operations, it pays to use a faster machine or a better compiler rather than a "more efficient" programming language.

The *security* of a programming language emanates primarily from its readability and its mechanisms for type checking (even across module boundaries). Independent of the application domain, therefore, a language with *static typing* should be preferred. Static typing means that for each expression the compiler can determine which type it will have at run time. Additional security risks include type conversions (type casts) and pointer arithmetic operations, which are routine for programming in C, for example. Run-time checks are also important for security, especially during the development phase. These functions normally belong in the domain of the compiler. Mechanisms for formulating assertions (e.g., in Eiffel) and features for exception handling (e.g., in Eiffel and Ada) also contribute to the security of a programming language.

*Portability* can be a significant criterion if a software product is destined for various hardware platforms. In such a situation it makes sense to select a standardized language such as Ada or C. However, this alone does not suffice to ensure portability, for any external modules belonging to the language also need to be standardized. This is a problem in the language Modula-2 because various compiler producers offer different module libraries. Beyond standardization, another criterion is the availability of compilers for the language on different computers. For example, developers of software for mainframes will find a Fortran compiler on practically every machine.

For interactive programs the programming language must also provide *dialog support*. For example, Fortran and Cobol offer only line-oriented input and output; highly interactive programs (that react to every key pressed) can thus be developed only with the help of specialized libraries. Some languages like Basic and Logo are particularly atuned to dialog with the user (and with the programmer), making these languages better suited for such applications. Object-oriented programming languages also prove well suited to the development of interactive programs, especially with the availability of a corresponding class library or an application framework (see Section 4.7).

For specialized tasks, *specialized language elements* can be decisive for the selection of a programming language. For technical applications, for example, the availability of complex number arithmetic (e.g., in Fortran) and in commercial domains fixed-point numbers with large ranges (e.g., in Cobol) can be important. For mathematical problems, matrix operations (e.g., in APL) can simplify the task, and translation and character string operations are elegantly solved in Snobol. The lack of such specialized language elements can be compensated for with library modules in modular languages. Object-oriented languages prove particularly suited to extending the language scope.

In addition to language characteristics, pragmatic considerations also play a role. The best programming language would be of little value if certain constraints preclude its use or make it impractical. Such potential factors include:

- Quality of the compiler
- Availability of libraries
- Availability of development tools
- Company policy
- External requirements

The *quality of the compiler* is decisive for the actual implementation phase. A good compiler should not only generate efficient code, but also provide support for debugging (e.g., with clear error messages and run-time checks). Particularly in the area of microcomputers, many compilers have been integrated in development systems. Here the user-friendliness of such systems must also be considered.

With modular programming languages, the *availability of libraries* for various application domains represents a significant selection criterion. For example, for practically all Fortran compilers, libraries are available with numerous mathematical functions, and Smalltalk class libraries contain a multitude of general classes for constructing interactive programs. The availability of libraries can also depend on the compiler used. For example, the Fortran library can also be used in C or Modula-2 if the compiler supports linking routines from foreign languages. On the other hand, there are libraries that are available only in compiled form and usable only in connection with a certain compiler.

Today's trend is toward the use of *tools* to support software development. Many tools intended for the implementation phase are bound to a particular programming language or even a certain compiler. Examples of such tools include structure-oriented editors, debuggers and program generators. For example, if tools like Lex and YACC (tools for the application of attribute grammars on UNIX machines) are to be employed, then an implementation in C becomes unavoidable; choosing another language would only be justified if it promises gains greater than the cost of forfeiting the tool.

Often a particular *company policy* influences the choice of a programming language. Frequently the language decision is made not by the implementors, but by managers that want to use only a single language company-wide for reasons of uniformity. Such a decision was made by the U.S. Department of Defense, which mandatorily prescribes Ada for all programming in the military sector in the U.S. (and thus also in most other NATO countries). Such global decisions have also been made in the area of telecommunications, where many programmers at distributed locations work over decades on the same product.

Even in-house situations, such as the education of the employees or a module library built up over years, can force the choice of a certain language. A company might resist switching to a more modern programming language to avoid training costs, the purchase of new tools, and the reimplementation of existing software.

Sometimes *external requirements* force the use of a given programming language. Contracts for the European Union increasingly prescribe Ada, and the field of automation tends to require programs in Fortran or C. Such requirements arise when the client's interests extend beyond the finished product in compiled form and the client plans to do maintenance work and further development in an in-house software department. Then the education level of the client's programming team determines the implementation language.

### 3.5.2 Programming style

After they have been implemented and tested, software systems can very seldom be used over a longer time without modifications. In fact, usually the opposite is true: as the requirements are updated or extended after completion of the product and during its operation, undetected errors or shortcomings arise. The implementation must constantly be modified or extended, necessitating repeated reading and understanding of the source code. In the ideal case the function of a program component should be comprehensible without knowledge of the design documents, only from its source code. The source code is the only document that always reflects the current state of the implementation.

The readability of a program depends on the programming language used and on the *programming style* of the implementor. Writing readable programs is a creative process. The programming style of the implementor influences the readability of a program much more than the programming language used. A stylistically well-written Fortran or Cobol program can be more readable than a poorly written Modula-2 or Smalltalk program.

The most important elements of good programming style are:

- Structuredness
- Expressiveness

- Outward form
- Efficiency

This refers to both the *design* and the *implementation*. We have applied these principles in the development of the examples thus far without pointing this out to the reader. Let us atone for this now.

Although efficiency is an important quality attribute, we do not deal with questions of efficiency here. Only when we have understood a problem and its solution correctly does it make sense to examine efficiency.

### 3.5.2.1 Structuredness

*Structuring* refers to decomposing a software system with the goal of mastering its complexity through abstraction and striving for simplicity and comprehensibility; this is *structuring in the large*. But structuring also refers to the selection of appropriate program components in the algorithmic formulation of subsolutions; we call this *structuring in the small*.

**Structuring in the large**. The principles for structuring in the large have been presented in detail in Sections 3.4.3 and 3.4.5 to 3.4.7. This process results in classes and methods for object-oriented decomposition as well as modules and procedures assigned to the modules. During implementation the components defined in the design must be realized in such a way that they are executable on a computer. The medium for this translation process is the programming language. For the implementation of a software system, it is important that the decomposition defined in the design be expressible in the programming language; i.e., that all components can be represented in the chosen language.

**Structuring in the small**. The understanding and testing of algorithms require that the algorithms be easy to read. Many complexity problems ensue from the freedom taken in the use of Goto statements, i.e., from the design of unlimited control flow structures. The fundamental idea behind *structured programming* is to use only control flow structures with *one input* and *one output* in the formulation of algorithms. This leads to a

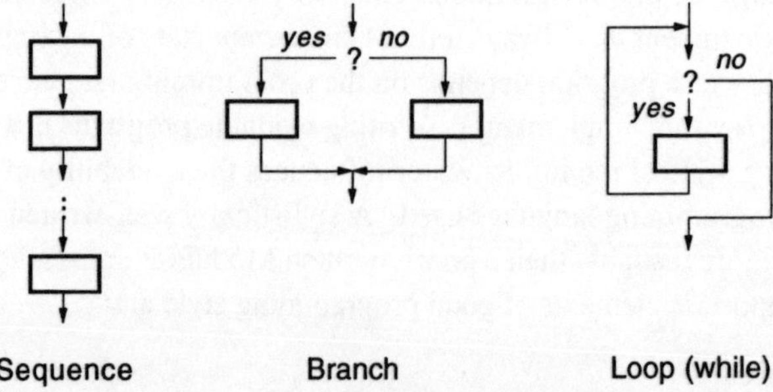


Figure 3.46: D-diagrams

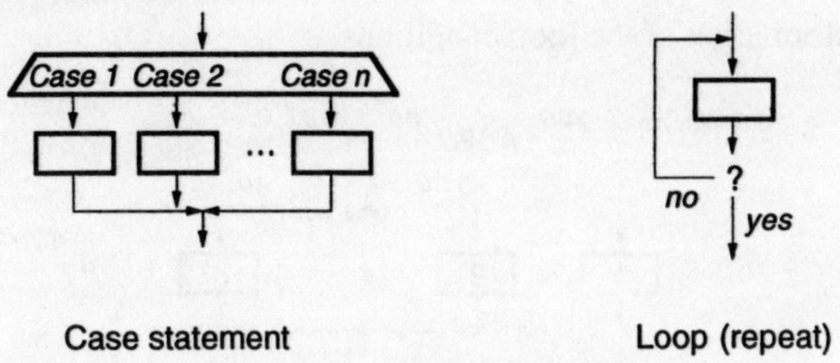


Figure 3.47: Additional control flow elements

correspondence between the static written form of an algorithm and its dynamic behavior. What the source code lists *sequentially* tends to be executed *chronologically*. This makes algorithms comprehensible and easier to verify, modify or extend.

Böhm and Jacopini [Böhm 1966] have shown that every algorithm can be represented by a combination of the control elements *sequence*, *branch* and *loop* (all of which have one input and one output). Figure 3.46 shows these control elements in the form of flow diagrams. Diagrams for algorithms consisting of only these elements are called *D-diagrams* (named after Dijkstra). In addition, we permit the elements depicted in Figure 3.47 because they have no negative impact on comprehensibility.

If we describe algorithms by a combination of these elements, no Goto statement is necessary. However, programming without Goto statements alone cannot guarantee structuredness. Choosing inappropriate program components produces poorly structured programs even if they contain no Goto statements.

The following three examples (see [Blaschek 1990]) show how unlimited control structures, as found often in practice, can be converted to structured solutions.

**Example 1**
*Given* the following (poor) program structure:

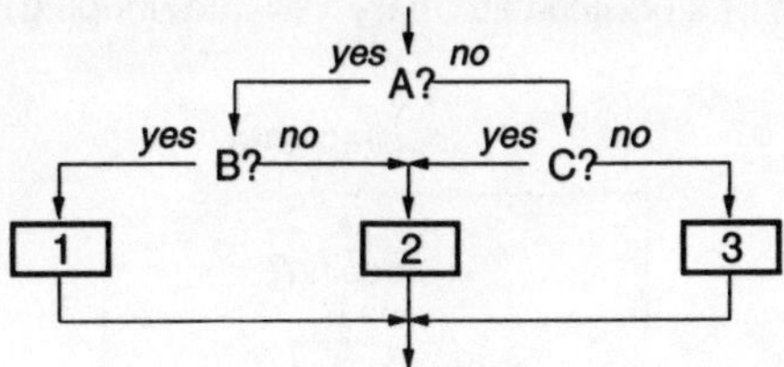


*find* a transformation to a structured form.

*Solution 1*: Transformation of the loop conditions

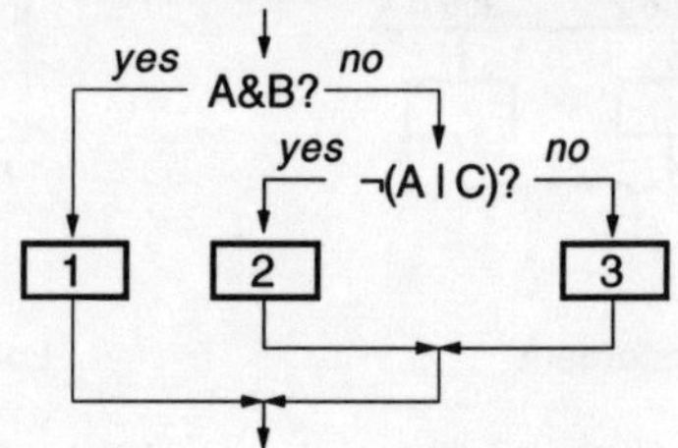


*Solution* 2: Code duplication

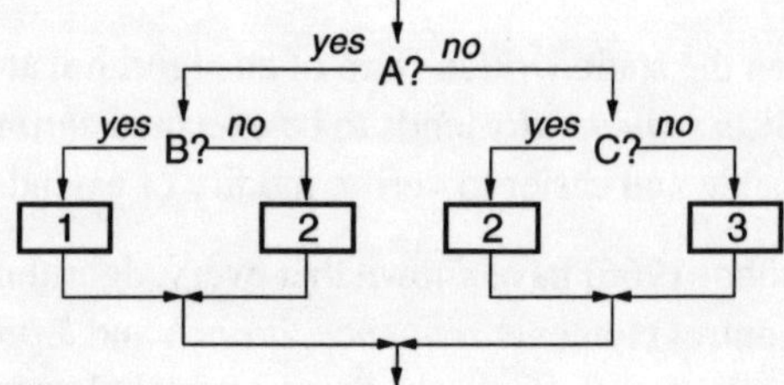


**Example 2**

*Given* is a so-called *n+1/2–loop* (*n* + 1/2 times), as frequently occurs in loop statements:

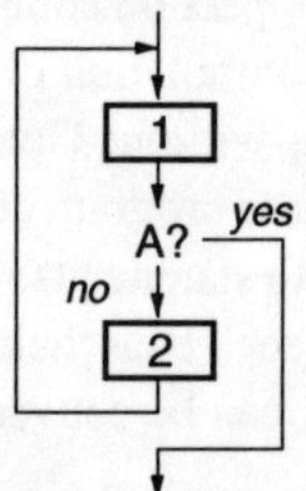


*find* a form of loop that adheres to the rules of structured programming.

*Solution 1*: Introduction of a boolean auxiliary variable (looping)

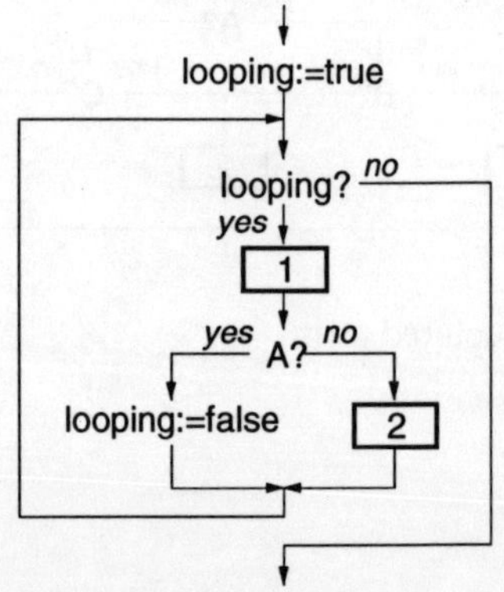

*Solution 2*: Code duplication

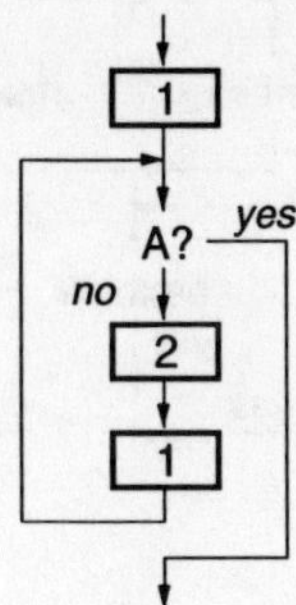


**Example 3**

*Given* the following program structure (call it a *cross structure*) which is often found in dialog programs:

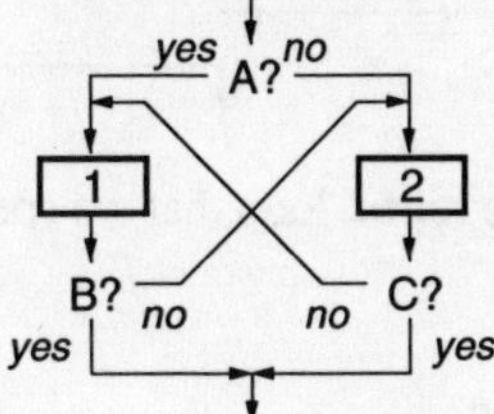


*find* a transformation that adheres to the rules of structured programming.

On closer examination of the structure we see that 1 and 2 are executed alternatingly and until B or C is true. This flow suggests a game between two players. First we draw to see which player will start (test A); after each round we must determine whether the game will continue with the other player or end. We can devise a structured solution for this algorithm by introducing an auxiliary variable next, which can assume the values 1, 2 or 0 depending on whether it is player 1's or player 2's turn or whether the game ends.

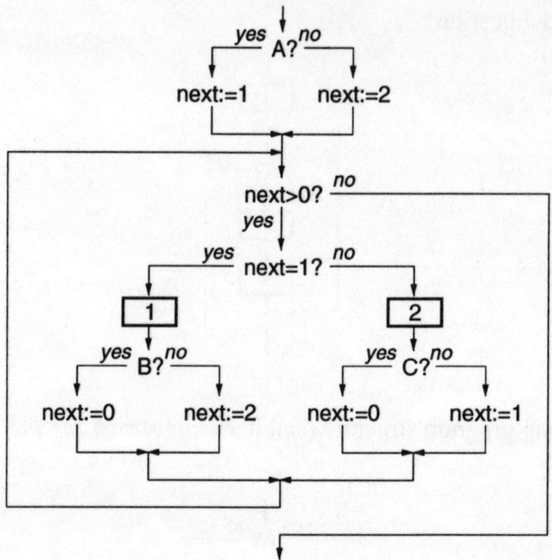


This structure corresponds to the repeat loop that we specified as an element of structured programming.

#### 3.5.2.2 Expressive power

The implementation of software systems encompasses the naming of objects and the description of actions that manipulate these objects. The *choice of names* becomes particularly important in writing algorithms.

Some sites have introduced such conventions as naming identifiers beginning with an acronym for the programming project or even with the initials of the programmer. Unfortunately, atrocious names like HPCJJSP (setpoint for project "Heat Pump Control", programmer Johnny Jones) are no rarity. Clearly such names encumber readability.

Hence we recommend vesting particular importance in the expressiveness of identifiers and abiding by the following rules:

- Choose expressive names, even at the price of long identifiers. The writing effort pays off each time the program must be read, particularly when it is to be corrected and extended long after its implementation. For local identifiers (where their declaration and use adjoin) shorter names suffice.
- If you use abbreviations, then use only ones that the reader of the program can understand without any explanation. Use abbreviations only in consistent context (avoid temp for temperature and temporary).
- Within a software system assign names in only one language (e.g., do not mix English and German).

- Use upper and lower case to distinguish different kinds of identifiers (e.g., uppercase first letter for data types, classes and modules; lower case for variables) and to make long names more readable (e.g., CheckInputValue).
- Use nouns for values, verbs for activities, and adjectives for conditions to make the meaning of identifiers clear (e.g., width, ReadKey and valid, respectively).
- Establish your own rules and follow them consistently.

Good programming style also finds expression in the use of comments; they contribute to the readability of a program and are thus important program components. Correct commenting of programs is not easy and requires experience, creativity and the ability to express the message concisely and precisely. We suggest the following rules for writing comments:

- Every system component (every module and every class) should begin with a detailed comment that gives the reader information about several general questions regarding the system component:
  - What does the component do?
  - How (in what context) is the component used?
  - Which specialized methods, etc. are used?
  - Who is the author?
  - When was the component written?
  - Which modifications have been made?
- Every procedure and method should be provided with a comment that describes its task (and possibly how it works). This applies particularly for the interface specifications.
- Explain the meaning of variables with a comment.
- Program components that are responsible for distinct subtasks should be labeled with comments.
- Statements that are difficult to understand (e.g., in tricky procedures or program components that exploit features of a specific computer) should be described in comments so that the reader can easily understand them.
- A software system should contain comments that are as few and as concise as possible, but as many adequately detailed comments as necessary.
- Ensure that program modifications not only affect declarations and statements but also are reflected in updated comments. Incorrect comments are worse than none at all!

These rules have deliberately been kept general because there are no rules that apply uniformly to all software systems and every application domain. Commenting software systems is an art, just like the design and implementation of software systems.

#### 3.5.2.3 Outward form

Beyond name selection and commenting, the readability of a software system also depends on its outward form. Hence we recommend the following rules for the outward form of programs:

- For every program component, the declarations (of data types, constants, variables, etc.) should be distinctly separated from the statement section.
- The declaration sections should have a uniform structure when possible, e.g., using the following sequence: constants, data types, variables, classes and modules, methods and procedures.
- The interface description (parameter lists for methods and procedures) should separate input, output and input/output parameters.
- Keep comments and source code distinctly separate.
- The program structure should be emphasized with indentation, for example:

```
...
REPEAT
   Read(char,eof);
   IF NOT eof THEN
      tl := tl + 1; text[tl] := char
   ELSE
      PrepareText(text, tl)
   END
UNTIL eof;
...
```

We have strived to apply these rules consistently throughout this book.

### 3.5.3 Incremental implementation

The consistent application of the prototyping-oriented approach to software development, as described in Sections 1.3 and 3.1.3, also affects the implementation phase. The development process becomes incremental. To discuss the effects on the implementation process, we again illustrate the individual activities of the software development process (Figure 3.48).

The upper part of Figure 3.48 depicts the phases of the development process corresponding to the life-cycle model, while the lower part of the Figure represents the approach and activities of the phases individually. The upper part of the illustration connects the individual phases with two kinds of arrows: the thin arrows symbolize the phase sequence and the thick arrows represent the cycles between the individual phases, a characteristic of the underlying model.

The basic idea of incremental implementation is to quasi merge the design and implementation phases rather than to uphold the strict separation of phases that the

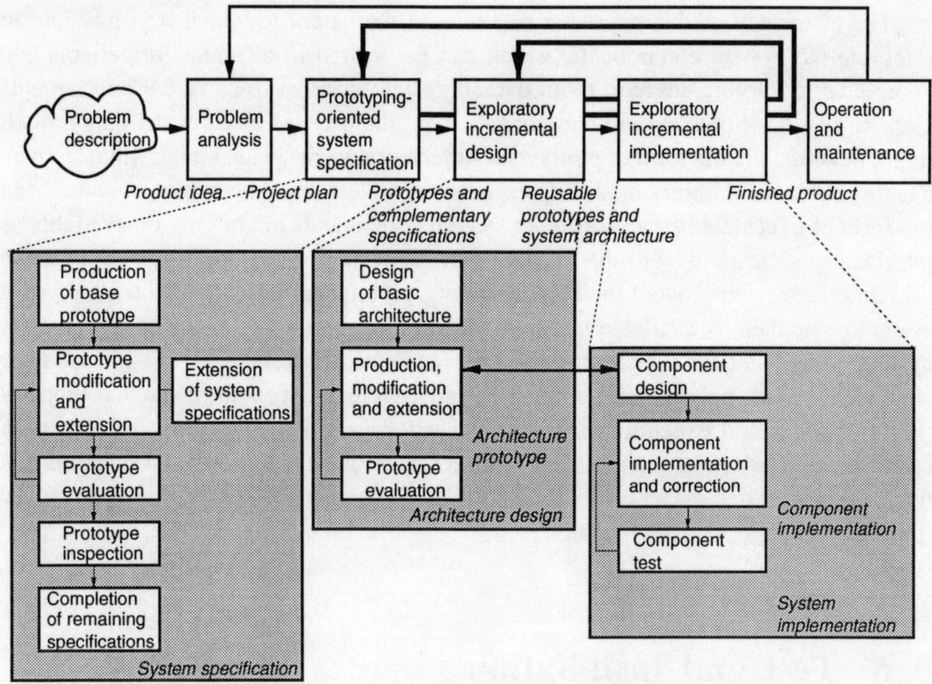


Figure 3.48: Prototyping-oriented incremental software development (compare [Bischofberger 1992])

classical sequential software life-cycle model requires. The recommendation of this approach is founded on the experience-based assumption that design and implementation decisions strongly affect one another, and thus a rigorous separation of design and implementation does not accomplish its goal. In many cases only the implementation can determine whether the decomposition structure of the design proves adequate for the problem.

Incremental implementation means that after each design step that is relevant to the architecture, the current system architecture is verified on the basis of real cases. This means that the interplay of the system components specified in the design (in the form of interface specifications) is verified. To make this possible, the system components (i.e., their input/output behavior) is simulated or realized as a prototype. Naturally the developer must devote thought to the implementation of individual components. The knowledge gained in the process, as far as possible, is translated directly into the implementation of the components, or documented for the subsequent implementation process. If there is any doubt concerning the feasibility of a component, then the design process is interrupted and these components are implemented. Only when their implementation and their embedding in the previous system architecture have been checked, is the design process continued, or the architecture is adapted according to the knowledge gained in the implementation of the component.

The efficiency of this approach depends on the extent to which it is possible to integrate the system components, which can be written in different formalisms and completed to varying degrees, to an overall system in order to carry out experiments close to reality. Some system components, e.g., the user interface or the data model, might be present in the form of prototypes; other components, which might stem from an existing component library or already exist as a complete implementation, are present in the form of executable code; still other system components might only be available as interface specifications. For the validation of the current system design, whenever the user interface is employed, the corresponding prototypes need to be activated. If a system component is available in compiled form, it needs to be executed directly. A system component for which only the interface specifications are available must be simulated. This is only possible with a software development environment that supports the integration and execution process for such *hybrid systems*. Describing such a development environment and its application scenarios would exceed the scope of this book. The interested reader can find both in [Bischofberger 1992].

## 3.6 Test and installation

The quality of a software product is influenced by the extent to which it fulfills the quality criteria *correctness* and *reliability* (see Chapter 2), i.e., the number of errors overall and the number of serious errors with respect to their consequences in the application of the software product. Every software product thus demands thorough testing.

The *goal of testing* is to detect as many errors as possible. By *error* we mean any deviation of the behavior of the software from that prescribed in the requirements definition. The *cause of an error* can reside in the specifications, in the design, or in the implementation; if the quality attribute robustness is fulfilled, then erroneous selection of input values cannot cause such an error. The quality-assurance measure *testing* accompanies the entire project. It involves the phases system specification, design, implementation and maintenance (testing modifications) and must also include testing the robustness of the system. We speak of a *test phase* in the software life cycle because we can only test the end product after completion of all preceding phases. However, in the following we discuss test activities distributed across all phases of the software life cycle.

*Debugging* is closely connected to testing. While testing is an activity that detects errors, debugging locates and corrects the *causes of errors*.

This section describes various test methods and discusses how testing and debugging should be carried out and documented. Finally, we prescribe measures necessary for the installation of a software product.

### 3.6.1 Test methods

Before we discuss various *test methods*, i.e., specify which activities are necessary for the systematic testing of a software system, we need to state what is to be tested: the *system specifications*, the *individual modules*, the *connections between modules*, the *integration of the modules* in the overall system, and the *acceptance* of the software product. First we describe what we mean by these tests and their associated goals; then we describe various test methods and strategies.

**Testing the system specifications**. The system specifications provide the foundation for the planning and execution of program tests. The comprehensibility and unambiguity of the system specifications is the prerequisite for testing a software system. The *goal of the specification test* is to examine the *completeness*, *clarity*, *consistency* and *feasibility of the system specifications*.

For the analysis of system specifications, Hughes and Michtom [Hughes 1976] suggest the technique of *cause and effect*. In this context *causes* are conditions or combinations of conditions that are prescribed or that have arisen; *effects* are results or activities. The specification test is intended to show whether causes (data, functions) are specified for which no effects (functions, results) are defined or vice versa. Prototypes of user interface and system components play an important role in testing the system specifications; they permit experimental inspection of the system specifications. The specifications test must always be carried out in cooperation with the user.

**Testing modules**. Modules encapsulate data structures and operations that work with these data structures. The *goal of the module test* is to identify all *deviations of the implementation from the module specifications*. Module testing requires first testing the individual functions and then their interplay. Generally modules are not independently executable programs; their execution requires the existence of other modules (due to the networking of modules through import and inheritance relationships). The test can only be executed if the *environment* of the module already exists or can be simulated. Part of the work in module testing consists of creating a suitable *test environment* that permits invocation of the module, examination of the results of its invocation, and simulation of modules yet to be developed (see Figure 3.49). Here the problem is keeping the test environment as simple as possible, for increasing complexity also raises the probability that the environment itself contains errors.

**Testing module connections**. The step following the module test is the *testing of subsystems*. A *subsystem* comprises a problem-specific collection of individual (tested) modules. The *goal* is to test the *connections between the individual modules* of a subsystem. The test encompasses checking the correctness of module communication and hardly differs in its approach from module testing. Subsystems also require the creation of test environments. After testing subsystems, several subsystems are combined to a (hierarchically superordinate) subsystem, and the connections between these subsystems are tested. This form of hierarchical test is also an *integration test*.

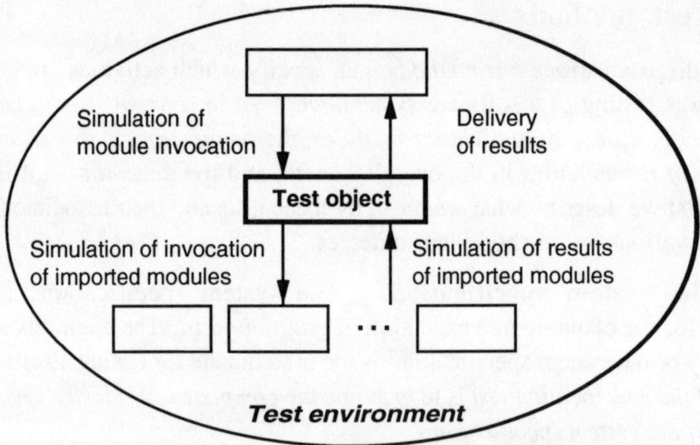


Figure 3.49: Test object and test environment

**Test of the overall system**. Here we test the *integration of all subsystems*. The goal is to detect all deviations of the system behavior from that in the requirements definition. Here the goal is not only to test the completeness of the user requirements and the correctness of the results, but also to test whether the software system is reliable and robust with respect to erroneous input data. The system's adherence to nonfunctional requirements (see Section 3.3.1), e.g., the required efficiency, must also be tested. The scope and number of tests as well as the *selection of appropriate test data* vary from case to case; the present state of the art offers no universal recipe for testing software systems. The effort vested in testing of the overall system must be in some proportion to the amount of damage that erroneous operation of the software systems can inflict.

**Acceptance test**. The development of a software product ends with the *inspection (acceptance test)* by the user. At inspection the software system is tested with *real data* under *real conditions of use*. The goal of the inspection is to uncover all errors that arose from such sources as misunderstandings in consultations between users and software developers, poor estimates of application-specific data quantities, and unrealistic assumptions about the real environment of the software system. Only this test unveils whether the actual application agrees with the requirements definition and whether the system behavior meets the user's expectations. Particularly the correct design of the interface between a software system and its users creates extreme difficulties for a software engineer – usually due to a lack of experience in the specialized application domain. The user friendliness (or hostility) of a software product is proven here. Thus user testing with real application cases is imperative. With prototyping-oriented software development, the user inspection begins during the specification phase.

In the following we describe various methods that support the above testing activities.

#### 3.6.1.1 Verification of algorithms

In designing a software system, the software engineer constantly confronts the questions of whether the chosen approach will actually lead to the required solution and whether the already developed components are correct, i.e., whether they fulfill the specifications. Ideally we would like to be able to prove at any time that for every imaginable input the algorithms included in the design and their interplay will deliver the expected results according to the specifications. Since today's large software systems permit the complete description of neither the input set nor the anticipated result set (due to combinatorial explosion), such systems can no longer be completely tested. Thus efforts must be made to achieve as much clarity as possible already in the design phase about the correctness of the solution.

It is clear that such proof of correctness cannot be handled without formal and mathematical tools. Mathematically oriented *verification techniques* are described in the works of McCarthy [McCarthy 1962], Naur [Naur 1966], Floyd [Floyd 1967], Hoare [Hoare 1969], Manna [Manna 1969], Knuth [Knuth 1973] and Dijkstra [Dijkstra 1976]. An overview of various methods for algorithm verification can be found in [Elspas 1972].

The use of a verification procedure forces the software engineer to reproduce all design decisions and thus also helps in finding logical errors. Here the aspect of the actual comprehension of an algorithm is at least as important as the proof of its correctness. *Verification* is an extremely useful technique for early detection of design errors and also complements the design documentation. Verification itself can be fallible, however; it cannot replace testing of a software product. The larger a software system is, the more difficult it becomes to carry out a complete verification.

Verification can be used successfully to prove the correctness of short and simple algorithms. For the production of larger software systems, the difficulties rise so sharply that it should be clear that verification fails as a practical test aid. Because software engineering primarily involves the production of *larger* software systems, this book does not present a detailed account of verification techniques.

#### 3.6.1.2 Static program analysis

*Static program analysis* seeks to detect errors without direct execution of the test object. The activities involved in static testing concern *syntactic*, *structural* and *semantic analysis of the test object* (compare [Ramamoorthy 1974] and [Schmitz 1982]). The goal is to localize, as early as possible, error-prone parts of the test object.

The most important activities of static program analysis are:

- Code inspection
- Complexity analysis
- Structural analysis
- Data-flow analysis

A useful technique for localizing design and implementation errors is *code inspection*. Many errors prove easy to find if the author would only read the program carefully enough. Unfortunately, however, the individual often lacks the motivation.

The idea behind code inspection is to have the author of a program discuss it step by step with other software engineers. Fagan [Fagan 1976] recommends a team of the following four persons:

(1) An experienced software engineer who is not involved in the project to serve as moderator
(2) The designer of the test object
(3) The programmer responsible for the implementation
(4) The person responsible for testing

The moderator notes every detected error and the inspection continues. The *task of the inspection team* is to *detect, not to correct,* errors. Only on completion of the inspection do the designer and the implementor begin their correction work.

The goal of *complexity analysis* is to establish metrics for the complexity of a program. These metrics include complexity measures for modules (e.g., according to McCabe [McCabe 1976] or Halstead [Halstead 1972]), nesting depths for loops, lengths of procedures and modules, import and use frequencies for modules, and the complexity of interfaces for procedures and methods [Blaschek 1985]. The results of complexity analysis permit statements about the quality of a software product (within certain limits) and localization of error-prone positions in the software system. However, complexity is difficult to evaluate objectively; a program that a programmer perceives as simple might be viewed as complex by someone else. Therefore, as the meaningfulness of complexity metrics is disputed, we refrain from detailed treatment and refer the interested reader to the cited literature.

The goal of *structural analysis* is to uncover structural anomalies of a test object. For example, structural analysis provides information about whether all statements of a program can be reached from the beginning of a program, whether the end of the program can be reached from all statements, whether a program contains loops with jumps, and whether the control flow contains impermissible structures.

*Data-flow analysis* is intended to help discover data-flow anomalies. It provides information about whether a data object has a value before its use and whether a data object is used after an assignment. Data-flow analysis applies to both the body of a test object and the interfaces between test objects.

#### 3.6.1.3 Dynamic testing

For *dynamic testing* the test objects are executed or simulated. The activities for dynamic testing include:

- Preparation of the test object for error localization

- Availability of a test environment
- Selection of appropriate test cases and data
- Test execution and evaluation

Dynamic testing is an imperative process in the software life cycle. Every procedure, every module and class, every subsystem and the overall system must be tested dynamically, even if static tests and program verifications have been carried out. Thus we handle the above activities of dynamic testing in Section 3.6.2 (test execution) in detail.

#### 3.6.1.4 Black-box and white-box tests

Every test object can be tested in two principal ways to determine whether it fulfills its specifications:

(1) Test of the input/output behavior without considering the inner structure of the test object (interface test)
(2) Test of the input/output behavior considering the inner structures (interface and structure test)

The first test method is called the *black-box test, functional test* or *exterior test*; the second method is called *white-box test, structure test* or *interior test.*

*Black-box tests* serve to detect deviations of a test object from its specifications. The selection of test cases is based on the specifications of the test object without knowledge of its inner structure. It is also important to design test cases that demonstrate the behavior of the test object on erroneous input data.

The black-box test provides no information about whether all functions of the test object are actually necessary or whether data objects are manipulated that have no effect on the input/output behavior of the test object. Such indicators of design and implementation errors emanate from the white-box test.

In the *white-box test* the test activities involve not only checking the input/output behavior, but also examination of the inner structure of the test object. The goal is to determine, for every possible path through the test object, the behavior of the test object in relation to the input data. For this method, test cases are selected on the basis of knowledge of the control flow structure of the test object. The selection of test cases must consider the following:

- Every module and function of the test object must be invoked at least once.
- Every branch must be taken at least once.
- As many paths as possible must be followed.

It is important to assure that every branch is actually taken. It does not suffice to merely assure that every statement is executed because, as the following example demonstrates, errors in binary branches might not be found because not all branches were tested.

The statement sequence:

```
IF condition THEN
    action1
END;
action2
```

should read:

```
IF condition THEN
    action1
    action2
END
```

This error would not be detected if only the execution of all statements were tested and only one test case with condition = TRUE were executed.

It is important to consider that, even for well-structured programs, in practice it remains impossible to test all possible paths, i.e., all possible statement sequences of a program. The example of a simple program structure from Pressman [Pressman 1987] depicted in Figure 3.50 shows this clearly. With automatic test data generation it is likewise impossible to test all paths because the number of test runs would be much too high.

Nevertheless, the white-box test is one of the most important test methods. For a limited number of program paths, which usually suffices in practice, the test permits correct manipulation of the data structures and examination of the input/output behavior of test objects.

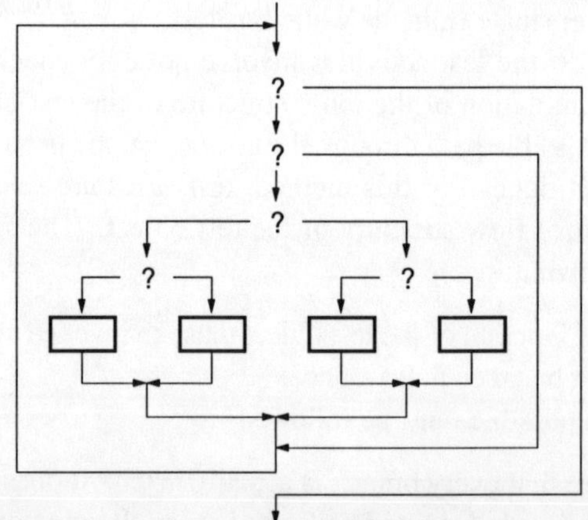


Figure 3.50: Control flow graph; for 10 iterations there are almost one million paths

#### 3.6.1.5 Top-down and bottom-up testing

The test methods discussed so far primarily involve module tests. We still need a strategy for testing complete software systems. While program design is usually approached top-down (i.e., outside-in), testing usually is the opposite. First the elementary components, the foundation of a software system, are tested and only then their integration. This approach is called bottom-up testing. However, following the principle of stepwise refinement, we can reverse the normal testing direction and test a software system progressively from the outside toward the inside. This is called top-down testing. Both methods have advantages and drawbacks and both are employed in practice.

For the *top-down test* the control module is implemented and tested first. Here imported modules are represented by surrogate modules. Surrogates have the same interfaces as the imported modules and simulate their input/output behavior. After the test of the control module, all other modules of the software systems are tested in the same way; i.e., their operations are represented by surrogate procedures until the development has progressed enough to allow implementation and testing of the operations. The test advances stepwise with the implementation. Implementation and test phases merge, and the integration test of subsystems becomes superfluous.

Applying this strategy has many advantages. Design errors are detected as early as possible, saving development time and costs because corrections in the module design can be made before their implementation. The characteristics of a software system are evident from the start, which enables a simple test of the development state and the acceptance by the user. The software system can be tested thoroughly from the start with real test cases without providing (expensive) test environments.

All this sounds very convincing and promises a panacea. However, practice has shown that this method also has serious *drawbacks*. Strict top-down testing proves extremely difficult because designing usable surrogate objects can prove very complicated, especially for complex operations. However, the simpler surrogate objects are kept, the less test cases can be simulated. Errors in lower hierarchy levels are hard to localize, yet they can affect the design of the overall system. Furthermore, in complex systems the user-relevant results are seldom output by the upper hierarchy levels of the software systems, but by the lower levels. The same applies to the control of human/machine dialogs because the operations can be distributed over the entire hierarchy. It is difficult to provide usable surrogate operations that are still easy to implement. Errors are hard to localize because many modules are involved from the start. Further drawbacks are that the entire software system must be loaded to test the lower levels and that appropriate test cases are hard to design.

The consistent application of the prototyping-oriented approach to software development, as previous sections have described, can largely eliminate the above difficulties because the test takes place before or at least along with the implementation. Errors are detected earlier and are easier to correct. Prototyping-oriented testing in combination with adequate tools to support the prototyping process (see Chapter 6) enables a top-down testing strategy. The approach has already been described in Section 3.5.3, "Incremental Implementation".

*Bottom-up testing* inverts the top-down approach. First those operations are tested that require no other program components; then their integration to a module is tested. After the module test the integration of multiple (tested) modules to a subsystem is tested, until finally the integration of the subsystems, i.e., the overall system, can be tested.

The advantages of bottom-up testing prove to be the drawbacks of top-down testing (and vice versa). The bottom-up test method is solid and proven. The objects to be tested are known in full detail. It is often simpler to define relevant test cases and test data. The bottom-up approach (assuming no prototyping-oriented incremental development strategy) is psychologically more satisfying because the tester can be certain that the foundations for the test objects have been tested in full detail.

The *drawbacks* of bottom-up testing are that the characteristics of the finished product are only known after the completion of all implementation and testing, which means that design errors in the upper levels are detected very late. This can have detrimental consequences because their correction induces modifications in lower levels and thus can require the repetition of all previous tests. Testing individual levels also inflicts high costs for providing a suitable test environment.

## 3.6.2 Test planning and execution

The selected test strategy can already influence the system design; this necessitates initiating rough test planning as early as possible – preferably in the system specification phase. *Test execution* requires careful preparation of *test objects and test cases*.

The test objects in the lower levels of software systems (modules or classes) should be tested by the implementors themselves; the integration of test objects, on the other hand, by other staff not directly involved in the implementation of the test objects. In the following we describe the most important activities involved in test planning and test execution.

### 3.6.2.1 Test planning

The purpose of *test planning* is to establish the tasks, goals and strategies for test execution. Test planning specifies the following:

- Test methods
- Test documentation
- Test objects and their quality requirements
- Test criteria to be fulfilled (number of test cases, percent of program paths to be tested, etc.)
- Type of inspection for individual test objects

- Test personnel
- Testing tools to be used

The test schedule provides the foundation for quality assurance and is a prerequisite for monitoring and controlling test execution on the part of the project leader. Thus the time spent in creating a highly detailed test schedule is well invested.

#### 3.6.2.2 Preparation of test objects for error localization

The execution *of a test object* should expose errors that were not detected during static tests. However, *error detection* generally does not encompass *debugging*, and *error diagnosis* can be an arduous process. The *preparation of test objects for error localization* is thus an important measure for rational production of software products. Although we cannot offer a universal recipe, we do present some useful methods.

The simplest and most natural approach is to follow the execution of a test object and to monitor its states (i.e., the values of important variables) at certain points. Modern programming environments provide tools to support both activities. In lieu of such tools, we recommend inserting switchable statements in the test object to follow the program's control flow and to monitor its state.

To *follow program execution*, it helps to protocol jumps to labels, cycles through loops, and the execution of certain statements. To *follow program states*, it must be possible at certain locations in the test object to output the values of important state variables and, e.g., the minimum and maximum values that a given variable assumes during the execution. To *monitor program states* means to employ indicators of whether a variable value goes above or below a set limit or whether index overruns and violations of conditions (assertions) occur that must be fulfilled at certain points in the test object.

#### 3.6.2.3 Selection of test cases and test data

We have already indicated that *exhaustive testing* is usually impossible, even for simple test objects. The number of combinations of input data (test cases) is so large even for simple test objects (compare Section 3.6.1.4) that such tests cannot be realized. The right selection of test cases to localize as many errors as possible with the available resources, time and budget thus requires a great deal of experience and intuition of the testers.

It is important to distinguish the terms *test data* and *test case*. Test data are the input data with which a certain test object is to be tested. The description of a test case consists of the specification of the test object and the functions to be tested, the specification of input values (test data), and the exact description of the results anticipated for these test data.

The selection of test cases for software product testing is a creative process. No all-purpose method can be prescribed. The reader can find useful tips in [Ostrand 1988]. Furthermore, in the following we provide the most important criteria for test case selection.

**Testing program components**. *Program components* (modules, functions) must be subjected to a structure test (compare 3.6.1.4). Here it does not suffice to design test cases that assure that every statement is executed at least once, as the following example from Kimm et al. [Kimm 1979] demonstrates.

In a program fragment to compute the maximum of three numbers:

```
IF x>=y THEN max := x ELSE max := y END;
IF z>=max THEN max := z ELSE max := y END;
```

with input data of this kind:

```
z>=x>=y and y>x and y>z
```

all statements are executed once and correct results are returned. The testing does not detect that input cases where *x* is the maximum cause an error.

The weakest criterion that should be fulfilled in the selection of test cases is that every program branch executes at least once. Yet even this does not suffice, as the above example demonstrates.

The test cases for a test object need to be selected in such a way that the following hold:

- The specifications must be fulfilled for all functional units and their interface behavior.
- All branches of the functional unit are executed.
- The smallest and largest values for all input data are considered (limits test).
- Every loop is tested with minimum and maximum loop condition values.
- All error outputs of the test object are tested.
- The reaction of the test object to arbitrary input data is tested (stress test, random test).

**Testing the integration of program components.** In testing the *integration of program components* the testers can assume that all the components have been tested, i.e., that all components are correct. The selection of test cases does not differ significantly from that of program components. Each program component is treated like a statement. The (sub)system to be tested is viewed as a collection of black boxes, and the test cases need to be selected such that the operations of all components are executed at least once. For the sake of comprehensibility, it pays to depict the relationships between test cases and the affected operations and program components in a table (Figure 3.51).

However, it does not suffice to design only enough test cases to execute all operations, especially if multiple operations work with the same data set. Then it becomes necessary to design test cases that test a combination of functions.

The goal of test case selection is the determination of input data combinations that are suitable for exposing as many errors of a test object as possible. Since absolute reliability of test case selection is practically unachievable, the quality of the test data has decisive importance.

Test case selection requires both *task-oriented criteria* (which depend on the specifications of the test object, but require no knowledge of the source code) and *structure-oriented criteria* (which require knowledge of the source code). The test cases should be very typical data sets, yet represent highly differentiated application cases. Before the execution of a test case, the anticipated results should be noted to avoid "proofreader fatigue", where the tester tends to mistake wrong results for correct ones. It is best to have a tool that compares expected results with actual ones. If a test case detects errors and corrections are made, all tests already completed need to be repeated. For this purpose all test cases need to be carefully archived. An extensive treatment of the test cases that are relevant in a particular context can be found in [Myers 1979].

### 3.6.2.4 Availability of a test environment

The dynamic testing of modules or subsystems requires the availability of a *test environment* to simulate the real application conditions for a test object. The test environment (see Figure 3.49) must contain all resources necessary to cover the following:

- (Repeated) execution of the test object
- Availability of input data (data to be read)
- Simulation of necessary but not yet available external resources (e.g., imported modules, operating system components, etc.) and their results (e.g., computed values, interrupts, processes, etc.)
- Display or output of results of a test execution

The test environment should be kept as simple as possible in order to avoid being a source of errors itself. However, it must enable the execution of a sufficient number of different tests.

| | Module 1 | | | | Module 2 | | | |
|---|---|---|---|---|---|---|---|---|
| Function | 1 | 2 | 3 | 4 | 5 | 6 | 7 | 8 |
| Test case 1 | X | X | | | | | | |
| 2 | | | X | | | | | |
| 3 | | | | | X | | X | |
| 4 | | | | X | | | | X |

Figure 3.51: Test case matrix

### 3.6.2.5 Test evaluation and diagnosis

After test execution, the test case descriptions help to determine whether the results of the test run agree with the anticipated results and whether all the functions in the test case description were actually executed. For an error detected during testing, there is still no indication of its source.

The next task is *error diagnosis*, or locating the cause of the error. The simplest approach is to follow the execution of a test object. Here we can use the aids for following program execution and monitoring its states in Section 3.6.2.2 and attempt to narrow down the error. Debugging is significantly easier if the test object has a modular structure with unambiguously defined interfaces. Then in many cases it suffices to observe the data at the interfaces and to isolate the erroneous program component. Within the erroneous module we then proceed to localize the error with control flow and state monitoring at a finer level.

Once an error has been localized and its cause diagnosed, there are often many ways to correct it. Before deciding on a particular option, consideration must be given to the effects the correction will have on other components of the test object. Here it helps to study not only the implementation of the test object but, above all, the more abstract design. *Error correction* demands particular care because it can introduce new (perhaps nastier) errors. The probability that a correction succeeds on first try is under 50% [Wolverton 1972]. After every error correction the test case that revealed the corrected error as well as all other test cases to which the test object was already subjected must be repeated.

In the absence of tools for following program control flow and for monitoring states, statements inserted to help in debugging should not be removed. It should be possible to reactivate them at any time.

### 3.6.2.6 Typical errors

Practice shows that certain errors occur repeatedly. Knowing these error sources can facilitate the localization and correction of errors. The following are examples of such errors:

- Failure to consider special cases (e.g., division by zero)
- Failure to handle limits
- Array index overflow
- Iterative loops that do not terminate
- Failure to initialize variables
- Erroneous logical expressions (especially in combination with a negation operator) in conditions
- Lack of agreement of number and type of parameters in formal and actual parameter lists (in languages with strict type checking and separate compilation, the compiler detects this error)
- Misuse of common data (data encapsulation avoids this error)

### 3.6.3 Test documentation

*Test documentation* is very important for the economical execution of the test phase, for quality control, and for the maintenance phase. For software production with division of labor, it also provides the basis for communications among the personnel involved in the testing. Test documentation should contain the following:

- Test plan
- Specifications of test cases
- Information on test environments used
- Test results of individual test runs
- Number and kind of detected errors
- Description of measures for error correction
- Information on the number of required test runs for each test object

Unfortunately the necessity of detailed test documentation still receives too little recognition in practice. This necessity ensues from the requirement to repeat all preceding test runs on a test object after a correction. This also applies for modifications in the maintenance phase. The test documentation should also provide material for statistics to improve planning of future projects.

### 3.6.4 Acceptance test and installation

The purpose of the acceptance test is to show the client that the now complete software product fulfills the requirements recorded in the requirements definition. Thus before the software's release for installation, an inspection must be carried out.

During inspection the behavior of the product is tested from the viewpoint of the user under real environmental conditions. The foundation for the selection of test cases is exclusively *acceptance criteria* specified in the requirements definition (and not the source code). Test case selection for the acceptance test is a difficult task and should be handled by the user; the user alone has authentic conceptions of the application domain. The inspection also includes testing the user documentation (see Section 3.7.1.1). If the client determines differences between user instructions specified in the user documentation and the operation required by the software product, this can require a change in the implementation. The inspection should also be protocoled in the test documentation.

On completion of the acceptance test comes the actual installation of the software product. In many application cases more or less large external data sets are manipulated. If the software product to be installed accesses such data sets (e.g., master data), then the respective files need to be initialized before installation (if this was not done before the acceptance test). This *initialization of files* (e.g., collection of master data) can be very work-intensive and can require the implementation of extensive data collection and checking programs. The development of these programs must be planned, executed and documented just as carefully as for the functional components of the software product, even if they are only needed at the time of installation.

After the installation the user should carry out a *performance test*. The goal of the performance test is to test the *nonfunctional requirements* (e.g., capacity utilization, response times for dialog systems, etc.) and the *stability (reliability)* of the software product, i.e., its behavior over a longer period of time.

# 3.7 Documentation and maintenance

As a rule, software products are not used by their developers, but by persons who neither were involved in the implementation nor have any knowledge in the area of software engineering. Software products also frequently need to be corrected during operation, adapted to changed environmental conditions or extended (collectively termed the *maintenance* of software products). The maintenance activity is likewise carried out by persons who were not involved in the development. Thus, as with other industrial products, the operation and maintenance of software products requires detailed *documentation*.

Practitioners often fail to recognize the importance of documentation, and many programmers see documentation work merely as a necessary evil that they try to avoid. However, if we consider the fact that today more than half of the costs of operating software products are incurred for maintenance work and that software maintenance costs are steadily rising (see Figures 3.52 and 3.53), then we must conclude that that we should strive to reduce the maintenance component of the costs of the software life cycle. This means increasing the modifiability and extensibility as well as the correctness and reliability of software. Documentation plays an important role here.

The examination of aspects regarding the documentation and maintenance of software products is thus an important element of software engineering.

The first of two parts of this section describes the content, the structure and the creation of the documentation of software products, and the second part describes aspects of maintenance.

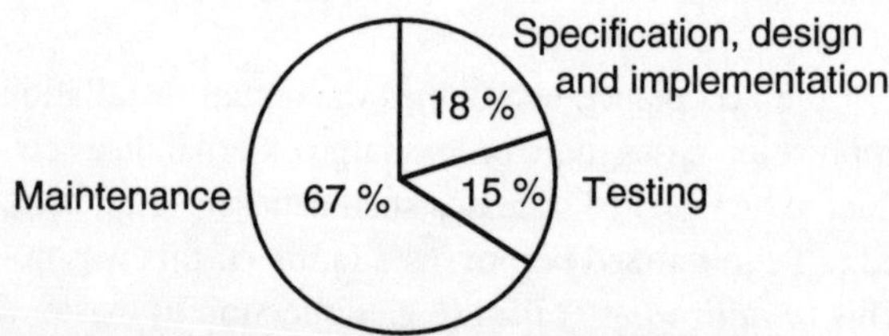


Figure 3.52: Relative costs of the phases of the software life cycle [Arthur 1988]

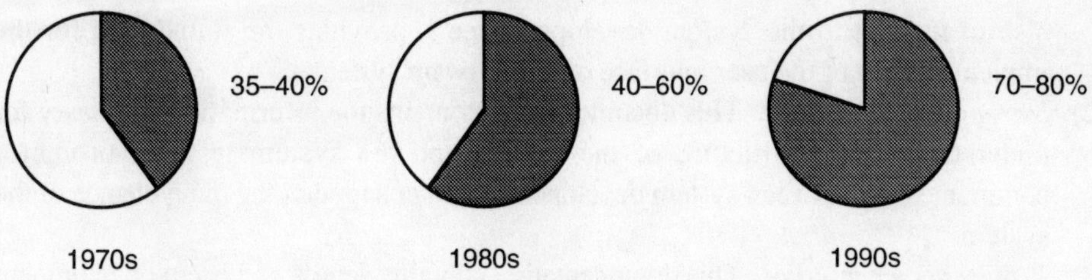


Figure 3.53: Share of maintenance in development costs [Pressman 1987]

### 3.7.1 The documentation of software products

During the development phases, *documentation* should enable communication among the persons involved in the development. After completion of the development phase it should support the use and the maintenance of the software product. In addition, documentation should record the project history for the purpose of calculating production costs and for improved planning of future projects.

The documentation should provide information about the following:

- The purpose and special characteristics of a software system
- Measures required for installation
- How to use the software system to solve its tasks
- How the software system was implemented and tested
- The organization of the production process and the development team, including difficulties that arose and costs that were incurred

The *readers* of documentation fall into three categories:

(1) *Users* of the software products and *interested parties*
(2) *Developers* of software products and *maintenance personnel* involved in modifications and extensions of the system
(3) *Managers* of software projects

In order to cover the differing informational needs of these three groups, the documentation should be divided into three sections corresponding to the respective readership. Care should be taken to include in each document only information relevant to its intended readership and to consistently omit everything else. The reader should not be bothered with information that does not relate to his tasks. Documentation should be *easy to read; it* should contain *as little information as possible*, yet *as much information as necessary*. Based on the three groups of readers, we distinguish the following kinds of documentation of software products:

(1) *User documentation.* This documentation contains all information for anyone who wants to get acquainted with the software system and for the user. It is naturally

also of interest to the system developer since it provides the foundation for the implementation of the user interface of the software system.

(2) *System documentation.* This documentation contains the information necessary for understanding the structure of the system and the system test. It promotes communication between system developers and later supports the maintenance of the system.

(3) *Project documentation.* This documentation contains details of system development from an organizational and financial viewpoint (project schedule and organization, logbook, costs of personnel, material and time, etc.). It helps to check the progress of the project and to compute project costs, and it provides information for future projects.

The following sections describe the content and structure of these three kinds of documents.

#### 3.7.1.1 User documentation

The *user documentation* must ensure the usability of the software product without the need for additional information. This document first generally describes the features of the software product and then offers everything that the user needs to know to use the software. This includes the following:

(1) General system description

The *general system description* covers the system's features, what it can and cannot do. This description should not include details. Its goal is to inform the reader about the purpose of the software system, its strengths and weaknesses, and the prerequisites for its operation. In particular, this document should contain information about the following:

- The purpose of the software system
- Necessary hardware and software resources
- How user/system interaction works
- The form of results
- Organizational and informational prerequisites
- Restrictions related to its implementation
- The flexibility and portability of the software system

(2) Installation and user instructions

The *installation and user's guide* should contain everything that the user needs to know in order to use the software system. The software system should be described as a black box and explanations should be limited to the user interface. This section contains the following:

- Prerequisites and instructions for the installation of the software system (e.g., required files, technical resources) and its embedding in the respective operating system
- A complete and easily comprehensible description of all system functions and the user actions they require
- Typical application examples for all system functions
- Specifications and explanations of the input data
- Presentation and explanation of results, preferably using examples
- Composition of error messages, references to error sources, and measures to correct errors

The user's guide should be divided into two sections. The first part provides an overview and should be written for sequential reading. The second part serves as a reference and should describe typical work with the software and the necessary system functions and user actions. This reference manual must therefore be organized to allow selective reading; the structure must support the rapid finding of any needed information. In addition, a reference card should present the most important information in concise form.

(3) Operator instructions (if necessary)
For software products that run on a host computer that is monitored by an operator, the user documentation must also contain operator instructions. The operator instructions describe all messages that the documented software system sends to the operator station, what triggers the message, and what reaction is expected of the operator.

The documentation is a particularly important component of a software product. The user friendliness of a software product derives not only from the design of the user interfaces, but also significantly from the content, structure and form of user documentation.

The user documentation should be formulated *concisely* and *precisely*, but *with redundancy*. It should be structured so that the reader is not forced to read the entire document in order to learn how to use the simplest functions. The structure of the documentation should allow the user to advance from the general to the specific and thus to slowly assimilate all the details that the system offers.

For software systems that support multiple groups of users with different user interfaces, it makes sense to produce separate user documentation for each group or to at least divide the document into self-contained sections that provide each user group with the necessary information (but no superfluous information relevant only to other groups).

The user documentation is a *reference book* and thus should contain an extensive table of contents and index.

Particular importance is vested in the *readability* of the user documentation – the user must be able to understand it. Therefore careful consideration must be given to appropriate language. Many users are not accustomed to reading strictly formal specifications. Hence it does not make sense, for example, to describe the syntax of an input language as a grammar in Backus-Naur form. If formalisms are needed for precise definition, then we must assume that these are unfamiliar to the user and need to provide detailed explanation before using them. The same applies for the use of domain-specific terms and graphic symbols from the area of software engineering; likewise they are not generally familiar and require explanation.

One important criterion for the quality and acceptance of the documentation is the *style* in which it is written. Although stylistic brilliance is a talent reserved for but a few, everyone is assumed to be capable of following simple rules of style. *Sommerville* [Sommerville 1985] suggests the following style rules:

(1) Use active rather than passive tenses.
(2) Do not use long sentences that present several different facts. It is much better to use a number of shorter sentences.
(3) Do not refer to information by reference number alone. Instead, give the reference number and remind the reader what the reference covered.
(4) Itemize facts wherever possible. It is usually clearer to present facts in a list rather than in a sentence.
(5) If a description is very complex, repeat yourself. It is often a good idea to present two or more differently phrased descriptions of the same thing.
(6) Don't be verbose. If you can say something in five words, do so, rather than use ten words to try to make the description seem more profound. There is no merit to quantity of documentation – quality is much more important.
(7) Be precise and define all terms you use. Computer terminology is very fluid and many terms have more than one meaning. Therefore if such terms (e.g., module, process) are used, make sure that your definition is clear.
(8) Keep paragraphs short As a general rule, a paragraph should contain not more than seven sentences. Our capacity for holding immediate information is limited, so by keeping paragraphs short all of the concepts of the paragraph can be maintained in short-term memory.
(9) Make use of headings and subheadings. Always ensure that a consistent numbering system is used for these.
(10) Use grammatically correct constructions and spell words correctly.

Ideally, user documentation should be accessible both in paper form and electronically as a component of the software product. User-driven selection of information is of great importance because usually the user has a general mastery of the system, but needs help with certain details (e.g., to execute seldom used system functions).

Information selection can best be supported by providing an extensive and well-planned index for the user documentation and an online help function. Whenever needed, the user should be able to call up information, e.g., for user interface elements

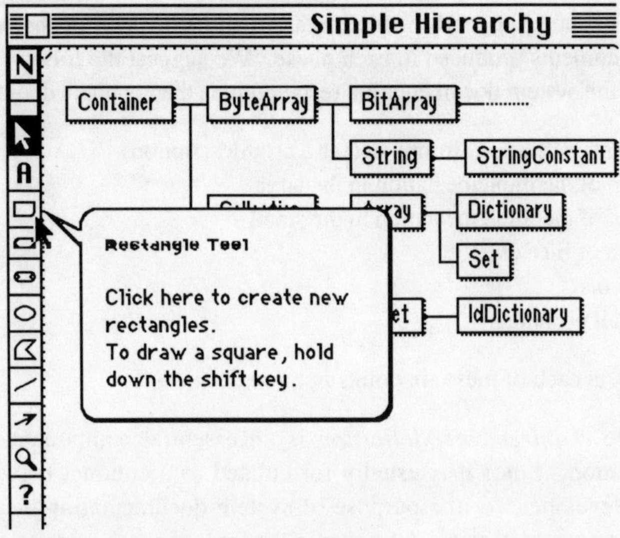


Figure 3.54: Online help function in a drawing program

such as function buttons and data elements (see Figure 3.54), on the screen. The preparation and formulation of such information is a time-intensive process that must be incorporated into the planning of a software project.

Modern user interfaces replace parts of the user documentation or significantly reduce its scope. The following properties of a program permit a reduction of the operating instructions:

- *Use of graphic symbols*
  The expressiveness of symbols is normally higher than that of verbal specifications.
- *Consistency of the user interface*
  If similar functions can be invoked in a similar way, they only need to be documented once.
- *Online help*
  If parts of the user's manual are directly integrated into a program, then a reference in the user's manual to the online help function suffices.
- *Undo functionality*
  If the user has the possibility to undo an executed action, then the description of the error behavior can be kept short.

#### 3.7.1.2 System documentation

The *system documentation* describes all details of the structure of a software system, the structure of its components, and the test activities. It should contain all information necessary for understanding the implementation, for communication between system developers, for debugging, and for modification and extension of the system. Thus it contains all documents produced in each phase. We suggest the following structure for the contents of the system documentation (each point is then explained in the sequel):

(1) Requirements definition (formulated as a task description)
(2) Description of the implementation in the large
(3) Description of the implementation in the small
(4) Description of files used
(5) Test protocols
(6) Listing of all programs

Now let us look at each of these six points in more detail:

(1) Clearly the *requirements definition* is an essential component of the system documentation. Since it is usually formulated as a contract between client and software developer, for the purpose of system documentation it makes sense to reformulate the requirements definition in the form of a task description.

For prototyping-oriented software development the requirements definition also includes all prototypes that were developed and any complementary specifications, especially if reusable prototypes are employed. With reusable prototypes, modification and extension activities must be undertaken at the prototype level, and the storage and documentation of these prototypes is important for maintenance (the primary purpose of this documentation).

(2) The *description of the implementation in the large* should describe the conception and fundamental structure of the software system and, as necessary, of its components in such a way that a software engineer can understand them. This description reflects how the overall solution emanates from the subsolutions of the chosen decomposition, which components were used to solve the problem, and their interface definitions. If the system design evolves with strict object-orientation or according to the principle of stepwise refinement and the individual design steps are commented accordingly, then this document emerges almost automatically during the design phase. It is important to document *not just the results*, but also the *genesis*, and to provide comments on particular difficulties that arose or that might arise during future modifications. This document must be neither too general nor too detailed. The reader must be able to infer from it the consequences of any modification of any system component.

For object-oriented software construction, this part of the system documentation contains in particular specifications of the utilized application framework or class library (see Section 4.7). Since the structure changes during the course of the software life cycle, it makes sense to provide this information by means of tools – class and structure browsers (see Chapter 6 “Software engineering tools”) that enable inspection of the source code and the associated documents – rather than as a document in paper form. This is the only way to ensure that this part of the system documentation is kept current.

(3) The *description of the implementation in the small* is generally easy to produce. It contains the descriptions of all components, preferably according to some uniform schema. If the implementation language separates interface and implementation descriptions (e.g., Modula-2), and if the conventions for commenting programs given in 3.5.2 are upheld, then part of this description of the implementation in the small is already available. The advantages here are that the description in the small is always current, maintenance of the documents presents no obstacles, and the scope of the documentation is small. For older programming languages that lack a class or module concept, offer no separation of interface and implementation, afford no means to formulate abstract data types, and offer no explicit description of import and export interfaces, the program listing does not suffice as documentation. Here we suggest the following documentation schema: Every module description consists of a descriptive header and a description body of the following form:

---

| | |
|---|---|
| *Name:* | name of the module |
| *Keyword:* | brief designation of the tasks of the module |
| *Import interface:* | specification of name, type and meaning of all imported operations and which module they belong to |
| *Export interface:* | specification of name, type and meaning of all exported operations |
| *Invocations:* | invocation instructions for all exported procedures with parameters and parameter types, including designation of input, output and input/output parameters |

---

*Tasks:*
This is a brief description of the tasks of the module.

*Abstract data structures*
If the module represents an implementation of a data capsule, we provide a description of the abstract data structures. Here we describe the characteristics of the data structure from the viewpoint of the module user and give no specifications about the concrete implementation.

*Exported procedures and internal procedures*
Here we describe the effects of the procedures of the module. If the procedure depends on its environment, we first describe the initial state. Then comes the description of the algorithm in a form appropriate to the complexity of the procedure. Then, if necessary, follows the description of the final state, i.e., of the state of the

environment after execution of the procedure. The procedure description must also contain all specifications relevant for the user concerning behavior in an error situation as well as notes on the treatment of special cases.

*Concrete data structures*
This is a description of the concrete implementation of the abstract data structures (assuming that the module manipulates abstract data structures).

*Module initialization*
Here we describe the initializations that take place in the module body. This item can be omitted if there is a separate initialization procedure.

For object-oriented programming, particularly for the sake of increasing reusability, it is especially important to describe the class interfaces with particular care (see also Section 4.3.4). We propose the following documentation schema:

---

| | |
|---|---|
| *Name:* | name of the class |
| *Keyword:* | brief description of the purpose of the class |
| *Inheritance interface:* | description of the components and messages that heirs can access |
| *Export interface:* | description of the components and messages that clients can access<br>The descriptions of the inheritance and export interfaces encompass the respective name, type and meaning of the components, as well as the name and parameters of the messages and instructions for their use and for overwriting methods (see also Section 4.7.4 "Organizational measures for the use of a class library"). |
| *Basis interface:* | description of the other classes from which the given class inherits |
| *Import interface:* | description of the other classes that were used for the implementation |

---

*Task:*
This is a brief description of the tasks of the class.

*Abstract data structure:*

Here we describe the abstract data structure that is realized in the class. We describe the characteristics of the data structure from the viewpoint of the class user and give no specifications about the concrete implementation.

*Methods:*
This describes the implementation of all methods to realize the corresponding messages. Often the methods are so small that detailed description proves superfluous.

---

The inheritance relationships – the knowledge of which methods are overwritten, and other mutual relationships between classes and the associated documents – are particularly important for the utilization of a class library and in the maintenance phase. These relationships cannot be documented and, especially, kept up to date in a conventional way with reasonable effort. Thus here, too, it makes sense to provide this information not in the form of documents on paper, but via hypertext tools (see [Sametinger 1991]).

Since object-oriented software construction emphasizes the use of class libraries and application frameworks and thus to some extent design decisions have already been made, the documentation of such libraries becomes particularly important. To ease reuse, it often makes sense to explain the utilization of individual components as well as their interplay by means of examples.

(4) If the software system to be described works with external files, a *description of files used* becomes necessary. Each file description contains the following information:

- File name
- Contents
- Sentence structure
- File organization
- Maximum file size
- Access privileges and means of access
- Form of possible read and write operations

(5) The *test protocol* covers all testing activities, the test data and the test results for all test cases. In particular this encompasses the following:

- A test schedule for the integration test and user's acceptance test
- A test schedule for each system component
- For each separately tested system component and each subsystem, documentation of the testing environment used (in case it is not provided by a tool)
- A protocol of all utilized test cases
- A protocol of the executed weakness analysis

The completeness of the test protocol is particularly important for quality control and for the repetition of test cases after a system modification. Unfortunately this is underrated in practice, and frequently there is no test protocol at all.

Since upon modification or correction of a program all previous test runs must be repeated to assure that the modification has no undesired side effects, the documentation of utilized test cases is particularly important. This is an extremely troublesome process that as a rule can only be handled with tool support. Tools for storing and repeating test scenarios thus also belong to the category of documentation tools; Bischofberger and Pomberger [Bischofberger 1992] describe an example in the software development environment TOPOS.

The *system documentation*, like the user documentation, should be written *concisely* and *precisely*. Generally there is too much rather than too little documentation. Extensive documentation is troublesome to read and frequently does not reflect the current state of a software product because management and maintenance become more difficult for the documentation than for the software product itself.

The above explanations of system documentation make it clear that sequential text and manually produced diagrams provide inadequate forms for system documentation. Meeting the multifold requirements on system documentation requires hypertext in combination with tools for information extraction from source code and for comfortable reading of hypertext documents. System documentation should thus be created in electronic form. (For more information on hypertext, we refer the interested reader to [Bigelow 1988], [Fidero 1988], [Garg 1988] and [Nielsen 1990].)

In contrast to user documentation, system documentation should employ *formal means of description*. Note here that all persons involved in the system documentation should use the same formalisms and representations so that the reader encounters a uniform style. The style rules in Section 3.7.1.1 also apply to system documentation.

System documentation should by no means be produced only after the test phase. It evolves continuously during the entire development. The above sections of the document emerge as follows:

(1) in the specification phase
(2) in the design phase
(3, 4, 6) during implementation phase
(5) in the specification and test phases

After completion of the software product, the documents emanating from the individual phases should be checked, complemented and corrected as needed and polished to stylistic uniformity.

#### 3.7.1.3 Project documentation

The *project documentation* contains information on project management and control. *Project management* requires uniformity of the means of communication, i.e., the setting of conventions and standards for all intermediate products resulting in the course of system development. *Project progress control* requires the existence of a project schedule and the clarification of the system development process. *Quality control* also requires the definition of standards for intermediate products and the determination of suitable checkpoints in the software development process. *Determining the production costs* of a software product requires careful documentation of costs for personnel, time invested, machine time, etc.

In particular, project documentation encompasses the following:

- A project plan that specifies the realization phases and the planned time spans.
- An organizational plan that specifies personnel assignment and management for the individual realization phases.
- The specification of those results (documents) that are required upon completion of each realization phase.
- The definition of project standards covering the specification of designs methods and test strategies, conventions for documentation, etc.
- A matrix of all documents belonging to the project containing information for each project on its development status (planned, under development, released), access rights and archiving.
- A record of invested work time, machine time and other costs.
- A project diary for protocoling meetings with the development team. The project diary provides information on the progress of the project, aids the project manager in project progress control, and contains valuable information on decisions that occurred long ago and whose justification the project manager might have forgotten.

To conclude this section, we want to re-emphasize that the documentation is an *integrated component* of a software system. Documentation does not have its own phase in the software life cycle; it is a component of all phases and is revised and complemented upon completion of implementation and testing activities. Every modification of a software system requires modification of the corresponding documentation. Efficient and simple management of the documents is a fundamental prerequisite for orderly documentation; therefore we recommend using computer-aided tools to produce such documentation (see Chapter 6).

### 3.7.2 Maintenance of software products

The *maintenance of software products* encompasses all activities that occur after the completion of development work on a software system. It is practically impossible to develop a software product that never requires maintenance. It is also impossible to prove the correctness of a software system by means of testing. Many errors arise only during actual operation and can only be corrected after the development phases.

Frequently during the operation of the software system new user requirements arise that also trigger system changes.

Software maintenance encompasses the following:

(1) Corrective improvements of the user interface and program optimization.
Only the operation of a software system reveals the actual quality of the user interface, the load, and the speed of execution of individual system components. Targeted modifications and optimizations can improve the run-time efficiency and the user interface (assuming that it was not fully realized as a prototype) to adapt them to actual requirements. We do not consider this error correction because the maintenance activity is not triggered by a deviation of the system behavior from that specified in the requirements definition, but reflects later correction requests by the user.

(2) The correction of errors that were not detected during testing.
Since it is impossible to test all program paths of a complex software system and all possible combinations of input data, errors are often detected only during the operation of a software product. Therefore they can only be corrected in the realm of software maintenance.

(3) Modifications triggered by new user requirements.
As a software system is in operation longer, additonal user wishes arise whose necessity or feasibility the user had originally doubted. Organizational restructuring or other in-house changes and the use of other software products also create new requirements on a software product.

Lientz and Swanson [Lientz 1980] term these three types of maintenance *perfective*, *corrective* and *adaptive* and state that about 65% of maintenance costs stem from the first type, 17% from the second and 18% from the third.

A reasonably exact estimate of the maintenance costs of a software product is practically impossible since the reasons for the maintenance cannot be predicted in advance and generally do not fall within the sphere of influence of the software developer.

As a rule, maintenance costs are underestimated. Studies by Lientz and Swanson [Lientz 1980], Pressman [Pressman 1987] and Arthur [Arthur 1988] show that maintenance costs consume more than half of the overall costs. Thus it pays to appreciate the importance of the quality attribute *maintainability* and to design software systems so that they are maintainable.

Implementing a *maintainable system* means guaranteeing modularity, structuredness, readability and testability and during the entire development process examining every decision with attention to the possibility and probability of future modification.

The techniques for software development presented in the previous sections are particularly aimed at assuring the maintainability of software products. The most important criteria for maintainability are the following:

(1) Comprehensibility
Here we mean the clarity of organization of the software system, the transparency of the decomposition of the overall system, and the structuredness of the system and its components. The decomposition and design principles discussed in Section 3.4.3 and in Sections 3.4.5 to 3.4.7 promote comprehensibility.

(2) Independence of components
The program components must be designed such that modifications have no effect on the environment. The guidelines for modularization given in Section 3.4.3 promote component independence.

(3) Programming language
Software systems implemented in a programming language that is acceptable from the viewpoint of software engineering (e.g., Modula-2 [Wirth 1985], Oberon-2 [Mössenböck 1991] or Smalltalk [Goldberg 1983]) are easier to read (and thus easier to maintain) than software systems written in programming languages that do not reflect the state of the art (e.g., Basic or RPG). The criteria for the selection of a programming language were given in Section 3.5.1.

(4) Programming style
The programming style determines the structure and the readability of the implementation. A software system is modifiable if it is easy to find the locations affected by a modification and if the program structure allows easy prediction of the ramifications of a modification. High-quality programming style was described in Section 3.5.2.

(5) Testability
After every modification the system must be tested anew. Thus it is important that the test objects prepared for debugging during the test phase remain available for maintenance. The same applies to the test environment of the individual components of a software system.

(6) Modifiability and extensibility
During software development we should assure that the existing system components are so designed that extensions are possible without touching the existing structure. However, it is necessary to design the program structure, the data structures and the file structures such that they are readily extensible. The technique of object-oriented programming explained in Chapter 4 ("Object-oriented programming") promotes the extensibility to an extent previously unknown.

(7) Documentation
The system documentation is an important prerequisite for the maintainability of software products. The comprehensibility of a software system largely depends on the quality of the system documentation. Software maintenance without system documentation and with maintenance personnel that were not involved in the development process is normally an expensive undertaking and sometimes even impossible. The data for tests to be carried out after a modification are likewise

information that the system documentation provides. The content and structure of the system documentation was discussed in Section 3.7.1.2.

Chapter 4

# Object-oriented programming

In the preceding chapters we have repeatedly spoken of the importance of object-oriented methods in software engineering. In Chapter 3 we showed how to design an object-oriented program system. The present chapter treats object-oriented programming in detail. First we examine object-oriented programming itself, giving special attention to inheritance. After a general treatment of the subject, we show how various programming languages have realized object-oriented principles. Since class libraries play a central role in object-oriented programming, we dedicate a section to them. Finally, we show how the design developed in Section 3.4.7.4 can be transformed to an implementation.

## 4.1 Why object-oriented programming?

A new method should only be used if it really promises advantages in terms of new possibilities or simply the avoidance of drawbacks of previous methods. Object-oriented programming can contribute to a reduction of the complexity of software products, promote the reuse of existing software components, and improve the flexibility of software systems. In the following sections we examine object-oriented programming and show how it helps to ameliorate the problems of conventional software development.

### 4.1.1 The complexity of software products

One of the major problems in conventional program development is the scarcely comprehensible complexity of the resulting products. A program system consists of a multitude of individual parts (procedures, data, files) and the relationships between them. The unpleasant aspect here is that the number of possible interconnections rises more than linearly with the number of components, as the sequence in Figure 4.1 shows.

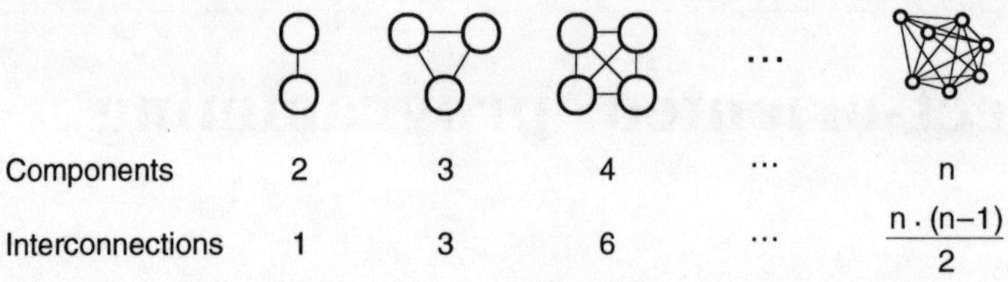

| Components | 2 | 3 | 4 | ... | n |
|---|---|---|---|---|---|
| Interconnections | 1 | 3 | 6 | ... | $\frac{n \cdot (n-1)}{2}$ |

Figure 4.1: Rise in complexity with increasing number of components

The quadratic rise in the number of possible interconnections means that the number of potential relations quadruples when the number of components doubles. In the realization of a software project, the developers need to understand not just the individual components, but also their interaction; this means that a program twice as large requires four times the analysis and implementation effort. The only escape from this dilemma is to reduce the interconnections, for example, by modularization. If we can structure a program with 16 components in four modules of four components each, then there are six possible interconnections within each module and another six interconnections between the modules. This makes 30 potential relationships – compared to 120 if all 16 components interact directly. This reaps a complexity reduction by a factor of four. Unfortunately, modularization also has its limits with extremely large systems because the number of modules rises so sharply that the module structure approaches incomprehensibility. Add to this the communication problems that ensue from the necessity to engage a large development team for the realization of such a large project.

### 4.1.2 Reuse

The complexity problem can be ameliorated by reusing existing components. Although the reuse of existing program components does not directly bring a reduction in complexity, it does relieve developers from unpleasant routine activities and enables them to concentrate on application-specific problems. Unfortunately, reuse in conventional program development is restricted to invoking procedures in prefabricated or self-accumulated libraries. If an existing component fails to meet requirements exactly, additional effort is required that can negate the advantages of such a procedure library. Fundamentally, three approaches are possible when an existing component does not match exactly:

- *New development.* Frequently it is easiest to develop the desired procedure from scratch. This takes time and costs money, but can have a positive effect on the quality of the product because errors in the original version are not repeated in the new development.
- *Adaptation.* Often the existing component can be modified so that it fulfills the needed function. To make this work requires good knowledge of the original. Even if a "minimal adaptation" seems so enticing, it does have its perils. One problem

arises from inadequate comprehension of the original, so that treacherous errors easily can creep in. Another problem is the multiplicity of versions. As soon as multiple variants of a component exist, they have to be managed. For later reuse, this encumbers the choice of the right component, and when an error is detected, corrections have to be made in all affected versions, so that the advantage of reuse can transform into a millstone of increased maintenance effort.

- *Double floor.* If the required procedure should perform more duty than the existing one, then sometimes a simple procedure can be implemented that uses the original one, but also fulfills the additional tasks. This is a case of actual reuse. This approach also has the advantage that the inner workings of the original need not be known. If modifications are made on the implementation of the original component (e.g., in the course of error correction), the extended procedure can continue to be used without modification.

With object-oriented programming, reuse can be significantly improved through targeted inheritance and adaptation of existing components. Furthermore, as shown in Section 3.4.7 on object-oriented design, a natural modularization of the overall system occurs almost automatically.

### 4.1.3 Flexibility and compatibility

While a conventional program consists of cooperating procedures, imagine an object-oriented program as a collection of communicating objects. The significant difference is that the data are no longer passive, but carry out actions themselves. An action executed by an object can consist of a state transition in the object or the activation of other objects. Objects are viewed as components that have a relationship to one another and exchange messages. Consider the comparison with technical components: For example, an electronic switching network can be seen as a network of objects, as Figure 4.2 shows.

A clock sends a pulse to a counter object. The counter reacts by increasing its value by 1. If the counter reaches the value 10, then it resets its value to 0 and sends a pulse to another object. The receiver object only needs to have the correct interface, i.e., at least one connection that can receive pulses of a certain voltage. How the receiver reacts is of no importance to the sender. Thus the output line of a counter could be connected to a second counter just as easily as to a blinking lamp. Likewise components that are unknown to date (perhaps under development) could later be connected to this line without changing the inner structure of the counter.

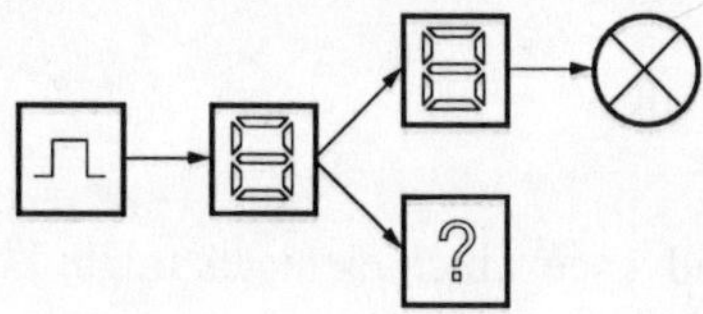


Figure 4.2: Electronic components as an object network

In conventional programming there is nothing that corresponds to this kind of flexibility. To program the processing of a counter pulse with conventional means, we could proceed as shown in the following program fragment:

```
TYPE
   Counter = POINTER TO CounterValue;
   CounterValue = RECORD
      value: [0..9];
      output: Counter
   END;

PROCEDURE ProcessPulse(c:Counter);
BEGIN
   WITH z^ DO
      IF value < 9 THEN
         value := value + 1
      ELSE
         value := 0;
         ProcessPulse(output)
      END
   END
END ProcessPulse;
```

This solution assumes that the output connects to a counter so that the operation ProcessPulse(output) can function. To assure that different elements can be connected to a counter requires a record type with variants, as in the following pattern:

```
TYPE
   ElementType = (counter, lamp, flipFlop);
   Component = RECORD
      CASE type:ElementType OF
         counter:   c:Counter
      |  lamp:      l:Lamp
      |  flipFlop:  f:FlipFlop
      END
   END;
   Counter = RECORD
      value: [0..9];
      output:Component
   END;
```

Since we cannot know in advance which elements might be connected to an output, a case distinction must be made in processing a pulse:

```
PROCEDURE ProcessPulse(c:Counter);
BEGIN
  WITH z^ DO
     IF value < 9 THEN
        value := value + 1
     ELSE
        value := 0;
        CASE output.type OF
             counter: ProcessPulse(output.c)
        |    lamp: Illuminate(output.l)
        |    flipFlop: Toggle(output.f)
        END
     END
  END
END ProcessPulse;
```

Such a case distinction is required wherever another component can be connected to the output of a component. These case distinctions are distributed over the whole program and take on similar form everywhere.

Particularly unpleasant is that to cover the addition of a new component (e.g., a buzzer or a relay) troublesome and error-prone modifications need to be made at every possible code location in the entire program system. Although this is a routine activity that can be handled almost without thinking, it is easy to miss one or more locations (maybe even a whole module). The effects drive home at run time, when the execution of a case statement cannot find a fitting alternative.

In the following sections we will show how this problem almost solves itself with the use of object-oriented methods.

## 4.2 Fundamentals of object-oriented programming

This section presents the foundations of object-oriented programming. We begin with explanations of the terms *object* and *class* and then pursue *dynamic binding*, *polymorphism* and *inheritance*. These concepts play a central role in object-oriented programming. Comprehending them is an absolute prerequisite for proper application of the technique.

### 4.2.1 The terms object and class

The term *object* is not new to programming. It is often used as a general designation for things that are not specified more precisely. For example, in descriptions of

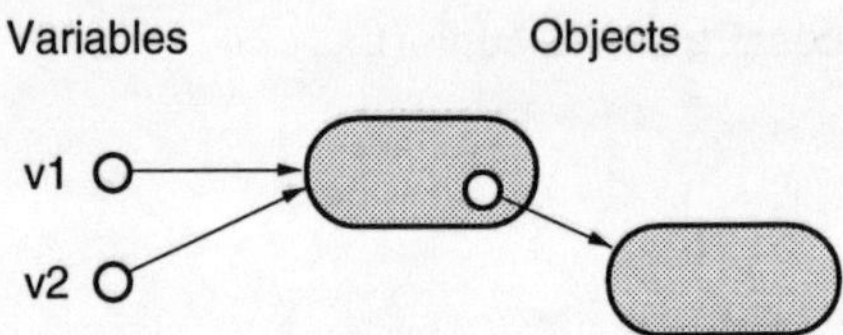


Figure 4.3: Variables and objects

programming languages we find the word object as a general designation for variables, constants, data types and procedures. In the realm of object-oriented programming, however, the term object has a clearly defined meaning. An *object* in our sense is characterized by having a *state*, the ability to carry out *actions*, and membership in an (object) *class*. A variable can contain a reference to an object (an *object reference*), as depicted in Figure 4.3.

Imagine objects as dynamically created data that are accessible via pointers and linked to one another. Still, we speak abstractly of a reference because the actual representation of objects at run time need not necessarily be realized with the help of pointers (e.g., indirect pointers or indices in object tables are common). An object can contain variables that reference other objects. This allows the formation of object structures of any complexity.

Different variables can also reference the same object. Here we speak of *object identity* because the objects referenced by v1 and v2 are identical. We could also say that v1 and v2 are different names for the same object, a situation termed the *alias effect*. Modifying an object via variable v1 also affects program segments that use v2. This can lead to misunderstandings and errors.

Each object has a clearly defined interface that specifies which operations are possible with it. Ideally, the state of an object is encapsulated and not accessible from the outside. If the state of an object is to be modified, this is possible only with the help of operations defined in the interface.

*Note:* In many object-oriented programming languages the object structure is a white box, relaxing the principle of information hiding. For security reasons, we discourage abusing the knowledge of the object structure for direct manipulation of objects. Thus in our discussions we always assume the existence of strict data encapsulation.

The operations specified in the interface amount to access routines as discussed in Section 3.4.3.2 on data encapsulation. Figure 4.4 depicts an object in this sense. The object represented here contains the three encapsulated variables x, y and z. Its interface defines the three operations P, Q and R, which can be invoked from outside. If the variable v references this object, then the operations v:P, v:Q and v:R are possible with it. Note that in using v we only know that these operations are available and how to use them; how they are realized remains hidden in the implementation of the object.

In the object model sketched here, every object has its own data and operations. In reality there are many objects of the same kind with the same interface, structure and

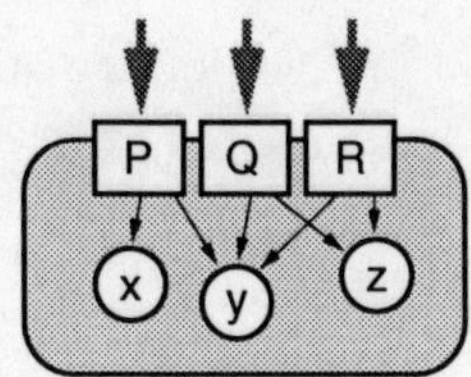


Figure 4.4: A simple object

behavior. These objects belong to the same class. Their commonalities need to be defined only once in a class description. In this respect classes correspond to abstract data types. We also use class names like type names and declare, for example, a variable v to be of class C in the form

```
VAR
   v: C;
```

In such a declaration we frequently designate v as a C object. The reader should understand that the variable does not contain an object, but a reference to an object.

A property of classes that transcends conventional data types is that they can be ordered hierarchically, as shown in Section 3.4.7.2. We define that every class can (but need not) be derived from another class and use the following notation to define a class interface:

```
INTERFACE OF NewClass;
INHERITS FROM OldClass;
   simpleOp;
   paramOp(param:paramType);
   functionOp: ResultType;
   paramFunctionOp(param:paramType):ResultType;
   ...
END NewClass.
```

An interface description thus begins with INTERFACE OF and the name of the defined class (here: NewClass). Then follows the specification of the existing class from which the new class derives. The keyword INHERITS states that this is an inheritance relationship. NewClass inherits the interface from OldClass, meaning that automatically all operations that were permitted with objects of class OldClass are also possible with class NewClass. The interface of the new class can be extended by defining additional operations for it. simpleOp is a parameterless operation and paramOp has one parameter of type paramType, whereby the parameter type naturally can be a class itself. The operation functionOp is a parameterless function procedure that returns a result of data type ResultType, and paramFunctionOp is a function with parameters. The following fragment shows our notation for the use of a class:

```
VAR
    obj: NewClass;
    param: paramType;
    result: ResultType;
...
obj := NewClass:new;
obj:simpleOp;
obj:paramOp(param);
result := obj:functionOp;
result := obj:paramFunctionOp(param);
```

In contrast to procedures in conventional programming, the operations defined here are bound to an object of the corresponding class. To execute the operation simpleOp requires the specification of the object that is to execute it. Shifting the focus from functions to the data finds expression in the language of the object-oriented way of thinking. The construct x:m expresses not that the operation m is to be applied to object x, but instead that object x is requested to execute the operation m. This request is called a *message*. m is not merely a message to object x, but a *request* to which the object must react. (The object itself determines the nature of this reaction.) In accordance with the usual terminology, we write x:m to mean that *object x is sent message m*. Sending a message amounts to a procedure invocation. The sender gives the receiver a task and can only continue working after the receiver has completed the task. This means that messages and message handling is sequential rather than parallel.

Variables are static quantities in the sense that the compiler can already reserve storage for them. By contrast, objects are dynamic quantities that come to life only at run time through explicit creation. Another difference between variables and objects is that variables have a name, but objects are nameless (and thus can only be referenced via variables). Every object-oriented language provides a mechanism for creating a new object and for assigning to a variable a reference to the new object. The notation we use comes from the language Smalltalk [Goldberg 1983]. We pretend that a class is also an object and imagine that every class reacts to the message new by creating an object of the class. Here we assume that the creation process occurs in two steps: first memory is reserved for the object and then the created object is requested to initialize itself appropriately. We assume that every class has an implemented message initialize that handles this task.

A *class definition* specifies the messages to which its objects will react. The nature of this reaction (i.e., which actions it executes on receipt of a certain message) and the structure of the objects is described in the *class implementation*. For now, we will employ the following notation:

```
IMPLEMENTATION OF NewClass;
   VAR
      comp: SomeType;

   simpleOp IS
   VAR
      local: AnotherType;
   BEGIN
      actions
   END simpleOp;
   ...
END NewClass.
```

The inheritance relation (i.e., from which class the new class derives) is already specified in the class definition; it need not be repeated in the implementation. Inheritance already determines that every object of class NewClass contains at least the components that objects of the class OldClass have. If additional components are needed for the implementation of the class, they can be introduced in the class through additional variable declarations. In our example all NewClass objects have an additional component comp.

Actions to be executed on receipt of a message are specified in a *method*. For each new message added to the class definition (e.g., simpleOp) there must be a method of the same name in the class implementation. A method has the same structure as a conventional procedure. It consists of local declarations and statements. One significant divergence from a procedure is that methods are always bound to a receiver object. Frequently the receiver object is used within methods as a receiver object for another message or as a parameter or a message to another object. Most object-oriented languages use the name self in such cases to designate the receiver of the just executed method, for example:

```
self:writeToFile(f);
list:append(self);
```

A class has two tasks: It provides a description of the *structure* and the *behavior* of its objects, and it serves to *create new objects*. In this sense a class is often called an object template or object factory. Another characteristic of classes is that they can be organized hierarchically. Figure 4.5 depicts the various relations between classes and their objects.

A variable *references* (informally: contains) an object. Multiple variables can reference one and the same object. Every object belongs to – *is a* member of – a class. Corresponding to their positions in the inheritance hierarchy, there exists an *is-a* relation between classes. This relationship is also extrapolated onto the relationship between objects and their classes (a is an Auto, even x is an Auto). The *is-a* relation is also often

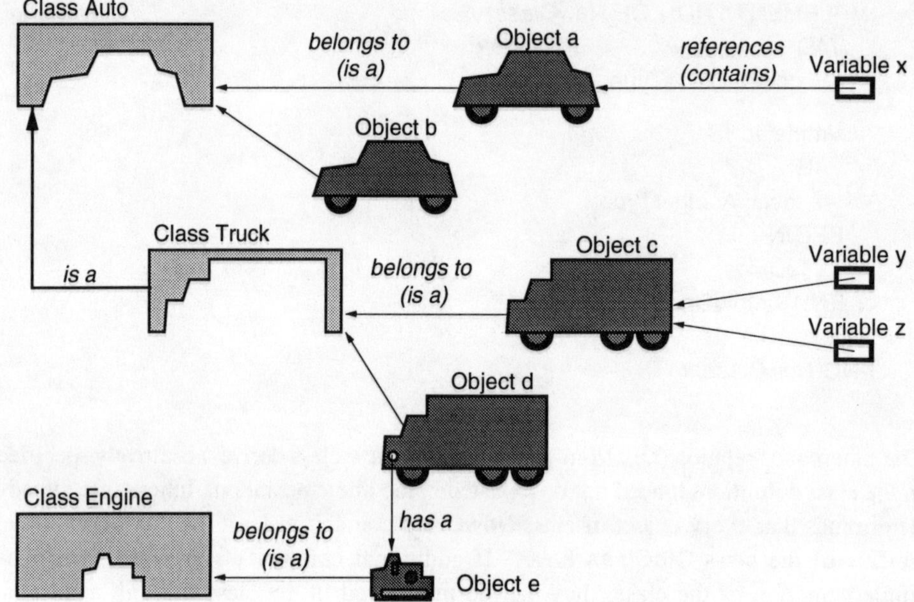


Figure 4.5: Relations between objects and classes

applied to indirect class membership. Object c, for example, also belongs to the class Auto (because a Truck *is an* Auto as well).

Another relation arises from the variables contained in objects. For example, object d contains a variable that references an Engine object. In object-oriented terminology this is designated as a *has-a* relation. It plays an important role in communication between objects and in the formation of complex object structures.

In the literature, objects are also called *instances* of classes and variables contained in objects are termed *instance variables*. In the following we use the terms *instance variable*, *object component* and *component* synonymously.

## 4.2.2 Dynamic binding

In conventional programming, simply examining the source code allows the reader to determine the effect of a procedure invocation at run time. Standard Pascal has but a single compilation unit; the invoked procedure is always located in the same source code file as the procedure invocation. Here the compiler can assure that the procedure invocation is translated to a jump instruction directly to the first statement of the procedure.

For programming languages with separate (e.g., Ada and Modula-2) or independent (e.g., C) compilation this is no longer possible because the invoked procedure can reside in a different compilation unit that might not even have been written yet. The compiler can no longer bind the procedure invocation to the statement to be executed; this binding must be resolved later (but still before the execution of the program) by the linker or the loader. In these languages the programmer can no longer check the effect of a procedure invocation, but must rely on the interface description of the procedure.

Object-oriented programming languages go one step farther, for the effect of each message depends on the type of the receiver object. The binding of a message to the method to be executed is determined anew each time at run time. This must be the case because there can be many methods with the same name. Thus some mechanism must assure that the correct method is executed when a message is sent.

When we speak of *binding* in the context of object-oriented programming, we mean the binding of an invocation (of a procedure or message) to a certain sequence of statements (procedure or method). The term *dynamic binding* thus always refers to the binding of methods to messages. In general, programming languages can be categorized according to when they bind:

| | Binding time | Static check | Language examples |
|---|---|---|---|
| early | compile time | yes | standard Pascal |
| ↓ | link time | partially | Ada, C, Modula-2 |
| late | run time | no | C++, Smalltalk, Eiffel |

In the first two cases the binding does not change at run time, hence we have *static binding*. By contrast, object-oriented languages employ *dynamic binding*. For most novices to object-oriented programming, dynamic binding represents an obstacle to comprehension because the same invocation at different times can have different effects. Likewise, dynamic binding proves a hindrance to error detection (for example, during a walk-through, a dry-run simulation of the program on paper) (see [Ponder 1992]). On the other hand, precisely this dynamic aspect opens new dimensions in programming.

For the sake of completeness we should mention that many conventional programming languages have language elements to realize dynamic binding. In standard Pascal, for example, a formal parameter of a procedure can be a procedure itself. Within the procedure this procedure parameter can be invoked, but which concrete procedure (actual parameter) is actually invoked is determined only on invocation at run time. Modula-2 goes one step further because any variable can be declared as a procedure. The following example shows how dynamic binding can be realized in Modula-2:

```
VAR
   action: PROCEDURE(Rectangle);    (* procedure variable *)
   r: Rectangle;
...
PROCEDURE Erase(r:Rectangle); BEGIN ... END Erase;
PROCEDURE Invert(r:Rectangle); BEGIN ... END Invert;
...
```

```
IF mode = clear THEN action := Erase ELSE action := Invert END;
...
action(r);    (* dynamic binding *)
```

Depending on certain conditions, various procedures (more precisely, their start addresses) can be assigned to the variable action. The effect of an invocation of action(r) depends in our case on whether the variable mode contains the value clear.

### 4.2.3 Polymorphism

In conventional programming languages, static typing has become the standard. It forces a programmer to declare all variables and thus to define their data type. This allows the compiler to check the correct use of a variable and thus to help avoid numerous errors. The data type of a variable not only determines which operations are possible, but also which values it can assume at run time. Most conventional languages permit a variable to assume only values of one and the same data type (its declared type) during its entire lifetime.

*Note:* Some programming languages (e.g., Pascal) permit the assignment of values of other data types to variables. However, before the actual assignment these languages always make an implicit conversion of the value to the data type of the variable. Therefore the variable itself always contains only values of the same data type.

In object-oriented programming many similar data types occur that permit the same operations. A variable v of class B, for example, permits all operations that are defined in class B. If we derive a new class C from B, then C objects permit the same operations as B objects (and possibly even more). This suggests allowing a C object wherever a B object is permitted. In other words, the variable v should be able to contain references not only to B objects, but also to C objects. At run time the variable v can assume various forms; hence we speak of *polymorphism* (Greek πολυς = many, μορφη = form).

Let us consider the class hierarchy developed in Section 3.4.7.4 and depicted in Figure 4.6. Since the classes Beam, Ball and ComplexPart directly, and the classes Fundament, Portal, Gripper and Robot indirectly, derive from the class Part, objects of these classes permit all operations that are allowed with an object of class Part. Nothing

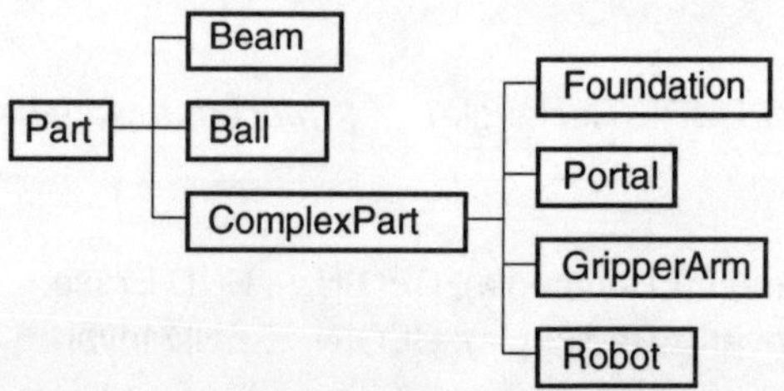


Figure 4.6: Class hierarchy of robot parts

prevents assigning an object of class Ball to variable v of data type (class) Part. This enables, for example, the operation v:move(0,100,50). The following example shows a possible application of polymorphism:

```
VAR
   v: Part;
   b: Ball;
   r: Robot;
...
IF x THEN v := b ELSE v := r END;
...
v:move(0,100,50);
v:drawFrontView(rect);
```

The effect of the statement v:move(0,100,50) depends on whether v contains a reference to a Ball or a Robot object. In operations with polymorphic variables, dynamic binding is always at work.

Note that we cannot predict whether the variable v really references a Robot object after the assignment v := r. The variable r might have been assigned an object of another class that was derived from Robot. In any case, we can be sure that the operations carried out with v are permissible.

While conventional languages always ensure that a variable of data types S contains a value of data types S (i.e., a reference to an object of class S) at run time, in object-oriented languages we must carefully distinguish between the *static* and *dynamic* data types of a variable. The static data type stems from the declaration, while the dynamic data type is the type (class) of the object which the variable references at run time. The dynamic data type thus derives from the run time history. The usual rules of polymorphism state that a reference to an object of (dynamic) class D can be assigned to a variable of (static) class S only if D = S or if D derives from S. This means that assignments are only permitted along the class hierarchy, in our representation from right to left. For example, the assignment b := v is forbidden because we cannot be sure that the variable v references a Ball object. However, this condition would need to be fulfilled because after this assignment an operation like b:setRadius(5) is possible.

Together, dynamic binding and polymorphism provide the foundation for the flexibility of object-oriented program systems. The relaxation of static compatibility rules allows an already completely developed program later to work with objects for which it was not originally intended. Even long-time object-oriented developers are repeatedly amazed when their programs can be enriched with originally unplanned functionality by simply adding a few new classes – and without modifications in the existing program itself.

The simulation of electronic components (see Section 4.1.3) can be solved simply and elegantly with object-oriented means. We need a class Component whose objects support at least the operation processPulse:

```
INTERFACE OF Component;
    ...
    processPulse;
    ...
END Component.
```

Any number of specific components can be derived from this class. For example, class Counter could be implemented as follows:

```
IMPLEMENTATION OF Counter;
    VAR
        value: [0..9];              -- momentary value of counter
        output: Component;          -- component connected at output
    connect (b:Component) IS
    BEGIN
        output := b
    END connect;
    reset IS
    BEGIN
        value := 0
    END reset;
    processPulse IS
    BEGIN
        IF value < 9 THEN
            value := value + 1
        ELSE
            value := 0;
            output:processPulse
        END
    END processPulse;
    ...
END Component.
```

A Counter object has two instance variables. The first represents the current value, or the state of the counter. The second instance variable contains a reference to the component that is connected to the output of the counter. The method connect connects an arbitrary component b with the output of the counter. The method reset returns the counter to its initial state. Processing a pulse can now be formulated very simply. Since the object referenced by the instance variable output certainly belongs to the class Component, we can be sure that it can execute the operation processPulse. However, we cannot predict the effect that the message processPulse will have at run time. The counter described here is so general that even components developed later can be connected to its output. Such flexibility would be very difficult to achieve with conventional programming.

### 4.2.4 Inheritance

While dynamic binding and polymorphism increase flexibility, inheritance enables object-oriented programs to be written with significantly less effort than comparable conventionally implemented programs. If a class already exists that provides significant functionality, a subclass derived from it can utilize this functionality.

For example, consider a small class B with the following interface and implementation:

```
INTERFACE OF B;
  P;
  Q;
END B.
```

```
IMPLEMENTATION OF B;
  VAR x, y: ...;
  P IS BEGIN ... END P;
  Q IS BEGIN ... END Q;
END B.
```

If we derive a new class C from class B without defining additional functionality, then objects of the new class exhibit behavior identical to that of objects of their base class. C objects have the same structure and behavior as B objects (see Figure 4.7).

```
INTERFACE OF C;
  INHERITS FROM B;
END C.
```

```
IMPLEMENTATION OF C;
END C.
```

Class C thus inherits all attributes of its base class B. To be more precise, we need to distinguish between interface inheritance and implementation inheritance, depicted in Figure 4.8.

Class C inherits the entire interface from B. This means that objects of class C permit the same operations as objects of class B – not more or less. Interface inheritance

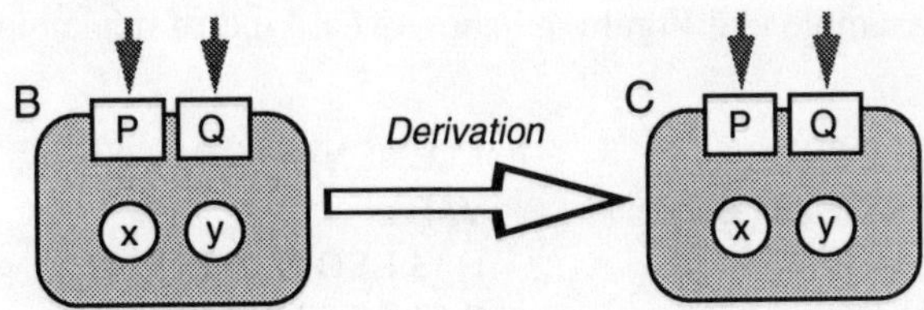


Figure 4.7: Inheritance of attributes through derivation

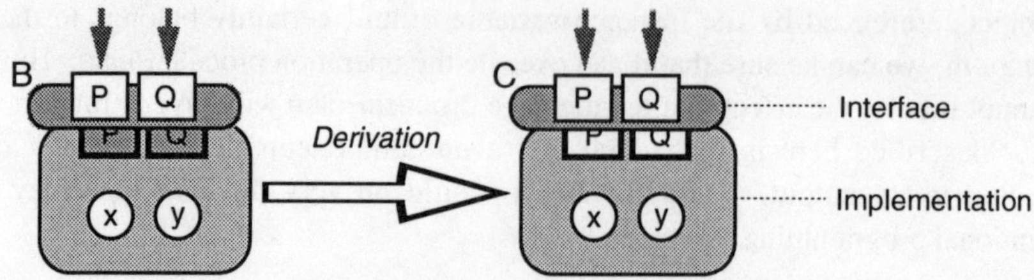


Figure 4.8: Inheritance of interface and implementation

thus affects the *functionality* that the subclass provides to its *clients* (the invoking program units).

Through implementation inheritance, class C also inherits the *behavior* and the *structure* of class B. In this case this means that C objects not only understand messages P and Q, but also that they react in the same way as B objects. Structure inheritance means that C objects, just as B objects, contain instance variables x and y, which is necessary for the realization of operations P and Q.

Behavior inheritance should not be misunderstood as code duplication for methods P and Q in class C. Quite the contrary, we could imagine behavior inheritance as if a C object knew that methods P and Q were already implemented in class B. Hence we have a binding between classes B and C which, among other things, assures that modifications of methods in a class also affect its derived classes without recompilation. These aspects are treated in more detail in Section 4.2.5 on the dynamic model.

Properties inherited from a class can later be extended and modified, whereby we again need to distinguish between interface and implementation inheritance:

- The interface can only be *extended*. This means that existing operations cannot be modified, but new operations can be added – otherwise polymorphism would not function.
- For every operation added to the interface, a method *must* be implemented to clarify which actions to execute on receipt of a message. Furthermore, new methods can be written for inherited operations, which is termed *overriding* the inherited method. If such a new method requires additional instance variables, they can be added in the derived class. As with the class interface, declarations of existing instance variables cannot be removed or modified.

The following example and Figure 4.9 show what kind of deviations are possible for class C:

```
INTERFACE OF C;               IMPLEMENTATION OF C;
  INHERITS FROM B;              VAR z: ...;                -- new component
  R;    -- new message          R IS BEGIN ... END R;      -- new method
END C.                          P IS BEGIN ... END P;      -- overridden method
                              END C.
```

In addition to inheriting operations P and Q from B, class C defines a new operation R, for which an implementation must also be provided. Class C inherits operation Q without modifications, but overrides operation P with a new method. Since methods P and R require a new instance variable, the structure of C objects is extended by element z.

Frequently an inherited method does not need to be fully overridden, but only extended by some actions. It would be a crass violation of the rules of reusability to write a new method that contains the same code as the original method along with some extensions. Instead, we first invoke the overridden method and then program the additionally required actions. For the example of a C method named P, an initial attempt could take the following form:

```
P IS
BEGIN
   self:P;
   additional actions
END P;
```

Unfortunately this cannot work, for dynamic binding assures that the invocation self:P again causes activation of method P of class C (because the current recipient object self is a C object). We would have attained an endless recursion instead of the required functional extension of a method. This means that the language elements introduced so far do not suffice. We need a message construct that enables the invocation of the overridden method. Based on similar language elements in existing object-oriented languages, we introduce the keyword base, which can take the place of self in a method invocation. base:P invokes the overridden method in the base class. Note, however, that the receiver object remains the same. If the overridden method P uses self, this is a C object (not a B object from the base class). The correct formulation of a functional extension thus takes the following form:

```
P:
BEGIN
   base:P;
   additional actions
END P;
```

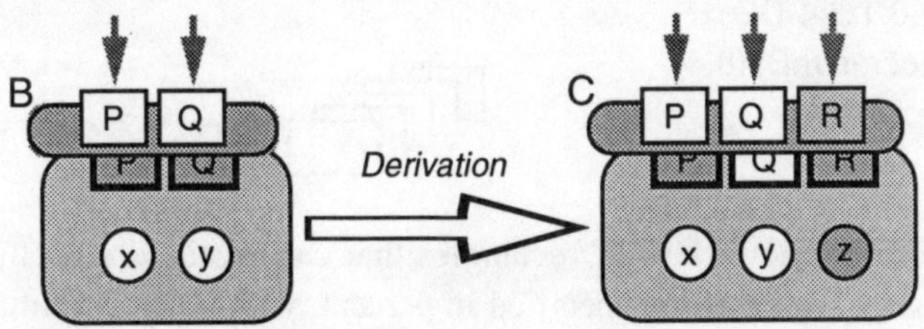


Figure 4.9: Extensions and modifications of derived classes; new and modified messages, methods and instance variables are depicted in gray

Let us now examine an example to clarify what we have presented in general and abstract form. We assume the existence of a class Rectangle with the following interface:

```
INTERFACE OF Rectangle;
  draw;                        -- draws a rectangle with white interior and black border
  erase;                       -- removes the rectangle from the screen

  left: Integer;               -- returns the position of the rectangle's left border
  top: Integer;                -- returns the position of the rectangle's top border
  width: Integer;              -- returns the rectangle's width
  height: Integer;             -- returns the rectangle's height

  moveTo (x,y:Integer);        -- moves the rectangle's top left corner to (x,y)
  moveBy (dx,dy:Integer);      -- moves the rectangle's position by (dx,dy)
  changeSize (w,h:Integer);    -- sets the rectangle's dimensions to (w,h)
END Rectangle.
```

As in previous examples, we provide separate operations to query and to modify the state of a rectangle. The first group of operations concerns the display of a rectangle, the second group the simple query of elementary attributes, and the third the modification of such attributes. However, we did not provide separate operations for the modification of each individual attribute, but combine these in one operation to modify the position and size of a rectangle. This simplifies global modifications because they require less messages. However, changing only the height of a rectangle demands first querying its width and then passing this width with the invocation of the method changeSize: myRect:changeSize(myRect:width, 50). Whether a developer chooses elementary or composite operations is largely a matter of taste. Still, the operations that will be carried out most frequently should be as easy as possible to invoke.

The above interface description remains incomplete despite the comments. It explains the effect of the individual operations, but leaves their interplay open. In particular, nothing has been said about the effect of the operations moveTo and changeSize if the rectangle is already displayed. Let us correct this shortcoming by defining that state transitions do not affect an existing display of objects. Thus, for example, we could draw a series of staggered rectangles with the following loop:

```
FOR i := 0 TO 4 DO
  myRect:moveBy(8,4);
  myRect:draw
END;
```

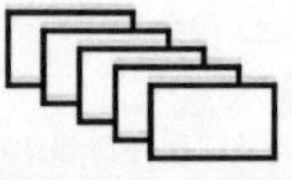

Now let us create a new class of rectangles that can be filled with the gray scale of choice. The gray scale will be specified in percent, with 0 being white and 100 black. Thus we will design a new class GrayRectangle, whose objects possess the additional attribute shade (returned below by the operation shade). All other attributes defined in class Rectangle will be retained, so that we can derive the new class from the existing one. As usual, we provide separate operations for querying and modifying the new attribute:

```
INTERFACE OF GrayRectangle;
INHERITS FROM Rectangle;
   shade: Integer;            -- returns the rectangle's shade (in percent)
   setShade (d:Integer);      -- sets the rectangle's shade to d%
END GrayRectangle.
```

Note that the operations inherited by Rectangle are not repeated in this interface definition; specifying INHERITS FROM Rectangle suffices to specify that GrayRectangle objects also permit the operations draw, erase, moveTo etc. For example, a GrayRectangle object called myGrayRect can be modified as follows:

```
FOR i := 0 TO 4 DO
   myGrayRect:moveBy(8,4);
   myGrayRect:setShade(i*25);
   myGrayRect:draw
END;
```

The interface definition does not conclude the development of the new class; we need to assure that the new operations can be executed. We suggest the following class implementation without further preliminary comments and follow it with explanatory notes of details that are important for comprehension.

```
IMPLEMENTATION OF GrayRectangle;

   VAR grayValue: INTEGER;  -- the rectangle's shade in percent          ①

   shade: Integer IS        -- return the rectangle's shade              ②
   BEGIN
      RETURN grayValue
   END shade;

   setShade (d:Integer) IS  -- sets the rectangle's shade to d%          ②
   BEGIN
      grayValue := d
   END setShade;

   draw IS                  -- draw the rectangle filled with gray       ③
   BEGIN
      base:draw;
      fill interior with gray
   END draw;
```

```
    initialize IS                    -- initialize the rectangle as w      ④
    BEGIN
        base:initialize;
        grayValue := 0
    END initialize;

END GrayRectangle.
```

*Notes*:

① The additional attribute shade must be described by a new instance variable, designated here as grayValue. Note that the class implementation declares only the *additional* components; at this point, because we have not provided the implementation of class Rectangle, we do not even know which instance variables define the position and size of a rectangle (and thus also of a gray rectangle). This knowledge proves unnecessary because we can query, for example, the width with the help of self:width.

② Since we added the operations shade and setShade to the interface, we also need to write methods for them. Their implementations are quite simple because only the value of the instance variable grayValue must be returned or set.

③ Since the rectangle is to be displayed differently, the draw operation needs to be overridden. We approach this by first activating the overridden method that displays the rectangle in white with a black border. Then the inside of the rectangle simply has to be filled with the proper shade of gray. We have omitted the exact formulation because the statements differ depending on the hardware and the graphic software.

④ Similar to the draw operation, we also need to override the initialization method. Recall that we assume that this method will be invoked automatically with each creation of an object of this class. Here, too, we begin with the invocation of the overridden method to initialize the instance variables of the base class. Next we initialize the new instance variable grayValue. In our example grayValue starts at value 0 for a white rectangle.

Note that the operations erase, moveTo, left, top, width, height, moveTo, moveBy and changeSize are not overridden. These methods can be inherited without modification. This situation is characteristic of object-oriented programming. The automatic assumption of inherited functionality results in savings in newly written code that are typical of object-oriented program systems.

### 4.2.5 Dynamic models for method lookup

In the previous section we noted that inheritance does not build on the duplication of inherited code, but that there is a binding between a class and its base class, so that an object "knows" from where it inherits methods. How does dynamic binding really work and how is inheritance realized? These questions often pose obstacles for novices to object-oriented programming. Thus in this section we attempt to cast light on the realization of these concepts. We begin with two models and then show how concrete programming languages actually realize these models.

If object x is to execute operation op (x:op), then the dynamic data type of x must be determined first; let us designate it as D. Then comes a method lookup whose goal is to find an appropriate method for the duple ['op', D]. Such a lookup could begin with either of the two criteria, providing the respective orientations of the two following models. The first model (which we term the *algorithmic model*) employs the method name as the primary criterion and looks for a class in which the method is implemented. Since the method can be implemented in multiple classes, the class must be found in which the method op that applies in D is implemented. The second model (termed the *layer model*) uses class D as the primary criterion and looks up the correct method for this class in a table.

The *algorithmic model* is based on the idea that each class specifies which methods it implements. Figure 4.10 shows the algorithm to select the correct method for a message op. When an object receives a message, the lookup begins by checking whether a corresponding method is implemented in the object's class (= dynamic data type of x). If so, it is executed, which can result in further messages (to the same object or to other objects). If there is no corresponding method, the lookup continues in the base class. If the method is not implemented there either, the lookup continues in the base class of the base class. In statically typed object-oriented languages (the only case considered so far) the method is found eventually. In object-oriented languages without static typing (e.g., Smalltalk [Goldberg 1983] and Self [Ungar 87]) the method might not be found at all. The attempt to continue the lookup in the base class determines that there is no further base class (see Figure 4.12). The lookup fails and the program terminates with a run-time error (in Smalltalk: message not understood).

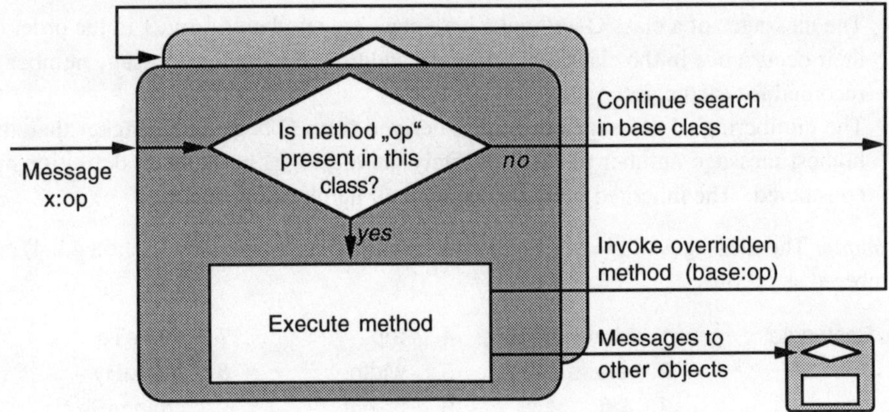


Figure 4.10: Algorithmic method lookup

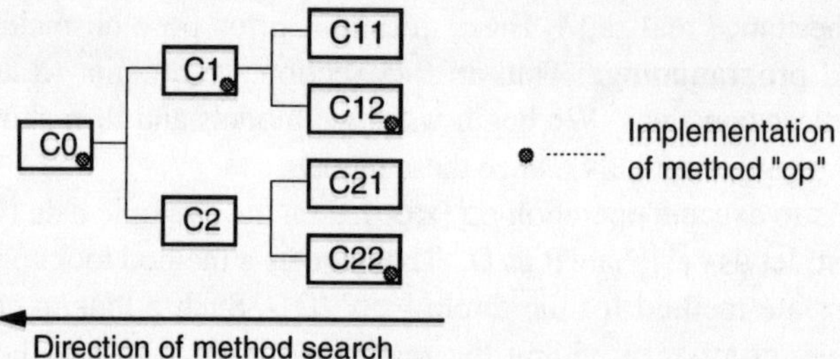


Figure 4.11: Method lookup in a class hierarchy

Figure 4.11 uses a simple class hierarchy to show how the method lookup works with various dynamic data types of the object associated with variable x. We assume that the method op is implemented in classes C0, C1, C12 and C22. If variable x contains a reference to an object of one of these classes, the method is found immediately. However, if the object is of class C11, e.g., the method is found in the base class C1. Analogously, the method is found in class C0 if the object is of class C21. If method op in class C22 contains an invocation base:op, then this invocation is first delegated to base class C2. Since the method is not implemented there, the lookup continues in base class C0. Thus a base invocation need not necessarily be executed in the direct base class.

*Important:* If the object belongs to class C21, the method in C0 is executed. However, if this method contains a self invocation with another message (e.g., self:op2), the method lookup begins with the dynamic data type of self, class C21! This means that even an inherited method need not always have the same behavior because it might use other methods that could be overridden.

The *layer model* is based on a completely different idea. The messages of a class are numbered, for example, according to the following schema:

- The message initialize receives number 0.
- The messages of a class C without a base class are numbered from 1 in the order of their occurrence in the class definition. In addition, the highest message number is recorded for each class.
- The numbering of messages in a class derived from C begins at 1 higher than the highest message number of class C. Only the messages in the class definition are considered. The inherited messages retain their numbers.

*Example:* The messages of classes Rectangle and GrayRectangle (see Section 4.2.4) are numbered as follows:

| Rectangle: | 1 draw | 4 top | 7 moveTo |
|---|---|---|---|
| | 2 erase | 5 width | 8 moveBy |
| | 3 left | 6 height | 9 changeSize |

Highest message number: 9

GrayRectangle: 10 shade 11 setShade

Highest message number: 11

For each class, a table is created; imagine this table on a transparent pane. The pane is divided into numbered columns; if a class contains a method for message number i, a sheet of paper with the source code of the method is adhered in column i. The complete methods table for a class results when, beginning with the root class, the panes of all base classes are stacked with the pane of the class itself on top (Figure 4.12).

Viewed from above, the multilayer table immediately shows which methods are executed for which messages. A method implemented in the current class is in the top layer, while inherited methods are behind one or more transparent panes. Figure 4.13 depicts an isometric view of this stack.

In this representation, the thin arrows pointing away from a method symbolize base invocations. As this shows, an invocation of an overridden method corresponds to removing all layers up to the one containing the invoked method; viewing the stack from the top again, the method that is now visible is executed. The thin gray arrow from method 4 of the base class to method 5 of the derived class shows what happens on invocation of self:msg5: The method lookup begins again in the current class, the dynamic data type of self.

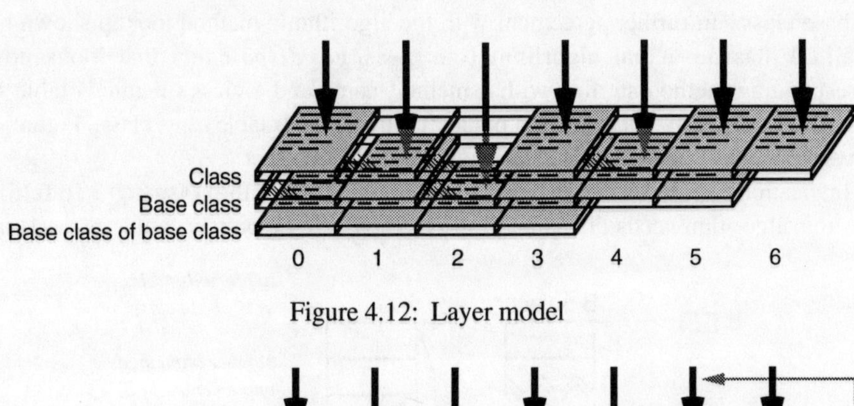


Figure 4.12: Layer model

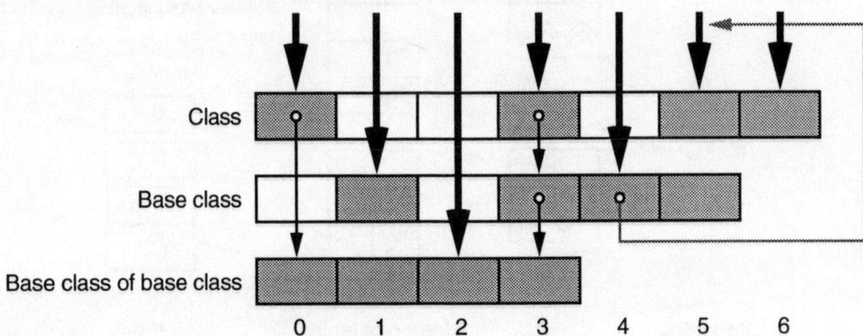


Figure 4.13: Method selection in the layer model

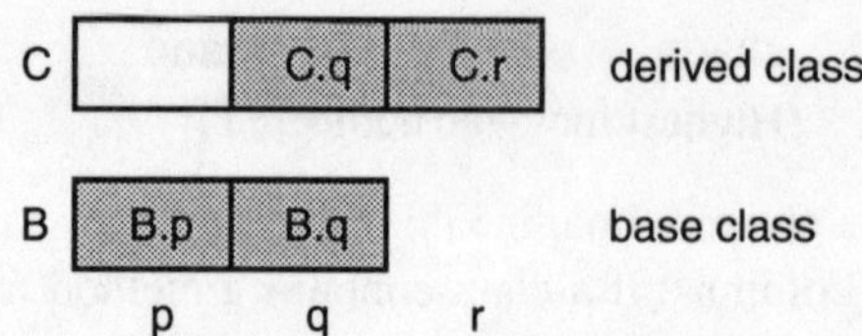


Figure 4.14: A simple example depicted as layer model

Although both these approaches are intended as thought models, they do correspond largely to today's usual realizations of dynamic binding. The remainder of this section shows how dynamic binding works in Smalltalk and C++ using the simple example in Figure 4.14.

Class C derives from class B, which implements methods p and q, whereby C inherits p and overrides q. C implements the additional method r, which cannot be applied to B objects. We employ the notation C.q for method q implemented in class C.

Smalltalk lacks explicit class interfaces and static typing. This makes sequential numbering of methods impossible and thus precludes the layer model for method lookup. Today's common Smalltalk systems use a methods table for each class; this table records the names and start addresses of all methods implemented in this class. If a method is not found in a class, the lookup continues in the base class as described in the algorithmic model. For this purpose the methods table contains a reference to the methods table of the base class. In further agreement with the algorithmic method lookup shown here, Smalltalk has an actual algorithm (the *message dispatcher*) that looks up the corresponding method starting with a method name and a class's methods table. To make this work, each object needs a pointer to the methods table of its class. Figure 4.15 shows the memory structure on creation of a B and a C object.

Invocation c:q causes the invocation of the lookup algorithm Dispatch. To fulfill its task, this algorithm needs the name of the method and the pointer to the methods table

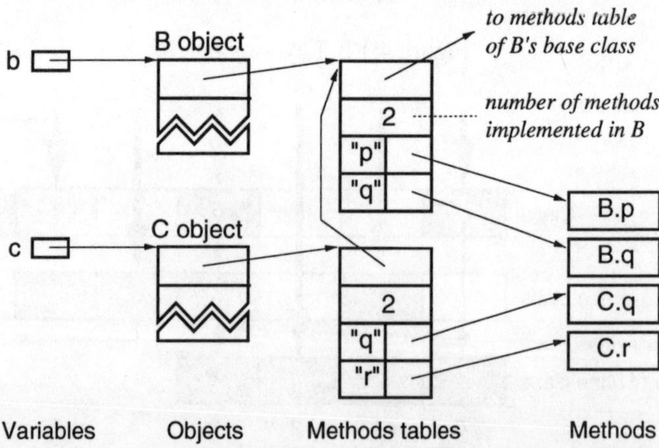


Figure 4.15: Memory model for algorithmic method lookup

where the lookup is to begin. In pseudocode this algorithm can be represented as follows:

```
Dispatch (↓name ↓tablePtr):
VAR codeAdr: Pointer;
BEGIN
    Lookup (↓name ↓tablePtr ↑codeAdr);
    WHILE codeAdr = NIL DO
        tablePtr := tablePtr^.baseTable;        -- find method table of base class
        IF tablePtr = NIL THEN HALT END;        -- no further base class
        Lookup (↓name ↓tablePtr ↑codeAdr);
    END WHILE;
    call method starting at codeAdr
END Dispatch;
```

The procedure Lookup searches in the methods table for the name of the method and returns the corresponding start address of the method (or NIL if there is no such method). Clearly the efficiency of this procedure depends almost exclusively on the efficiency of the name lookup. Usually method names are represented numerically and stored in hash tables.

Algorithmic method lookup suffers from relative sluggishness because for each message a procedure must be invoked to determine which method is to be executed. However, an advantage is the compactness of its methods tables due to inherited methods not being represented. Another advantage is the enormous flexibility to which Smalltalk owes its popularity. This approach makes it possible to add to a class a new method, which is immediately inherited by all derived classes.

Most hybrid languages (e.g., C++) use the layer model. It works with indexing in *complete* methods tables that contain all methods, including the inherited ones. The methods are numbered as described above. Each class receives a methods table with enough entries to cover all methods it contains. Since methods can now be identified directly with their indices, names are not needed. The example employed above for algorithmic method lookup produces the memory structure shown in Figure 4.16 with the layer model.

Here, too, every object has a pointer to the methods table of its class. However, here we no longer need a class's link to its base class or the number of methods in the table. On invocation b:q the lookup in the methods table begins at position 2 (the method number of q) and the method at the start address recorded there is executed. If, as in Figure 4.16, the object associated with variable b belongs to class B, then method B.q is activated; if b references a C object, C.q is invoked because method q is overridden in C. Compared with conventional statically bound procedure invocation, dynamically bound method invocation with the layer model costs three additional memory operations. This is very little in comparison to an algorithmic method lookup.

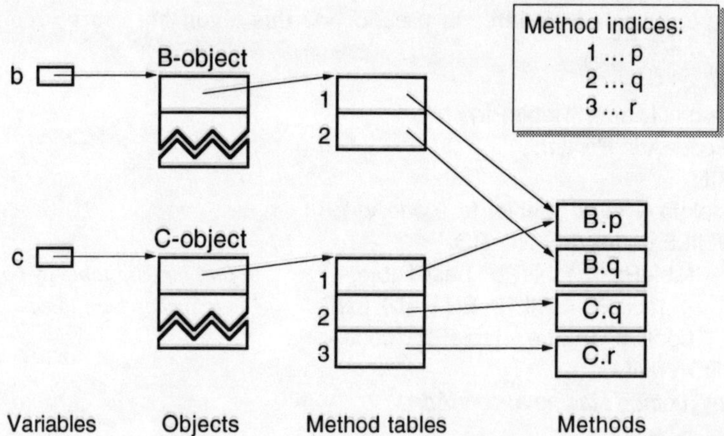


Figure 4.16: Memory model with method indexing (layer model)

In practice, methods tables are used for more than just the realization of dynamic binding. Since each class has its own methods table, it seems natural to expand the table to a class description that contains further information about the class and its objects. In addition to methods, the table normally contains:

- The name of the class
- A link to the base class
- Sizes of objects of the class
- Notes on object structure (e.g., for garbage collection)

Such information about classes and objects that does not concern the values of the instance variables is called *meta-information*. It makes it possible at run time to determine the name of an object's class or to determine whether an object directly or indirectly belongs to a given class. Unfortunately the scope of available meta-information varies greatly in different languages. For example, while a class test is a regular component of some languages, others lack this feature.

## 4.3 Kinds of inheritance

Inheritance is a concept so central to object-oriented programming that we dedicate this section to discussing some particular kinds of inheritance that are supported in certain programming languages. In particular, we treat the following points:

- Simple and multiple inheritance
- Protected inheritance
- Restricted inheritance
- Access rights

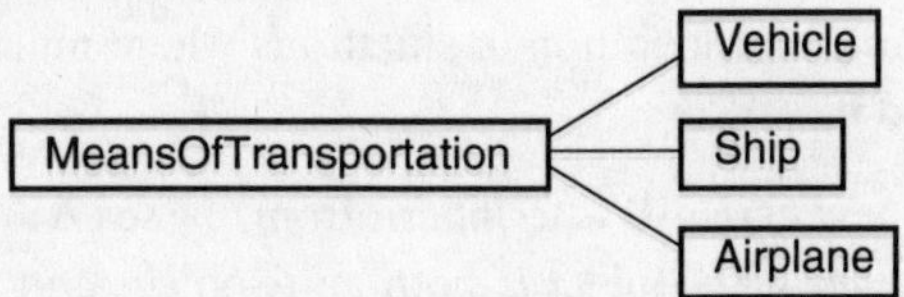


Figure 4.17: Class hierarchy of means of transportation

Above all, we intend to show that object-oriented concepts are interpreted and supported differently in various languages. This is particularly unpleasant for object-oriented design because the designer must already know in the design phase which language features will later be available for implementation.

### 4.3.1 Simple and multiple inheritance

Thus far, in designing a new class we have always used only *one* base class. We call this *simple inheritance* . In the real world we repeatedly encounter things that cannot unambiguously be assigned to one class, but actually belong to multiple classes simultaneously. For example, if we try to set up a class hierarchy of means of transportation, we might start with the simple hierarchy depicted in Figure 4.17.

These classes can then be refined to any depth as shown in Section 3.4.7.2 with the Vehicle example. If we want to incorporate an amphibious vehicle or a seaplane in our hierarchy, we encounter real problems because we can rightfully maintain that an amphibious vehicle belongs to both the class of vehicles and the class of ships. This conflict extends beyond the is-a relation to include the attributes of the classes and the operations possible on their objects. Hence a ship has a draft and an airplane a maximum flight weight, but a seaplane has both. This suggests that we might want to inherit from *both* base classes. In our example this leads to the class hierarchy in Figure 4.18.

#### 4.3.1.1 Criteria for multiple inheritance

The literature often cites examples from the real world (such as a houseboat, which we discuss later) to demonstrate the usefulness of multiple inheritance . Although such examples prove illustrative, unfortunately they contribute nothing to a critical evaluation of the practical value of multiple inheritance. Hence in the following we use an example from the world of programming to show where multiple inheritance proves useful. First,

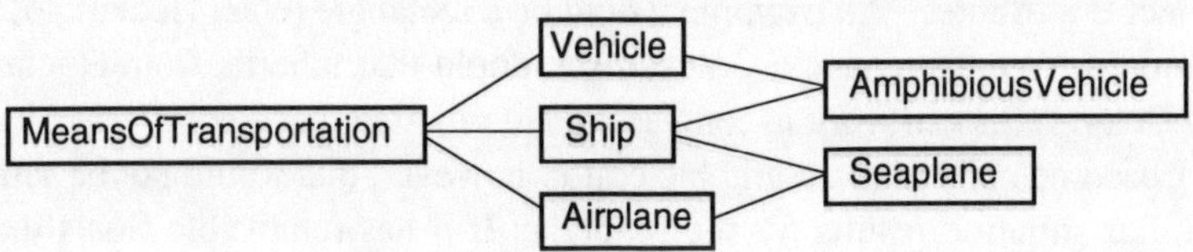


Figure 4.18: Class hierarchy with multiple inheritance

however, let us give some consideration to situations where multiple inheritance can be used and where to avoid it:

- *Is-a relation.* If a new class AB is to inherit from classes A and B, then we first need to study whether every AB object *is* both an A object *and* a B object. Only then should multiple inheritance be used. The amphibious vehicle already leaves room for discussion, since most likely it will be used primarily as a vehicle, but one that can also travel on water. Likewise a houseboat *is* primarily a boat that *has* a house or is used as such. The matter is even clearer with a seaplane: It *is* an airplane in any case, but it can land on water. One aid in deciding whether to use multiple inheritance is the compound noun that frequently sparks the idea to use multiple inheritance. The noun at the end always expresses the primary characteristic, while preceding words only define the basic term more precisely (compare, e.g., houseboat and boathouse).
- *Code reuse.* For multiple inheritance to bring noticeable benefits to programming, it must demonstrate particularly high reuse of code. If all or most operations can be inherited from only one of the base classes under consideration, then multiple inheritance is probably misguided. Stated differently, if nothing is inherited from one class, it should not be a base class.
- *Interface inheritance.* Deriving a new class from an existing one means inheriting not just code but also the interface. In the case of multiple inheritance, this means that the interface of a new class AB consists of the union of the interfaces of the base classes A and B (plus any extensions). This leads to the conclusion that multiple inheritance is appropriate wherever the sum of operations possible with the base classes approximates what is expected of the new class. Many make the error of inheriting too much, which causes unnecessary inflation of the interface of the new class with functionality that is superfluous or undesired.
- *Compatibility.* If a new class C derives from class B, then (dynamic) C objects are compatible with variables of (static) data type B. With multiple inheritance this means that objects of the new class AB can be assigned to A as well as B variables. This requires careful consideration of whether an object of the new class makes sense in the context of *every* base class. For example, if the use of an AB object at some location where a B object is expected proves unintended or undesired, some other form of realization should be considered.
- *Object identity.* During its entire lifetime, an object always belongs to one and the same class. This should be considered if multiple inheritance is to be used to give an A object B attributes. An example would be a rectangle (class Rectangle) that is to be colored. We can create a ColoredRectangle that inherits from Rectangle and from Color. This can work as long as we are satisfied that a colorless rectangle can never become colored. In a graphic editor, however, this would not be satisfactory. A similar situation results for the seaplane: If it has removable floats that can be replaced by wheels, then it must maintain its identity, but change its class

membership. However, such a mutation is impossible (except in some specialized languages).

One example of multiple inheritance emerges if we want to map the contents of a disk storage medium (magneto-optical disk or CD-ROM) onto objects. The atomic components are files (class File) which are either at the top level of the disk (class Disk) or in a directory (class Directory). By factoring common attributes, we arrive at three abstract classes:

- NamedItem: Disks, files and directories all have a name. The naming conventions (permitted characters, maximum length) tend to be uniform for all three classes.
- Container: Disks and directories, in contrast to a file, can contain any number of files or further directories (as long as the storage capacity suffices).
- Element: Directories and files share that they are contained in a container. They can be moved from one container to another, copied or removed (which is not possible with a disk).

These considerations naturally lead to the class hierarchy in Figure 4.19. This class hierarchy is not an artificial example that we present here to demonstrate the usefulness of multiple inheritance. Indeed, it evolved in the realm of a research project as an initial solution for the design of a class library. Now let us test to what extent the criteria listed above are fulfilled for multiple inheritance in the case of the class Directory:

- *Is-a relation*. A Directory is both a Container (because it can contain additional parts) and an Element (because it is itself in a Container). Neither of the base classes has precedence over the other, and neither can be challenged readily.
- *Code reuse*. In Container all methods are realized to determine how many and which entries compose a Directory, and to check the existence of an entry with a certain name. In Element we have all methods for moving a Directory to another Container and for checking to which Container the Directory belongs. A Directory can thus inherit essential methods from both base classes.
- *Interface inheritance*. All operations possible with Container and Element objects are also possible and sensible with Directory objects. This is not surprising because the abstract base classes evolved from the factoring out of commonalities of the classes now derived from it.

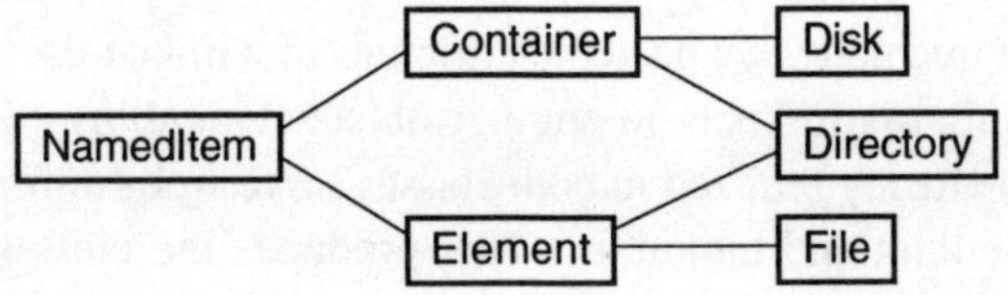


Figure 4.19: Multiple inheritance in the modeling of disk storage

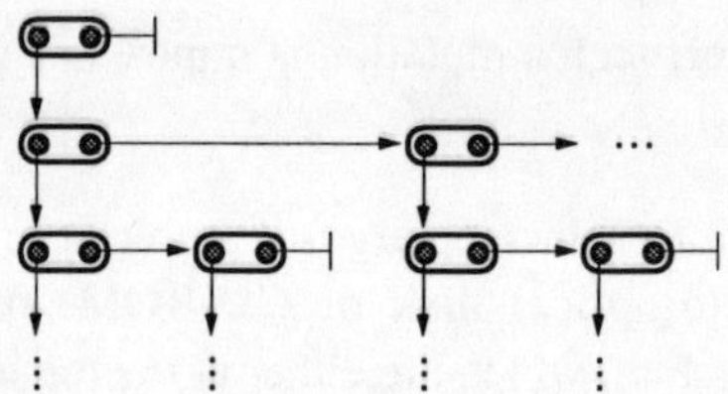

Figure 4.20: Realization of trees as linked nodes

- *Compatibility*. A Directory can serve both as a Container and as an Element. For example, in its Container context it can be manipulated like a Disk, and in its Element context it can be moved like a file to another container.
- *Object identity*. A Directory is created to collect files within a disk and retains this purpose until it is deleted. In particular, it is never transformed into a disk or a file.

A directory behaves like a textbook example and fulfills all requirements for inheriting from two base classes. Nevertheless, it is not a typical example of the usage of multiple inheritance nowadays because in the design of the above hierarchy we were guided by interface considerations and viewed the objects as black boxes. This is unavoidable if we want to exploit polymorphism and still strive for clear interfaces with matching parameters and operation types. Consider, for example, the interfaces of the Directory operations parent to determine the containing Container and the operation contains to check whether it contains a certain Element:

```
parent: Container;                  -- can return either a Disk or a Directory
contains(e:Element): Boolean;       -- e can be either a File or a Directory
```

The interfaces clearly show which objects are involved in these operations; using them can scarcely bring surprises that the compiler will not detect due to incompatibility.

In practice, multiple inheritance is seldom used to achieve clear interfaces and clean abstract concepts; instead, the goal tends to be to reuse as much written code as possible. The emphasis tends to be not interface inheritance but implementation inheritance. An example is the Eiffel class Tree (originally TREE) in [Meyer 1988]. Meyer does not distinguish between trees and tree nodes (actually, the designation TreeNode would be more appropriate). A tree node is realized as a linked element with a link to its right sibling. Furthermore, a tree node is a linked list in which its children are stored (see Figure 4.20).

To implement a tree node, we need the attributes of a linked list (LinkedList) and one attribute of a node that is linkable to another object (Linkable). The operations (and instance variables!) already realized in both classes serve well for forming trees, so Tree inherits from LinkedList and Linkable. This produces the class hierarchy shown in Figure 4.21.

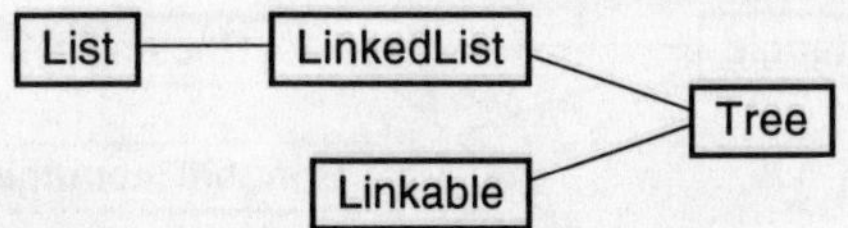


Figure 4.21: Multiple inheritance in modeling tree nodes

Note that classes List and Linkable have no base classes. Such *independent classes* are very important for comfortable reuse through multiple inheritance, as we shall see later in the subsection on conflict resolution under 4.3.1.4.

#### 4.3.1.2 Mix-In

Independent classes are frequently used only to describe attributes which are then imposed on classes via multiple inheritance. For example, with multiple inheritance we could create the variations depicted in Figure 4.22 from the classes Rectangle and Circle with the help of the attribute classes Gray and Shaded.

We term this approach *mix-in* because new attributes are mixed into existing classes. The hierarchy diagram in Figure 4.23 shows the multiplicity of inheritance relationships that ensue. This example was provided only for didactic reasons; in practice, mixing in attributes should be avoided if there is the possibility that at run time one and the same object at some time might have a certain attribute and then later lose it, or that it might gain an attribute. Multiple inheritance always defines attributes for an entire class (in the everyday as well as the object-oriented sense) of objects. It is not suited for decorating an existing object with a new attribute. This amounts to a state transition for the object and can only be realized with instance variables (e.g., shadow, shadow width and shadow color) that are modified by means of corresponding methods.

#### 4.3.1.3 Repeated inheritance

A special form of multiple inheritance is *repeated inheritance* as employed in Eiffel [Meyer 1988]. Here a class can inherit not only from multiple *different* base classes, but also repeatedly from *the same* base class. In most object-oriented languages repeated inheritance can only occur indirectly. We also used it in the above Directory example

| | no shadow | with shadow |
|---|---|---|
| no gray | | |
| with gray | | |

Figure 4.22: Rectangles and circles with various attributes

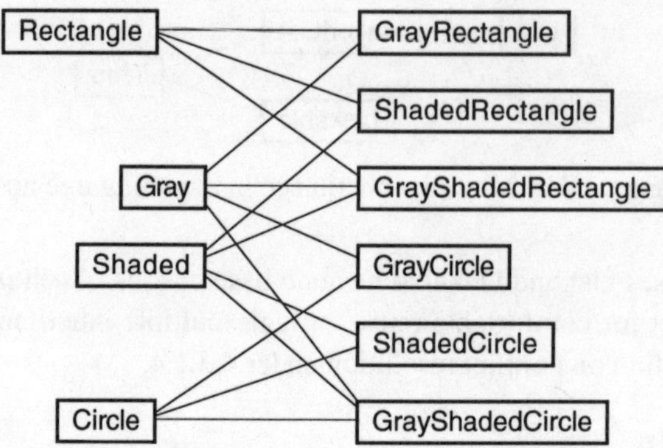


Figure 4.23: Class hierarchy for rectangles and circles with various attributes

without expressly calling attention to it: The class Directory inherits from the class NamedItem via two routes (via Container and Element). Eiffel also permits direct repeated inheritance. For example, the class DualEmployee (persons who work at two jobs) can be realized with repeated inheritance, as Figure 4.24 shows.

We have represented repeated inheritance here with two links between the base class and the derived class. Repeated inheritance is said to be justified here because a doubly employed person really *is* an employee in a double sense. The dual employee has two employers, two supervisors, two personnel numbers, two sets of hiring data, two job descriptions and two incomes. However, the problem arises of what should occur when a DualEmployee object receives the message personnelNumber (defined in class Employer). Which of the two personnel numbers should be returned? A similar problem arises with indirect repeated inheritance. We will treat this question in more detail in the subsequent section under conflict resolution.

Furthermore, in this example we must note that a dual employee need not remain a dual employee for a lifetime and probably was not always one. Such a class is thus at best suited for modeling a census or a poll at a certain time, but not for a directory of residents of a city because a dual employee would otherwise have to change class membership upon quitting one company and thus becoming a simple employee (again).

### 4.3.1.4 Simple versus multiple inheritance

Over time many object-oriented languages have been developed and numerous conventional languages have been extended with object-oriented elements. While the first object-oriented languages provided only simple inheritance, some later languages were equipped with multiple inheritance features. Some object-oriented languages (e.g., C++) were only extended for multiple inheritance later. Today we observe a general

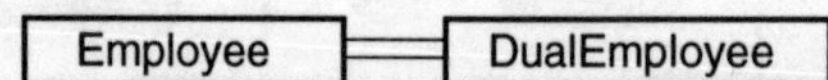


Figure 4.24: A simple example of repeated inheritance

trend toward multiple inheritance, but the critical voices are also becoming ever louder. The question of whether we need multiple inheritance or whether it should be avoided due to its associated problems is a favorite subject of discussion among experts. Thus we can hardly write about object-oriented programming without treating this question. We should note at the start of the discussion that the authors were also originally fascinated by the possibilities of multiple inheritance. However, over time, both in practice and by studying newer programming languages, we have become convinced that simple inheritance suffices quite well, which the Smalltalk libraries impressively demonstrate. We even go so far as to say that we consider multiple inheritance a dangerous instrument that is frequently abused and all too often not comprehended fully. In the following subsections we justify this opinion.

*Complexity*

Simple inheritance produces a class hierarchy that is always a *tree* or a *forest* of trees (in the event of no common root class). As soon as we involve multiple inheritance, these simple structures become *directed acyclical graphs* (DAGs). If a hierarchy contains many classes, this creates a tapestry that is difficult to comprehend and use. This is already reflected in the difficulty in graphically representing the relationships between multiply inheriting classes. The example in Figure 4.23 provides a sample with its gray and shadowed rectangles and circles. This problem in depicting multiple inheritance has practical ramifications: Most software tools to support object-oriented programming (*class browsers*) depict the class hierarchy graphically (or at least as an indented list). This is easy to implement for simple inheritance, and the user also easily comes to terms with it.

Another complexity problem arises with *method lookup*. To look up the implementation of a certain method for simple inheritance, it suffices to search the (linear) inheritance chain to the root. For multiple inheritance the predecessors of *one* class already form a complex graph that has to be searched systematically. This significantly encumbers the programmer both in debugging and in studying someone else's program. Not only for the programmer, but also for the compiler that has to translate the program to machine language, this task is anything but simple. The layer model presented in Section 4.2.5, "Dynamic models for method lookup", is not applicable to multiple inheritance in this simple form, and algorithmic method lookup becomes more complex (and slower) because at each stage the lookup continues not just in one base class, but parallel in multiple branches of the base class graph. Experience with languages supporting multiple inheritance has shown that multiple inheritance slows execution and costs storage – sometimes even if the programmer does not employ multiple inheritance at all!

*Conflicts*

The second problem accompanying the use of multiple inheritance arises when a class AB inherits an operation from each of its base classes A and B with the same name m. Which method should an AB object execute when it receives the message m? We have a conflict that only the programmer can resolve. We find three fundamental approaches in various programming languages:

① Method m must be *overridden* in class AB. In this implementation method m of only one of the base classes can be invoked. This requires a base construct for specifying the desired base class, e.g., with base[A]:m. Naturally it is also possible to sequentially invoke method m from *both* base classes. However, this kind of conflict resolution functions only if m from A and m from B have the same interface. If the number of parameters differs or even a parameter type does not match, then these are *different* operations that cannot be overridden with *one* method.

② At least one of the inherited m methods must be *renamed* in the inheriting class. For example, the method inherited from B can be renamed mb. This means that an AB object ab now understands messages m and mb, whereby ab:m causes the invocation of the method inherited from A and ab:mb of that from B. In many cases this is desired because we want to have both operations. However, there are situations that easily cause confusion: If object ab is assigned to variable b of static class B, operation mb is not possible with variable b (because the renaming applies only to class AB), but naturally b:m is permitted. However, this invocation does not have the effect of ab:m, but that of ab:mb.

③ The conflict resolution is left to the *clients* of class AB. Both methods are inherited, but the client of an AB variable must explicitly specify which method is meant with each use, e.g., by an invocation of the form ab[A]:m. More precisely, the conflict is not resolved, but only passed on to the client. Things get particularly unpleasant when such a conflict cannot be resolved by a one-time qualification, for example, because class A itself has already multiply inherited method m; then the base class specification must be repeated in the form ab[A][D]:m.

Conflicts of method names prove particularly troublesome if both base classes A and B have a common root (Figure 4.25). This is a case of indirect repeated inheritance. This means that every method defined in C or in any of its base classes triggers a conflict in AB. This is true even if the methods are not overridden in A or in B, in which case we know that there is only one implementation of each. Keep in mind that at a later time a method in one of the classes A or B could be overridden after all, which would invalidate class AB. Renaming one of the methods for conflict resolution does not prove a suitable means in this case because we only want to provide the inherited operation once. In the Directory example, class NamedItem will provide one method to query the name, one for

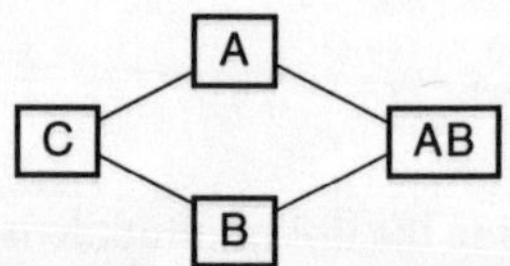


Figure 4.25: Rhombus structure for multiple inheritance

renaming, and one for deleting. All these operations are only needed once in class Directory as well; and they should have the same names there. Thus the only remaining resolution of such conflicts is overriding. Yet if a class hierarchy has a root class with only 20 methods, then in every multiply inherited class at least these 20 methods (probably even more) must be overridden. With 15 such classes we have 300 methods that have to be implemented only for the sake of conflict resolution.

*Repetition of components*
Another problem arises with repeated inheritance regarding whether the components of the repeatedly inherited class should be duplicated. Both sides of this question can be argued convincingly: The example of the dual employee supports the duplication of components because the dual employee needs the work-related specifications twice. The Directory example counters duplication because the name defined in NamedItem should only be inherited once (a Directory has only *one* name). The AmphibiousVehicle mentioned above, which also repeatedly inherits from MeansOfTransportation (Figure 4.18), is an example showing that we need both duplicate and unique components: The brand, series number, owner and other registration data are components that we need only once. The range, fuel consumption and permissible load depend on whether the vehicle is operated on land or in water and are thus needed twice. To be able to make such differentiations purposefully requires above all a suitable language feature, which makes the programming language more difficult to master. It is particularly unpleasant that the implementor of a repeatedly inheriting class needs to know which components are inherited via different paths. This means that the principle of information hiding must be disabled so that the programmer can define which components are unique and which are duplicates.

For these reasons we recommend avoiding multiple inheritance whenever possible. Practice has shown that we can get along quite well without it. This is reflected in the fact that most class libraries are built on simple inheritance. Furthermore, many programming languages permit only simple inheritance; a design based on multiple inheritance would have to be implemented differently in such languages. The following section describes how to emulate multiple inheritance with simple inheritance and the considerations that play a role here.

#### 4.3.1.5 Emulating multiple inheritance

Sometimes a developer is confronted with the task of implementing a design based on multiple inheritance in a language that supports only simple inheritance. This can occur, for example, if multiple inheritance seems to actually impose itself in a certain situation or if the task calls for porting a program that uses multiple inheritance to another language that does not support it. Then the developer must circumvent multiple inheritance. There are various options for doing this, the practicability of which depends on the reasons for using multiple inheritance in the first place.

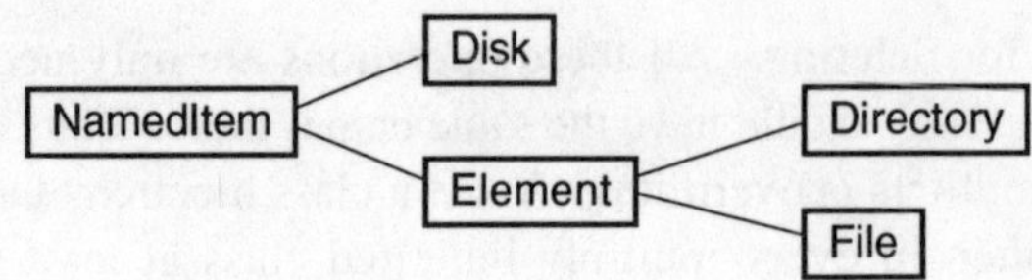


Figure 4.26: Result of redesign to remove multiple inheritance

From a software engineering viewpoint, the best option is a complete redesign of the program. Naturally this requires significant effort, but it leads to a clean solution without tricks. The best approach to redesign is to create a different abstract model for each class with multiple inheritance. For the Directory example we could simply define a disk as a storage medium that *has* a directory (the root directory). Then a disk would no longer be a Container, and Directory would be the only class derived from Container. The class Container thus becomes superfluous because we no longer need an abstract intermediate layer to combine the common attributes of Disk and Directory. With the omission of this class the class hierarchy becomes somewhat simpler (Figure 4.26).

This restructuring naturally also has ramifications for the usage of these classes. Assuming that we could previously query the number of elements directly contained on a disk d simply with d:nElements, now we first have to procure the directory of the disk and then determine the number of elements in it with (d:rootDirectory):nElements. For an object of class Element we can no longer say unconditionally that it is contained in a Directory (previously Container). Because the root directory of the disk no longer resides in a further directory, we need to take measures to prevent it being moved to another directory, for example. Hence a Directory object needs to know whether it is contained in a further directory.

Often multiple inheritance is used only to inherit some additional operations. In such mix-in cases, the desired effect can be achieved by simply extending the class by the respective methods. If this needs to be done for multiple classes, this implies code duplication, which object-oriented programming actually strives to avoid. One possibility is to partially deviate from object-oriented principles and to invoke conventional procedures in the additional methods to handle the required operations.

If multiple inheritance is employed to give objects additional attributes, instance variables provide a solution. This is suggested by the observation that the gray and shadowed rectangles and circles *have* a shade of gray and a shadow. The is-a relation (the rectangle *is* a shadowed object) is transformed to a has-a relation. This reduces the number of classes to two, Rectangle and Circle, both of which can have a shade of gray and a shadow. Shadowless objects can now be realized with various conventions, for example, by using an invisible shadow (hidden completely behind the original) or by giving the instance variable representing the shadow the value NIL. (The latter solution requires that all operations on this instance variable must test whether the value is NIL.)

In any case, such modifiable instance variables provide flexibility in the usage of the objects. This creates powerful classes that can be reused in many different applications.

However, it does have two drawbacks: first, it requires many case distinctions to test which attributes a certain object has because class membership no longer reflects these attributes; second, during reuse all possible components might not be used, so that a lot of dead weight could be dragged along.

A frequent error in the use of multiple inheritance is that a has-a relation is misunderstood as an is-a relation. For example, a houseboat *is* not a house, but a boat that *has* a structure to be used as a house. A tree node (Tree) *is* an object that can be linked to others (Linkable), but it *has* a list of its children (LinkedList). This leads to a circumvention of multiple inheritance known in technical jargon as a *wrapper*. The developer selects a primary base class that best fits the is-a relation. The other relations are transformed to has-a relations by extending the object with components of the other base classes. If class AB previously had two base classes A and B, the developer might choose base class A and realize the B attributes (similar to the shadowed rectangle) with an instance variable b in class B. Every method defined only in B must be incorporated in AB as well; in the corresponding method the task is delegated to the B object contained in the AB object. A method m in class AB could take the following form:

```
m (x: Something) IS
BEGIN
   b:m(x)              -- Forward message to b
END;
```

In this solution we sacrifice the compatibility of AB objects with variables of data type B. Fortunately this is not even necessary because it makes no sense anyway to assign to a variable of class B an object only because it *has* a B.

In our opinion, multiple inheritance should be handled very critically. Striving from the start for a design without multiple inheritance can spare the developer difficulties later. The possibilities for emulating multiple inheritance presented here should thus be seen in the same light. Multiple inheritance is analogous to structured programming: it is much easier to write a well-structured program from the start than to impose structure afterwards on an unstructured program.

## 4.3.2 Protected inheritance

In a well-planned object-oriented design, not only the overall program system but also its integral parts, the objects, are structured according to the modularization principle, whereby the methods represent the components that make up the functionality of the object. A new object is built by adding new components and replacing existing ones. Here several base methods are frequently used in many other methods. In pure object-oriented languages these include such elementary operations as copying objects. These elementary operations are normally implemented only once at the root of the class hierarchy. These methods should not be overridden because many other methods (which

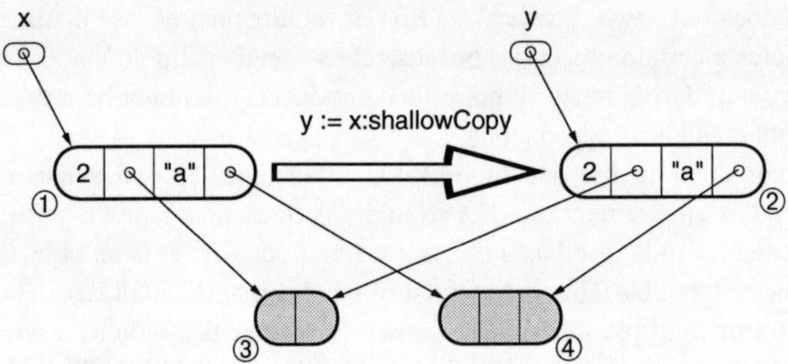


Figure 4.27: Result of the message shallowCopy

we might not even know) depend on certain behavior. This indicates the need for a way to protect methods from accidental overriding.

An example of such a critical operation is shallowCopy, a method to produce a copy of an object whose instance variables have the same values as those of the original, a *shallow copy*. Any references to other objects are retained in the instance variables of the copy (to the same objects as in the original). Figure 4.27 depicts the result of such a copy operation.

After the statement y := x:shallowCopy, objects ¿ and ¡ associated with x and y are *equal*, but not *identical*. The two references within the object do refer to *identical* objects ¬ and √. If object ¬ represents an attribute of object ¿, then a change in its state affects not only ¿ but also ¡.

shallowCopy (sometimes called clone) is a critical method because it is used by all other copy operations (in Smalltalk, e.g., deepCopy and copy). Overriding shallowCopy could cause a catastrophe and must be avoided. In most programming languages there is a way to prevent the overriding of methods. This usually amounts to extensive commentary that explains that this method must not be overridden and why not. Few languages offer a language element with which a method can be protected effectively against overriding, for example:

```
INTERFACE OF C;
  method1;
  method2 PROTECTED;
  ...
END C.
```

In this case, during compilation of a class derived from C, the compiler can reject an attempt to override method2 as not permissible. Without such a possibility there is no means to prevent the accidental overriding of the method. The only solution in hybrid languages is to implement the operations to be protected not as methods but as conventional procedures. To create a copy of an object x, the programmer must write y := ShallowCopy(x) instead of y := x:shallowCopy. The difference is less a matter of syntax than of fundamental nature: this approach produces an external algorithm that affects an object *from the outside*. For more complex operations this violates the principle of information hiding. In addition, the possibility to create a shallow copy of an object cannot be read from the interface description of the class.

### 4.3.3 Restricted inheritance

Often inheritance is used simply to inherit as much functionality as possible from an existing class. This can turn into overkill because too many operations are inherited that are not needed in the derived class. Within a project this is not so bad – apart from the inherited dead weight – because conventions and suitable documentation can assure that nobody uses the extraneous methods. A class designed for reuse must not contain any such potentially dangerous operations because there is no assurance that future users will abide by the conventions described in the documentation.

We will explain this situation with the help of a simple example. We assume the existence of a class Array for dynamic arrays with the following interface:

```
INTERFACE OF Array;
INHERITS FROM Object;
    size: Integer;                        -- returns the number of elements
    changeSize (newSize:Integer);         -- changes the extent of the array
    put (index:Integer; elem:Object);     -- places elem at position index
    get (index:Integer): Object;          -- returns the element at position index
END Array.
```

On the basis of this class a stack (Stack) is to be implemented. We approach the problem from the consideration that a Stack *is* an Array where elements can be appended or removed only at one end. A possible implementation could take the following form:

```
INTERFACE OF Stack;
INHERITS FROM Array;
    push (elem:Object);
    pop: Object;
END Stack.

IMPLEMENTATION OF Stack;

    VAR sp: Integer;                  -- stack pointer

    push (elem:Object) IS
    BEGIN
        sp := sp + 1;
        IF sp > self:size THEN self:changeSize(sp + 10) END;    -- enlarge stack
        self:put(sp,elem)
    END push;
```

```
    pop: Object IS
    BEGIN
        IF sp = 0 THEN HALT END;
        sp := sp – 1;
        RETURN self:get(sp + 1)
    END pop;

    initialize IS
    BEGIN
        sp := 0
    END initialize;

END Stack.
```

This solution is correct in the sense that the required operations can be carried out with Stack objects. But it fails to fulfill the condition that a stack permits appending and removal *only at one end* because in addition to the operations push and pop the operations put and get inherited from Array are available. With the method changeSize it even becomes possible to make a stack smaller than its fill-level variable sp indicates.

It would be justified to argue that the base class was poorly selected because a Stack *is* not an Array, but should only *have* an Array to store its elements. We will see later that this criticism provides a starting point for a better solution, but let us retain the selected inheritance for the time being.

To prevent the user of class Stack from utilizing the methods get, put and changeSize, we need a way to restrict the interface defined by the combination of inheritance and new operations. Since the primary goal is to deny the availability to clients of some of the operations inherited from the base class, we term this *restricted inheritance*, which amounts to renouncing an inheritance.

There are two fundamental approaches to achieving the desired effect. The first is based on reducing the inherited interface. This variant is realized in Eiffel, for example, which allows the explicit declaration in each class of which methods are to be *exported* (made available to clients). The inheritance diagram in Figure 4.28 shows this approach.

The methods get and put can be used in Stack, but they are not accessible to clients. If a new class is derived from the class Stack, then a new export statement there can redefine the visibility of inherited methods. For example, the method pop could be hidden, while get might be made available again.

At first glance the export mechanism provides exactly what we need. The following example shows operations that are permitted and forbidden with a Stack object:

```
VAR s:Stack; e:Object;

e := s:get(3);          -- forbidden; not exported
s:push(e);              -- permitted
```

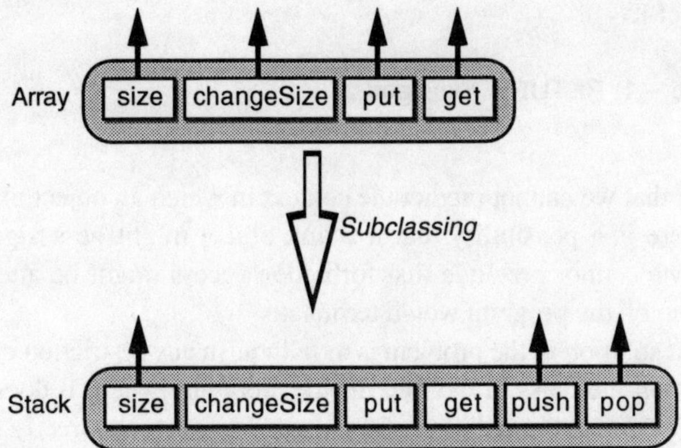


Figure 4.28: Reduction of the interface by explicit export; methods with arrows are exported

Considering polymorphism casts a different light on the subject when we modify the above example as follows:

```
VAR a:Array; s:Stack; e:Object;

a := s;                    -- polymorphic assignment

e := a:get(3);             -- permitted
a:push(e);                 -- forbidden; undefined
```

In accordance with the usual rules of polymorphism, a Stack object can be assigned to an Array variable, and the operation get is permitted with an Array variable. Therefore the (permitted) statement a := s; e := a:get(3); has the same effect as the (forbidden) statement e := s:get(3). A crafty developer of a client can thus circumvent such interface restrictions at will.

The second approach is the *invalidation* of inherited methods. Here the interface is inherited, but the implementor of the derived class assures that the methods cannot be invoked. A popular measure is to override the method so as to output an error message and terminate the program, for example:

```
get (index:Integer): Object IS
BEGIN
    Write('Attempted to call get for a Stack'); HALT
END get;
```

Although this does not prevent the use of the Stack method get, it at least assures that the error will not remain undetected to inflict greater damage at some later point. With this solution note that the get method can no longer be used from within Stack. Instead, the overridden method of the base class must be invoked:

```
pop: Object IS
BEGIN
   sp := sp – 1; RETURN base:get(sp + 1)
END pop;
```

One problem is that we cannot predict the context in which an object of a new class will be used. If there is a possibility that a Stack object might be assigned to an Array variable, then we cannot preclude that forbidden access might be attempted with this variable, whereupon the program would terminate.

The cleanest solution to the problem is to relinquish any restriction of inheritance and instead to position the class in the inheritance hierarchy where it does not inherit any unnecessary or undesired operations. Stack could be derived directly from Object, for example, and thus be defined as a sibling of Array. In order to utilize the Array functionality, an instance variable elements is added to Stack; any needed Array operations (in our example, only size) are delegated to this component. The following implementation shows how this functions:

```
INTERFACE OF Stack;
INHERITS FROM Object;
   size: Integer;
   push (elem:Object);
   pop: Object;
END Stack.

IMPLEMENTATION OF Stack;
   VAR
      elements: Array;
      sp: Integer;

   size: Integer IS
   BEGIN
      RETURN elements:size          -- delegate message to the array
   END push;

   push (elem:Object) IS
   BEGIN
      sp := sp + 1;
      IF sp > elements:size THEN elements:changeSize(sp + 10) END;
         -- enlarge stack
      elements:put(sp,elem)
   END push;
```

```
    pop: Object IS
    BEGIN
        IF sp = 0 THEN HALT END;
        sp := sp – 1; RETURN elements:get(sp + 1)
    END pop;

    initialize IS
    BEGIN
        elements := Array:new;          -- allocate the array of elements
        sp := 0
    END initialize;

END Stack.
```

With this solution a Stack object really provides only the operations that we expect of it. The only significant changes remaining in the implementation are that the method size must be implemented (because it can no longer be inherited) and that an Array object must be generated during initialization. There is also a restriction for the client because it can no longer process Stack objects in an Array context.

### 4.3.4 Access rights

Object-oriented programming represents an excellent modularization technique because every class is used like a module in the conventional sense for the solution of all subproblems that arise in connection with a certain data type. A class also functions like an abstract data type because the components contained in its objects are hidden toward the outside.

A class typically contains many relatively small methods, many of which are only used internally and not intended for use by clients. Thus, in addition to the ability to restrict access to components, we need a way to determine the access rights for methods. We discussed one aspect of this problem in Section 4.3.3.

In conventional programming a module has two interfaces, an import and an export interface (compare Section 3.4.3.1, "Guidelines for modularization"). These two interfaces provide the connection for the client (export) and to the modules used (import). With inheritance in object-oriented programming, we have two additional interfaces (see Figure 4.29).

The class depicted in gray in Figure 4.29 has the usual export interface to the client at the top and import interface to classes used at the bottom. We are primarily interested in the export interface because it provides information on how objects of the class can be used. The import interface is only of interest if we want to modify the class. The base and heir interfaces are analogous. The base interface is a special kind of import interface and thus only of interest to clients inasmuch as the base class determines the export interface of a class derived from it.

In deriving a new class from an existing one, the heir interface plays a central role. Alone through the possibility of base invocations, the heirs have a broader interface available than do the clients. In addition, in deriving a new class, we often find that the operations exported from the base class prove inadequate or only awkwardly fulfill the goals. Another aspect comes into play due to the multitude of small methods that typically evolve from object-oriented design. Large methods should be decomposed into multiple smaller ones so that they (and the subfunctions they embody) can be overridden in derived classes in a targeted way. If heirs and clients have the same interface, this means that the individual methods also have to be provided to the client. Since these are usually very specialized and in part dangerous operations, this is undesirable.

Thus we need a language feature to explicitly control access rights to certain methods. At least we should be able to specify which of the following access modes a method permits:

- Public (accessible to clients),
- Protected (accessible to heirs) or
- Private (only usable internally)

Some programming languages permit such declarations. Examples include C++ and Omega [Blaschek 1991]. In addition, C++ permits making certain methods accessible only to certain clients (*friends*). Eiffel permits only the declaration of a method as public or not; independent of this declaration, *all* methods are accessible to the heirs – Eiffel has no protected methods. In Oberon-2 [Mössenböck 1991] access rights are defined not for classes but for modules. An exported method can be invoked outside a module and all other methods only within. Since in Oberon-2 multiple classes can be implemented in a module, this language provides a mixed form of the access rights listed above. Some languages offer no possibility to influence access to individual methods. For example, in Object-Pascal and Smalltalk all methods are public.

As with methods, it can be practical to define access rights for instance variables. Thus far we have always assumed that instance variables – in adherence to the principle of information hiding – should be encapsulated. However, this can be troublesome if

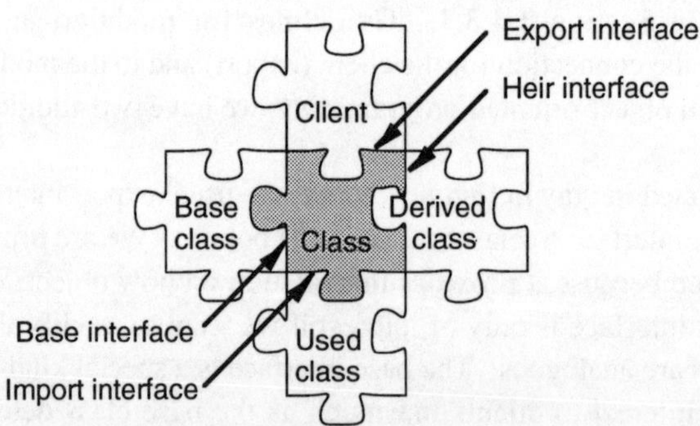


Figure 4.29: The interfaces of a class

we want to derive a new class from an existing one. One remedy is to define two access routines for each relevant instance variable for testing and for modifying the instance variable. The invocations of these routines take time, so many languages offer the possibility to access the instance variables directly. Here we have the same categories of access rights as for methods. In the above languages the access rights for instance variables are handled as for methods. The only exception is Smalltalk, where all instance variables are always protected, in contrast to Smalltalk methods.

### 4.3.5 Covariance and contravariance

Some object-oriented languages permit not only the overriding of inherited methods, but also to a restricted extent the overriding of interfaces. They permit a redefinition of data types of arguments or function results. Such modifications must, however, adhere to certain rules. The data types defined in the base class can be generalized or specialized. The specialization of a data type in the derived (more specialized) class is termed *covariance*; generalization is called *contravariance*. This section shows how and where covariance and contravariance can be employed in object-oriented programming. First let us examine which problems arise if we do not have these mechanisms available.

Some methods always return an object of the same (dynamic) type as the receiver object. Examples include the copy operations such as shallowCopy (Section 4.3.2). The creation of a copy of an object can be implemented already in the root class of the hierarchy. The only prerequisite is that dynamic storage must be reserved and it must be possible to query the storage space and address of an object at run time. The following fragment sketches how the method shallowCopy can be implemented in class Object.

```
INTERFACE OF Object;
...
   shallowCopy: Object;
   byteSize: Integer;
   address: Pointer;
...
END Object.

IMPLEMENTATION OF Object;
...
   shallowCopy: Object IS
   VAR
        newObject: Object;
        objSize: Integer;
        srcAddr, destAddr: Pointer;
   BEGIN
        objSize := self:byteSize;
        newObject := new object with objSize bytes;
```

```
            srcAddr := self:address; destAddr := newObject:address;
            copy objSize bytes from srcAddr to destAddr;
            RETURN newObject
        END shallowCopy;
    ...
    END Object.
```

Thus we have a simple tool for making any number of duplicates of an existing object with the same contents. However, the definition in the class interface has a flaw: the method shallowCopy is defined so that it always returns an object of (static) data type Object. Thus if we duplicate a Rectangle object, the statement newRect := oldRect:shallowCopy (whereby both oldRect and newRect should be declared as Rectangles) causes a compilation error because the compiler only knows that the invocation oldRect:shallowCopy returns a value of data type Object. This could also be a circle or a stack, but according to the rules of polymorphism such objects cannot be assigned to a Rectangle variable.

A polymorphic assignment along the class hierarchy thus leads to a dead end with the means available to us so far because we can assign any object to a variable of data type Object, but we can never again assign this object to a variable of its actual (dynamic) data type. Therefore most programming languages provide language features that permit such an assignment anyway. C++ and Object-Pascal use a *type cast* (a data type conversion). The reader should be aware that this operation is uncertain because only at run time (if at all) can the determination be made of whether an object matches the data type of the variable to which it is assigned.

For example, if we use a type cast of the form T(x) to transform object x to a T object, a run-time error can occur if x is not compatible with data type T. Depending on the programming language, the error might be detected during the type cast and the program could be terminated in a more or less orderly fashion, or an indirect error that is difficult to localize could occur because operations arc carried out with object x for which it is not designed.

If the method shallowCopy always returns an object of the same type as the receiver, some languages have a particular feature to express this. Eiffel uses the construct like Current, and Omega has the special identifier Same for this purpose. Applied to the shallowCopy example, this leads to the following class definition:

```
INTERFACE OF Object;
...
    shallowCopy: Same;
...
END Object.
```

With this definition the assignment x := x:shallowCopy can always be used without problems because now the compiler knows that the operation shallowCopy returns an object of the same type as variable x.

Naturally certain conditions have to be met for the Same construct to be really type safe. A method with the result type Same must be designed so that it returns only values of the pseudotype Same in every RETURN statement. This could be:

- self (the receiver object is naturally of type Same)
- the result of a message to self, whereby the message must be defined with the function type Same

The case described here, where the data type of the result object must match the data type of the receiver object, is a special case of covariance. Consider the following simple example. We assume the definition in class B of operation m with function type X:

```
INTERFACE OF B;                  IMPLEMENTATION OF B;
   m: X;                            m: X IS
END B.                              VAR x: X;
                                    BEGIN ... return x END m
                                 END B.

INTERFACE OF C;                  IMPLEMENTATION OF C;
INHERITS FROM B;                    m: X IS   -- method m is overridden
-- no interface changes             VAR y: Y;
END C.                              BEGIN ... return y END m
                                 END C.
```

In class C, derived from class B, method m is overridden such that it always returns an object of class Y. To make this work, Y must derive from X. The following program fragment shows why this is so:

```
VAR b:B; c:C; x:X;
...
b := c;
x := b:m;
```

Since a C object can be assigned to a B variable, method m must *always* (i.e., even if it is overridden in a class derived from B) return an object that can be assigned to an X variable, and this includes the objects of class X and all its derived classes.

Although we now know that method m in class C always returns a Y object, the following program fragment is not permissible:

```
VAR c:C; y:Y;
...
y := c:m;
```

The reason is in the usual compatibility rules: the definition of method m (which was inherited from class B) specifies its function type as X, and X objects cannot be assigned to a Y variable. We can remedy this by modifying the definition of the method in class

C. Such interface modifications are possible in Eiffel and Omega. In Eiffel we employ a redefinition, for which we introduce the following notation:

```
INTERFACE OF C;
INHERITS FROM B;
   REDEFINE m: Y;
END C.
```

Here we specify that method m in class C (and likewise in all its derived classes) no longer returns just an X object, but a Y object. This declaration applies not only to class C, but to all its derived classes. From this declaration the compiler knows that method c:m returns a Y object. The assignment y := c:m is now permissible.

Since with increasing specialization the result class likewise can only be further specialized (but never generalized), this is called *co*variance*:* the modification of the function class can only occur in the same direction as the modification of the receiver class, i.e., from the base to a derived class.

The reverse case is also possible. If method m in class B expects an argument of class Y, its implementation can be more general than in class C, which is derived from B, so that now X objects can be handled. The following class definitions show how this is meant (whereby we again assume that class Y derives from X):

```
INTERFACE OF B;                     INTERFACE OF C;
   m (arg:Y);                       INHERITS FROM B;
END B.                                 REDEFINE m (arg:X);
                                    END C.
```

Here we have *contra*variance because the modification of the argument class takes place in the opposite direction to the change in the receiver class.

If the function or argument type of an operation in a derived class is modified, this is a modification of the interface. Since the class interface represents a contract between the implementor of the class and its users, the implementation of the corresponding method must ensure that the assurances in the interface (the method definitely returns a Y object or the method can also process an X parameter) are fulfilled. Since this cannot be expected from an inherited method (which assumes a different interface), the method must be re-implemented. In the special case of covariance with function type Same, the method can be implemented so that it also fulfills the assurance that it always returns an object of the same type as the receiver, even in derived classes. The following example shows a method grayCopy, which returns a copy of a graphical object that differs from the original only in that it is filled in gray:

```
grayCopy: Same IS
VAR theCopy: Same;            -- the Copy is to be of the same type as self
BEGIN
   theCopy := self:shallowCopy;   -- shallowCopy returns a Same object,
```

```
        theCopy:setShade(50);           -- the assurance is fulfilled.
        RETURN theCopy
    END grayCopy;
```

Unfortunately, most object-oriented languages do not provide this type of covariance, so that the programmer must circumvent the incompatibilities caused by the lack thereof by means of type casts. Only in untyped languages such as Smalltalk and Self is this no problem because they lack static data types and thus have no type incompatibility at compile time.

## 4.4 Genericity

Collection classes, which enable collections of any number of objects, present another source of compatibility problems. Every good class library contains such generally applicable classes, for example, for processing lists, sorted lists and sets. Classes Array and Stack in Section 4.3.3 belong to this category. Here we repeat the interface of class Array, which we use as an example below:

```
INTERFACE OF Array;
INHERITS FROM Object;
    size: Integer;
    changeSize (newSize:Integer);
    put (index:Integer; elem:Object);
    get (index:Integer): Object;
END Array.
```

In this class definition we are not primarily concerned with completeness and adequacy. For example, many general operations are generally already defined in an abstract class (such as Collection), from which all other collection classes (including Array) derive. Therefore the operation size would typically no longer appear in the interface of Array. However, we are not concerned with such details here; instead, we want this class interface to show how objects of class Array can be used and what problems can arise thereby.

The definition of class Array expresses that an array can contain objects of any class. Moreover, one array can contain objects of *different* classes. This is a significant increase in flexibility compared to conventional programming languages like Ada, C and Modula-2, where arrays consist only of homogeneous elements. We owe this genericity to polymorphism, which permits us to pass any object as actual parameter wherever a formal parameter of data type Object is specified. Naturally, this functions only if every class derives directly or indirectly from Object. The following program fragment shows how an array can be composed of completely different objects:

```
VAR
    rect: Rectangle;   circ: Circle;
    stk: Stack;   arr, otherArray: Array;
BEGIN
    arr := Array:new;   arr:changeSize(20);
    ...
    arr:put(1,rect);   arr:put(2,circ);
    arr:put(3,stk);   arr:put(4,otherArray);
```

Here we can store references to a rectangle, a circle, a stack and even another array as elements in arr. Since the array now consists of references to objects of different classes, we call it a *heterogeneous data structure*. Note especially that an array can contain references to arrays as elements. Even the statement arr:put(5,arr) would be permissible.

A problem arises only if we want to retrieve individual elements from the array. Then the genericity avenges itself because in the operation get we can make only the most general (and thus meaningless) assurance that it returns an object of class Object. Even if we know exactly that the first element of the array is a rectangle, the assignment rect := arr:get(1) remains impermissible because the invocation could just as well return a circle, a stack or an array. The assignment x := arr:get(i) is thus only valid if the variable x is declared statically as Object, for only then can we guarantee that variable x always references a matching object.

As noted in the previous section, the only remedy is to use a type cast to convince the compiler to accept the assignment: rect := Rectangle(arr:get(1)). The problem that we create in the process is that the type cast can fail at run time if a mismatched object has meanwhile shifted to position 1 of the array.

Usually the flexibility afforded by class Array is not the main reason for the use of Array objects; in a single array we normally only want to store homogeneous (or at least similar) objects. The following list shows several applications of object arrays:

- All open windows (class Window) of a dialog program
- Customers (class Customer) of a mail order firm
- Books (class Book) of a library
- Graphic elements (class GraphicObject) of a drawing

In the case of the library, the array might contain strictly Book objects. But it is also possible that several other classes with special attributes derive from Book (e.g., Dictionary, Novel). However, the array will certainly not contain customers, windows or graphic objects. In conventional languages, this can be expressed easily in the declaration:

```
VAR arr: ARRAY [1..1000] OF Book;
```

This is because these languages have not just an array type, but a language element for the definition of new array types with any kind of elements. In the following we explain how a similar effect can be achieved in object-oriented languages.

The key to adapting a class to different situations is genericity. Some conventional programming languages (e.g., Ada) allow assigning formal type parameters to program components (usually modules and procedures). They serve as templates from which usable components are made by replacing the formal data types with actual ones. This method can be applied in object-oriented programming to classes as well. A generic class Array, for example, could be defined as follows:

```
INTERFACE OF Array(Element);
INHERITS FROM Object;
   size: Integer;
   changeSize (newSize:Integer);
   put (index:Integer; elem:Element);
   get (index:Integer): Element;
END Array.
```

The operation put now expects an argument of class Element, and the operation get returns an object of class Element. The class Element is not a specific class, but represents any class to be passed with the use of Array. The following program fragment shows how to create an array of graphical objects and draw all its elements.

```
VAR
   arr: Array(GraphicObject);
   rect: Rectangle;   circ: Circle;
   graph: GraphicObject;
   i: Integer;
BEGIN
   arr := Array(GraphicObject):new;   arr:changeSize(20);
   arr:put(1,rect);   arr:put(2,circ);
   ...
   FOR i := 1 TO arr:size DO
        graph := arr:get(i);
        graph:draw
   END;
```

Class Array cannot be used without parameterizing because it first requires the specification of which elements the array is to contain. Here we use similar notation to that of a procedure invocation and write the name of the desired element class in parentheses after Array. The result is a specialized class with the same definition and implementation as Array, whereby each occurrence of the formal parameter class Element is replaced with GraphicObject. The resulting class definition thus takes the following form:

```
INTERFACE OF GraphicArray;
INHERITS FROM Object;
    size: Integer;
    changeSize (newSize:Integer);
    put (index:Integer; elem:GraphicObject);
    get (index:Integer): GraphicObject;
END GraphicArray.
```

As this definition shows, the operation put now expects a parameter of class GraphicObject, and get returns an object of this class. Hence the compiler can do the following:

- Assure that only graphic objects can be entered in the array with the help of put (in particular, no customers or books are permitted)
- Guarantee that the operation get always returns a graphic object, whereby type casts become superfluous

The nongeneric form of Array permitted elements of any class. The only prerequisite was that classes of elements had to be derivatives of Object, which we assumed as given. Likewise a generic Array can be a heterogeneous collection of objects; however, the set of permitted element classes is restricted to a subtree of the inheritance hierarchy. The declaration Array(Object) corresponds exactly to the nongeneric variant.

In conventional programming languages the use of genericity usually means a duplication of the compiler-generated code. This is because the possible elements (e.g., integers, characters and strings) have different sizes, and thus different code must be generated for their assignments and comparisons. In object-oriented languages this is unnecessary because all objects are identified by references of the same size. This means that the same machine code can be employed for all variants of a generic class. Furthermore, the operations possible with the elements need no longer be limited to assignments and comparisons. If therc is a root class Object, then all the elements in question certainly support at least the operations defined in Object. The following method shows how to compute the storage space allocated for an array and all its elements.

```
allocatedSpace: Integer IS
VAR
    space, i: Integer;
BEGIN
    space := base:allocatedSpace;     -- memory allocated to the array itself
    FOR i := 1 TO self:size DO
        space := space + (self:get(i)):allocatedSpace
    END;
    RETURN space
END allocatedSpace;
```

Here we assume that method allocatedSpace is already defined in class Object, so that it can be applied to all potential elements. Thanks to dynamic binding, this will also function for all future parameterizations.

Note that the creation of a new class by parameterization of a generic class has nothing to do with deriving a new class from a base class. The variants of a generic class share no inheritance relation and are thus not assignment compatible to one another. If class Array derives from Collection and class Collection derives from Object, then parameterization of these classes with the concrete element classes GraphicObject, Rectangle and Book produces the inheritances hierarchy in Figure 4.30.

An array of books *is a* collection of books. This relation results from the derivation of class Array from Collection. One would assume that an array of rectangles should also be an array of graphic objects because a rectangle is a graphic object. Although this might be true in a colloquial sense, it creates problems when we consider polymorphism. Consider the following program fragment:

```
VAR
    graphArr: Array(GraphicObject);
    rectArr: Array(Rectangle);
    circ: Circle;   rect: Rectangle;
BEGIN
    ...
    graphArr := rectArr;
    graphArr:put(3,circ);
    rect := rectArr:get(3);
```

If an array of rectangles can be assigned to a variable of type Array(GraphicObject), then it can subsequently be used as though it could contain arbitrary graphic objects. For example, as shown above, a circle could then be added to the array. In the rectangle context it would then be possible to assign this circle to a variable of type Rectangle. The reverse case (i.e., the assignment rectArr := graphArr) causes similar compatibility problems. We leave the proof to the reader.

In languages without static typing, genericity plays no role; it is only useful in such languages where the compiler checks the correct use of objects. Unfortunately, many object-oriented languages with static typing do not support genericity. To circumvent the problems described here, C++ and Object-Pascal leave only the type-cast remedy.

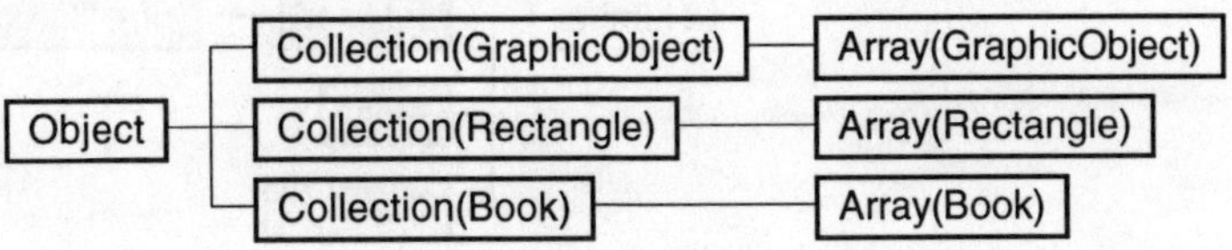


Figure 4.30: Class hierarchy with genericity

# 4.5 Pure object-oriented and hybrid languages

Object-oriented programmers often discuss the question of whether elementary values such as numbers and characters should be viewed as objects. Some experts believe that object-oriented programming brings undisputed advantages in some situations, but that many problems are better solved with conventional (i.e., procedural) programming. Their primary argument is usually efficiency. Their opponents see object-oriented programming as a universal tool that can be used everywhere advantageously.

Various programming languages also reflect this difference in attitude. Languages that view all data as objects are termed *pure object-oriented*, while languages in which objects and conventional data coexist are called *hybrid*. In the following sections we discuss several important differences and arguments for and against pure object-orientation.

## 4.5.1 Uniformity

The primary advantage of object-orientation is its greater generality, especially if the class hierarchy has a root class Object. The elementary data types are classes that indirectly derive from Object. Figure 4.31 shows the corresponding part of the class hierarchy of Smalltalk as an example.

A commonality of almost all elementary data types is that their elements are ordered (i.e., comparable with the operators < and >). We thus combine them in a subtree under the abstract class Magnitude. The numeric data types are collected under the class Number, where all arithmetic operations are defined.

A particular advantage of pure object-orientation is that all elementary classes inherit from Object. This makes all operations defined in Object also applicable to objects of the elementary data types. For example, Smalltalk has an operation printString defined in Object that provides an object description in the form of a printable character string. This operation can also be applied to numbers. For example, the message 123:printString returns the character string "123".

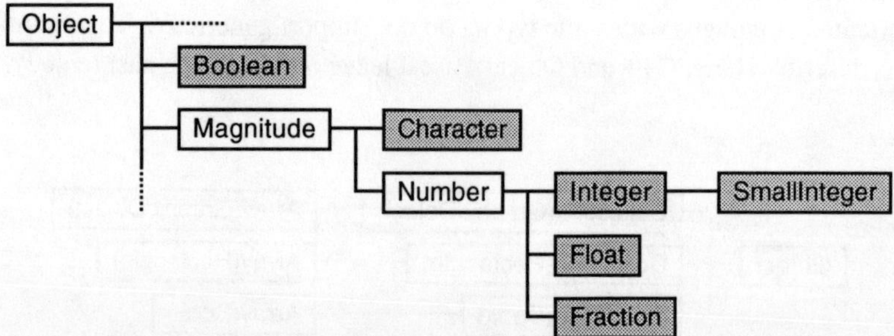


Figure 4.31: Positions of elementary data types in the Smalltalk class hierarchy

Since the objects of elementary classes provide all operations defined in Object, they can be used everywhere where an object of type Object is permitted (in Smalltalk, everywhere). In particular, this means that elementary objects can also be stored in a Collection object. Thus, for example, class Stack can be used for actual objects (such as of class GraphicObject) as well as for numbers. This is not the case in hybrid languages because numbers are not objects and thus not compatible with Object variables.

Finally, elementary classes can serve as base classes for new classes. For example, a special character class Kanji for Japanese characters can be derived from the general class Character. Although this possibility is seldom exploited, it is available.

## 4.5.2 Efficiency

An increase in generality and flexibility is usually associated with a loss of efficiency, and this is also the case in pure object-oriented languages. To understand the reasons for this loss of efficiency, let us consider how hybrid languages improve efficiency.

The major advantage of a hybrid language is that elementary data and objects have different representations in memory. While an object variable contains a reference (normally a word-length pointer) to the actual object, a variable of an elementary data type can contain the value itself. Figure 4.32 shows various memory representations. While an object always requires indirect access to the actual data, elementary data can be accessed directly. In addition, objects are usually created dynamically, which (static) elementary data do not require because their memory requirements and addresses are known at compile time.

Another advantage of hybrid languages results from elementary data types' exclusion of polymorphism. The compiler can thus require that a variable declared as Integer always receives an Integer value. Thus the compiler does not need dynamic binding and can even optimize frequently occurring constructs (for example, the statement i := i + 1). This profoundly increases efficiency because of the particular frequency of operations with elementary data types (especially integers).

However, knowing about the efficiency of elementary operations in hybrid languages often leads programmers to renounce the use of objects and to program conventionally in

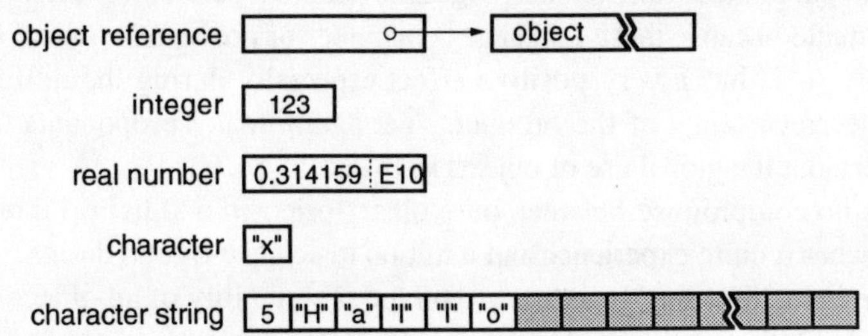


Figure 4.32: Representations of objects and elementary data in memory

supposedly time-critical program parts. Unfortunately, this often leads to overreaction because time-critical parts can seldom be identified during program design.

### 4.5.3 Operators as messages

Since in pure object-oriented languages all data are objects, methods must also be provided for all operations permissible with them. This goes so far that even the arithmetic operations such as addition, subtraction and comparison are activated with messages. To adapt these operations to the object-oriented way of thinking, the operators are defined as binary messages identified with a special character instead of a name. This has the advantage that a programmer can invent new operators and override inherited ones. The definition (especially the new definition) of operators by the programmer is termed operator overloading.

However, many programmer consider the viewing of operators as messages as frantic excess. It takes some adjustment to accept that the expression `2 * x` is a request to object `2` to multiply itself by the argument `x` and to return the result. This proves particularly difficult if the operands are of different classes. In the expression `2 * x` the whole number `2` is the executing object, while in `x * 2` object `x` is responsible for the computation. If `x` is a real number, then dynamic binding activates a different method and the operation can produce a different result. Hence we lose the commutativity of multiplication. Matters become worse if all binary messages have the same priority. In Smalltalk sequential operators are executed strictly from left to right, so that the expression `2 + 3 * 4` returns 20 rather than 14. This disables our accustomed operator precedence rules and can produce unpleasant surprises. Therefore the language Self has a special rule that forbids sequences of operators and operands without parentheses. This requires writing (2 + 3) * 4 or 2 + (3 * 4) instead of 2 + 3 * 4, which precludes such precedence errors.

### 4.5.4 Consistency

Hybrid languages offer the choice between conventional and object-oriented features. This confronts the developer with the decision of which thought model to use in which situations. In pure object-oriented languages the path to a pure object-oriented solution is almost automatic because these languages encumber or prevent the use of conventional subsolutions. This has a very positive effect especially during the design phase and promotes the consistency of the product. Yet again, many proponents of the hybrid approach consider the global use of objects as overkill.

There is no compromise between pure object-oriented and hybrid thought models. Both approaches require experience and intuition to achieve a good design. The problem in hybrid design is deciding case by case on the preferability of an object-oriented or a conventional solution; in pure object-oriented design the craft is not to overshoot the mark.

### 4.5.5 Object-oriented thinking

Most hybrid languages are object-oriented extensions of conventional programming languages. An argument for these languages is that they are easy to learn for a programmer already experienced in the base language. The strength of this argument can be seen, for example, in the fact that object-oriented programming only achieved worldwide attention with the hybrid language C++, although the principle was known a decade earlier and already practicable in the pure object-oriented language Smalltalk. The trend to object-oriented extensions of existing languages continues. We can assume that the near future will bring at least one object-oriented variant of every procedural language.

Another argument for hybrid languages in this sense is that we need only the following additional language elements to enable object-oriented programming:

- A class type (usually with a syntax similar to structure types)
- The ability to derive new class types from existing ones
- Methods (usually with a syntax similar to procedures)
- A message construct (comparable to procedure invocations)
- A predefined identifier for the message receiver (e.g., self)
- More tolerant context restrictions for assignments to permit polymorphism

While it proves relatively easy to learn the new object-oriented language elements, utilizing them without the required background knowledge is problematic. For example, in practice we observe how C programmers treat a C++ compiler as just a new version of the old C compiler. They see no reason to deviate from their accustomed way of working, and they justifiably fear the new language elements. For someone who wants to learn object-oriented programming, a hybrid language can prove to be a hindrance because the novice is repeatedly tempted to fall back on conventional programming techniques to solve subproblems.

Particularly for the novice, a sink-or-swim approach with a pure object-oriented language proves worthwhile. This forces the programmer to relinquish old ways of thinking. Experience has shown that problems occur not in learning and understanding an object-oriented language, but more so in learning object-oriented thinking. For learning purposes, we therefore recommend a pure object-oriented language such as Smalltalk even if the working languages will later be a hybrid language like C++.

## 4.6 Object-oriented programming languages

The history of object-oriented programming began in the 1960s with the programming language Simula [Dahl 1966], a special language for simulating events in the real world. Although Simula already introduced the terms class and object, no one then spoke of object-oriented programming. This changed with Smalltalk [Goldberg 1983], the first pure object-oriented language. Smalltalk is still considered as *the* object-oriented programming language because of its pure object-orientation. This is reflected in that today's widespread object-oriented terminology stems almost exclusively from Smalltalk literature and that almost all newer object-oriented languages in some way borrow from Smalltalk. Figure 4.33 depicts the development and the influences of the most important object-oriented languages. The languages shaded in gray are object-oriented; those in white are the predecessors from which they emerged or adopted features. Most object-oriented languages have block structures and thus emanate from Algol.

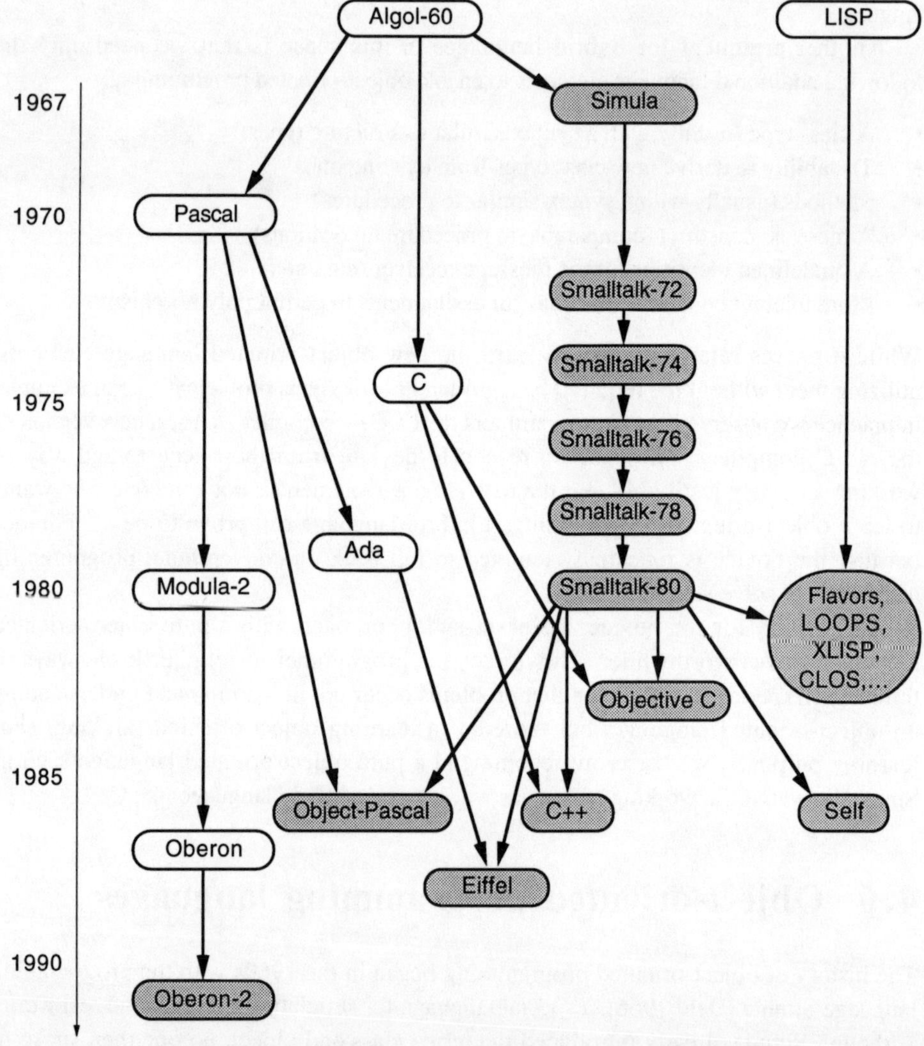


Figure 4.33: The family tree of object-oriented languages

Table 4.1: Selection criteria for object-oriented languages

| Language | Selection criteria |
|---|---|
| Smalltalk | Grandparent of almost all object-oriented languages; pure object-oriented; no static type information. |
| C++ | Worldwide dissemination; static and dynamic objects; high efficiency; flexibly definable access rights. |
| Object-Pascal | Minimalism; strong reliance on existing Pascal elements; methods handled as record components. |
| Eiffel | Independent development without direct model; multiple and repeated inheritance; assertions, preconditions and postconditions. |
| Oberon-2 | Extensible record Types; type-bound procedures; type test and type guard. |

The left branch of the diagram shows the languages developed by Niklaus Wirth. Pascal, the most important structured programming language, was succeeded by Modula-2 as a module-oriented language. From Modula-2 came Oberon [Reiser 1992], which was extended in 1991 to Oberon-2 [Mössenböck 1991], a real object-oriented language. Object-Pascal [Schmucker 1986] is an object-oriented extension of Pascal. Two object-oriented languages evolved from C: C++ [Stroustrup 1986] and Objective C [Cox 1986]. Objective C borrows more from Smalltalk than C++, which contains many of its own language elements that do not exist in other object-oriented languages.

The right branch shows the function programming language Lisp and some of its object-oriented derivatives. The ellipsis indicates that this family of languages has significantly more members. This is surprising because they unify two completely contradictory language concepts, static functional and dynamic object-oriented thought models.

Among the newer languages Oberon-2, Eiffel and Self play a particular role because their object-oriented concepts rely little on existing languages. While Oberon-2's inheritance and dynamic binding build on record types and type-bound procedures, Eiffel focuses on multiple inheritance and genericity, and Self replaces classes with prototypes and inheritance with delegation.

We make no claim of completeness in our diagram. New object-oriented languages with new concepts and object-oriented dialects of existing languages continue to evolve. For example, Modula-3 has been presented as an object-oriented extensions of Modula-2, and object-oriented elements for the language Ada were already under discussion in 1992.

The following subsections discuss the object-oriented elements of five representative languages. Here we cannot strive for full coverage; instead, we want to give an overview of the languages and to show the multitude of concepts that they realize. Table 4.1 indicates the languages we chose and the aspects that led to their choice.

### 4.6.1 Smalltalk

Smalltalk was developed in the Xerox's Palo Alto Research Center (PARC). The language evolved from a Learning Research Group study that began in the 1970s. The actual goal of the study was to collect ideas about the form of communication between people and computers in the year 2000. The staff of the research group were not satisfied with a study alone, but developed a programming language and a corresponding operating system. The ideas that were realized then continue to influence (even more than ever) how we interface with computers. For example, these researchers introduced the mouse as input medium, the organization of the screen in overlapping windows, and the input of commands with pop-up menus.

The first Smalltalk version was completed in 1972 (hence the name Smalltalk-72). The language was revised every two years, producing the versions Smalltalk-74, -76, -78 and -80. When people speak of Smalltalk today, they usually mean Smalltalk-80 [Goldberg 1983].

Smalltalk uncompromisingly follows object-oriented principles; hence in Smalltalk *everything* is an object – even classes and statement sequences. Smalltalk has three kinds of messages:

- *Unary messages* consist of an identifier written after the receiver object. For example, the expression alpha sin designates the unary message sin to the object alpha. It corresponds to the Pascal expression SIN(alpha) and can be compared to a unary function invocation.
- *Binary messages* consist of a special character or a sequence of special characters written between the receiver object and the lone argument. Examples include 25 + x and x ~= y. In the first example 25 is the receiver object and x is the argument of the message +. A binary message corresponds to an operator in a conventional programming language.
- *Keyword messages* consist of one or more keywords that each end with a colon. An argument follows each colon. Examples include the expressions 'AEIOU' at:i and nameList at:5 put:'Adele'. The first example sends the message at: with argument i to character string 'AEIOU'; in the second example the message is at:put:, the receiver object is the variable nameList, and the arguments are the number 5 and the character string 'Adele'. A keyword message corresponds to a procedure invocation with multiple parameters in a convention programming language, e.g., At('AEIOU',i) and AtPut(nameList,5,'Adele'). Note that the colons are components of the message names. They indicate how many parameters a message has and where they are to be applied; hence they are also pronounced (e.g., "at colon put colon").

One peculiarity of Smalltalk is that the language contains no statements for governing control flow. Instead, *blocks* can be formed, which are objects containing any sequence of statements. A block is formed by enclosing a sequence of statements (separated by periods) in square brackets, for example:

```
[alarmCount := alarmCount + 1. bell ring]
```

On formation of the block, the statement sequence is only combined to an object, but not yet executed. Like any other object, the block can be assigned to a variable, for example:

```
alarm := [alarmCount := alarmCount + 1. bell ring]
```

In this way statement sequences can be stored for later use. To execute them, we send the block object the unary message value. The expression alarm value thus causes an evaluation of the statement sequence, whereupon the variable alarmCount is incremented by 1 and the bell rings.

Blocks represent a very powerful concept. For example, they can be used to parameterize objects. An object can be linked to a block that is executed whenever the object receives a certain message. Blocks are also used for flow control. For example, objects of class Boolean understand the messages ifTrue: and ifTrue:ifFalse:. The following examples show some simple control flow structures and their Pascal counterparts:

```
Smalltalk                              Pascal
--------------------------------------------------------------------------
x>limit ifTrue: [x := limit]           IF x>limit THEN x := limit

x<y                                    IF x<y
   ifTrue: [min := x. max := y]           THEN BEGIN min := x; max := y END
   ifFalse: [min := y. max := x]          ELSE BEGIN min := y; max := x END

n timesRepeat:                         FOR i := 1 TO n DO
   [Transcript nextPut: $– ]              Write('–')

[x>0] whileTrue:                       WHILE x>0 DO BEGIN
   [y := y * 2. x := x – 1]               y := y * 2; x := x – 1
                                       END
```

In the first example the expression x>limit returns a True or a False object. A True object reacts to the message ifTrue: by evaluating the argument (i.e., the block [x := limit]), while the message ifTrue: has no effect for a False object. The situation is similar for the message ifTrue:ifFalse:. A True object evaluates the first argument and a False object the second.

Not only elementary data and statement sequences but also classes are objects in Smalltalk. Every object knows to which class object it belongs. The class objects are also used to create new objects by sending a class the message new, to which the class reacts by reserving the storages space for a new object and initializing the new object appropriately. For example, the statement nameList := List new creates a new list.

Since classes are objects as well, they also belong to a class. The class of a class is a *metaclass*; just as a class determines the structure and behavior of its objects, a metaclass determines the structure and behavior of its (only) object, the class. Since the metaclass is also a class and thus also an object, it also belongs to a class, which again is an object that belongs to a class. This theoretically produces an endless chain of metaclasses. In Smalltalk this chain is terminated by a class of all classes – a mathematical impossibility, as a proof by contradiction quickly shows. In Smalltalk this does not create a contradiction because all metaclasses have the same behavior and thus can be described by a common metaclass named MetaClass, which also defines its own behavior.

Smalltalk was originally defined as a language with simple inheritance. The flexibility of the language is often presented as an argument that multiple inheritance is superfluous. Nevertheless, some Smalltalk versions with multiple inheritance have evolved meanwhile.

Smalltalk affords no possibility to define classes with a piece of text. The class hierarchy, the structure of objects, and the methods are all defined interactively with a *browser*. A method is displayed in a window and can be edited there. The following example shows the definition of the method timesRepeat: of class Integer in Smalltalk:

```
timesRepeat: aBlock
   "execute the argument aBlock as many times as the receiver specifies"
   | count |
   count := self.
   [count > 0] whileTrue: [aBlock value.  count := count – 1].
```

The header specifies the name of the method and the name of the formal parameter. The text enclosed in double quotation marks is a comment that describes the function of the method. The vertical bars surround the declaration of the local variable count. Note that neither the parameter aBlock nor the local variable count is defined by type. In Smalltalk declared variables are not associated with a data type; an object of any class can be assigned to any variable. In using a variable it might occur that the object associated with the variable is of a different class than expected. For example, the compiler cannot check the statement x timesRepeat: y for semantic correctness. At most it can report an error if no method named timesRepeat exists in any known class. At run time this can mean that y is not a block object and thus does not understand the message value (sent within timesRepeat:). Likewise x could be a character string, so that the message timesRepeat: could not be processed. In either case the program terminates with an error message ("message not understood").

Despite the lack of static typing, Smalltalk is a type-safe language because all incompatibilities are checked and detected – although possibly only at run time. It is very difficult to write a Smalltalk program that leads to a crash with severe consequences. Here Smalltalk's memory management makes a significant contribution. In Smalltalk all objects are allocated dynamically, but there is no language mechanism for explicit deallocation of memory. Because of the extreme networking of objects, it is difficult to know when memory for objects can be deallocated. Explicit memory deallocation would always bear with it the danger that references still exist to objects that no longer exist (dangling pointers). Smalltalk's automatic garbage collection assures that memory occupied by objects that can no longer be reached is deallocated.

### 4.6.2 C++

The language C++ [Stroustrup 1986] was developed by Bjarne Stroustrup at AT&T Bell Laboratories in the mid-1980s. The primary goal of this development was not to make C an object-oriented programming language, but to create a better C (hence the original name ABC). Above all the lack of type safety was to be ameliorated. The design of the language strived to maintain upwards compatibility with C so that existing C programs could be ported to C++ with minimum effort. This upwards compatibility represents a strength for C++, since it made the language attractive for C programmers who wanted to venture into object-oriented programming. However, its great similarity with C is also the main target of criticism of C++ today. C has many hidden traps such as pointer arithmetic and (hidden) type casts, that for compatibility reasons also had to be assimilated in C++. Thus a programmer must maintain extreme discipline in order to achieve high security.

The most important new feature in C++ compared to C is the possibility of defining abstract data types. An abstract data type is declared like a structure that can also contain functions. The following declaration shows a simple abstract data type for an integer counter.

```
class Counter {
   private:
      unsigned in val;
   public:
      Counter() { val = 0; }      // constructor
      void Increment() { val++; }
      void Decrement() {val--; }
      unsigned int Value() {return val; }
};
```

An abstract data type is defined with the keyword class. The above definition differs from a class in our sense, however, in that it does not enable dynamic binding. To effect dynamic binding of a method, it must explicitly be declared as virtual, which we did not do in the above example. The choice of declaring methods as virtual or nonvirtual is typical of C++. The programmer has the choice of the greater flexibility of dynamic binding or the greater efficiency of static binding. This choice is also a source of errors because accidentally omitting the keyword virtual can give a program a completely different meaning if inheritance with overridden methods is involved.

The first method of the class has the same name as the class itself. It is a *constructor* that is responsible for the initialization of newly created Counter objects. Depending on requirements, there can be multiple constructors with different parameter lists. For example, a second constructor could be defined to initialize Counter objects with a start value different from zero:

```
Counter(unsigned int init) { val = init; }
```

With the help of such constructors, objects can be initialized appropriately upon declaration. The counterparts to constructors are *destructors*, which are automatically activated upon (explicit) deallocation of an object's storage. A destructor also has the same name as the class, but begins with a tilde (e.g., ~Counter). Destructors can ease garbage collection with the use of complex object structures, but they are no substitute for automatic garbage collection.

As the Counter example already shows, instance variables and methods can be defined with different access rights (in the sense of Section 4.3.4). The parts declared after the keyword public are accessible to clients, while those after private can be used only within the class. A third kind of access rights is protected, which hides the respective parts from clients, but makes them available to heirs. Furthermore, C++ enables the definition of *friend classes* and *friend functions*, which receive more access rights than normal clients. In object-oriented programs such classes occur relatively frequently when cooperating classes are developed simultaneously.

In C++ an object can be declared statically or created dynamically. The following comparison shows these two kinds of usage with the example of a counter object.

| Static | Dynamic |
|---|---|
| Counter c; | Counter * c |
| ... | c = new Counter(); |
| c.Increment(); | c –> Increment(); |
| ... | ... |
| printf("\ncounter=%u", c.Value()); | printf("\ncounter=%u", c –> Value()); |
| | delete c; |

The left example declares the variable c statically. With the invocation of the procedure containing this declaration, the object is created and initialized with the help of the constructor. On termination of the procedure the memory occupied by the object is deallocated after activation of a destructor (if present). The right example declares the variable c dynamically (i.e., as a pointer to a Counter object). Before we can work with the variable, a pointer to a Counter object must be assigned to it. This can be done with the help of new Counter(), for example. This construct creates a Counter object at run time and executes the constructor to initialize it. While a static object can be used like a structure, method invocations with dynamic objects require a different notation. When the object is no longer needed, its storage must be deallocated with the help of the delete statement, which first activates a destructor (if present).

C++ allows the use of a type cast to assign any object to a variable of a certain type, as the following example shows.

```
T v;
...
v = T(x);
```

As was the case in C, this operation is not safe; the subsequent use of v can lead to errors that are hard to detect if the variable x did not contain a T object. Unfortunately, C++ offers no possibility to check the dynamic class of an object associated with a variable.

In the original language definition, C++ offered only simple inheritance. Since then the language has been repeatedly revised and extended with multiple inheritance, among other things. With multiple inheritance in C++, name conflicts must be resolved by explicit qualification in method invocations. An object derived with multiple inheritance in C++ is treated as the union of two object of the two base classes (with additional new components). This results in duplication of the root class components when deriving with multiple inheritance from two classes that share a common root.

A complete description of all object-oriented concepts of C++ would exceed the scope of this book since the possibilities this language offers are multifaceted. This is itself a danger for the novice because C++ encompasses so many language concepts that a programmer should keep in mind.

### 4.6.3 Object-Pascal

The language Object-Pascal is notable for its minimality. Its significant attributes include an object type (an extension of the record type), a methods construct (an extension of procedures), a new standard function Member, and two keywords to designate receiver objects within a method (SELF) and for the invocation of methods of the base class (INHERITED). These few new language elements enable object-oriented programming in our sense.

More precisely, Object-Pascal is not the name of an individual language, but a collective name for object-oriented Pascal extensions that in part differ considerably. We describe MPW Pascal [Schmucker 1986], a Pascal dialect developed by Apple for the Macintosh programming environment MPW (Macintosh Programmer's Workshop). Borland's Turbo-Pascal also contains object-oriented elements beginning with version 4.5. The concepts of this language deviate significantly from MPW Pascal and resemble C++ more.

In Object-Pascal classes are described with the help of an object type. The following example shows one way to define and implement in Object-Pascal the Counter class introduced in the previous section on C++.

```
TYPE
   Counter = OBJECT
      val: INTEGER;
      PROCEDURE ICounter;
```

```
        PROCEDURE Decrement;
        PROCEDURE Increment;
        FUNCTION Value: INTEGER;
    END;

PROCEDURE Counter.ICounter;
BEGIN
    val := 0
END;

PROCEDURE Counter.Increment;
BEGIN
    val := val + 1
END;

PROCEDURE Counter.Decrement;
BEGIN
    val := val – 1
END;

FUNCTION Counter.Value: INTEGER;
BEGIN
    Value := val
END;
```

The type declaration describes only the structure of a Counter object and the operations it permits. The methods are implemented separately (which is also possible in C++). We actually could have omitted the function Value to test the momentary counter value. Object-Pascal does not support the principle of information hiding, so that every client can access and modify the components of a type declaration. This extreme drawback can only be compensated with extreme discipline in the use of objects.

Since Object-Pascal lacks constructors and destructors, programmers write an explicit initialization method, which by convention bears the same name as the class preceded by the letter I. The following program fragment demonstrates the usage of objects in Object-Pascal.

```
VAR
    c: Counter;
...
NEW(c);
c.ICounter;
c.val := 5;
c.Increment;
...
```

```
Writeln("counter=", c.Value)        or: Writeln("counter=", c.val)
DISPOSE(c);
```

The standard procedure NEW was extended for Object-Pascal so that it can be used for variables of object types. The invocation NEW(c) creates a new Counter object (because c's static data type is Counter) and assigns the variable c a reference to this object. Object variables in Object-Pascal always contain a reference to an object or the value NIL. There are no static objects as in C++. Nevertheless, the same syntax as for records was retained for accessing instance variables and for sending messages. As in C++, in Object-Pascal storage for objects that are no longer needed must be deallocated explicitly using the standard procedure DISPOSE.

Object-Pascal offers a simple way to determine whether an object belongs to a certain class. The function invocation Member(x,T) determines whether the current contents of an object variable x is an object of class T or a class derived therefrom. Such checks are necessary whenever an object x is to be assigned to a variable v of type T, as the following example shows:

```
VAR x: ...; v: T;
...
IF Member(x,T) THEN v := T(x);
```

The expression T(x) is a type cast that leads to a run-time error if x is not a T object. This error can be prevented by a preceding type check.

In the design of Object-Pascal, highest priority was placed on simplicity. This emerges from the fact that Pascal was extended by only a few language elements to support object-oriented programming. For this reason multiple inheritance was also omitted.

### 4.6.4 Eiffel

The programming language Eiffel [Meyer 1988] was originally developed by Bertrand Meyer as an in-house tool of his Interactive Software Engineering company. After good experience with the language, he decided to market the product. One of the primary goals in Eiffel's development was high safety of the resulting programs. For this reason Eiffel language elements to formulate assertions, preconditions and postconditions, and invariants, as well as a mechanism for exception handling.

Although Eiffel is a hybrid language, it was a new development from scratch. Eiffel is no object-oriented extension of any existing programming language. Eiffel's many individualistic language concepts make it difficult to compare Eiffel to other languages. With respect to object-oriented concepts, Eiffel offers multiple and repeated inheritance as well as genericity. There are only two statements for flow control, an If statement and a Loop statement that functions like a While loop. The following example demonstrates how to formulate the Counter class (shown in C++ and Object-Pascal above) in Eiffel.

```
class COUNTER export
    increment, decrement, value

feature
    val: INTEGER;

    increment is
    do
        val := val + 1;
    end;
    decrement is
    require
        val>0
    do
        val := val – 1;
    end;

    value: INTEGER is
    do
        Result := val
    end;

end
```

Keywords are written in lower case in Eiffel, type names in upper case. Accessibility of a class's features to clients is defined separately for each class. This visibility can be redefined anew in every derived class. In a class derived from COUNTER, the instance variable val could be exported while the invocation of the method increment is forbidden.

In the usage of a class, Eiffel does not distinguish between instance variables and methods. Both are simply defined as features. It is even possible to redefine a method as an instance variable in a derived class.

In the above example we required that the counter value be nonnegative. Such restrictions can be specified in Eiffel as preconditions and postconditions of methods. For method decrement we defined a precondition in a require section. The preconditions and postconditions in Eiffel are viewed as elements of the contract between the implementor and the clients of a class. The implementor is required to fulfill the postconditions if the client assures the preconditions. These restrictions are tested before/after the method invocation and produce a run-time error if they are not fulfilled. In addition, for a whole class a set of invariants can be specified that must be fulfilled before and after each method invocation. Such checks can be situated anywhere within methods as well with check statements.

If a run-time error occurs (for example because an assertion was not fulfilled), an exception handling mechanism is activated. Every method can contain a rescue part in which an attempt can be made to correct the error and repeat execution of the method with a retry statement. This type of exception handling is designated error-safe because it guarantees that a method is only returned to the caller if it has fulfilled its contract.

The following example demonstrates the use of a COUNTER object in Eiffel.

```
local
    c: COUNTER
do
    c.Create;
    c.increment;
    ...
    output.putstring("counter =");
    output.putint(c.value);
```

In Eiffel, too, object variables contain references to the actual objects. To initialize the variable c with a COUNTER object, we write c.Create. This is a curiosity because the notation appears to indicate that we are sending an object linked to c (which does not exist yet) the message Create. All variables in Eiffel are initialized with defined start values. This also applies for the instance variable val of COUNTER objects, which is automatically initialized to zero. If another start value is required, the Create method must be overridden.

Eiffel has no mechanism for the explicit deallocation of an object's storage. There is a special method x.Forget, but it does not clear the object corresponding to x from memory; it only breaks the link between the variable x and its object. x.Forget thus corresponds to the statement x = 0 in C++ and to x := NIL in Object-Pascal. Objects that are no longer needed are cleared with automatic garbage collection. In the run-time system developed together with Eiffel, garbage collection occurs parallel to program execution. As the amount of free memory declines, efforts intensify to free memory by disposing of objects that can no longer be reached.

Eiffel offers multiple and repeated inheritance. Conflicts arising due to multiple inheritance are resolved by renaming features. Renaming is also possible without a conflict, for example, in order to give a method in a derived class a more expressive name. Since Eiffel possesses no language element for invocation of an overridden method, renaming also provides a means to enable such invocations: First the inherited method m is redefined (the Eiffel expression for re-implementation of a method); then it is renamed (e.g., old_m). In the overriding method the overridden one can then be invoked with the name old_m.

Eiffel has its own mechanism for defining abstract classes. An abstract method contains the attribute deferred instead of a statement sequence, and the whole class is also declared with this attribute. This definition means that for a variable x of this class the operation x.Create is illegal.

Eiffel also supports the definition of generic classes. An example is the class ARRAY[T], in which the parameter T describes the element type of the array. Eiffel's genericity is notable because the abstract parameter type can also be used for parameterizing base classes. For example, the generic class FIXED_LIST[T] inherits from ARRAY[T] and from LIST[T].

### 4.6.5 Oberon-2

The language Oberon-2 was developed at the Eidgenössische Technische Hochschule (ETH) in Zurich. Niklaus Wirth simplified the language Modula-2, enhanced it with the concept of type extension, and named the new language Oberon [Reiser 1992]. Hanspeter Mössenböck extended Oberon by introducing type-bound procedures to create the language Oberon-2 [Mössenböck 1991].

Oberon-2 proves noteworthy because this language employs two conventional concepts to enable object-oriented programming. Objects in Oberon-2 are record variables, and classes are record types that, contrary to conventional records, can be extended with new components and thus permit the derivation of new types. Methods in Oberon are special procedures that are bound to a record type. Methods have a parameter list and an additional *explicit* parameter that specifies the receiver object. The following example shows two record types and their corresponding bound procedures.

```
TYPE
  Date = RECORD
     year: INTEGER;
     month, day: SHORTINT
  END;
  Time = RECORD (Date)
     hour, minute: SHORTINT
  END;

PROCEDURE (VAR d:Date) Write;
BEGIN
  Out.Int(d.year,0); Out.Char("–");
  Out.Int(d.month,0); Out.Char("–");
  Out.Int(d.day,0)
END Write;

PROCEDURE (VAR t:Time) Write;
BEGIN
  t.Write^; Out.Char(" ");
  Out.Int(t.hour,0); Out.Char(":");
  Out.Int(t.minute,0)
END Write;
```

In Oberon-2 the receiver object is specified before the procedure name. Within the procedure this object can thus be addressed with the name specified in the procedure header; a predefined identifier like Smalltalk's self becomes superfluous in Oberon-2.

An invocation of an overridden procedure is indicated with the caret ^ after the procedure name.

Like C++, Oberon-2 permits the use of static and dynamic objects. A variable of type Date contains a static object, while a variable of type POINTER TO Date contains a dynamic object, a reference to a Date object. The derivation relation between the record types Date and Time is passed on to the corresponding pointer types DatePtr = POINTER TO Date and TimePtr = POINTER TO Time. A variable of type TimePtr can thus be assigned to a variable of type DatePtr, and in this way polymorphism can be achieved. The following example demonstrates how the counter example can be formulated with dynamic objects in Oberon-2:

```
TYPE
   CounterPtr = POINTER TO Counter;
   Counter = RECORD
        val: INTEGER
   END;

PROCEDURE (VAR c:Counter) Init;
BEGIN
   c.val := 0
END Init;

PROCEDURE (VAR c:Counter) Increment;
BEGIN
   c.val := c.val + 1
END Increment;

PROCEDURE (VAR c:Counter) Decrement;
BEGIN
   c.val := c.val – 1
END Decrement;

PROCEDURE (VAR c:Counter) Value: INTEGER;
BEGIN
   RETURN c.val
END Value;
```

Contrary to most other object-oriented languages, methods (i.e., type-bound procedures) are not defined together with the class type. This avoids redundancy; however, the interface of a class is spread across a whole module. As in Eiffel, a dedicated tool extracts from the source code of a module the interfaces of the classes it contains.

The following example demonstrates the usage of a Counter object in Oberon-2:

```
VAR
   c: CounterPtr;
...
```

```
NEW(c);
c.Init;
c.Increment;
...
Out.String("counter =");
Out.Int(c.Value(),0);
```

A dynamic object must be created as in Object-Pascal with the standard procedure NEW. However, automatic garbage collection handles the deallocation of storage for objects that can no longer be reached.

Another similarity to Object-Pascal is that Oberon-2 supports testing the dynamic type of variables and provides *type guards* to assure that at run time a variable is of a certain dynamic type. The following program fragment shows how this mechanism helps to test the type of an object.

```
VAR x: ...; v: T;
...
IF x IS T THEN v := x(T) ... END
```

A variant of this type test is Oberon-2's WITH statement. After a preceding test of the type, it permits the usage of a variable in an entire statement sequence as if it had been declared as its current dynamic type. If data types T1 and T2 are both derived from type T0, for example, then the following WITH statement would be legal:

```
VAR x:T0;
...
WITH x:T1 DO
    (* x is dynamically at least of type T1; use x as T1 object *)
| x:T2 DO
    (* x is dynamically at least of type T2; use x as T2 object *)
ELSE
    (* x is neither a T1 nor a T2 object *)
END;
```

Oberon-2 supports flexible definition of access rights to instance variables and methods. However, the access rights are defined not for the clients of a class, but for clients of a whole module, which can contain multiple classes. Exported record types are marked with an asterisk. However, this does not automatically mean that all instance variables of objects of this type are visible outside the module. Access rights to instance variables and methods can be specified separately, again with an asterisk marking public instance variables with unrestricted access rights. If write access to an instance variable is to be forbidden, this can be indicated with a minus sign. In the Counter example, for example, we could omit the procedure Value and write-protect the instance variable val instead:

```
TYPE
    CounterPtr* = POINTER TO Counter;
    Counter* = RECORD
        val–: INTEGER
    END;
...
PROCEDURE (VAR c:Counter) Init*;
...
```

Since access rights are defined at the module level, multiple dependent classes can be implemented in one module. The access rights restrictions then do not apply for mutual access of these classes within the module. For use within the module, for example, write access is possible to the instance variable val of a Counter object. Oberon-2 also permits the export of the pointer type without the corresponding record type. Then the clients have no access to the contents of the object.

In Oberon-2 the standard numeric types are hierarchically ordered. These five types are ordered according to their domains as follows:

$$\text{SHORTINT} \subseteq \text{INTEGER} \subseteq \text{LONGINT} \subseteq \text{REAL} \subseteq \text{LONGREAL}$$

A number of type SHORTINT can be assigned to a variable of any other numeric data type because the values of this data type can also be represented in all other types. Mixed operations with numbers of various data types are possible. The result is then always of the smallest type that the types of the two operands encompass.

## 4.7 Class libraries

The question of which programming language is the best has always been a favorite subject among computer scientists. Such remained the case as object-oriented programming came into vogue. In fact, the clear conceptual differences among the various object-oriented languages keep fueling the fires of discussion. Above all, the question of whether C++ is *the* object-oriented programming language repeatedly sparks intense emotions. Practitioners seem convinced that C++ is unavoidable for practical reasons, while software engineers warn of the dangers of this language. Meanwhile ever more people are adopting the view that the programming language used is only of secondary importance compared to a good class library. This opinion is not unfounded, because the concepts inherent in a class library often exert more influence on the programmer's thought model than the concepts of the programming language itself.

Preceding chapters have shown that object-oriented programming provides an excellent tool for the creation of reusable program components. We need to distinguish between the following two kinds of reuse:

- *Intra-application reuse* is the reuse of a class in the same program for which the class was originally created. This kind of reuse already demonstrates benefits with relatively small projects. It usually arises from application-specific classes that are needed in multiple variants, whereby a large portion of the functionality remains constant. Likewise abstract classes whose general attributes are inherited by multiple heirs lead to a high degree of code reuse within a program.
- *Inter-application reuse* is the multiple use of a class in mutually independent programs. It occurs primarily when existing general classes (e.g., ones accompanying the compiler) are used repeatedly, or when a class created in project P is used again in a succeeding project Q to solve the same or a similar problem.

Intra-application reuse requires no particular measures. It evolves as a by-product of a clean design. Since the classes used are tailored to the current problem description, however, no inter-application reusability ensues.

Inter-application reusability is a different story. Normally it does not occur as a random product, but must be carefully planned. Even if a well-designed class is so general that it promises benefits in other projects, it does no good if some ambitious programmer hoards it in a private drawer. The goal of a class library is to make potentially reusable classes for later reuse in other projects. Typically, large class libraries do not ensue from simply collecting more and more reusable classes over time. Usually a base library with generally useful classes accompanies a compiler for an object-oriented language.

The market for class libraries is steadily growing today. For a novice to object-oriented programming, an existing class library provides the best means to attain high productivity quickly. There are several reasons for this. First, even the smallest class library can be a solid foundation for the development of further classes. New classes can be derived from existing ones, or an implementation can simply use the existing classes. Second, a novice to object-oriented programming can hardly be expected to deliver excellent designs. Yet developing generally usable classes requires this ability. An open library (whose source code is available) also offers a first-class reference for learning object-oriented programming style. Over and over again, experienced object-oriented programmers say that they acquired much of their knowledge through class libraries.

Since every class represents an abstract data type, it enhances the programming language with new functionality. This indicates that a class library represents an additional abstraction level above the programming language. This is particularly evident in pure object-oriented programming languages. Smalltalk, for example, lacks language elements for loops or for adding two numbers. The class library provides all such functionality. The particular advantage of this additional abstraction level is that it can be extended by the programmer as needed and adapted to local requirements. The programmer designs a personal language, so to say, on the basis of an existing programming language. This makes it clear why the importance of the programming language takes a back seat to that of the class library.

The extension of a language with the help of classes does have some drawbacks, too. Class design becomes languages development. However, the design of a language demands special talent that every programmer cannot be expected to have. This presents the danger of the evolution of complex virtual languages that cannot be mastered.

A class library also demands fundamental changes in how the software developer works. While it frees the programmer from bothersome routine work and spares the developer the reinvention of the wheel because frequently needed operations (for example, sorting and searching) are already implemented in the library and can be reused repeatedly. The developer's main work thus transfers from algorithmic detail to the integration of components to increasingly larger units. This transition is not always free of problems for the developer because most people have a love of detail but little sense of complex interconnections.

## 4.7.1 Categorizing classes

The classes of a class library can be categorized according to various criteria. These criteria determine which classes prove suitable under which conditions for the solution of which problem descriptions.

An important classification criterion that often affects a whole library is its *origin*, i.e., whether a class is a purchased product or an in-house development. The advantage of an in-house development is clearly the intimate knowledge of the implementation of the class. This need not be the case for an externally developed class because some class libraries are distributed only in compiled form to protect the copyright.

The availability of the source code is an invaluable benefit for understanding a class library and its concepts or for nailing down an error. However, the source code brings with it a danger because of the temptation to undertake unauthorized modifications of classes to adapt them to local requirements. Such intrusions are avenged in the negative effects on maintainability. If the modified class is used in only one of several projects, then two variants exist, nullifying any actual reuse. If the modifications are to be assumed in all project, it must be clear what kind of side effects this can have. Furthermore, a serious problem arises if the producer releases a new version of the class library. If the modifications in the original class were not precisely documented, they can hardly be transferred to the new library. A similar problem also results with in-house classes. Section 4.7.4 discusses this aspect in the context of the required organizational measures for class libraries.

Classes can also be categorized according to their *development status*. As with all professionally produced software products, classes pass through three stages before they are considered complete:

- *Delta*. A class that is still under development is categorized as a delta version. During development it is repeatedly tested in a real environment. If the development takes place in a larger development staff, then such incomplete intermediate products are exchanged between programming teams in regular intervals. The designation as delta version serves within the development staff as an indicator that the class is very likely to undergo modifications.

- *Alpha.* Once a class fulfills it significant requirements, it is passed to (possibly external) testers with the request for criticism. This testing does not aim to detect errors as much as to uncover conceptual shortcomings. An alpha version approaches the final product, but interface modifications can still take place.
- *Beta.* After a class is complete in the opinion of its development team, it is designated as a beta version and released for its trial by fire. Now the interface is viewed as given; the goal is to detect and remedy functional flaws.

A program that has transcended these development stages is considered complete and distributed as a product. Likewise, for an application-specific class the development process is terminated at this point. If a class is intended for later reuse, however, then the stabilization phase begins now (compare Section 3.1.5, "The object-oriented life-cycle model"). A class can only be tagged as reusable after it has proven itself in various environments. Multiple reuse within the same program does not suffice because the requirements that the class must meet remain too similar. A class intended for reuse is thus temporarily declared as immature and then observed in subsequent projects.

Reuse might reveal that a class has insufficient generality. Typical errors include operations that were overlooked or too extensive methods that have to be completely overridden in deriving new classes. In addition, implementation errors can surface during reuse because some partial functionality was tested insufficiently in previous projects or perhaps not needed at all. Since the class is often reused by programmers other than its developer, comprehension difficulties might arise that indicate either a poorly thought out concept or inadequate documentation of the class.

Only after the class has survived a number of reuses without modification is it classified as stable or mature. When reusing a class with this seal, a programmer can generally assume that it is largely error-free and will create no problems worth mentioning during reuse. This is the strength of class libraries on the market, because they were developed by experienced programmers and have hundreds of reuses behind them.

Another criterion for categorizing classes is their *purpose*. The following list shows the categories into which class libraries typically fall.

- *Standard classes.* This category is found only in class libraries for pure object-oriented languages in which the elementary data types are realized as classes. A typical characteristic of a standard class is that it represents certain elements of the underlying programming language. For example, in Smalltalk the number 123 is of class SmallInteger and #value is of class Symbol. Standard classes are thus inseparably bound to the programming language.
- *Data structure classes.* Even a very small class library contains classes for collecting objects into larger organizational units. Examples include Array, List, Set and

Dictionary. Which classes a library provides depends in part on the respective programming language. Smalltalk and Eiffel, for example, lack language elements for creating arrays. A class library for these languages thus certainly contains a class Array. A class library for C++ need not provide such a class because C++ (as C) supports array declarations.

- *Operating system classes.* This category encompasses classes for communication with the hardware (e.g., File and Stream) and for using special functions of the underlying processor and operating system (e.g., Process and Resource). Most class libraries try to abstract away from the actual operating system and hardware. This has the advantage that class interfaces do not depend on the target machine.
- *User interface classes.* Most larger class libraries contain many classes for communication with the user. Examples include Window, View, EventHandler, Menu and Command. These classes prove especially important for the implementation of interactive programs with graphical user interfaces. We treat this aspect of class libraries in Section 4.7.3, "Application frameworks".
- *Graphic classes.* This category normally contains all classes related to the display of objects on the screen. This includes graphic elements (e.g., Line, Circle, Rectangle and Icon) as well as attributes of graphic elements (e.g., Color and Pattern). Some class libraries omit these classes and provide a procedural collection of graphic operations instead.
- *Application-specific classes.* This group encompasses classes for the solution of problems from specific domains. Examples include Statistics for statistical evaluations, EventQueue for simulations, and Account for commercial tasks.

## 4.7.2 Structure of class libraries

As the previous section noted, a class library is usually tailored to a certain implementation language. Still, nearly all class libraries borrow from the Smalltalk library, which has scarcely lost in importance in a decade and a half.

The various class libraries differ, sometimes drastically, in their scope and goals. Some compilers come with only a core library for data structures that encompasses not more than twenty classes. Other libraries contain 100 classes for a variety of purposes, whereby they usually emphasize graphic and user interface classes. There is no ceiling on the scope of class libraries. Some libraries have 300 or more classes. For example, the class library ET++ ([Weinand 1988] and [Weinand 1989]) for C++ contains some 350 classes.

In evaluating a class library, we must be aware that size alone cannot guarantee better or more comfortable reusability. Some libraries provide a separate class for every possible variation, while others use parameterizable classes that prove more versatile in their applicability. For example, a class library can contain a class Window and a class GrowWindow for windows of fixed and variable size, respectively, while another library makes do with one Window class whose objects can optionally be fixed or variable in

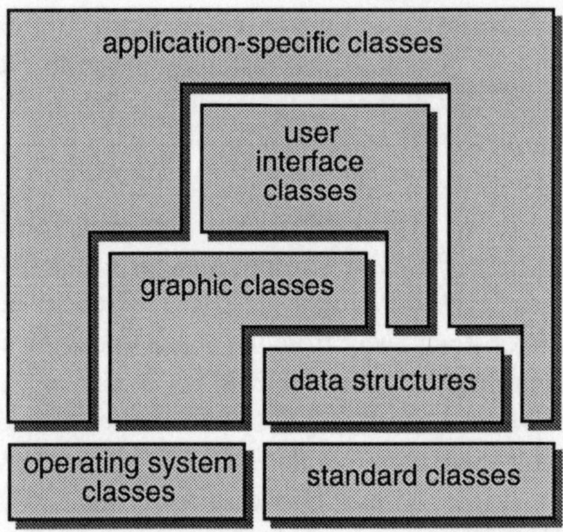


Figure 4.34: Structure of a class library

size. The former case results in small, specialized classes, while the second case has large classes with a multitude of methods.

One interesting regularity of class libraries is that their classes contain on average ten implemented methods. This statistic is largely independent of the size of the library. A class library with 200 classes would thus contain about 2000 methods. If the classes of a library share a common root, then this root class usually contains 10 to 50 methods that are available in all derived classes.

The individual classes of a library generally have strong dependencies. There is usually a group of fundamental classes that other classes use. These fundamental classes include ones realizing data structures that most other classes require, but that themselves require no other classes. Figure 4.34 shows a typical structure of a class library in functional blocks.

The strong interdependencies of the classes in a library means that parts of the class library can hardly be used out of context. For this reason, various class libraries cannot be unified to a larger library. This is primarily because the concepts of different libraries generally deviate too strongly from one another. Another problem arises because various class libraries build on similar but incompatible base classes. The only chance to purchase problem-oriented classes would be in the form of a collection of classes especially developed as an extension of an existing library.

### 4.7.3 Application frameworks

A collection of classes particularly designed for reusability in a certain application domain is termed a *framework*, a skeleton that already provides a structural plan for the solution of an entire class of problems. A framework is more than a class library because it contains not just elementary components, but also the significant algorithms for problem solving. A framework thus consists of a collection of carefully harmonized classes that can be specifically extended to attain required functionality. The significant aspect is that the most important design decisions have already been made by the producer of the framework. The user of a framework is well advised to become familiar with the ideas behind the design and to adapt new components to the framework concept. In the context of frameworks we speak of design reuse because not only code, but a completely designed architecture is reused.

Frameworks can be used in a broad range of application domains. Wherever various tasks of a class of problems can be solved in a similar way, a program framework can be created that already has the basic structure. For example, there are frameworks for telecommunications, process automation, and compiler construction. Most frequently, however, frameworks are used to build interactive programs with graphical user interfaces. Such programs are easy to use, but all the harder to implement. This suggests realizing ever recurring operations (i.e., moving windows, reacting to menu commands, scrolling in windows, saving and printing documents) once in a framework so that the framework can easily be extended with application-specific components. The result is a general application program termed an *application framework.*

The main difference between a class library and an application framework is that the class library serves as a foundation on which new programs are built bottom-up; an application framework *is* already an executable program with the most important control functionality. For certain purposes it uses general classes that the programmer can replace with more specialized ones. Figure 4.35 depicts schematically how programs are designed with a class library and with an application framework.

An application framework need not necessarily be developed and used with object-orientation. Conventional methods also permit the writing of a framework whose general part can be replaced on demand by more specialized procedures or modules. This

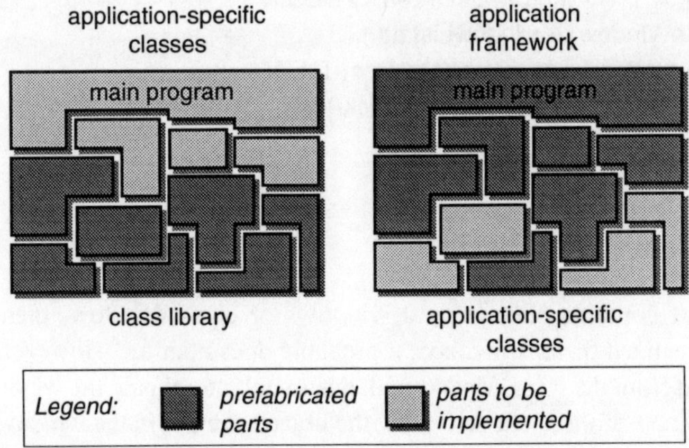


Figure 4.35: The position of a class library and an application framework in the program hierarchy

means, however, that the entire program system has to be copied and specifically modified at certain locations by inserting one's own procedure invocations. Although the source code of the program framework is reused, many similar copies evolve through reuse and must be separately managed and maintained.

Object-oriented programming leaves the framework as is. To create a new program with it, a new class is derived from the class Application (which determines the behavior of the overall system). Then a small main program creates an object of the new class derived from Application and transfers control to it (typically by sending the message run). The actual application-specific functionality is not in the class Application, but in extensions of other classes of the application framework.

Let us explain how to add new functionality to the framework using one subaspect, the display of application-specific information in a window. The application framework is generally executable without application-specific extensions. Then it is just a program that can manage any number of (empty) windows. Every window is represented in the program by an object of class Window. If a window is to be displayed, then the window frame is drawn first with the help of the underlying window system. Next a message is sent to the Window object (e.g., drawContent), with which the object is requested to display its contents in a certain rectangle. In class Window the corresponding operation is implemented with an empty method. An application framework keeps a list of all currently open windows. Thus a general routine can determine in which window a mouse click occurred. The click is then delegated to the respective window by sending the Window object a message, for example, handleClick. The following procedure suggests a general handling of a mouse click at position clickPos (from class Point).

```
IF clickPos:inMenuBar THEN
    Selection of a menu command
ELSE
    FOR i := 1 TO windowList:size DO BEGIN
        theWindow := windowList:at(i);
        IF theWindow:contains(clickPos) THEN
            theWindow:handleClick(clickPos);
            RETURN
        END -- IF
    END -- FOR
END -- ELSE
```

If windowList contains only general windows of class Window, then the method handleClick realized there is invoked; it probably does nothing. However, new classes can be derived from the class Window and, due to polymorphism, the window list can be filled with objects of these classes. How the objects are put in the window list depends on the design principles of the application framework and is not discussed further here. What is important is that the variable theWindow can contain a mix of objects of different classes, including ones that were not even predictable at the time of the implementation of the application framework. Dynamic binding assures that the methods defined in the new classes are invoked instead of Window methods. Probably the method contains will never be overridden because it is universally applicable to all windows. The method handleClick, on the other hand, now provides window-specific actions. Note especially that some application frameworks are distributed only in compiled form, yet they can still be extended with new functionality.

As in so many other areas of object-oriented programming, among application frameworks the Smalltalk system played a pioneering role. Smalltalk introduced the *MVC model*, which has since been copied in numerous variations in other application frameworks. The letters M, V and C stand for *model*, *view* and *controller*. A graphical user interface in Smalltalk consists of these three components, as shown in Figure 4.36.

The MVC model is based on the observation that things are almost always displayed on the screen and processed by user input, or at least this is the execution of an interactive program from the viewpoint of the user. Actually the program always contains data structures that represent the screen display. These data structures are the *model* of the reality that is represented in a window on the screen. Thus the screen displays a certain *view* of the model. A dedicated View class handles this display. User input must be processed in a way appropriate to the view. Interpreting the input and executing the corresponding actions are the tasks of the *controller*, represented by a Controller class.

Due to the close coupling of a view and the meaning of user input, View and Controller classes always exist in pairs. Specific classes are derived from the framework classes View and Controller. As a rule, the model lacks a general base class and thus also a common interface for various models. Smalltalk's MVC model also supports the

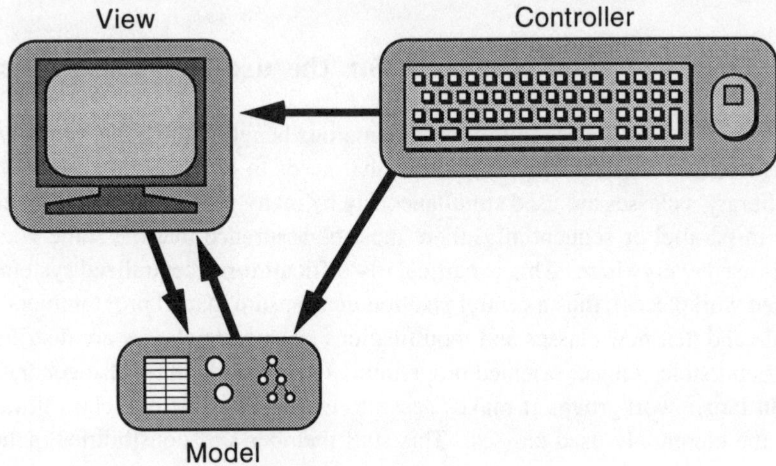


Figure 4.36: The MVC model

simultaneous display of a single model in multiple views, processed by different controller classes. Any change in the model leads to automatic update in all views with a mechanism called *change propagation.* A model "knows" in which views it is displayed and informs them of any changes.

Some newer application frameworks deviate from the MVC model. They employ the observation that View and Controller classes always occur pairwise and so also leave the handling of user input to the View classes. In these frameworks user input is read in the main program, which delegates the interpretation and processing of input to the View objects. An example of such an application framework is MacApp [Schmucker 1986].

Application frameworks not only prove useful to the program developer, but also bring benefits to those who use the programs so developed. Because the application framework takes on a large part of the processing of user input and visual representation, programs produced with the same framework have a uniform look and feel. This promotes the consistency of user interfaces across multiple programs. For most computers, guidelines exist for the design of user interfaces; the programmer should adhere to these guidelines in order to assure high acceptance of developed products. An application framework supports the programmer here because it already provides significant parts of the user interface.

The combination of application frameworks with prototyping tools holds particular promise. The application framework provides the general program structure and the prototyping tool permits interactive design of the user interface of new program components, for which classes are generated that can be integrated into the application framework. If manual adaptation should be necessary for the classes generated by the prototyping tool, this is not realized directly in the classes, but in derived classes. In this way the prototyping tool can be used repeatedly to remodel the user interface, but manual adaptations are retained. An example of such a tool is DICE [Pree 1990].

### 4.7.4 Organizational measures for the use of a class library

Although the users of a class library reap numerous benefits, there is a price. A class library is itself a complex software product that needs to be managed and maintained. Since a library's classes are used simultaneously by many programmers and in multiple projects in parallel or sequentially, there must be assurance that the same version of classes is used everywhere. This is particularly difficult for decentralized systems (e.g., networked workplaces); thus a central position must ensure that all programmers remain up to date and that new classes and modifications of existing classes are distributed as quickly as possible. Object-oriented programming saves work, but it also generates new work. In larger workgroups it makes sense to employ at least one class librarian to manage the commonly used classes. This staff member's responsibilities include the following activities:

- *Updating the class library.* Usually a commercial product provides the core of a class library. Such commercially distributed libraries are continuously maintained by their producers. New versions of the core library must thus be incorporated in the overall library, which can affect running projects and other classes. The producer of class libraries normally assure the compatibility of new versions with older ones, but updates can still necessitate modifications. For example, if classes were written locally to circumvent shortcomings in the class library, then such classes could become superfluous. Highly functional extensions of a class library can also meant that problems can now be solved simply. Part of the job of the class librarian is to announce such modifications and to alert programmers of possible consequences.
- *Adding new classes.* When a project produces a new class that can be assumed to be reusable in other projects, this class cannot simply be added to the library by its developer. This would create chaos in short time. Every incorporation of a class into the class library must be handled or at least monitored by the class librarian, whose responsibilities include checking whether the class is compatible to the classes already archived in the library and whether it is appropriately documented. Newly integrated classes also have to be cataloged and announced to other programmers to help make the step from reusability to actual reuse. This cataloging becomes even more important as the scope of the library increases.
- *Establishing guidelines.* The classes of a library must fulfill certain guidelines, including rules for naming classes and methods, documentation and commenting conventions, regulations for structuring methods, and conventions for visibility and access rights. Not only formal but also objective guidelines must be observed. For example, new classes should be usable in a similar way as existing ones to minimize the learning effort. The general guidelines must be established by the class librarian (in cooperation with the users of the class library), whereby the purchased core library should serve as the foundation.
- *Cooperation in class design.* New reusable classes sometimes arise by chance, but as a rule they are consciously planned. This is particularly true when a company produces certain software products (e.g., business programs, process controls or network software). The purchased core library seldom contains appropriate classes for specialized problem domains, so that the company must first create a foundation on which to build in the future. The design of such classes requires the cooperation of the class librarian to assure observance of guidelines from the start. Furthermore, because such classes are of general interest, other programmers should submit criticisms and suggestions as early as possible.
- *Monitoring immature classes.* Classes recently added to the class library are temporarily marked as immature. They must be monitored to determine how they prove themselves in future reuse. This is easier said than done because the class librarian usually only receives feedback if something does not work. Thus from time to time the librarian must check which classes are used where and which

problems have occurred. A protocol must be kept of these observations so that the state of all new classes is always known.

- *Change control.* If an error occurs during the reuse of a class, then the class must definitely not be corrected in the original version. First the librarian must determine whether the class was used properly and whether incorrect use is due to inadequate documentation of the class. In this way many reported software errors can be dismissed. If an actual error has occurred, then naturally it must be fixed and the corrected class must be put in the class library. Here the librarian must check whether the class is used in other projects. If so, the other teams must also receive the new class without delay. The librarian might also determine that the class has been used in already completed projects, in which case the correction must be assimilated there as well. Such corrective modifications are particularly relevant for products with maintenance contracts.
- *Assistance in the use and maintenance of classes.* The class librarian needs to know all the details of the library. The librarian should not be seen as just some average programmer who was degraded to purely administrative work. Indeed, the librarian must have profound knowledge in the field of object-oriented programming to be able to answer all questions. For critical classes, the class librarian should be integrated in the development process.

The more programmers work with a class library, the more extensive and important are the administrative tasks associated with the class library. In small teams (whose members have constant personal contact) cooperation can amount to each member specializing in one part of the class library. In large software divisions with one hundred or more staff members, this becomes difficult, and even a single class librarian cannot handle the job. Instead, large programming staffs should have a dedicated class library team that is also responsible for in-house development of generally useful classes. This results in a division of the programming staff into object specialists and application programmers. The specialists are not directly involved in running projects, but produce tools that the application programmers can use. Unfortunately, organizing such a specialist group usually encounters resistance from management because the group does not produce quantitatively measurable profit. However, the specialist group is important because its work enables the application programmers to achieve higher productivity.

A few years ago publications were writing about future outlooks that promised an immense market for specialized classes. The offered classes were to be listed in catalogs (comparable to mail-order catalogs) and described in data sheets. The reuser would then only have to select the classes relevant to a current project. More recently such predictions have ceased. Object-oriented practice is more sober because classes developed independently at different sites very likely will not be compatible. The literature continues to report about sublibraries for special purposes, with claimed compatibility to every class library developed for a certain programming language, but

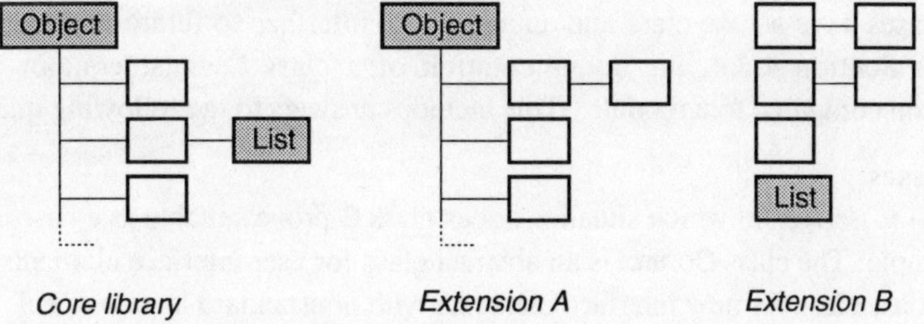


Figure 4.37: Extensions of a class library

such promises must be viewed with caution. Figure 4.37 depicts some of the difficulties associated with such special-purpose sublibraries.

If a sublibrary has a common root (as in Figure 4.37, extension A), then this root class very likely has an interface that is different from that of the root class of the core library. Mixing these libraries creates conflicts that can hardly be resolved. If the root classes have different names, then a parallel hierarchy can be constructed, but the objects of the extension are no longer compatible with objects of the core library.

If a sublibrary consists of a loose collection of classes (as in Figure 4.37, extension B) and all its classes are provided as source code, then the classes can be integrated into the core library. However, this requires manual modifications of the classes, which again creates difficulties in adjusting on release of a newer version of the sublibrary. In addition, the implementation of the purchased classes probably contains collection classes (e.g., List) that are distributed with the sublibrary, but are also present in the core library. A conflict results. Keeping the new classes (and renaming them if necessary) results in a duplication of functionality in the merged class library. On the other hand, using the core library classes instead of the new ones again requires massive intervention into code of the purchased sublibrary.

The only real chance for the purchase of new classes results when a vendor offers an extension for precisely the class library that a company uses. Since this generally requires the recompilation of the purchased classes in the context of the installed library, even this works only if the new classes are distributed as source code. Most professional class producers avoid this, however, out of fear of infringement of copyright.

A further restriction ensues because class libraries are generally written for a specific programming language. Only in the most seldom of cases are the classes compiled with different compilers compatible. Among the reasons is that the concepts of different programming languages deviate drastically. A C++ class library that uses static objects and assumes multiple inheritance, for example, cannot be used in Eiffel or Object-Pascal programs. One exception is the application framework MacApp, which was deliberately designed for use with Object-Pascal and C++.

For a class to be reused, it must be adequately documented (see Section 3.7.1.2). Since classes share much similarity with modules, the same guidelines apply for classes.

Since classes have a base class and an additional interface to future derived classes, as shown in Section 4.3.4, the documentation of a class C must contain additional information compared to a module. This includes answers to the following questions:

**For classes:**

- *When to derive:* In which situations does class C prove suitable as a base class?
  Example: The class Control is an abstract class for user interface elements. It serves as a base class for new interface elements with nonstandard look and feel.
- *How to derive:* Which constraints need to be fulfilled if a new class is derived from class C?
  Example: The class TextView works together with the class TextController. If a class with different behavior is to be derived from TextView, a parallel class to TextController must also be derived.

**For methods:**

- *When to override:* May a method be overridden? If yes, under what conditions?
  Example: The method shallowCopy must not be overridden under any circumstances because its standard behavior is assumed in other methods.
  Example: The method draw is defined abstractly in the class Image; therefore it must always be overridden if the derived class is to be concrete.
  Example: The method writeToFile must be overridden if the derived class defines additional instance variables.
- *How to override:* What must be observed in overriding the method?
  Example: In overriding the writeToFile method, first invoke the overridden method before additional instance variables are defined.
  Example: The overridden method isEmpty must return the value TRUE if the list contains no element.

The documentation of a class C should also include information about classes used within C, so that reusers of class C will know which classes they will need additionally to use class C. This can be important information if the goal is to save memory and thus to use as few classes as possible. This category also encompasses notes on run-time behavior.

Example: The class List is realized as a linear linked list. Searching through the list from start to finish is quite efficient, while searching in reverse order takes a long time. If you need a list that will be processed in both directions, use the class DoubleList instead; it works with a doubly linked list.

When object-oriented programming is first introduced to a workgroup, there can be psychological problems regarding the acceptance of a class library. Two aspects play a role here. On the one hand, many programmers tend to solve subproblems themselves rather than use a class provided by another programmer. Especially for small problems, the learning effort is perceived as too high; programmers believe that they can solve the problem themselves in less time. This is termed the NIH effect (not invented here). The second problem is that some programmers are reluctant to have someone look over their shoulders. A good product of a programmer or a department is seen as a personal achievement that is no one else's business. Sometimes management, perhaps intentionally, promotes this kind of behavior by encouraging competitive thinking between programmers or even whole departments. In addition, making a class generally available demands additional effort because the class must be tested more intensively and documented better. However, this effort is not to the benefit of the implementor or the department, but helps other programmers who reap the rewards of others' work.

Integrating a class library into daily work can be promoted with simple organizational measures. For example, some companies pay reuse premiums that primarily benefit those who create reusable products, but also those who reuse them. For example, the class librarian might handle the job of compiling a list of the most frequently reused classes and their authors. Naturally this approach also has weaknesses because it encourages manipulations such as reusing a befriended programmer's classes without actually needing them, only to help secure the annual premium. Fortunately, other measures, less strictly organized, can also help achieve the reuse goal. These include, for example, promoting team spirit and turning away from group-oriented cost computation.

One very significant factor is time, because the real benefits of object-oriented programming with class libraries can only be harvested with increasing experience on the part of the individual programmer. Due to the learning curve, productivity is still low in the first months because object-oriented thinking must be learned and class library explored. After about a half year we can expect programmers to be secure in using object-oriented programming and to be fully exploiting the class library.

## 4.8 Prototyping with object-oriented programming

An extensive class library contributes to a reduction in new written code. This can be exploited in a software project to support rapid prototyping. This section examines how class libraries can be employed for the production of prototypes for individual components of a program system. In this context, prototypes serve not to design the user interface, but to model the system architecture and to test individual system functions. The idea is to employ complex classes from the library for solving certain subproblems, whereby originally no consideration is given to efficiency. We demonstrate this with a simple example.

A subtask of a program system is to manage lists of names that are to be kept sorted and not recur. New elements thus always need to be inserted at the correct position in a list. We assume the existence of a class NameList with the following interface:

```
INTERFACE OF NameList;
INHERITS FROM Object;
   size: Integer;                       -- returns the number of names in the list
   add (name:String);                   -- appends a new name to the end
   delete (i:Integer);                  -- removes the name at position i
   at (i:Integer): String;              -- returns the name at position i
   replace (i:Integer; name:String);    -- replaces the name at position i
   contains (name:String): Boolean;     -- checks whether name is in the list
   sort;                                -- alphabetically sorts the list
   ...
END NameList.
```

We can implement a sorted name list by simply deriving a new class from the existing one and overriding the methods that violate the constraints (sorted and free of duplicates). In this example this affects only the methods add and replace. If no new operations need to be added, the interface of class NameList can be inherited:

```
INTERFACE OF SortedUniqueNameList;
INHERITS FROM NameList;
END SortedUniqueNameList.
```

In the methods add and replace the existing operations can be used, making the class implementation quite simple:

```
IMPLEMENTATION OF SortedUniqueNameList;

   add (name:String) IS
   BEGIN
      IF not self:contains(name) THEN      -- avoid duplicates
         base:add(name);                   -- append name ...
         self:sort                         -- ... and re-sort
      END
   END add;

   replace (i:Integer; name:String) IS
   BEGIN
      self:delete(i);                      -- remove old name
      self:add(name)                       -- insert new name at sorted position
   END replace;

END SortedUniqueNameList.
```

The add method first checks whether the name already exists in the list. If so, nothing needs to be done; otherwise the overridden method is used to append the name, and then the list is re-sorted to put the new name at the correct position. Note here that the

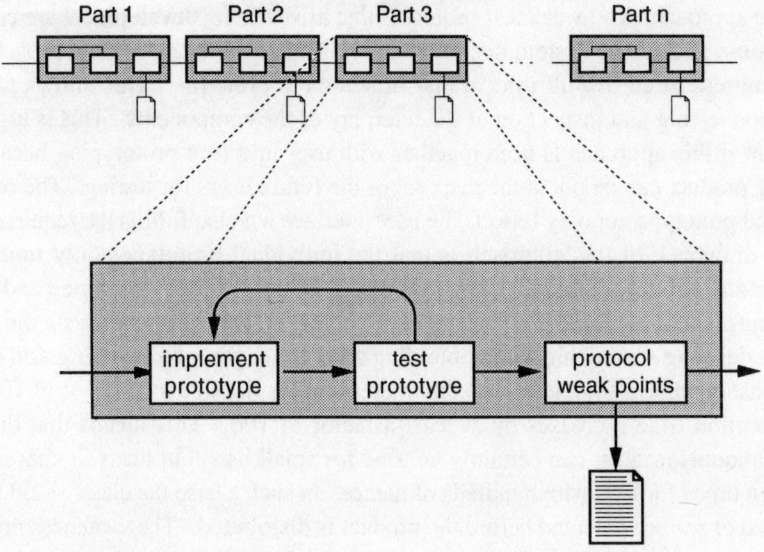


Figure 4.38: System design with object-oriented prototypes

invocation of add employs a base invocation, while sorting uses a self invocation. The effect is the same, but using self has the advantage that the sorting method can be overridden in a class derived from SortedUniqueNameList (e.g., with a better sorting algorithm). The add method thus automatically uses the new sorting operation. The replace method simply replaces the old name and inserts the new one with the help of add. Thus the list remains sorted and duplicates are avoided (e.g., in case we should try to replace the second name in the list ["A", "B", "C"] with "A").

The brevity and simplicity of the new class make it easy to check its correctness. The implementor need not contend with searching and sorting operations, but can concentrate on relevant matters. We get by with surprisingly little program code (here only 17 lines for definition and implementation combined) and can be quite sure that we have made no errors. Naturally, we must trust in the correct implementation of the base class because otherwise we would also inherit its errors. If the base class has been classified as mature, then its correctness can be assumed.

The new class can be used immediately wherever sorted name lists are needed. In the implementation of the overall system, we are not hindered by details and can progress to the next subtask. The development of a program system thus proceeds as depicted in Figure 4.38.

A prototype is produced for a component as rapidly as possible. This step has three parts: the implementation, the (local) component test and protocoling of weaknesses already known upon implementation (e.g., high memory requirements, slow execution, lack of generality). These weaknesses are not corrected, however, unless they affect the functioning of the component. Instead, the next component is immediately tackled with the same approach. The weakness protocols that arise during development are collected and become part of the system documentation. The advantage of this approach is the rapid progress to an overall system that functions in principle. This allows for early integration testing and inspection of the interplay of the components. This is especially important if this approach is used together with user interface prototyping because the resulting product can be put at the disposal of the future users for testing. The resulting functional prototype not only reflects the user interface but also fulfills the required tasks.

The drawback of this approach is that the individual prototypes only function in principle and still have a number of weaknesses. In our example the sorted addition of new names (and thus also the replacement of names) is slow. Depending on the quality of the underlying sorting algorithm, building a list of length $n$ by invoking add $n$ times has at least quadratic complexity, so that increasing the list size by a factor of 10 means that execution time increases by at least a factor of 100. This means that the class SortedUniqueNameList can certainly be used for small lists, but leads to unacceptable execution times for lists with hundreds of names. In such a case the class would have to be revised or re-implemented before the product is distributed. The weakness protocols provide the necessary support for such corrections. Nevertheless, it is not necessary to iron out all weaknesses since some conditions have no impact on the problem. For example, we might establish that sorted name lists contain at most ten entries, so that a more efficient implementation would bring no noticeable improvement.

In applying this approach, it should be clear that the project-specific prototypes are seldom suitable for interapplication reuse. Although they can be used repeatedly within the project, class prototypes are seldom so general that they can be incorporated into the class library. We should also add that class prototypes can only be used where object-oriented decomposition was carried out and a similar class is needed. This means that this approach proves unsuitable for extremely algorithmically oriented subtasks and also requires an extensive library with numerous project-specific classes.

## 4.9 Implementation of the design example

This section shows how to use object orientation to program the classes designed in Section 3.4.7.4 to display a portal robot. We use our accustomed abstract notation and stay with elementary concepts, so our realization can be transferred into any concrete object-oriented programming language without problems.

Figure 4.39 again shows the class hierarchy that evolved from our design process. Using the Abbot design method, we extracted these classes from the verbal specifications of the task. Hence we modeled the robot from the viewpoint of the user. The reader might wonder why we introduced separate classes for singular objects (of which only one is instantiated; e.g., ball, portal and robot). One reason is that all parts share a common interface. We can exploit polymorphism and dynamic binding to use different parts (e.g., Ball and Beam) uniformly. Another reason is that complex robot parts share class components. For example, (as we show below) the classes Foundation, Portal, Gripper and Robot share certain methods and thus can be implemented in a common base class, which promotes reuse of code. In this context we refer the reader to Section 4.9.9, which evaluates the object-oriented solution in detail.

We begin with the general classes Part and ComplexPart and then tackle the classes derived from them. The numbers in Figure 4.39 indicate the sequence in which the classes were designed. In each of the following subsections we first provide the definition and implementation of the respective class and then share some comments on them. To avert dependencies on certain graphics packages, we omit the actual graphic operations to display the parts in the methods and only specify their effect verbally.

Various classes use the data types Position and Rectangle, which we do not realize as classes but declare as record types as follows:

```
TYPE
  Position = RECORD           -- real-world coordinates
        x: Integer;           -- x-coordinate, increasing to the right
        y: Integer;           -- y-coordinate, increasing to the back
        z: Integer            -- z-coordinate, increasing upwards
     END;

  Rectangle = RECORD    -- screen coordinates
        x: Integer;           -- left edge
        y: Integer;           -- top edge
        b,h: Integer          -- width and height in pixels
     END;
```

Our decision for record types makes the class implementations easy to port to hybrid languages. In a pure object-oriented language these data types would require us to provide simple classes.

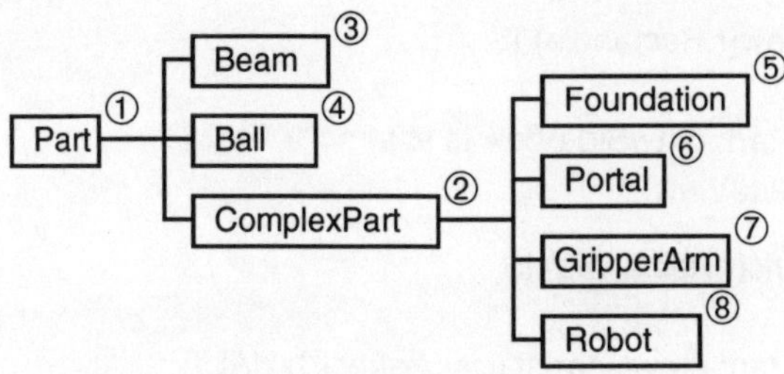


Figure 4.39: Class hierarchy of robot parts

### 4.9.1 Class Part

```
INTERFACE OF Part;
INHERITS FROM Object;
   move (dx,dy,dz:Integer);          -- relative movement of part in space
   drawFrontView(r:Rectangle);       -- front view in rectangle r
   drawTopView(r:Rectangle);         -- top view in rectangle r
   drawSideView(r:Rectangle);        -- side view in rectangle r
   drawIsometric(r:Rectangle);       -- isometric view in rectangle r
END Part.
```

We derive the class Part directly from the root class Object. This means that the class Part inherits at least the method initialize from Object, so this does not appear in the interface definition of Part. If new instance variables are defined in a class, the method initialize must be appropriately overridden to assure that the instance variables are initialized on instantiation. In the class Part this is not the case, but some of its derived classes (e.g., ComplexPart, Beam and Ball) do require such initialization.

The methods of the class Part are very simple:

```
IMPLEMENTATION OF Part;

   move(dx,dy,dz:Integer) IS
   BEGIN
      Write("Part: move is abstract"); HALT
   END move;

   drawFrontView(r:Rectangle) IS
   BEGIN
      Write("Part: drawFrontView is abstract"); HALT
   END drawFrontView;

   drawTopView(r:Rectangle) IS
   BEGIN
      Write("Part: drawTopView is abstract"); HALT
   END drawTopView;

   drawSideView(r:Rectangle) IS
   BEGIN
      Write("Part: drawSideView is abstract"); HALT
   END drawSideView;

   drawIsometric(r:Rectangle) IS
   BEGIN
      Write("Part: drawIsometric is abstract"); HALT
   END drawIsometric;
```

```
END Part.
```

Part is an abstract class. The operations specified in its interface refer either to coordinate transformations (move) or to display (draw...). The corresponding methods cannot be implemented here. We want to assure that the classes will be overridden and so provide an implementation that outputs an error message and then terminates the program. To output the error message, we use the procedure Write, which we use like the corresponding Pascal procedure. In a pure object-oriented language this procedure invocation would need to be replaced with a suitable message.

### 4.9.2 Class ComplexPart

```
INTERFACE OF ComplexPart;
INHERITS FROM Part;
   partsCount: Integer;               -- returns a count of simple parts
   simplePart(num:Integer): Part;     -- returns the simple part at index num
   addPart(p:Part);                   -- appends a new simple part
   removePart(num:Integer);           -- removes the simple part at index num
END ComplexPart.
```

The class ComplexPart derives directly from Part. We define only the additional methods that are needed to compose a complex part from simple parts and to change the composition of the complex part.

```
IMPLEMENTATION OF ComplexPart;

   VAR
      partsList: ARRAY [1..20] OF Part;
      number: Integer;

   initialize IS
   BEGIN
      base:initialize;
      number := 0
   END initialize;

   partsCount: Integer IS
   BEGIN
      RETURN number
   END partsCount;

   simplePart(num:Integer): Part IS
   BEGIN
      IF num < 1 OR num > number THEN
         Write("Invalid part index ",num); HALT
```

```
        END;
        RETURN partsList[num]
    END simplePart;

    addPart(p:Part) IS
    BEGIN
        IF number = 20 THEN
            Write("Complex parts can contain at most 20 simple parts"); HALT
        END;
        number := number + 1;
        partsList[number] := p
    END addPart;

    removePart(num:Integer) IS
    VAR i:Integer;
    BEGIN
        IF num < 1 OR num > number THEN
            Write("Invalid part index ",num); HALT
        END;
        number := number – 1;
        FOR i := num TO number DO partsList[i] := partsList[i + 1] END
    END removePart;

    move (dx,dy,dz:Integer) IS
    VAR i:Integer;
    BEGIN
        FOR i := 1 TO number DO partsList[i]:move(dx,dy,dz) END
    END move;

    drawFrontView(r:Rectangle) IS
    VAR i:Integer;
    BEGIN
        FOR i := 1 TO number DO partsList[i]:drawFrontView(r) END
    END drawFrontView;

    drawTopView(r:Rectangle) IS
    VAR i:Integer;
    BEGIN
        FOR i := 1 TO number DO partsList[i]:drawTopView(r) END
    END drawTopView;

    drawSideView(r:Rectangle) IS
    VAR i:Integer;
```

```
    BEGIN
        FOR i := 1 TO number DO partsList[i]:drawSideView(r) END
    END drawSideView;

    drawIsometric(r:Rectangle) IS
    VAR i:Integer;
    BEGIN
        FOR i := 1 TO number DO partsList[i]:drawIsometric(r) END
    END drawIsometric;

END ComplexPart.
```

A complex part contains a list of simple parts. We have realized this list conventionally as an array instead of using an Array class. The restriction to 20 elements is arbitrary, but can be circumvented because a complex part can recursively contain additional complex parts. A complex part that itself contains 20 complex parts can thus manage up to 400 simple parts.

Since the class ComplexPart defines new instance variables, they need to be initialized appropriately on instantiation of a new object. Thus we override the method initialize that is inherited from Object by simply initializing the instance variable number with the value 0. The array partsList need not be initialized because the implementation assures that there can be no access to the elements of a newly created complex part. Before the initialization of the instance variable, the initialization method of the base class is invoked. The class Part has no such method, and in Object this method is implemented as an empty method because there is no instance variable requiring initialization. The base invocation therefore has no effect. Nevertheless, it must not be omitted because we cannot ensure that a later modification of the class Part might not add an initialization method. Note: Knowing the implementation of the base class must not be abused.

ComplexPart is a concrete class. We can use objects of this class for simple management of several other parts. The methods abstractly defined in class Part must be overridden here. The implementation of these methods is simple. A message to a complex part is simply delegated to all its component simple parts. Note that at this time we do not know what kind of parts there will be in the future. Dynamic binding makes the class ComplexPart independent of later extensions.

### 4.9.3 Class Beam

```
INTERFACE OF Beam;
INHERITS FROM Part;
    startVal: Position;          -- returns the position of start of beam
    endVal: Position;            -- returns the position of end of beam
```

```
    thickness: Integer;            -- returns thickness of beam
    setStart(pos:Position);        -- sets starting position of beam
    setEnd(pos:Position);          -- sets end position of beam
    setThickness(d:Integer);       -- changes thickness of beam
END Beam.
```

A beam has three significant instance variables that determine its position and appearance on the screen. For each instance variable, we have a method for querying and one for changing the value.

```
IMPLEMENTATION OF Beam;

    VAR
        pos1,pos2: Position;       -- starting and end positions
        thick: Integer;            -- thickness of beam

    initialize IS
    BEGIN
        base:initialize;
        pos1.x := 0;  pos1.y := 0;  pos1.z := 0;
        pos2.x := 0;  pos2.y := 0;  pos2.z := 0;
        thick := 100
    END initialize;

    startVal:Position IS
    BEGIN
        RETURN pos1
    END startVal;
    endVal:Position IS
    BEGIN
        RETURN pos2
    END endVal;

    thickness:Integer IS
    BEGIN
        RETURN thick
    END thickness;

    setStart (pos:Position) IS
    BEGIN
        pos1 := pos
    END setStart;

    setEnd (pos:Position) IS
```

```
        BEGIN
            pos2 := pos
        END setEnd;

        setThickness (d:Integer) IS
        BEGIN
            thick := d
        END setThickness;

        move (dx,dy,dz:Integer) IS
        BEGIN
            pos1.x := pos1.x + dx;  pos1.y := pos1.y + dy;  pos1.z := pos1.z + dz;
            pos2.x := pos2.x + dx;  pos2.y := pos2.y + dy;  pos2.z := pos2.z + dz
        END move;
        drawFrontView (r:Rectangle) IS
        BEGIN
            Draw a line within rectangle r
        END drawFrontView;

        drawTopView (r:Rectangle) IS
        BEGIN
            Draw a line within rectangle r
        END drawTopView;

        drawSideView (r:Rectangle) IS
        BEGIN
            Draw a line within rectangle r
        END drawSideView;

        drawIsometric (r:Rectangle) IS
        BEGIN
            Draw a line within rectangle r
        END drawIsometric;

    END Beam.
```

We describe a beam with two positions and a thickness. The positions cannot be initialized practically; hence we assign to both the coordinates (0,0,0). The initialization value for thickness is 100; since all values have real-world dimensions and units are in millimeters, the value 100 (10 cm) seems to be an appropriate initialization value for the beam. For the sake of completeness, this initialization value should be documented in the class interface as well so that clients know about the appearance of a newly created beam.

We only describe the drawing operations verbally. Except for the isometric view, they are not difficult to implement. The main work is in converting real-world

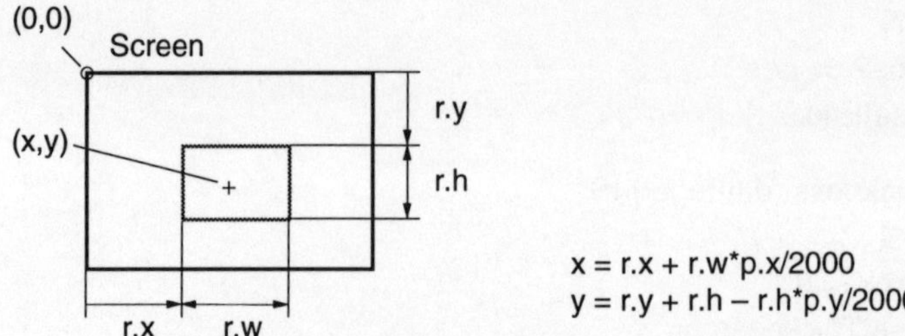


Figure 4.40: Computation of screen position from position in space

coordinates to screen coordinates (whose origin is the left top corner). Figure 4.40 uses the example of the front view to show how position *p* in real-world space is converted to screen coordinates *x* and *y* within rectangle *r*.

The factor 2000 emanates from the specifications in the task descriptions, where real-world coordinates are restricted to a 2000 mm cube. Accordingly, the thickness of the beam must be scaled on the screen with a factor r.w/2000.

### 4.9.4 Class Ball

```
INTERFACE OF Ball;
INHERITS FROM Part;
  center: Position;              -- returns the center of the ball
  radius: Integer;               -- returns the radius of the ball
  setCenter(pos:Position);       -- sets the center of the ball
  setRadius(r:Integer);          -- sets the radius of the ball
END Ball.
```

A ball is analogous to a beam: It has two instance variables that can be queried and set independently.

```
IMPLEMENTATION OF Ball;

  VAR
     cent: Position;   -- center
     rad: Integer;     -- radius

  initialize IS
  BEGIN
     base:initialize;
     cent.x := 0;  cent.y := 0;  cent.z := 0;
     rad := 100
  END initialize;
```

```
    center: Position IS
    BEGIN
        RETURN cent
    END center;

    radius: Integer IS
    BEGIN
        RETURN rad
    END radius;

    setCenter (pos:Position) IS
    BEGIN
        cent := pos
    END setCenter;

    setRadius (r:Integer) IS
    BEGIN
        rad := r
    END setRadius;

    move (dx,dy,dz:Integer) IS
    BEGIN
        cent.x := cent.x + dx;  cent.y := cent.y + dy;  cent.z := cent.z + dz
    END move;

    drawFrontView (r:Rectangle) IS
    BEGIN
        Draw a circle within rectangle r
    END drawFrontView;

    drawTopView (r:Rectangle) IS
    BEGIN
        Draw a circle within rectangle r
    END drawTopView;
    drawSideView (r:Rectangle) IS
    BEGIN
        Draw a circle within rectangle r
    END drawSideView;

    drawIsometric (r:Rectangle) IS
    BEGIN
        Draw a circle within rectangle r
    END drawIsometric;

END Ball.
```

Like a ball, a beam is an elementary part. Most of the work is precisely in these parts, while all other classes can then use the operations implemented here. The drawing operations require similar scaling to that in beam, and likewise the radius of the circle must be adapted to screen coordinates.

### 4.9.5 Class Foundation

```
INTERFACE OF Foundation;
INHERITS FROM ComplexPart;
   setup (l,w:Integer);          -- initialization with length l and width w
END Foundation.
```

The foundation is a complex part and thus provides all operations needed to draw and display it. We simply add a new initialization method setup to give the foundation a credible starting value. This initialization method must not be confused with the standard method initialize; while the standard initialize fulfills a purely technical purpose (the method ensures that all objects begin their life in an orderly state), our new method setup is problem-oriented (setting up the relationship to the real world).

```
IMPLEMENTATION OF Foundation;

   setup(l,w:Integer) IS
   VAR
       rail:Beam;
       pos1,pos2: Position;
   BEGIN
       self:initialize;
       pos1.x := 0;  pos1.y := 0;  pos1.z := 0;
       pos2.x := l;  pos2.y := 0;  pos1.z := 0;
       rail := Beam:new;
       rail:setStart(pos1);  rail:setEnd(pos2);
       self:addPart(rail);
       pos1.y := w;  pos2.y := w;
       rail := Beam:new;
       rail:setStart(pos1);  rail:setEnd(pos2);
       self:addPart(rail);
   END setup;

   move (dx,dy,dz:Integer) IS
   BEGIN
       -- nothing to do!
   END move;

END Foundation.
```

To initialize the foundation, we first invoke the method self:initialize, which assures that the parts list is empty. Then two beams (rails) are instantiated and appended to the parts list with the help of self invocations. Note here that the class Foundation requires no knowledge of the implementation of the base class ComplexPart.

Since the foundation is stationary, we override the method move with an empty method. We can view the message move as an attempt to move the object. The foundation does not react because it is anchored in the floor, just as a real foundation does not move if we try to shift it by hand.

The methods setup and move suffice to design a foundation that meets our requirements. The drawing operations can be inherited as they are from the base class ComplexPart. However, this inheritance also brings us methods for changing a complex part, so that a foundation could be redesigned by a client by invoking the methods addPart and removePart. In addition, the immobility of a foundation can be circumvented by invoking the method simplePart for each rail and using the methods setStart, setEnd and move for repositioning. To preclude this, we would have to override these methods with empty methods or invocations of HALT. This would also disable the design of a foundation with self:addPart, and base:addPart would have to be invoked instead.

### 4.9.6 Class Portal

```
INTERFACE OF Portal;
INHERITS FROM ComplexPart;
   setup (h,w,x0:Integer);        -- initialization with height h, width w
                                  -- and origin x0
END Portal.

IMPLEMENTATION OF Portal;

   setup(h,w,x0:Integer) IS
   VAR
      front,back,top:Beam;
      pos1,pos2: Position;
   BEGIN
      self:initialize;
      pos1.x := x0;  pos1.y := 0;  pos1.z := 0;
      pos2.x := x0;  pos2.y := 0;  pos1.z := h;
      front := Beam:new;
      front:setStart(pos1);  front:setEnd(pos2);
      self:addPart(front);
      pos1.y := w;  pos2.y := w;
      back := Beam:new;
```

```
            back:setStart(pos1);  back:setEnd(pos2);
            self:addPart(back);
            pos1.y := 0;  pos1.z := h;
            top := Beam:new;
            top:setStart(pos1);  top:setEnd(pos2);
            self:addPart(top);
        END setup;

        move (dx,dy,dz:Integer) IS
        BEGIN
            base:move(dx,0,0)
        END move;

    END Portal.
```

The portal is analogous to the foundation. During initialization three beams are instantiated and appended to the parts list. Contrary to the foundation, the portal is movable, although only along the *x* axis, i.e., left and right. This constraint is easy to implement by interpreting the invocation move(dx,dy,dz) so that the *y* and *z* coordinates are not changed. On receipt of the message move(20,30,–15), we modify it to move(20,0,0) and forward the message in this form to the simple parts with the method move of ComplexPart.

### 4.9.7 Class Gripper

```
    INTERFACE OF Gripper;
    INHERITS FROM ComplexPart;
      setup (l:Integer; pos:Position);  -- initialization with l and position pos
    END Gripper.

    IMPLEMENTATION OF Gripper;

      setup(l, pos:Integer) IS
      VAR
          arm:Beam;  hand:Ball;
          pos2: Position;
      BEGIN
          self:initialize;
          pos2 := pos;  pos2.z := pos.z + l;
          arm := Beam:new;
          arm:setStart(pos);  arm:setEnd(pos2);
          self:addPart(arm);
          hand := Ball:new;
          hand:setCenter(pos);
```

```
        self:addPart(hand);
    END setup;

END Gripper.
```

The implementation of the class Gripper is even simpler than that of class Portal because a gripper consists of only two parts and has no restrictions on its mobility, so that even the method move of the base class ComplexPart can be inherited.

### 4.9.8 Class Robot

```
INTERFACE OF Robot;
INHERITS FROM ComplexPart;
    setup (l,w,h:Integer;pos:Position);    -- initialization with length l, width w,
                                           -- height h and position pos
    gripperPosition: Position;             -- returns the position of the gripper
END Robot.
```

Like a foundation and a portal, a robot has a special initialization method; in addition, it has a method to determine the current gripper position.

```
IMPLEMENTATION OF Robot;
    VAR gripperPos:Position;               -- current gripper position

    initialize IS
    BEGIN
        base:initialize;
        gripperPos.x := 0;  gripperPos.y := 0;  gripperPos.z := 0
    END initialize;

    setup (l,w,h:Integer;pos:Position); IS
    VAR
        found: Foundation;
        port: Portal;
        grip: Gripper;

    BEGIN
        found := Foundation:new;
        found:setup(l,w);
        self:addPart(found);
        port := Portal:new;
        port:setup(h,w,pos);
        self:addPart(port);
        grip := Foundation:new;
```

```
        grip:setup(h,pos);
        self:addPart(grip);
        gripperPos := pos
    END setup;

    gripperPosition: Position IS
    BEGIN
        RETURN gripperPos
    END gripperPosition;

    move (dx,dy,dz:Integer) IS
    BEGIN
        base:move(dx,dy,dz);
        gripperPos.x := gripperPos.x + dx;
        gripperPos.y := gripperPos.y + dy;
        gripperPos.z := gripperPos.z + dz
    END move;

END Robot.
```

A robot consists of a foundation, a portal and a gripper. During initialization the robot assembles itself from these parts. Since a robot also should be able to return the current position of its gripper, it must know where to get this information. One possibility would be the following method:

```
    gripperPosition: Position IS
    VAR
        grip: Gripper;
        hand: Ball;
    BEGIN
        grip := Gripper(self:simplePart(3));
        hand := Ball(grip:simplePart(2));
        RETURN hand:center
    END gripperPosition;
```

In addition to the type casts for type conversion, this method has the disadvantage that it makes assumptions about how a robot and a gripper are constructed. If in the future the gripper arm assumes a more realistic appearance and the gripper is no longer represented by a ball, then this method ceases to function. Thus it makes sense to keep track of the position of the gripper separately and to update it with each movement.

### 4.9.9 Evaluation of the object-oriented solution

We could have designed the robot display conventionally, for example, using stepwise refinement, and implemented it with procedures. After the object-oriented solution in

Sections 4.9.1 to 4.9.8, the reader might wonder what advantages it has over a conventional solution. This section emphasizes the most important features of the object-oriented solution.

*Amount of code*

The implementation consists of eight classes with 46 methods containing a total of 105 lines of executable statements. This makes an average of 4.75 methods and 13 executable statements per class; the methods average only 2.33 statements. The implementation is quite compact, even though inheritance was used only within the classes developed here. The use of a class library could have brought additional savings, especially in the class ComplexPart. The brevity of the classes and their methods has a positive effect on readability and reduces error-proneness.

*Generality*

Of the eight classes, two (Beam and Ball) serve to realize elementary parts. Four classes (Foundation, Portal, Gripper and Robot) are application-specific. These classes contain the actual functionality for the solution of the problem. The class Part is abstract; it only defines the interface common to all parts. The class ComplexPart is a generally usable class for assembling parts, and more specific classes can be derived from it. Of the eight classes we have four general and four application-specific classes. Such grouping can hardly be achieved with conventional means.

*Encapsulation*

The individual classes can be used without knowledge of their internal realization. In particular, no direct access is required to instance variables of the objects. It is even possible to change the realization of the parts list in the class ComplexPart without affecting its derived classes. The object-oriented design produced a natural decomposition into individual components with clearly defined interfaces.

*Modifiability and extensibility*

Due to the strict encapsulation, modifications can be made in individual classes without affecting other classes. In particular, the structure of the robot can be modified with but a few changes in the class Robot. To adapt to a new graphic system, only the display methods in the elementary classes would have to be re-implemented. Thus modifications and extensions can be made locally in the corresponding classes. Due to the data-oriented decomposition, components that need modification are easy to find. Robot variants can be realized by deriving new classes from the class Robot. However, if *all* parts are to be provided with additional functionality, *all* classes might have to be extended.

*Reusability*

The class hierarchy can be extended with new classes for special parts (e.g., a more realistic gripper). For extensions we can use the abstract class Part (for deriving new elementary parts) and the class ComplexPart (for composite parts). Since the class Part is abstract, all its methods must be overridden; hence we can inherit from it the interface, but not the implementation. By contrast, from the class ComplexPart all operations for managing the parts list can be inherited, which constitutes real reuse. The class ComplexPart can also be reused without deriving a new class if multiple new parts are to be managed. Likewise the elementary classes can be reused for similar simulation tasks.

## 4.10 Quantitative and qualitative aspects

Object-oriented programming repeatedly inspires the question of what benefits it brings and at what cost. The following sections answer this question at least in part. An exhaustive answer is impossible because comparative data are too scarce and too uncertain.

For example, time savings in program development can only be estimated roughly. To achieve realistic comparative data would require an extensive project being realized with object-oriented as well as conventional means. At a professional production site this is impossible for cost reasons, so that such comparisons can only be carried out in research institutes. Even there the question is how to approach such a comparison. It certainly does not make sense to have the same team implement the project first with conventional and then again with object-oriented means (or vice versa) because the experience gained in the first implementation would certainly help to achieve a shorter project duration the second time around. This would also be the case if the project were implemented twice conventionally. The only sensible variant is to award the same project to two independent teams, making certain that the two groups have the same level of experience.

The size and kind of project also have a significant influence on the results of the comparison. In an extremely algorithmically oriented project, object orientation will not reap the same rewards as in a project where many different kinds of data need to be processed. If the data are very simple and lack sufficient structure, as in many simple business applications, object-oriented programming can have little effect on project duration.

Technical metrics such as code size and execution time of programs are easy to compare because these dimensions can already be measured on relatively small programs (to some extent even in individual statements). However, here too, factors such as the programming language and the class library play a significant role. Thus such metrics also allow considerable room for error.

The following sections treat the quantitative and qualitative impact of object-oriented programming. Here we designate positive aspects with + and negative ones with −. If no mentionable effects can be determined or if positive and negative aspects balance each other, we mark the item with ◎.

### 4.10.1 Quantitative comparison

In general, quantitative statements prove difficult because differences in programming style, programming languages and class libraries result in significant deviations. To exclude extreme values, the following metrics refer exclusively to hybrid languages and class libraries of medium size (some 100 classes). The impact of object-oriented programming is specified as a percentage, where we use the metrics of a corresponding conventional solution as the reference size at 100%. Hence the specification 120% means an increase by one fifth.

The specified metrics are based on the experience of the authors, their colleagues and their cooperation partners in years of object-oriented software development. The foundation for these metrics is numerous projects in the areas of software engineering tools, information systems, automation software, object-oriented programming languages, class libraries and application frameworks. The overall scope of these program systems encompasses more than 500,000 lines of code in various programming languages (especially C++, Eiffel, Oberon, Object-Pascal and Smalltalk).

#### 4.10.1.1 Impact on the size of program code

One interesting metric is the influence of object-oriented programming on the size of program code. Here we must distinguish between written code and reused code from a class library.

\+ *Code to be written: 25 – 50%*

The most important impact of object-oriented programming is the savings in code that needs to be written. This metric plays a significant role because it is directly proportional to programming effort and thus to project duration. The use of an application framework has particular ramifications, enabling savings of up to 90% because the solution to many standard problems becomes superfluous. Such extreme values can often be achieved in small projects in which, for example, an existing application must only be adapted to new requirements. If a program contains many algorithmically oriented components, the savings are more conservative.

Even without the availability of a class library, users of object-oriented programming can anticipate a reduction in self-written code. The savings rise with the size of the project due to intra-application reuse of classes. As a rule, with more careful design (especially by factoring out common object components) and better harmonizing of classes to each other, object-oriented programming yields more reuse than does modular programming.

– *Total program code: 120 – 300%*

Although less new code must be written, the size of the imported code rises. This involves primarily inherited classes, but also directly or indirectly used classes. The metrics specified here refer to the use of a class library compared to the use of a module library for modular programming. Depending on the scope of a class library and the interconnection of its classes, this factor can vary dramatically. If only classes for data structures are used, then the size of imported code is only a few percent of total code, but at the same time less savings in self-written code can be expected. If an application framework is employed, then frequently a multitude of classes are imported indirectly that are not needed for the solution of the actual problem. These classes usually provide additional functionality that would mean an immense development effort without the use of an application framework. Another factor that affects the size of imported code is the generality of the classes that are used and inherited. To make a class as generally reusable as possible, additional methods need to be provided which also contribute to the size of the code even if they are not needed.

#### 4.10.1.2 Effects on execution time

The effects of object-oriented programming on *execution time* are easier to measure objectively than the impact on code size. We can measure the time needed for a method invocation and for a procedure call and compute a factor. The same applies to accessing instance variables. Automatic garbage collection, if present, can also affect execution time because searching for superfluous objects takes additional time. Effects on the overall execution time are more difficult to determine because they depend significantly on the quality of the class library and on programming style.

- *Method invocation: 105 – 120%*
  Due to dynamic binding, the overhead for a method invocation is greater than for a procedure call. Note, however, that the overhead for parameter passing and the stack-like management of the procedure invocation chain is the same in both cases. The specified numbers refer to a parameterless invocation, whereby for method invocation we assume method lookup with indexing. Dynamic method lookup costs a multiple thereof, which must be particularly noted in some pure object-oriented programming languages because they often use this approach.
- *Accessing instance variables: 100 – 1000%*
  Regarding access to instance variables, we assume the use of pointers to dynamic data in the conventional program as well. If the object-oriented programming language permits external access to instance variables, then the resulting machine code does not differ from access to components of dynamic data in conventional languages. Such access occurs in object-oriented programs even when instance variables of the receiver object are used within a method. Access induces more overhead, easily by a factor of ten, if it employs a method invocation. However, this increase in access time also arises in conventional programs with data encapsulation and with the use of abstract data types.

– *Automatic garbage collection: 105 – 150%*
The overhead for automatic garbage collection depends on several factors: the number and sizes of objects, available memory, the rate of creation of new objects, and naturally the technique employed for garbage collection. Normally the overhead for automatic garbage collection amounts to not more than 5% of total run time. That this increase in overhead is so small can be credited to ingenious techniques that particularly take into consideration that object-oriented programs employ many objects with short life spans. However, most garbage collection techniques suffer from the drawback that garbage collection can occur precisely during the most computation-intensive phases because this is when the most objects are created. This can sometimes lead to intermissions that are unacceptable, e.g., in real-time applications. To avoid this drawback, incremental techniques have been developed that, parallel to the actual program, hunt unreachable objects and deallocate their storage. This parallelism avoids unwanted intermissions, but also slows normal program execution.

◎ *Overall execution time: 80 – 120%*
Although multiple individual factors impact negatively on execution time, usually the overall execution time of a program and the response times for interactive programs display no slowdown for three reasons. First, programming in hybrid languages does not use objects exclusively. A method contains not only additional method invocations but also normal statements. In addition, the use of many local variables and elementary data types means that there can be long stretches that do not require dynamic binding or access to instance variables. The second reason is that good class libraries employ highly efficient techniques. For example, sets of objects can be realized as hash tables. Searching for an element in a set is a matter of constant time regardless of set size. Using such classes can bring efficiency gains that take on not just percentage but exponential proportions. The third reason is that dynamic binding induces less overhead than a sequence of tests. Conventional programs require many case distinctions that do not occur in object-oriented programs.

The impact of object-oriented programming on *memory requirements* at run time of a program depends on multiple factors. Naturally the program code plays a role, but methods tables and the use of dynamic objects also come to bear in object-oriented programming.

– *Program code: 120 – 200%*
The increase in memory requirement caused by program code, like the size of imported code, depends greatly on the class library. Although the amount of self-written code declines, more classes are imported, so that the bottom line for program code could be double that of a conventional program. These numbers must be taken with a grain of salt because they depend greatly on the compiler and linker. For

example, some linkers identify unused classes and methods and omit their code from the finished program.

◎ *Method tables: 101 – 110%*
The size ratio of methods tables to program code depends on how many operations are possible with objects of a class and how extensive the methods are on average. If the root class implements 20 methods, then each class has at least these 20 entries in its methods table, even if the methods are not overridden. For 30 classes this amounts to 600 entries. If there are numerous small methods, then there are additional entries that again are transferred to all derived classes. Nevertheless, the proportion of total memory required for method tables is generally negligible.

– *Dynamic objects: 100 – 120%*
Dynamic objects require more memory for their management. This applies especially with automatic garbage collection, which requires storing additional information on the structure of objects. If an object table containing all objects is used as well, then the memory overhead can amount to one fifth of the storage allocated to the objects themselves. On the other hand, with simple memory management, objects produce no more overhead than other dynamic data.

## 4.10.2 Qualitative comparison

This section summarizes points that have already been raised elsewhere. We group the qualitative aspects into those that affect the course of the project and those that influence the quality of the final product.

### 4.10.2.1 Impact on the course of the project

The positive effects of object-oriented programming on the course of a software project result primarily from the reduction of the semantic gap, the high level of reuse and the resulting reduction in program code that needs to be written. As expected, most of the drawbacks result from the overhead related to the management of a class library.

+ *Planning*
The reduction in the semantic gap and the high level of reuse enable better preproject estimates of which parts of the project will prove most work-intensive. A constant amount of overhead for routine activities largely go by the board. Since the design takes place in part schematically (primarily with the use of an application framework) and a reduction in testing overhead can be expected, more flexibility results for scheduling.

+ *Organizational overhead*
Because of the reduced design and implementation effort, smaller teams can be employed. This eases the communication among those involved in a project and the coordination of subtasks.

+ *Design and implementation*
  Object-oriented design is largely methodical. This reduces the leeway that could otherwise lead to poor decisions. The design has a cleaner structure and is more systematic. Object-oriented programming thus promotes uniform style, which means that programmers previously not involved in the design can integrate themselves into a running project more quickly. The chronological merging of design and implementation proves a significant advantage. This results in intermediate products in short time, which serves to motivate project staff members.
+ *Division of labor*
  Object-oriented design leads to sharply delineated class definitions and is thus a modularization technique. The individual classes can be developed independently by different programmers or teams. Another form of division of labor emerges in larger institutions when a dedicated groups handle such responsibilities as preparing elementary classes and concepts, library management, library maintenance and application programming.
+ *Prototyping*
  Due to the low implementation effort, (reusable) prototypes can be developed in less time for individual system components. Even without appropriate tools, user interface prototypes can be produced manually with justifiable effort.
– *Familiarization*
  Programmers with many years of experience are usually so rooted in functional thinking that the transition to object-orientation proves very difficult. A familiarization phase lasting several months must be expected.
– *Management of class libraries*
  For the benefits of class libraries to take effect, they must continuously be kept up to date. The required effort rises with the number of users of the library, with its scope and with the number of projects that are being realized with it.
– *Cost accounting*
  Due to reuse, the costs of a software project can no longer be clearly assigned to one group. A class emanating from a project can cause costs during its development; these costs can be particularly high if the goal is reuse of the class in succeeding projects because reusability requires additional effort that no longer relates to the current project. Only in subsequent projects does the invested work bear fruit. The case is analogous for the effort invested in managing the class library. These costs must be viewed as general costs distributed among all projects.

#### 4.10.2.2 Impact on the quality of the final product

Object-oriented programming not only makes work easier, it also improves the quality of the resulting product. This effect ensues primarily from the use of thoroughly tested classes from the class library and the use of application frameworks. The following are the effects of object-oriented programming on the quality attributes presented in Section 2.1.

- *Correctness and reliability*
  Since the correctness of a program system hinges on the correctness of its components, the probability of correctness rises sharpy with the use of proven components. The components of a class library have generally survived repeated reuse, so that their correctness can be seen as quite high (ideally 100%). The more code that can be reused from a class library, the lower is the probability of errors in the overall system. Using application frameworks has a further positive effect on correctness because they usually come with a cookbook with clear guidelines on how to attain a certain goal. Upholding these guidelines helps to avoid typical errors. Since the reliability of a program also depends on its correctness, this quality attribute also gains from the reuse of error-free components. Experience shows that the stabilization phase in software systems developed with object-orientation tends to be significantly shorter than for conventionally implemented systems. Reductions by 70% are certainly within the realm of possibility.
- *User friendliness*
  In particular, the use of an application framework delivers noticeable improvements in user friendliness. This is primarily because the framework already contains components for communication with the user that would otherwise require considerable programming effort. The framework provides functionality that would tend to be omitted in conventional programming to reduce programming effort. Furthermore, a framework furnishes a user interface that is typical for the target platform, so that the user encounters an accustomed interface and the learning effort declines. Since most application frameworks supply undo and redo functionality, they promote the robustness of programs. The only aspect that object-oriented programming does not significantly influence is adequacy. Although dynamic binding and polymorphism make programs more flexible and more general, there is the inherent danger that – because it is so easy to do – the software product provides too much functionality, which distracts the user from the actual task at hand.
- *Maintainability*
  The encapsulation of objects and the locality of operations (because all operations possible with a set of objects are unified in a class) support error localization and make extensions easier. In addition, object-oriented programming promotes uniform programming style, so that familiarization with a foreign program creates less problems. Furthermore, using an application framework forces adherence to global design criteria that are familiar to all programmers working with it. This fosters uniform overall structure of programs and thus significantly reduces the familiarization effort. Polymorphism and dynamic binding support the extensibility of programs, and clear modularization positively influences testability.

- *Efficiency*
  As shown above, object-oriented programming has a negative impact on execution time and memory requirements. However, in view of the achievements in hardware development, ever faster computers and rising memory resources, these costs prove negligible.
- *Portability*
  Due to the dependency of most class libraries on a certain hardware platform and operating system, porting a program system of one class library to another can induce considerable overhead, which can be increased by the necessity of conceptual changes. Although there are application frameworks that run on different platforms, reducing porting effort to recompilation of the source code, these frameworks have their own interface concepts. The ported programs can thus seem quite foreign on the target platform. Another problem in porting object-oriented programs stems from the conceptual differences underlying different programming languages. Porting a C++ program to Smalltalk or vice versa, for example, goes far beyond a syntactic transformation, requiring fundamental adaptation to the concepts and thought model of the other language.

Chapter 5

# Project management

The production of complex software products generally involves a group of people with different tasks and varying expertise. To attain the goal that we set in our definition of the term *software engineering* – the *economic production* of software products – the organizational measures for on-schedule and economic production of software products need to be just as well thought out as the technical measures for product development.

Frequently software products are completed later than the target release date and with significantly higher costs than estimated at the start of the project, or software projects fail completely. The causes often reside at the organizational level. The following are the most important reasons:

- *The lack of project planning, project organization and project standards*
  Due to their complexity, software projects need to be planned and organized especially carefully. Programmers are individualists who see themselves as craftspeople and do not like to put all their cards on the table. This proves to be a disturbing factor in software development involving a division of labor. Furthermore, the lack of a systematically created project plan, no specification or enforcement of an approach, and missing project standards and milestones for project progress checks can have devastating effects on large software projects because shortcomings in the quality of individual system components and schedule delays are detected much too late.
- *Incompetent project leadership*
  The project leadership is usually organized strictly hierarchically, and the manager is often a software engineer with little experience in organization and calculation, or a qualified manager with little or no experience in the area of software engineering.

- *Lack of up-to-date documentation*
  Documentation is very frequently neglected in the course a project. This impedes communication among people involved in the project and prevents project progress control.
- *Lack of project progress and quality control*
  More complex software systems consist of subsystems which consist of components that are generally implemented by different people. Quality shortcomings in individual components usually require expensive corrections that lead to cost overruns and missed deadlines. Neglecting project progress and quality control can lead to the interruption of further project progress due to the delay in the completion of individual system components; this in turn can overturn the overall project planning.
- *Lack of cost control*
  Without running control of the costs of a project, it is impossible to assure early detection of errors in cost assessments and of bottlenecks in the course of the project and to take appropriate measures.

Particularly when a group of people is involved in the production of a software product, organizational considerations prove just as important as technical factors. However, care must be taken to not overshoot the target. Frequently the management of a software project takes priority over the technical solution. All too often the failure of a software project is blamed on inadequate management, although the actual cause was insufficient technical expertise. Consequently, we have deliberately kept this chapter short. The following sections sketch the goal and tasks of project management as well as aspects of costs estimation and project organization. For more information, we refer the reader to the literature on the subject (e.g., [Balzert 1985], [Pressman 1987], [Frühauf 1988] and [Denert 1991]).

# 5.1 The goal and tasks of project management

The *goal of project management* is to ensure that a software product that meets the quality specifications of the requirements definition is produced on schedule and at economically justifiable cost with the planned resources (e.g., personnel, equipment, tools). The primary tasks of project management are *planning*, *organization* and *technical* and *economic control* of project execution.

**Planning**

Exact project planning, appropriate to the size of the project, is of deciding importance for the successful execution of a software project. The scope of the planning and the effort invested in it depend on the following:

- *Task description*
  A project with a short, clear requirements definition and corresponding staff experience in similar projects is significantly easier to plan than a project with a vague task description that can only be clarified with prototyping and that has no corresponding models.
- *Project size*
  The difficulty of planning rises with an increasing number of people and other resources involved (e.g., development machines, interfaces).
- *Experience and qualifications of the project team*
  The qualifications of the project staff members, their experience, their degree of knowledge in the application domain, and their ability to cooperate are important planning parameters.
- *Constraints for the project*
- *Development methods* used

The *goal of planning* is to establish deadlines, costs, personnel requirements, and measures for quality assurance of the software product to be developed. This necessitates organizing software projects so that the individual tasks are largely independent of one another and so that these tasks can be carried out with testable results in teams as small as possible, with economically justifiable investment of time and technical resources. The phase model in Chapter 3 provides the basis for organizing the project.

The *result of the planning* thus consists of the following:

- Organizational plan and personnel schedule
- Timetable for each phase of the software project
- Cost schedule
- Documentation schedule
- Testing schedule and planning of measures for quality assurance for all intermediate products and for the final product

Measures for planning, testing and documentation were presented in Chapter 3. Measures for cost estimation (for timetable and cost planning) and organizational planning are treated later in this section.

### Organization

Software products differ from other technical products in that they are intellectual products whose design and construction cannot be as easily distinguished as those in other technical products. For this reason, conventional organizational forms do not apply directly to the development of software products. Therefore we lack uniform organizational models for software development. Nevertheless, we can identify the following as the most important *organizational tasks* of project management:

- Assignment of teams or individuals to phases (or subphases) of the software development process
- Composition of teams (members, form of organization, leadership)
- Exact specification of tasks, rights and duties of all persons involved in the project
- Establishment of project standards, methods to be used (prototyping, object-oriented design) and measures to provide software tools
- Regulation of communication (setting meetings, documentation guidelines, etc.)
- Providing resources (computers, office materials, money and rooms)

In addition to the classical hierarchical organizational models, as we know them from other technical projects, with their limited suitability for software development, there are several approaches for organizational models that positively influence productivity and control in software development. One well-known example is the organizational model of Baker and Mills [Baker 1979]. Section 5.4 treats both this model and the hierarchical organizational model in more detail.

**Technical monitoring**

Even careful and extensive planning is nearly worthless without continuous control of the achievement of the goals prescribed in the planning. The goal of *technical monitoring* is to check both *quantitatively* and *qualitatively* the *technical attributes* of the intermediate products of the individual phases.

*Quantitative* monitoring checks whether the development goals are being met according to the timetable. *Qualitative* monitoring checks whether an intermediate product fulfills its functionality as specified in the requirements definition and its quality requirements.

*Technical monitoring* encompasses not only checking whether certain technical goals have been achieved, but also triggering corrective measures if a goal has not been achieved.

**Economic monitoring**

*Economic monitoring* likewise has *quantitative* and *qualitative* aspects. Quantitative monitoring must check for cost overruns, while qualitative monitoring determines whether the completed intermediate products fulfill the contract conditions.

*Cost control* is only possible if corresponding cost accounting is carried out. Project management must therefore assure that all incurred costs are recorded and documented.

Experience shows that monitoring the economy of a software project is normally more difficult than technical monitoring. While developers normally succeed in completing a planned program at some time with adequate technical quality and in putting it into operation, very seldom do the schedule and budget estimates fall anywhere near reality.

*Schedule* and *cost estimates* for software products are difficult tasks. Therefore, before we turn to organizational models, let us consider some fundamental statements about the difficulties of software project management and about problems of and possibilities for cost estimation.

## 5.2 Difficulties in project management

The following are the fundamental difficulties of managing software projects:

- *Uniqueness of software systems*
  As a rule, software systems are developed only once. Experience from previous projects tends to be too scant to make reliable cost estimates. Such cost estimates are usually based on the scope of the software system to be developed, as estimated by an experienced software engineer (as a multiple of the number of program statements). Clearly this provides an unreliable basis for calculations.
- *Multitude of possible solutions*
  There are practically an unlimited number of possibilities for solving a given problem. The development of software products is not subject to the strict constraints that apply for other technical products (e.g., standards and material attributes). For software products, the limits stem from complexity and thus are difficult to determine in advance.
- *Individuality of programmers*
  Even with the state of the art in software engineering, software development remains more of a craft than a science. Software engineers are individualists with large differences in capability; this makes it particularly difficult to estimated personnel costs. In addition, individualists usually resist being forced into an organizational corset.
- *Rapidity of technological change*
  The speed of technological development in hardware and software encumbers both planning and organization of software projects. Sometimes during the development of a large software system, new, more powerful components (e.g., graphic monitors and window management systems) appear on the market that render the conception of the system obsolete after its design and force redesign. This can completely overturn existing planning. The project might also employ new software tools whose benefits are difficult to assess in advance.
- *The immaterial nature of software products*
  The invisibility of software products encumbers their control. It is difficult to assess how much of a software product is actually finished, and the programmer has many possibilities for disguising the actual state of development. Control tasks are more difficult to carry out than with other technical projects.

## 5.3 Cost estimation

The necessity of cost estimation stems from the requirements of scheduling and cost planning. For lack of precise methods, cost estimation for software development is almost always based on a comparison of the current project with previous ones. Due to the uniqueness of software systems, the number of comparable projects is usually quite small, and empirical data are seldom available. But even if there are exact cost records of comparable projects, these data are based on the technical and organizational conditions under which the comparable project was carried out at that time. The technical and organizational conditions are variable parameters, which again makes empirical data from comparable projects only an unreliable basis for estimates.

Of the cost estimation models developed so far, the best known are the *COCOMO Model*, the *Putnam Estimation Model* and the *Function Point Model*. The interested reader will find descriptions of these approaches in [Boehm 1981], [Putnam 1978], and [Albrecht 1983]. These models have found only very modest acceptance in practice because of the above difficulties.

Since there are no general standards, the factors influencing the estimate must be observed very carefully. The most important factors for cost and time estimates are the following:

- Experience and qualifications of the estimator
- Type of software (e.g., function-, data- or object-oriented, time-critical software with high efficiency requirements, control and monitoring software with high quality requirements)
- Anticipated complexity (e.g., number of components (modules, classes), number of component couplings, number of methods per class, complexity of methods)
- Expected size of program (number of statements)
- Experience and qualifications of personnel (e.g., project experience, programming experience, knowledge of methods, experience in use of tools, knowledge of problem domain)
- Techniques and tools to be used (e.g., planning, design and documentation techniques, test strategies and tools, programming languages)
- Number of staff members

This list of factors shows how difficult they are to quantify. Estimators generally proceed by first estimating the size of the software system to be developed, e.g., in the number of program statements. For cost estimation, they multiply the results of the size estimate by an empirical value for the cost of a program statement, and for time estimation they divide the size estimate by an empirical value for programming performance of staff member per time unit (e.g., month, year). These estimates are unreliable for several reasons:

- Estimating the number of program statements is extremely difficult, requires much experience on the part of the estimator, and usually misses the mark.
- The extreme variance in the performance of programmers means that even specifying average values cannot be better than imprecise. A study by Schnupp and Floyd [Schnupp 1976] determined the following relationship between the best and worst programming experience (referring to the same task):

| | |
|---|---|
| program size | 5 : 1 |
| coding time | 25 : 1 |
| required testing time | 26 : 1 |
| required computation time | 11 : 1 |
| execution time of finished program | 13 : 1 |

A significant, often neglected factor for cost estimation is the size of the development team. Brooks [Brooks 1975] states that the time requirement for each task handled in a team consists of two basic components:

(1) Productive work
(2) Communication and mutual agreement of team members

If no communication were necessary among team members, then the time requirement $t$ for a project would decline with the number $n$ of team members: $t \approx 1/n$. However, if we assume that each team member must exchange information with one other and that the average time for such communication is $k$, then the development time follows the formula:

$$t \approx \frac{1}{n} + k\binom{n}{2} \approx \frac{1}{n} + k \cdot \frac{n^2}{2}$$

Brooks himself expresses the consequence: "Adding manpower to a late software project makes it later."

Most empirical values for cost estimation are in-house and unpublished. The literature gives few specifications on empirical data, and these often diverge pronouncedly. The values also depend greatly on the techniques and tools used.

The experience of the authors reflects the following distribution of the time invested in the individual phases of software development (including the documentation effort by share) according to the selected approach model and implementation technique:

*Approach model*: classical sequential software life cycle
*Implementation technique*: module-oriented

| | |
|---|---|
| problem analysis and system specification | 25% |
| design | 25% |
| implementation | 15% |
| testing | 35% |

*Approach model*: prototyping-oriented software life cycle
*Implementation technique*: module-oriented

| | |
|---|---|
| problem analysis and system specification | 40% |
| design | 25% |
| implementation | 10% |
| testing | 25% |

*Approach model*: object- and prototyping-oriented software life cycle
*Implementation technique*: object-oriented

| | |
|---|---|
| problem analysis and system specification | 45% |
| design | 20% |
| implementation | 8% |
| testing | 27% |

Naturally these values can only be used as rough guidelines. They change with technological development as new programming paradigms and tools rationalize software development. We hope that the precision and reliability of such empirical values will increase.

# 5.4 Project organization

This section first describes the classical hierarchical organizational model and discusses its drawbacks for software development. Then we present an alternative organizational model, the chief programmer team.

## 5.4.1 Hierarchical organizational model

There are many ways to organize the staff of a project. For a long time the organization of software projects oriented itself to the hierarchical organization common to other industrial branches. Special importance is vested in the decomposition of software development into individual phases. A responsible leader is assigned to each of the phases, which are led and controlled by the project leader and which, depending on the size of the project, are led and controlled either by a single person or by a group leader. The project manager normally also has a project management staff with advisory and administrative tasks. The larger the project, the greater is the number of hierarchy levels in the organizational schema. Figure 5.1 shows an example.

The *project manager* represents the project team outwardly and maintains the contacts to the client. The project manager's tasks and responsibilities encompass personnel selection, assignment and management, planning of and division of labor for the project, project progress checks, and appropriate measures in case of cost or schedule overruns.

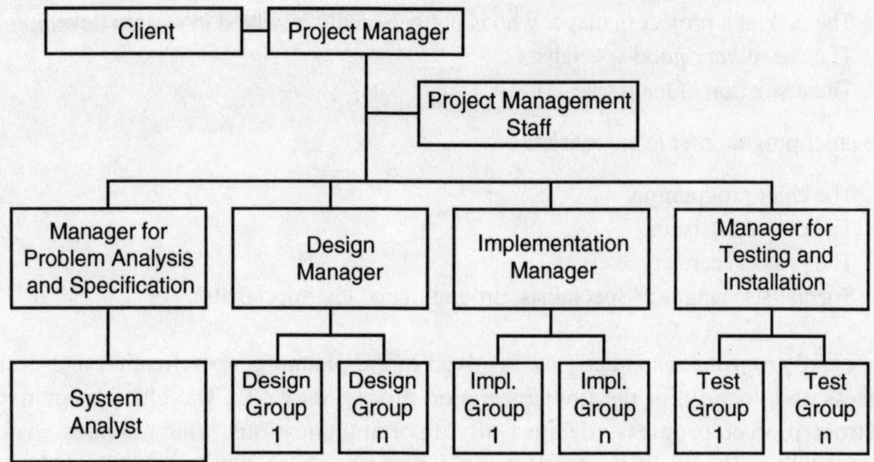


Figure 5.1: Organigram for a software project

The *project management staff* includes personnel who advise the project manager in task-specific questions, provide support in administrative tasks concerning project progress checks, prepare project standards, provide the necessary resources, and carry out training for project team members as needed.

The *managers at the middle management level* are responsible for planning, execution and control of phase-related activities of the software life cycle (see Chapter 3).
The form of organization shown in Figure 5.1 has some serious weaknesses:

- The project manager is too far removed from the actual programming and thus can only handle planning and control tasks inadequately.
- The multilevel organizational hierarchy encumbers communication and project progress checks. Particularly software projects demand problem-free communication within the project team for successful completion of the project.
- The Peter Principle easily takes hold in a hierarchy; i.e., each employee tends to rise one level above actual competence. Project personnel strive for their level of incompetence, and their actual qualifications cannot be exploited.

The organizational model presented in the next section attempts to ameliorate these weaknesses.

## 5.4.2 The chief programmer team

Baker [Baker 1972] first introduced this organizational model, which attempts to avoid the weaknesses of the hierarchical organizational model. Its most important characteristics are:

- The lack of a project manager who is not personally involved in system development
- The use of very good specialists
- The restriction of team size

The chief programmer team consists of:

- The chief programmer
- The project assistant
- The project secretary
- Specialists (language specialists, programmers, test specialists).

The *chief programmer* is actively involved in the planning, specification and design process and, ideally, in the implementation process as well. The chief programmer controls project progress, decides all important questions, and assumes overall responsibility. The qualifications of the chief programmer need to be accordingly high.

The *project assistant* is the closest technical coworker of the chief programmer. The project assistant supports the chief programmer in all important activities and serves as the chief programmer's representative in the latter's absence. This team member's qualifications need to be as high as those of the chief programmer.

The *project secretary* relieves the chief programmer and all other programmers of administrative tasks. The project secretary administrates all programs and documents and assists in project progress checks. The main task is the administration of the project library.

The chief programmer determines the number of *specialists* needed. Specialists select the implementation language, implement individual system components, choose and employ software tools, and carry out tests.

Figure 5.2 depicts this organizational model. The advantages of this form of organization are the following:

- The chief programmer is directly involved in system development and can better exercise the control function.
- Communication difficulties of pure hierarchical organization are ameliorated.
- Reporting concerning project progress is institutionalized.
- Small teams are generally more productive than large teams.

The drawbacks of this form of organization are:

- It is limited to small teams. Not every project can be handled by a small team.
- Personnel requirements can hardly be met. Few software engineers can meet the qualifications of a chief programmer or a project assistant.
- The project secretary has an extremely difficult and responsible job, although it consists primarily of routine tasks, which gives it a subordinate position. This has significant psychological disadvantages. Due to the central position, the project secretary can easily become a bottleneck.

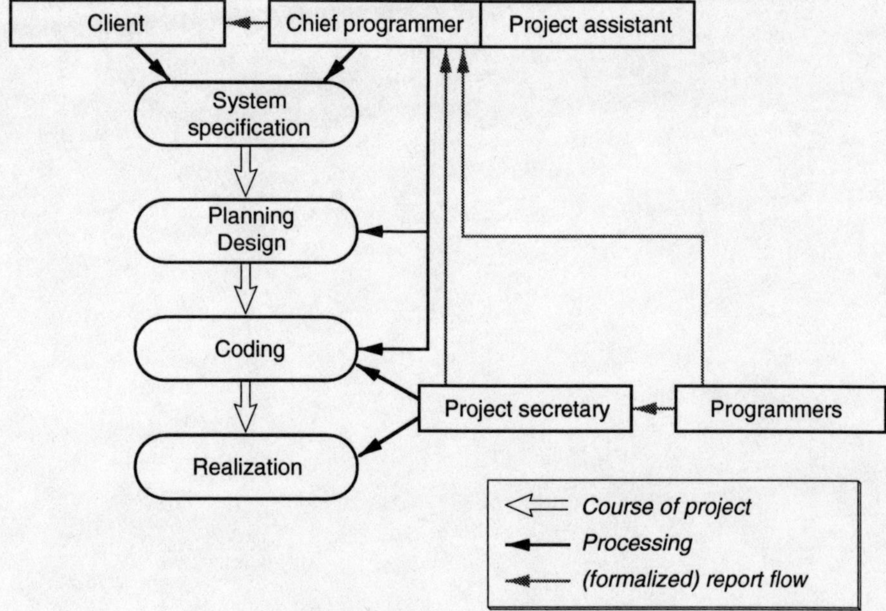


Figure 5.2 Chief programmer project organization from Baker and Mills [Baker 1979]

- The organizational model provides no replacement for the project secretary. The loss of the project secretary would have grave consequences for the remaining course of the project.

Regardless of the drawbacks of the chief programmer organizational model, experience has shown that small teams consisting of experienced software engineers work significantly more productively, reliably and on-schedule than large software factories.

Chapter 6

# Software engineering tools

Chapter 3 explained how the phase models bring order to the completion of software projects by dividing the development process into phases. For each phase of the software life cycle we specified corresponding goals and activities and discussed methods and techniques for achieving these goals. To meet the requirements of an engineering discipline, software engineering must also provide appropriate tools. By *tools* we mean programs that simplify or accelerate the production, testing, maintenance and documentation of software products or improve their quality (see [Rechenberg 1985b]). This means that an important area of software engineering is developing tools to support the software development process and providing techniques for implementing such tools.

In the early stages of information processing, the only tools available to programmers were assemblers, linkers and loaders. Parallel to the introduction of time-sharing systems and workstations, a whole range of software tools appeared: simple and complex; ones tailored to a specific task and ones supporting a certain phase of the software life cycle; etc.

Today's software tools are evolving to support a broad range of the activities of the software life cycle. Across the broad spectrum of features of such multipurpose tools – called software development environments or CASE systems (Computer Aided Software Engineering) – there is no consensus. Unfortunately, many software development environments on the market today do not meet the requirements of programmers and are often technically antiquated and difficult to operate. They seldom have the quality attributes that we define in Chapter 2. Here prototyping and object-oriented software development also (indeed, particularly) produce revolutionary improvements of the situation.

In this chapter we do not describe particular products, but only sketch which tools are provided by software development environments and how they support the activities of the software development process. First we describe elementary tools and then discuss which phase-related and phase-transcending tools are necessary for rationalization and quality improvement in software development.

## 6.1 Elementary tools

Here we identify several *elementary* tools that should be available in every software development environment. They already significantly simplify software production. In particular, these include the following:

- Tools for elementary file management
- Tools for simple analysis and documentation work

### 6.1.1 Tools for elementary file management

The software development process generates a multitude of documents (specifications, prototypes, source code, program descriptions, test files, etc.) that have to be managed. This requires phase-transcending tools (see Section 6.3) whose realization can be facilitated by the availability of elementary tools that can also be used independently. Such tools include the following:

- *Tools for data backup and file comparison*
  Managing files, especially to save the development history, requires archiving multiple generations of files and determining whether and how the generations differ. Thus tools for automatic file backup and for file comparison prove very useful. Every change in a file should automatically trigger a backup of the old file status.
- *Tools for file compression and expansion*
  To save storage capacity, backup files should be compressed and then expanded on demand.
- *Tools for assigning access privileges*
  For software development with division of labor, the consistency of documents is particularly important; in particular, there must be assurance that only the owner of a given file can modify it, while other project team members can only read it or use it without modification. This necessitates tools for assigning access privileges for files. Such elementary tools for file management are normally provided by the operating system.

### 6.1.2 Simple analysis and documentation tools

Simple *analysis* of software systems, *error localization*, checking adherence to project conventions (e.g., number of comments, prescribed complexity limits), and quality control all require information about structural characteristics and the frequency of certain program constructs. This information emanates from tools for the analysis of the *static program profile* (see also [Rechenberg 1984b] and [Blaschek 1985]). In particular, these tools should provide the following information:

(1) Structural characteristics

- Complexity metrics (e.g., as proposed by McCabe [McCabe 1976] or Halstead [Halstead 1972])
- Nesting depths for loops
- Identification of modules, classes, procedures and variables that are declared but not used
- Identification of instance variables and methods that are inherited but not used
- All objects not initialized
- All statements that cannot be reached from the start of the program (dead code)
- All statements from which program termination is impossible

(2) Number of program constructs

- Length and number of classes and modules, methods and procedures
- Number of loops
- Number of GOTOs
- Length and number of comments

To ease studying the program code, the *uniformly structured* output of program listings can prove very useful. If the required uniformity cannot be achieved through the discipline of the programmers and is not enforced by other tools (e.g., structure-oriented editors), all program listings can be brought into uniform format by means of a *formatter* or *pretty printer* (see, e.g., [Blaschek 1989]).

## 6.2 Phase-related tools

Phase-related software tools should support methods that are employed in the individual phases of the software life cycle. They should assist in the early detection and correction of errors, support documentation and quality assurance of the products emanating from the individual phases, and rationalize the production process.

### 6.2.1 Tools for problem analysis

The classical techniques for problem analysis (questionnaires, interviews, observations, etc.) were discussed in Section 3.2. We need not only tools that ease and standardize the documentation of analysis results, but also tools that support the analysis itself.

*Documentation of the analysis results* requires comfortable *word processing* tools (their requirements are covered in Section 6.2.6) as well as tools for *graphical representation of data and information flow*.

Especially for commercial and production-oriented applications, analysis begins with examining both the functionality and the data flow. This requires tools for creating and managing *data-flow diagrams*, preferably in graphical form. These tools should permit editing data-flow diagrams on-screen and support outputting them to a printer.

Prototyping helps to overcome communication difficulties between software engineers and users. Prototyping tools are described in Section 6.2.2. Frequently, *data dictionaries* are used as well, mandating tools for their management with functionality for entering, deleting, finding and modifying data descriptions.

In Section 3.2 we referred to SADT [Ross 1985] and SA [DeMarco 1978] as specialized methods for the analysis phase. Other methods frequently cited in the literature include PSL/PSA (see [Pressman 1987]) for classical analysis and the Coad/Yourdon approach [Coad 1990] for object-oriented analysis. Generally these methods can only be used practically with the availability of software tool support. A high-grade software development environment should offer tools for as many of these methods as possible.

Chapter 3 indicated that, as a rule, the problem analysis phase is so dependent on the problem domain that it makes no sense to propose a generalized model for problem analysis. Naturally this also affects the development of analysis tools. For the problem analysis phase there exist very few tools, and those available are quite specialized.

## 6.2.2 Tools for system specification

Due to the importance of an unambiguous, complete and contradiction-free system specification for a software project, there have been repeated efforts to define specialized *specification languages*. As yet there has been no satisfactory solution, and no such specification language has achieved a real breakthrough.

Another approach to supporting system specification is prototyping, a technique handled in detail in Sections 1.3, 3.1, 3.5 and 4.8. Contrary to other techniques for qualitative and organizational improvement of the software development process, prototyping absolutely requires the use of tools. The tools used are central to both the production as well as the modification and extension process for software prototypes (see Figure 6.1).

Typical classes of tools for prototyping in the specification phase are the following:

- Generators
- Fourth generation systems
- Hypertext systems

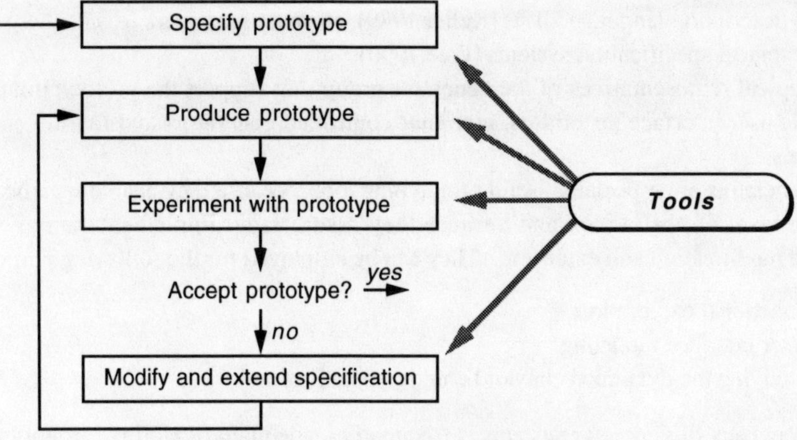


Figure 6.1: The prototyping process

## Generators

Generator systems typically consist of two components: an editor for creating the specifications and a generator/interpreter/compiler/run-time system for syntax checking, transformation of the specification into an executable prototype, and executing the prototype (see Figure 6.2).

In the ideal conception the prototype developer would simply have to specify *what* must happen without having to worry about *how* the executable system is realized. The implementation of the prototype is the task of the generator; the system developer has no influence on the implementation.

An important characteristic of a generator as a tool for prototype production is the abstraction level of the specification. Examples of specification languages include the

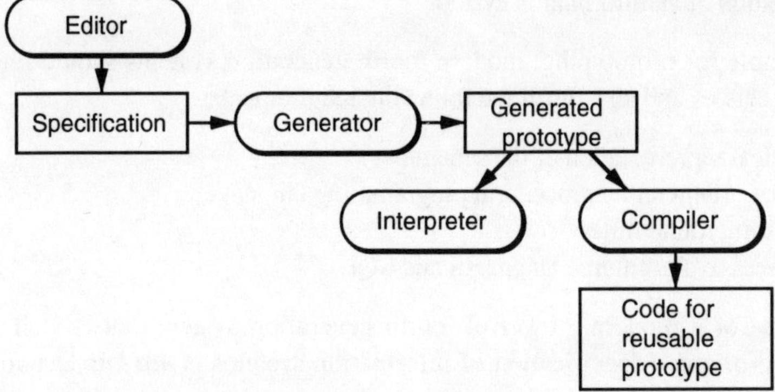


Figure 6.2: Generator systems for prototyping

dialog description language UISL [Keller 1989], attribute grammars [Rechenberg 1985a] and graphical specification systems [Pree 1990].

Typical representatives of the generator group that support the prototyping process include user interface generators, grammar-controlled generators and fourth generation systems.

Generators are especially useful prototyping tools because they enable specification at a high level of abstraction and because they assure rapid implementation as well as simple modification and extension. They can be employed for the following purposes:

- Functional exploration
- User interface modeling
- Studying the dynamic behavior behind a specification

The drawback of generator systems is frequently inadequate flexibility: prototypes that cannot be described in the specification language cannot be generated, even if the deviations are minimal. Another disadvantage of generators is that they frequently generate implementations that are inefficient.

**Fourth generation systems**

The increasing use of computers also increases the requirements for file storage. Database-centered information systems are often central components of an application. The domain of information systems often suffers from significant problems in specification and efficiency. This suggests handling the specification of information systems in a prototyping-oriented manner.

Creating prototypes for information systems requires tools for the following activities:

- (Interactive) definition of data models and database schemata
- Interactive design of user interfaces
- Database generation
- Simulation of an information system

To be suitable for prototyping, modern fourth generation systems should integrate the above tool classes and also fulfill the following requirements:

- Graphical representation of the schema
- Symbol-oriented, nonprocedural programming language
- Short turnaround times
- Interfaces to algorithmic languages and SQL

An example of a modern, powerful fourth generation system that is well suited for prototyping-oriented specification of information systems is 4th Dimension ([Renner 1989]). Fourth generation systems can be used for the following activities:

- Functional exploration
- User interface modeling
- Report creation
- Data modeling
- Database design
- Experimental verification of the dynamic behavior of the planned information system

Likewise *data definition languages* (DDLs) support the production of prototypes. However, they offer less comfort for the developer than graphical schema editors. The expressive power of DDLs sometimes exceeds the possibilities of graphical representation. To create the schema specification, DDLs frequently provide a normal text editor. The drawback here is that structural errors are detected only on generation of the database.

**Hypertext systems**

Smith and Weiss [Smith 1988] define hypertext as "an approach to information management in which data is stored in a network of nodes connected by links". Hypertext systems support the comfortable creation of links between information units and the layout of screen masks with a graphical editor.

Hypertext systems encompass the following:

- Graphical mask editors
- Tools for specification of user interface elements (e.g., windows, buttons, icons, menus)
- Tools for specification of information units (e.g., sets, arrays, lists)
- Tools for specification of run-time behavior at a higher level of abstraction
- Browsers to manage prototype components that have been created

Hypertext systems prove suitable as prototyping tools and find application in the following areas:

- Functional exploration
- User interface modeling
- Data modeling (to a limited extent)
- Experimental verification of the dynamic behavior of a planned information system

Beyond a coarse classification of prototyping tools on the basis of the above list, a number of criteria are important for their characterization and evaluation (see [Keller 1989]). The following criteria are not mutually independent, scarcely measurable, and only partially objective; they simply provide a foundation for the characterization and evaluation of such tools.

- *Required user knowledge*. What knowledge is expected of the user: procedural language, use of procedure libraries, specification language, use of graphical specifications tools, etc.?
- *Time invested before first prototype*. Is there a standard application that can easily be transformed into an executable prototype? How work-intensive is the first specification?
- *Underlying user interfaces*. Are they textual or graphical? Do they support a standard? Do they support only certain classes of applications? How much semantics and functionality do the generated user interfaces contain? Are the underlying user interfaces rigid or configurable?
- *Specification of user interfaces*. At what level of abstraction (e.g., as finite automata, hypertext, context-free grammar, etc.) does specification take place? What means are used for specification (formal language; graphical WYSIWYG editor with direct manipulation, etc.)? How are static components (layouts) and dynamic parts (flows, state transfers) specified?
- *Using the generated prototypes*. Can the prototypes be extended to complete applications? Do they serve only as a program framework? What information can be reused and how (simple cut and paste of code fragments; higher methods such as manipulation of user interface components like dialog patterns, dialog frameworks, screen layouts, etc.; support from object management system)?
- *Support of extensions*. How much effort does extension require if it only affects the user interface and if it affects the functionality? Are compile-link-go cycles necessary or is the system interpreter-based? Can the user interface be modified at run time (e.g., design of context-dependent menus, graphical display of generated data, user-dependent dialog structure)? Is the consistency of the created files and document assured?
- *Manner of functional extension*. Can the functionality of prototypes be extended stepwise? In the case of a generator, are extensions handled at the specification level or must they be implemented in the generated code? What is the quality of the generated code (readability, structuredness, etc.)? Can code generation be parameterized (choice of language and dialect, formatting)? How is it possible to address the user interface from functional components of the prototype? Can functional extensions, exception situations, etc. be simulated? Is it possible to create prototypes that execute some operations and only simulate others (hybrid execution)? What interfaces are available to database systems?
- *Development environment*. In which development environment can the prototyping tool be used and how is it integrated in this environment? Can information be exchanged between the prototypes and other documents (e.g., via the data dictionary)? Which software tools (dynamic debugger, version management tools, testing tools, profiling tools, etc.) and programming languages are available? Beyond the prototype, can the prototyping tool generate other documents (help files,

documentation, protocols and statistics on user behavior, etc.), and how can these be used?

- *Quality of the prototyping tool.* How does the prototyping tool score in terms of efficiency, reliability, complexity and learnability?
- *Implementation of prototyping tool.* On which concepts is the implementation based? Is the prototyping tool itself extensible?

### 6.2.3 Design tools

The design of a program system encompasses roughly the following activities:

- Decomposition of the overall system into subsystems and specification of the mutual effects between the subsystems
- Decomposition of subsystems into components and specification of the requirements on these components, i.e., specification of the component interfaces
- Design of algorithms for individual system components

In object-oriented system design we attempt to take as many system components as possible from an existing class library and use them as they are or adapt them to the problem at hand (by subclassing), or even to base the design on the base architecture of an application framework. Design thus requires tools for the following:

- *Documentation* of design results
  Efficient project completion and especially the maintenance of software products require careful, comprehensible and complete documentation of the system structure and all design decisions. This necessitates tools that support design documentation.
- *Validation* of design results
  An error-free design of the system architecture seldom succeeds on first try, and, in the sense of the prototyping-oriented system design suggested in Chapter 3, the design should continuously be validated throughout the project with experiments with a prototype of the architecture. This necessitates tools for architecture prototyping.
- *Efficient reuse* of existing design (class libraries and application frameworks)
  Planning and using application frameworks, available classes, and abstract data types is of central importance in an object-oriented approach. This necessitates tools that support the use of class libraries.

Tools for documentation of design results should have the following features:

- *Multiple document capability* allowing parallel processing of several design documents
- Broad *freedom* in formulating the system design, e.g., graphical representation of data models (entity/relationship diagrams) and hierarchical relationships (class structures)

- Comfortable *modification* and *extension* of existing documents
- Support in *consistency checks* of interfaces
- Check of *syntactic correctness* of design representations with the use of special formalisms
- *Hypertext capability* to link the design description with other documents, e.g., from the specification and implementation phases

Tools for validation of design results should have the following features:

- Possible simulation of the information flow between the designed components in order to verify the completeness and consistency of the component interfaces
- Possible linking of the system architecture with the user interface prototype to assure the consistency of the validation process
- Support for an incremental design and the implementation process
- Automatic protocoling of all validation activities and possible replay of already executed experiments with the system architecture

Tools for efficient reuse of available designs should have the following features:

- Comfortable browsing possibilities for quickly finding existing components and for recognizing interconnections and mutual effects between components
- Possibility to inspect system components at different abstraction levels (informal component description, interface description, implementation)
- Comfortable access to documents with notes on the use of components and instructions on which measures the designer or implementor expects for the integration of such components

### 6.2.4 Implementation tools

The implementation phase requires tools for translating the design into an executable program: primarily editors, compilers and linkers. Naturally other tools also prove useful in the implementation phase. For example, lists and diagrams repeatedly help to maintain an overview, and debuggers aid in testing individual components and in localizing errors. These tools are described in the corresponding sections on testing and documentation tools (6.2.5 and 6.2.6).

The use of editors amounts to some 90% of on-screen work. This makes it clear that the quality of an editor plays an important role in the problem-free completion of a software project. Hardware developments have led to the almost exclusive use of full-screen editors that are operated by direct manipulation. This means that the text is processed directly on-screen.

Beyond an editor's efficiency, the following features play a particular role in writing programs:

- *Multiple document capability* allowing parallel processing of several programs
- Fast and easy *copying* between text documents
- *Unlimited text size* for expansive source code and lists
- *Quick and flexible positioning* within source code
- High *security*, especially protection against unintended modification
- *Search and replace* functionality, including across document borders

Although even simple text editors fulfill their purpose for program development, editors with specialized language support prove particularly useful because they help avoid errors and enable faster and more comfortable work. For example, a combined editor and compiler permits careful syntax checks of the program without leaving the editor. If error locations are marked directly in the source code, this saves searching in error lists.

Even more useful are editors that support the actual writing of programs. For example, a simple macro function can be used to insert individual statements or a template for a whole procedure into the source code. Another improvement is syntax-driven and structure-oriented editors that know how a program needs to look and displays the program in uniform form (such as with systematic indentation). Such language-specific editors suffer from the drawbacks that they are often applicable to only one programming language and that many programmers resent being spoon-fed by the rigid layout.

*Formatting tools* called *pretty printers* provide a means to assure a uniform look of programs. They augment programs with either a fixed or a parameterized structure [Blaschek 1989]. Such tools provide uniform indentation of program components, thus increasing the readability of programs written by other programmers.

For recurring similar tasks, *program generators* can be used. Simple tools of this type are program template generators that create empty programs with uniform program headers and place holders for comments. Naturally tools that automatically generate an entire program (or at least parts thereof) from a formal description of a task prove more useful. However, since tasks occurring in practice differ dramatically, such tools prove suitable for only a few application domains. Examples include generators for user interface modules and compiler compilers for program translation tasks.

To help maintain an overview in particularly large program systems, *browsers* have proven their worth, allowing display and inspection of the structure of programs in graphical form or as text. Such browsers are particularly useful for object-oriented programs. They graphically display the class hierarchy and provide information on which methods are implemented in which classes. Usually such browsers are coupled with editors, so that the displayed methods can also be edited and new methods can be added.

Beyond the editor, the most important tool is the *compiler*, which translates source code into machine language programs. The quality of the compiler has an important influence on the production process and naturally also on the final product itself. Developers today expect the following characteristics from a good compiler:

- *Correctness and reliability*. Testing and the associated error localization are some of the most troublesome activities of software development. The developer must be able to rely on the compiler's translation of given source code into semantically equivalent machine code. Otherwise there could never be certainty whether a detected error stems from the program or the compiler. In addition, the compiler must be able to fulfill its tasks even under extreme conditions (e.g., very large programs).
- *Speed*. The compiler must be fast to expedite the often repeated edit-compile-go cycles.
- *Generation of efficient code*. The generated code should be compact and as fast as possible. A good compiler is able to make numerous optimizations. For example, frequently used variables are stored in registers, repeatedly occurring subexpressions are computed only once, and loops are optimized. If a compiler generates highly efficient code, the higher programming language can also be used for time-critical program parts instead of assembler.
- *Good error handling*. A compiler must reject erroneous programs. Although there have been experiments with error-correcting compilers, experience has shown that the corrections seldom reflected the intentions of the programmer. In the event of an error, the compiler must deliver precise information about the cause of the error and mark the error location. Compilers integrated with editors can terminate compilation upon the first error and request correction on the part of the programmer, while a stack-oriented editor should immediately find as many errors as possible.
- *Recognition of run-time errors*. The code generated by the compiler should be able to recognize the most important types of errors. These include variable range overrun, division by zero and index overrun with arrays. In case of an error, program execution should abort and return a detailed error message that helps to localize the error in the source code. Since such run-time checks cost time, it should be possible to suppress them in the finished program.
- *Standardization*. If the language to be translated by the compiler is standardized, then the compiler should be able to handle at least the language as defined in the standard. If the compiler also permits language extensions, then these should optionally be markable as errors. This permits assuring that programs adhere to the language standard and can easily be ported to other machines.

To run a modular program, we first need to link the modules with a *linker*. In some development systems the linker is part of the compiler; however, certain computers have a uniform linker that is independent of the source language. Both systems have advantages and drawbacks. A linker integrated into a compiler can detect and report language-dependent inconsistencies between the modules, while a linker that belongs to the operating system supports heterogeneous program systems (i.e., written in multiple source languages). At any rate, a good linker today is expected to be able to detect unused program parts and eliminate them.

If the interface of a module changes, all modules that use this interface must be recompiled, whereby errors might surface because individual modules still have to be adapted to the new interface. Such recompilations can be automated with tools. An example is the UNIX tool *make*, which has served as a model for many similar tools on other platforms. Make uses a description of dependencies between modules and checks which modules need to be recompiled on the basis of their modification time. With the help of such tools, inconsistencies between modules can be avoided even if the compiler and the linker offer no such support.

### 6.2.5 Testing tools

In larger projects the effort and expense of testing can exceed the actual implementation investment. This is the case because in properly executed testing all test cases already carried out need to be repeated after each program modification to ensure that no new errors have crept in. Testing tools can change this situation little. At best they can provide support in the preparation and execution of individual tests and in the correction of errors.

Testing tools fall into the categories *static* and *dynamic*. Tools for static testing (*static tools*) extract information from the program source code (without executing the program); tools for dynamic testing (*dynamic tools*) analyze the program flow itself.

Preparing a white-box test requires exact knowledge of the program structure. Here *static tools* can provide an overview of important characteristics of the program system. These tools include generators that produce lists from program code. The following lists prove useful for a white-box test.

- *Module lists* help to retain an overview of all modules of a software system and the import/export relationships existing between them. They are useful both in preparing module tests and in the integration test.
- *Cross reference lists* indicate which variables are used in which procedures. These lists can be used in testing the mutual effects of program components and prove to be a valuable aid in error localization, especially if variable values are destroyed by unauthorized access.
- *Procedure invocation lists* show which procedures are invoked by others. They prove helpful in testing the interplay of procedures in the integration test, but also provide valuable support in an individual test. If a procedure *P* is used by three procedures *X*, *Y* and *Z*, then this procedure is normally invoked under three different sets of circumstances that should be tested separately.
- *Control flow graphs* show the control flow structure of a procedure by combining series of statement sequences to blocks. Thus they provide information about which program branches are executed during a test.

The most important *dynamic tools* include debuggers, which allow a programmer or tester to follow program flow in order to find the causes of errors. In more complex programs, error localization becomes unthinkable without suitable tools. A good debugger should support the following functionality:

- *Program termination.* On occurrence of a run-time error (e.g., range overflow), program execution should be aborted and the debugger should be activated. This identifies errors at the earliest possible time.
- *Display on source code level.* All information should be displayed in the same form in which the source program was formulated. Error locations should be marked in the source code, memory locations should be designated by their variable names, and memory contents should be displayed in accordance with their type.
- *Procedure invocation chain.* When an error occurs, it helps to know as much as possible about the immediate history of a program's execution. This includes at least the procedure invocation chain, which indicates from where the procedure containing the error was invoked. This also makes it possible to trace invalid parameter values back to their source.
- *Explicit invocation.* The debugger should be explicitly invokable from the program. Such invocations can be used, for example, to monitor changes in variable values before the actual error occurrence.
- *Continuation, single-step execution and breakpoints.* The debugger should allow continuation of a program after an explicit debugger invocation. It should also be possible to set breakpoints where the debugger is to interrupt the program. Another useful function is single-stepping, where execution proceeds one statement at a time and the effects can be checked.
- *Dynamic data structures.* If data structures are involved that are linked via pointers, the debugger should enable following the pointers. Thus an explicit invocation of the debugger can replace a series of auxiliary expressions interjected into the source code.
- A debugger for object-oriented languages should allow inspection of *object structures* as well as displaying and monitoring relationships between objects. A debugger with such functionality provides valuable help not only in localizing errors but also in comprehending programs.
- *Changing memory contents.* The debugger should also allow modifying erroneous values in memory (naturally on the source code level). This allows temporary correction of an error during a test run and continuation of the test.

Other dynamic tools include instrumentation tools that insert additional statements in programs. Such statements can be used for counting procedure invocations and for checking path coverage, for example, but also for automatic protocoling of test runs and for testing assertions. Such a tool is described in [Dobler 1991].

### 6.2.6 Tools for documentation and maintenance

*Documentation tools* are necessary in several (usually in all) phases of the software life cycle. Many users with different needs use these tools, so their design must be well thought out, their operation must be simple in terms of concept, and they must work together with other tools. Comfortable word processing tools must have the following features:

- Basic functions for inserting, deleting, finding and copying text
- Different typefaces
- Simultaneous display and processing of multiple documents or parts of a document
- Flexible positioning in a document
- Word processing functions such as justification, centering and typeface changes
- Integration of text and graphics
- Print preview of documents
- Creation of hypertext documentation

The *maintenance* of software products involves localizing and correcting errors. *Version management* of libraries is a delicate matter that requires tool support. Such tools should provide the following functionality:

- Creation of a new version
- Assignment of version numbers to documents and vice versa
- Comparison of two versions of a document
- Automatic documentation of differences between versions

Thus the implementation and testing tools described in Sections 6.2.4 and 6.2.5 prove particularly important for the maintenance phase. Maintenance produces new versions of software products with a multitude of associated documents.

## 6.3 Phase-transcending tools

By phase-transcending tools we mean tools that support project management, and the combination of phase- and management-related tools known as software development environments.

### 6.3.1 Project management tools

This category of tools should provide functionality for management of all products arising in the course of the project (project standards, documents, tables, schedules, programs, etc.) and for monitoring project planning and progress, as well as for following cost developments.

The prerequisite for such tools is a common database that assures that all project team members can manipulate only those products for which they have access privileges and that all team members work only with the current version of each product.

The *basic functions* of these tools include:

- Creation and management of project and resource schedules, e.g., network plans
- Creation and management of calculations schemata
- Creation and processing of documents
- Assignment of project standards, i.e., of document styles of the product, document frames, etc.
- Display, modification, analysis and linking of documents
- Assignment of attributes such as version numbers, access rights, document styles, release status, etc.
- Creation and management of configuration descriptions

### 6.3.2 Software development environments

As with other projects for the production of technical products, for the production of software products we need tools to support the production process. These tools should be usable in a coordinated way, i.e., embedded in a development strategy (as discussed in previous sections of this book). An ideal software development environment integrates all the individual tools described above, so that they not only can be used individually, but can operate on a common database and present themselves to the developer as an enclosed development system. Such a development environment encompasses the following:

- A set of project management tools
- Prototyping tools for various prototyping activities (e.g., user-interface and architecture prototyping)
- Design tools to support functional, data-oriented and object-oriented decomposition
- A set of implementation and testing tools (such as editors, compilers for various programming languages, interpreters, debuggers, object structure browsers)
- Documentation and maintenance tools
- Comfortable browsing tools

Here it is important that the tools be easy to operate and efficient and provide a consistent user interface, that results can be exchanged between tools, and that the software development environment builds on modern hardware and a powerful operating system.

# Conclusion

Contrary to other technical products, software has no material restrictions. This freedom leads to the development of ever larger and more complex software systems; software developers even seem to be fascinated with the complexity of their products. However, the development of large software systems proves difficult and poses so many problems that the term *software crisis* has become part of our standard vocabulary. This inspires dreams of new methods and tools that deliver some amelioration, a great leap forward, or even a revolutionary breakthrough on the software development sector; such methods and tools could be prototyping, object-oriented programming, CASE systems, or something entirely novel. However, sober consideration reveals that we are still far from the realization of such dreams and that we can hardly expect such a quantum leap in the near future. Certainly new methods like those we describe in this book can make things easier, improved, more certain and simpler, but we cannot make complexity vanish. We should not expect miracles. Developing large software systems will remain a difficult task that demands a high measure of creativity and expertise from the developer.

# References


[Abbott 1983] Abbott R. J.: *Program Design by Informal English Descriptions*; Comm. of the ACM, Vol. 26, Nr. 11, 1983

[Aho 1986] Aho A. V., Sethi R., Ullman J. D.: *Compilers – Principles, Techniques, and Tools*; Addison Wesley, 1986

[Aho 1972] Aho A. V., Ullman J. D.: *The Theory of Parsing, Translation, and Compiling*; Prentice Hall, 1972

[Albrecht 1983] Albrecht A. J., Gaffney J. E.: *Software Function, Source Lines of Code and Development Effort Prediction: A Software Science Validation*; IEEE Transactions on Software Engineering, Nov. 1983

[ANSI 1984] *ANSI/IEEE Std. 830-1984 Software Requirements Specification*; IEEE 1984

[Apple 1987] Apple Computer, Inc.: *Human Interface Guidelines: The Apple Desktop Interface*; Addison-Wesley, 1987

[Arthur 1985] Arthur L. J.: *Measuring Programmer Productivity and Software Quality*; Wiley & Sons, 1985

[Arthur 1988] Arthur L. J.: *Software Evolution: A Software Maintenance Challenge*; John Wiley & Sons, 1988

[Baker 1972] Baker F. T.: *Chief Programmer Team Management of Production Programming*; IBM Systems Journal 11/1, 1972

[Baker 1979] Baker F. T., Mills H. D.: *Chief Programmer Teams*; in: *Classics in Software Engineering*; Yourdon Press, 1979

[Balzert 1985] Balzert H.: *Moderne Software-Entwicklungssysteme und -werkzeuge*; Wissenschaftsverlag, 1985

[Balzert 1990] Balzert H.: *CASE – Systeme und Werkzeuge*; Wissenschaftsverlag, 1990

[Bauer 1975] Bauer F. L.: *Software Engineering*; in: *Software Engineering as an Advanced Course*; Springer, 1975

[Betts 1987] Betts B. et al.: *Goals and Objectives for User Interface Software*; Computer Graphics, Vol. 21, Nr. 2, 1987

[Bigelow 1988] Bigelow J.: *Hypertext and CASE*; IEEE Software, Vol. 5, Nr. 3, 1988

[Bischofberger 1992] Bischofberger W., Pomberger G.: *Prototyping-oriented Software Development*; Springer, 1992

[Blaschek 1985] Blaschek G.: *Statische Programmanalyse*; Elektronische Rechenanlagen 2, 1985

[Blaschek 1989] Blaschek G., Sametinger J.: *User-Adaptable Prettyprinting*; Software—Practice and Experience, Vol. 19(7), 1989

[Blaschek 1990] Blaschek G., Pomberger G.: *Introduction to Programming with Modula-2*; Springer, 1990

[Blaschek 1991] Blaschek G.: *Type-Safe Object-Oriented Programming with Prototypes – The Concepts of Omega*; Structured Programming, Vol. 12/4, Springer, 1991

[Boar 1984] Boar B.: *Application Prototyping*; John Wiley & Sons, 1984

[Boehm 1976] Boehm B. W., et al.: *Quantitative Evaluation of Software Quality*; Proc. of 2nd Internat. Conf. on Software Engineering, IEEE Comp. Soc., 1976

[Boehm 1978] Boehm B. W., et al.: *Characteristics of Software Quality*; North Holland, 1978

[Boehm 1979] Boehm B. W.: *Software Engineering*; in: *Classics in Software Engineering*; Yourdon Press, 1979

[Boehm 1981] Boehm B. W.: *Software Engineering Economics*; Prentice Hall, 1981

[Boehm 1988] Boehm B. W.: *A Spiral Model of Software Development an Enhancement*; IEEE Computer 21, 1988

[Böhm 1966] Böhm D., Jacopini G.: *Flow Diagrams, Turing Machines and Languages with only two Formation Rules*; Comm. of the ACM, Vol. 9, 1966

[Bons 1982] Bons H., van Megen R.: *Zur Festlegung von Qualitätszielen als Grundlage der Qualitätsplanung und -Kontrolle*; German Chapter of the ACM, Bericht 9, 1982

[Booch 1991] Booch G.: *Object-Oriented Design with Applications*; Benjamin/Cummings, 1991

[Brooks 1975] Brooks F. P.: *The Mythical Man-Month. Essays on Software Engineering*; Addison-Wesley, 1975

[Buxton 1969] Buxton J. N., Randell B. (Eds.): *Software Engineering Techniques*; Report on a Conference, Rome, Brussels: NATO Scientific Affairs Division, 1969

[Connell 1989] Connell J. L., Shafer L. B.: *Structured Rapid Prototyping*; Yourdon Press, Prentice Hall, 1989

[Coad 1990] Coad P., Yourdon E.: *Object-Oriented Analysis*; Prentice Hall, 1990

[Cox 1986] Cox B.: *Object-Oriented Programming: An Evolutionary Approach*; Addison-Wesley, 1986

[Dahl 1966] Dahl O., Nygaard K.: *Simula – An Algol-based Simulation Language*; Comm. of the ACM, Vol. 9, Nr. 9, 1966

[DeMarco 1978] DeMarco T.: *Structured Analysis and Systems Specifications*; Yourdon Press, 1978

[Denert 1991] Denert E.: *Software-Engineering – Methodische Projektabwicklung*; Springer, 1991

[Dennis 1973] Dennis J. B.: *Modularity*; Lecture Notes in Economics and Mathematical Systems Nr. 81; Springer, 1973

[Dennis 1975] Dennis J. B.: *The Design and Construction of Software Systems*; in: *Software Engineering As An Advanced Course*; Springer, 1975

[Dijkstra 1968] Dijkstra E. W.: *Goto Statements Considered Harmful*; Comm. of the ACM Vol. 11, 1968

[Dijkstra 1969] Dijkstra E. W.: *Structured Programming*; Software Engineering Technique, Report on a Conference; Rome, 1969

[Dijkstra 1972a] Dijkstra E. W.: *The Humble Programmer*; Comm. of the ACM, Vol. 15, No. 10; New York, 1972

[Dijkstra 1972b] Dijkstra E. W.: *Notes on Structured Programming*; Academic Press, 1972

[Dijkstra 1976] Dijkstra E. W.: *A Discipline of Programming*; Prentice Hall, 1976

[Dobbins 1987] Dobbins J. H., Buck R. D.: *The Cost of Software Quality*; in: *Handbook of Software Quality Assurance*; Van Nostrand Reinhold, 1987

[Dobler 1990] Dobler H., Pirklbauer K.: *Coco-2 – A New Compiler-Compiler*; ACM Sigplan Notices, Vol. 25, Nr. 5, 1990

[Dobler 1991] Dobler H., Huber G.: *Dynamic Analysis of Modula-2 Programs*; Proc. of the Conference "Modula-2 and Beyond", 1991

[Elspas 1972] Elspas B., et al.: *An Assessment of Techniques for Proving Program Correctness*; Computing Surveys 4, 1972

[Fagan 1976] Fagan M. E.: *Design and Code Inspections to Reduce Errors in Program Development*; IBM Systems Journal, Vol. 15(3), 1976

[Fairley 1985] Fairley R.: *Software Engineering Concepts*; McGraw-Hill, 1985

[Fidero 1988] Fidero J.: *Hypertext: A Grand Vision*; BYTE, Vol. 13, Nr. 10, 1988

[Floyd 1967] Floyd R. W.: *Assigning meanings to programs*; Mathematical Aspects of Computer Science, Vol.19, 1967

[Floyd 1984] Floyd C.: *A Systematic Look at Prototyping*; in: *Approaches to Prototyping*; Springer, 1984

[Frühauf 1988] Frühauf K., Ludewig J., Sandmayr H.: *Software-Projektmanagement und -qualitätssicherung*; Teubner, 1988

[Gane 1979] Gane C., Sarson T.: *Structured Systems Analysis: Tools and Techniques*; Prentice Hall, 1979

[Garg 1988] Garg P. K., Scacchi W.: *A Hypertext System to Manage Software Life-Cycle Documents*; Proc. of the 21st Annual Hawaii International Conference on System Science, Vol. 2: Software, 1988

[Goldberg 1983] Goldberg A., Robson D.: *Smalltalk-80: The Language and its Implementation*; Addison-Wesley, 1983

[Goos 1973] Goos G.: *Hierarchies*; in: *Software Engineering as an Advanced Course*; Springer, 1973

[Halstead 1972] Halstead M. H.: *Natural Laws Controlling Algorithm Structure*; Sigplan Notices Vol.7, No. 2, 1972

[Heitz 1988] Heitz M.: *HOOD: A Hierarchical Object-Oriented Design Method*; Proc. of the Third German Ada Users Congress, Gesellschaft für Software Engineering, 1988

[Hoare 1969] Hoare C. A. R.: *An Axiomatic Basis for Computer Programming*; Comm. of the ACM, Vol.12, 1969

[Hughes 1976] Hughes J. K., Michtom J. I.: *A Structured Approach to Programming*; Prentice Hall, 1976

[IEEE 1989] Institute of Electrical and Electronic Engineers: *Software Engineering Standards*, IEEE, 1989

[Jackson 1975] Jackson M. A.: *Principles of Program Design*; Academic Press, 1975

[Jackson 1983] Jackson M. A.: *System Development*; Prentice Hall, 1983

[Johnson 1975] Johnson S. C.: *YACC – Yet Another Compiler-Compiler*; Technical Report Nr. 32, Bell Laboratories, 1975

[Kastens 1982] Kastens U., Hutt B., Zimmermann E.: *GAG: A Practical Compiler-Generator*; Lecture Notes in Computer Science 141, Springer, 1982

[Keller 1989] Keller R. K.: *Prototypingorientierte Systemspezifikation*; Verlag Dr. Kovac, 1989

[Kerth 1987] Kerth N. L.: *The Use of Multiple Specification Methodologies on a Single System*; in: Proceedings of the Fourth International Workshop on Software Specification and Design, Monterey, 1987

[Kimm 1979] Kimm R., et al.: *Einführung in Softwareengineering*; Walter de Gruyter, 1979

[Knuth 1965] Knuth D. E.: *On the Translation of Languages form Left to Right*; Information and Control 8, 1965

[Knuth 1968] Knuth D. E.: *Semantics of Context-free Languages*; Mathematical Systems Theory 2, 1986

[Knuth 1973] Knuth D. E.: *The Art of Computer Programming*; Vol. 1-3, Addison-Wesley, 1968, 1969, 1973

[Kopetz 1976] Kopetz H.: *Software-Zuverlässigkeit*; Carl Hanser, 1976

[Koskimies 1984] Koskimies K.: *A Specification Language for One Pass Semantic Analysis*; Sigplan Notices 19, 6, 1984

[Laurel 1990] Laurel B. (ed.): *The Art of Human-Computer Interface Design*; Addison-Wesley, 1990

[Lewis 1976] Lewis P. M., Rosenkrantz D. J., Stearns R. E.: *Compiler Design Theory*; Addison-Wesley, 1976

[Lientz 1980] Lientz B. P., Swanson E. B.: *Software Maintenance Management*; Addison-Wesley, 1980

[Manna 1969] Manna Z.: *The Correctness of Programs*; Journal of Computer and System Science, Vol. 3, 1969

[McCabe 1976] McCabe T. J.: *A Complexity Measurement*; IEEE Transactions on Software Engineering, SE-2, 1976

[McCall 1977] McCall J. A., et. al.: *Factors in Software Quality*; Vol. I, Concepts and Definitions of Software Quality, 1977

[McCarthy 1962] McCarthy J.: *Towards a Mathematical Science of Computation*; Proc. IFIP Congress, Amsterdam; North-Holland Publications, 1962

[Meyer 1988] Meyer B.: *Object-oriented Software Construction*; Prentice Hall, 1988

[Mössenböck 1991] Mössenböck H., Wirth N.: *The Programming Language Oberon-2*; Structured Programming, Vol. 12, Nr. 4, 1991

[Myers 1979] Myers G. J.: *The Art of Software Testing*; John Wiley, 1979

[Naur 1966] Naur P.: *Proof of Algorithms by General Snapshots*; BIT 6, 1966

[Naur 1969] Naur P., Randell B. (Eds.): *Software Engineering*; Report on a Conference, Garmisch, 1968; Brussels: NATO Scientific Affairs Division, 1969

[Nielsen 1990] Nielsen J.: *The Art of Navigation through Hypertext*; Comm. of the ACM, Vol. 33, Nr. 3, 1990

[Ostrand 1988] Ostrand T. J., Balcer M. J.: *The Category-Partition Method for Specifying and Generating Functional Tests*; Comm. of the ACM, June 1988

[Parnas 1972] Parnas D. L.: *On the Criteria to be Used in Decompositing Systems into Modules*; Comm. of the ACM, Vol. 15, No. 12, 1972

[Parnas 1974] Parnas D. L.: *Software Engineering or Methods for the Multi-Person Construction of Multi-Version Programs*; Lecture Notes in Computer Science, Programming Methodology, Springer, 1974

[Ponder 1992] Ponder C., Bush B.: *Polymorphism Considered Harmful*; Sigplan Notices, Vol. 27, Nr. 6, 1992

[Pomberger 1986] Pomberger G.: *Software Engineering and Modula-2*; Prentice Hall, 1986

[Pomberger 1991] Pomberger G. et al.: *Prototyping-Oriented Software Development – Concepts and Tools*; Structured Programming, Vol. 12, Nr. 1, 1991

[Pree 1990] Pree W.: *DICE – An Object-Oriented Tool for Rapid Prototyping*; Proc. of TOOLS Pacific '90, Sydney, 1990

[Pressman 1987] Pressman R. S.: *Software Engineering. A Practitioner's Approach*; McGraw-Hill, 1987

[Putnam 1978] Putnam L.: *A General Empirical Solution to the Macro Software Sizing and Estimating Problem*; IEEE Transactions on Software Engineering, Vol. 4, Nr. 4, 1978

[Ramamoorthy 1974] Ramamoorthy C. V., et al.: *Reliability and Integrity of Large Computer Programs*; Lecture Notes in Computer Science - Fachtagung Prozeßrechner 1974; Springer, 1974

[Ramamoorthy 1982] Ramamoorthy C. V., et al.: *Techniques in Software Quality Assurance*; Proc. of the German Chapter of the ACM, Vol. 9; Teubner, 1982

[Rechenberg 1984a] Rechenberg P.: *Attributierte Grammatiken als Methode der Softwaretechnik*; Elektronische Rechenanlagen 26, 1984

[Rechenberg 1984b] Rechenberg P.: *Werkzeuge zur statischen Programmanalyse*; Proc. Compass '84, VDE-Verlag, Berlin, 1984

[Rechenberg 1985a] Rechenberg P, Mössenböck H.: *Ein Compiler-Generator für Mikrocomputer*; Carl Hanser, 1985

[Rechenberg 1985b] Rechenberg P.: *Editorial* zu *Werkzeuge der Softwaretechnik*; Elektronische Rechenanlagen 27, 2, 1985

[Rechenberg 1990] Rechenberg P.: *Programming Languages as Thought Models*; Structured Programming, Vol. 11, Nr. 3, 1990

[Reiser 1992] Reiser M., Wirth N.: *Programming in Oberon – Steps Beyond Pascal and Modula*; Addison-Wesley, 1992

[Renner 1989] Renner M.: *4th Dimension Design Reference*; ACIUS Inc., 1989

[Ross 1985] Ross D. T.: *Applications and Extensions of SADT*; IEEE Computer, Vol. 18, Nr. 4, 1985

[Royce 1970] Royce W.: *Managing the Development of Large Software Systems: Concepts*; WESCON Proceedings, 1970

[Rumbaugh 1991] Rumbaugh J., et al.: *Object-Oriented Modeling and Design*; Prentice Hall, 1991

[Sametinger 1991] Sametinger J.: *DOgMA: A Tool for the Documentation and Maintenance of Software Systems*; Report, Dept. of Software Engineering, Johannes Kepler Universität Linz, 1991

[Schmauch 1994] Schmauch S.H.: ISO 9000 for Software Developers, ASQC Quality Press, 1994

[Schmitz 1982] Schmitz P., et al.: *Software-Qualitätssicherung – Testen im Software-Lebenszyklus*; Vieweg, 1982

[Schmucker 1986] Schmucker K. J.: *Object-Oriented Programming for the Macintosh*; Hayden, 1986

[Schnupp 1976] Schnupp P., Floyd C.: *Software*; Walter de Gruyter, 1976

[Schoman 1977] Schoman K., Ross D. T.: *Structured Analysis for Requirements Definition*; IEEE Transactions on Software Engineering, SE-3, 1977

[Smith 1988] Smith J. B., Weiss S. F.: *Hypertext*; Comm. of the ACM, Vol. 31, Nr. 7, 1988

[SoftTech 1976] SoftTech Inc.: *An Introduction to SADT: Structured Analysis and Design Technique*; Woltham, Massachusetts. SoftTech Inc., 1976

[Sommerville 1985] Sommerville I.: *Software Engineering*; Addison-Wesley, 2nd edition, 1985

[Stroustrup 1986] Stroustrup B.: *The C++ Programming Language*; Addison-Wesley, 1986

[Ungar 1987] Ungar D, Smith R. B.: *Self: The Power of Simplicity*; Proceedings of OOPSLA '87, 1987

[Waite 1984] Waite W. M., Goos G.: *Compiler Construction*; Springer, 1984

[Wallmüller 1990] Wallmüller E.: *Software-Qualitätssicherung*; Carl Hanser, 1990

[Wallmüller 1995] Wallmüller E.: *Ganzheitliches Qualitätsmanagement in der Informationsverarbeitung*; Carl Hanser, 1995 (soon to be available in English)

[Warnier 1974] Warnier J. D.: *Logical Construction of Programs*; Van Nostrand Reinhold, 1974

[Wasserman 1990] Wasserman A. I. et al.: *The Object-Oriented Structured Design Notation for Software Design Representation*; IEEE Computer, Vol. 23, Nr. 3, 1990

[Weinand 1988] Weinand A., Gamma E., Marty R.: *ET++ – An Object-oriented Application Framework in C++*; Proceedings of OOPSLA '88, 1988

[Weinand 1989] Weinand A., Gamma E., Marty R.: *Design and Implementation of ET++, a Seamless Object-oriented Application Framework*; Structured Programming 10, 2, 1989

[Wilson 1990] Wilson D.A.: *Class Diagrams: A Tool for Design, Documentation, and Testing*; Journal of Object-Oriented Programming, Vol. 3, Nr. 1, 1990

[Wirfs-Brock 1989] Wirfs-Brock R., Wilkerson B.: *Object-Oriented Design: A Responsibility-Driven Approach*; Proceedings of OOPSLA ´89, 1989

[Wirfs-Brock 1990] Wirfs-Brock R., Wilkerson B., Wiener L.: *Designing Object-Oriented Software*; Prentice Hall, 1990

[Wirth 1971] Wirth N.: *Program Development by Stepwise Refinement*; Comm. of the ACM, Vol. 14, No. 4, 1971

[Wirth 1985] Wirth N.: *Programming in Modula-2*; Springer, 1985

[Wirth 1986] Wirth N.: *Compilerbau*; Teubner, 1986

[Wolverton 1972] Wolverton R. W., et al.: *Assessment of Software Reliability*; TRW Software Report (TRW-SS-72-4) California, 1972

[Yourdon 1979] Yourdon E., Constantine L.: *Structured Design*; Prentice Hall, 1979

[Zave 1984] Zave P.: *The Operational versus the Conventional Approach to Software Development*; Comm. of the ACM, Vol. 27, No. 2, 1984

# Index